# MOMENT OF MADNESS

# MOMENT OF MADNESS

## The People vs. Jack Ruby

by ELMER GERTZ

with a Preface by

JON R. WALTZ, Professor of Law
at Northwestern University School of Law

FOLLETT PUBLISHING COMPANY
Chicago   New York

Library of Congress Catalog Card Number: 68-18507

First Printing

Manufactured in the United States of America

T-5868

# PREFACE

*It is a piece of idle sentimentality that truth, merely as truth, has any inherent power denied to error, of prevailing. . . .*
A misleading *dictum* of John Stuart Mill.

I HAVE A THEORY, or perhaps it is only an opinion, about the law and lawyers and their power to get at facts fairly and adequately. It is that the purposes and the actual workings, and the flaws, of our legal truth-determining machinery can best be demonstrated not in all-encompassing treatises, which are almost inevitably too broad and too thin, but rather in knowledgeable and close dissections of particular litigated cases. I do hold, on the basis of this theory, that Anthony Lewis' study of Earl Gideon's case, *Gideon's Trumpet*, is worth a hundred books with such promissory titles, to mention a recent one, as *The Lawyers*. It was on the basis of this theory of mine that a few years ago Stanford's Professor John Kaplan and I, aided by the Walter E. Meyer Research Institute of Law, undertook our study entitled *The Trial of Jack Ruby*. And the same theory impels me to say that the book in your hand by Elmer Gertz, focusing principally on the post-trial proceedings in the Ruby case, is an important and useful effort.

Since I have espoused it publicly and often, I believe that before saying more I should mention another notion that might at first appear to cut sharply across the one just stated. This notion, which was invented by the legal profession long before I was thinking about such things, is that practicing lawyers ought not to go about advertising themselves and their doings. There are many reasons for this notion, now embedded in ornate ethical canons, and one of them is that the general public might get it in its head that the best-publicized lawyer is the best—a conclusion the invalidity of which has repeatedly been proved, the trial of Jack Ruby being at once a dramatic and a distressing case in point. So there is a dilemma which might seem to be posed directly by the publication of *Moment of Madness*: attorney Elmer Gertz participated fully and with great vigor in the very proceedings which he has chronicled in this book.

The dilemma is a bothersome one—although it obviously has vexed me far more than it has some hustling members of the practicing legal profession. We can best see how the law functions and malfunctions by considering particular law cases. Sometimes—certainly not invariably—the person best qualified to describe a consequential case is the lawyer who participated in it. But if he writes a book about it, at least while still engaged in making his living by practicing law, is he automatically to be lumped with the J. W. Ehrlichs, the Bellis and the Nizers as a wanton self-publicizer?

It all depends. In part it depends on motive. Was the lawyer-author's sole or primary purpose the generation of more law business of the sort about which he has written? When a practitioner of the law fills a volume with fragmentary accounts of cases that serve to establish nothing more than that he has somehow won a lot of them, when he embroiders the dust jacket with solicited testimonials to his own powers in a recurrent type of litigation in which he specializes, his motive is clear enough—and reprehensible. In a related way it depends, too, on the significance of the cases to be discussed by the participant in them and upon the objectivity with which the lawyer-author approaches his project. Can he be first a partisan advocate and then the calm student of his own work or will leftover passions induce him to mislead? Some trial lawyers cannot speak objectively of their own cases, win, lose, or draw; the hope for dispassionate discussion never draws a living breath.

It seems to me that it comes down to this: if the case, fully concluded, is for some reason important; if the author-participant writes of it to give and not to get; if he imparts information that might otherwise be lost and if he does so with all the objectivity he can muster, then an accommodation between the apparently conflicting notions that I have mentioned is proper.

On these grounds such an accommodation is in order here. Elmer Gertz has not had the opportunity, and I trust never will, to specialize in the defense of convicted killers of presidential assassins. (Ironic death has closed Jack Ruby's case.) And I do not think Gertz looks for more cases of this or similar sort even if they were to be had. In the first place, he is not a specializing criminal lawyer, although he plainly comprehends how to move around in that highly special area. In the second place, the pursuit of more cases like Jack Ruby's would—judging by what actually happened— mark out a rapid route to starvation, which is a condition that few lawyers actively invite. (And Gertz, though something of a cross between Don Quixote and an ethical Clarence Darrow, has never indicated an aversion to nourishment.) But more significantly, Elmer Gertz—although the advocate in him glimmers through occasionally—has written with substantial objectivity from a unique fund of knowledge about a case that strikes me as being of genuine importance to all who care about the law in the United States.

The Ruby case has significance not because the accused was intrinsically important as a man. He was not, just as most of the members of his drama—Judge Joe B. Brown, Melvin M. Belli, Joe Tonahill, Henry Menasco Wade—are unimportant. Putting aside certain neuropsychiatric signs, Jack Ruby was a paradoxical man in ways that often stamp unexceptional men. He operated cheap nightclubs and wanted "class." (It was this love of "class" that attracted Ruby, fatally, to the garish Melvin Belli.) A prim man who moralized with his fists, Ruby detested "punks" and "characters" and beat them up. But, according to one of his employees, "he'd help anyone who came along and needed food or a place to stay." He was incessantly on the prowl, as

Wills and Demaris put it in their revealing *Jack Ruby,* for
the "big deal that would make him a big man," but he
veered away from projects just as they began to show
promise. He ran after people with power and toadied to
them, fawning, pressing upon them unwanted favors,
squirming into their slice of the limelight. Still, it was said,
"the one thing Ruby does not want is to be a clown." The
man wanted dignity and a measure of respect. He was not a
political man (his businesses seemed to consume his
thoughts) and yet he was moved, in Gertz's "moment of
madness," to execute the asserted murderer of a controversial President. In the main, then, it was Ruby's act, and not
the man himself, that was important; the extraordinary act
of an unexceptional man set important things in motion.

It put in motion this country's machinery of courtroom
justice, our most formal means for getting at truth. Inextric-
ably bound up with Lee Harvey Oswald's apparent crime,
Ruby's act of extermination contributed also to setting in
motion investigative processes of unprecedented dimensions,
for we wanted to know whether Oswald and Ruby were
alone in their deeds. These less formalistic processes included not only the work of the President's Commission on
the Assassination of John F. Kennedy but that of countless
free-lance investigators bent upon discrediting that Commission on the one hand and, on the other, establishing that
Kennedy's death was the product of an intricate conspiracy
that counted Ruby as a participating member. Elmer Gertz
is interested in both of these consequences of Jack Ruby's
extraordinary act. He believes, as I do, that they hold out
clues concerning the efficacy of our formal and informal
methods of ascertaining truth in as full a fashion as fairness
will allow.

Few criminal matters to be tried by a jury under our
adversary trial system were more likely than the Ruby case
to test that system for latent defects. The matter of Jack
Ruby was a laboratory case, extreme in its every aspect. It
carried the extreme penalty, its notoriety was extreme, the

trial judge was extremely obtuse, the defense was extremely sophisticated, the prosecutors were extremely efficient, chief defense counsel Melvin M. Belli was, well, extremely extreme. I shall mention only two of the reasons that these factors make the Ruby case a subject of fascination for observers of the trial and appellate process.

First, Ruby's case would test as never before the ability of our criminal justice apparatus to accord fairness to the accused in a publicized matter. Jack Ruby had been without question history's most public assassin. Not only was his shooting of Lee Harvey Oswald witnessed by those who were crowded into the basement of the Dallas Police and Courts Building on the twenty-fourth of November, 1963; television cameras recorded the event, and an estimated eighty million persons, including eleven of Ruby's jurors, observed the killing contemporaneously or on videotape reruns. Thereafter Ruby inherited the news media attention that would have been his victim's. And then into a case already bathed in publicity strutted a chief defense counsel, Melvin Belli, whose presence in virtually any case was carefully calculated to escalate attention. Thus Ruby's jurors eventually took with them into their deliberation room not only the relevant data that had been shaped by the rules of evidence and conveyed to them during the trial, but also the myriad material and immaterial things that they knew, or thought they knew, long before they had been impaneled.

Second, the Ruby trial offered a matchless opportunity to test the law's ability to assimilate useful contributions from other disciplines, particularly those of psychiatry. As layer after layer of Ruby's somewhat bizarre makeup was peeled away, his case posed an increasingly obvious chance to wed law with science in an attempt to find a courtroom solution to that most troublesome of medical-legal questions, the insanity defense to a charge of crime. Dr. Roy Schafer, the highly regarded Yale psychologist, had suggested, on the basis of extensive psychological testing, that Ruby suffered from organic brain damage, possibly associated with psy-

chomotor epilepsy. Dr. Martin L. Towler, a University of
Texas neurologist, diagnosed Ruby a psychomotor epileptic
on the basis of electroencephalograms which conformed to
a brain-wave pattern recently labeled the "psychomotor variant type of seizure discharge" by the eminent Chicago elec-
troencephalographer, Dr. Frederic A. Gibbs. Melvin Belli's
chief psychiatric expert, the late Manfred S. Guttmacher of
Johns Hopkins, believed that at the time of the Oswald killing Jack Ruby had been in the throes of a functional psychotic episode of a type that had been described by Karl
Menninger. Belli himself thought that Ruby's was "the most
perfect psychiatric defense backed by diagnostic reports I
have ever seen." He later proclaimed that ". . . our medical
case, after it all came together, was a thing of beauty. . . ."
But a Dallas jury, consuming only two hours and nineteen
minutes to do it, arrived at a verdict of guilty of murder with
malice and assessed the punishment at death.

The American legal system foundered badly at the trial
level in Jack Ruby's case. A national news magazine referred
to it later as "a legal disaster." Professor Lawrence Friedman, writing in the *Wisconsin Law Review,* called the Ruby
trial "an American tragedy" and stated, "The American
system of trial by jury was itself on trial, and the verdict was
adverse." In his view the trial judge and Belli, among others,
"stood indicted of incompetence or worse." Martin Mayer,
writing in *Commentary* before the results of Jack Ruby's
appeal were known, was speaking of the trial when he said
that "everything to be learned from it is discouraging." A
Washington *Post* writer thought that the Ruby case "raised
fundamental doubts about our system of criminal justice."
And there were repercussions abroad. Sir Denis Brogan, the
English historian, remarked that "Texas justice, if not quite
Jeddart justice, is certainly not justice as administered in the
Old Bailey. . . [and] will be a source of superior delight to
the already smug enough English bench and bar."

There is ample support for these gloomy comments in the

official transcript of Ruby's trail and in my own study, with
Kaplan, of the trial phase of this case. The unpredictable
judge refused to change the location of the trial to more
temperate terrain, defense counsel inexplicably failed to seek
a continuance of the trial date and publicity overwhelmed
the participants. Regarding the insanity defense, Dr. Guttmacher wanted to talk about organic brain damage and
Menninger's "episodic dyscontrol"; Melvin Belli wanted to
talk about epilepsy and fugue states and to finger yards of
"demonstrative" electroencephalograms. The witness's diagnosis and his interrogator's theory of the case passed like
ships in the night: there was no wedding of law and science
at the trial of Jack Ruby.

The legal system that foundered outrageously at the first
level of Ruby's case shortly thereafter righted itself and, in
so doing, arguably vindicated itself in large measure. Gertz's
book describes, in rich detail, how the law's appellate processes lent themselves to dispelling the stench of Ruby's
trial. I will not tread upon the author's territory by pre-
viewing the involved steps that led, not long before the accused's death, to reversal of his conviction and the ordering
of a new trial. I shall, however, say that I know of no book,
Anthony Lewis's included, that so fully illuminates what
for most nonlawyers has remained an almost total mystery,
the criminal law's procedures following trial, conviction and
sentence. This is not to say that everything the author illuminates is admirable. As I have indicated, Gertz is dissect-
ing, and dissections bring up the ugly with the rest; here
and there it can even be suggested that Gertz's scalpel has
slipped and that he has cut himself. Pure perfection could
not be achieved by so simple an expedient as the Ruby family's firing of Melvin Belli. But of this much I am convinced:
this book was worth the writing, for it is important that we
understand, now and in years to come, precisely what happened—from start to finish—in the law's formal disposition
of Jack Ruby's complex case. Gertz, in his Foreword,

describes the case as "nearly incomprehensible," but it is much less so with the publication of his book.

I have said that Jack Ruby's act led to something at least as worthy of scrutiny as his own trial and its legal aftermath. It was immediately responsible, in part, for unchecked rumors of a pernicious sort. It was astounding enough that a President of the United States had been murdered, apparently by a self-proclaimed Marxist and Castroite; Ruby's killing of the murder suspect two days later under what seemed the most desperate circumstances was incredible. Into this vacuum rushed an assortment of conspiracy theories. At first no one possessed any firm notion as to whether the suspected cabal had a leftist or a rightest origin; the citizenry of Dallas sensed a Communist plot, while the rest of the world leaned toward a right-wing theory. In either case, if Oswald were a pawn in a larger scheme, Ruby's silencing of him might indicate an extension of the conspirators' activities. Such speculations led to the initiation by Lyndon B. Johnson of a less structured and more sweeping investigatory process than Ruby's own trial could possibly be.

The Warren Commission, so dubbed in common parlance because of Chief Justice Earl Warren's chairmanship, found no evidence that Jack Ruby's shooting of Oswald had been part of a larger pattern. This and other facets of the Commission's work inspired critical commentary by a few responsible analysts such as Edward Epstein, author of the flawed but valuable *Inquest*. Publication of the Commission's Report and supportive exhibit volumes also summoned forth what Warden John Sparrow of All Souls College, Oxford—a scholarly lawyer not given to hyperbole—has denominated a "host of crack-pots and rabble-rousing publicists, of 'patriots' with a self-appointed mission." These "demonologists" (another label applied by Sparrow) produced a stream of tumultuous criticisms of the Report and concocted phantasmagorical conspiracy theories that embraced, among others, a protesting Ruby. The most vocal of the "demonologists" has been a man by the name of Mark Lane, who in 1966 published a best-selling collection of speculations entitled *Rush to Judgment*. Included toward the end of *Moment of Madness* is Elmer Gertz's comparative analysis of the Warren Commission Report and the published works of its critics, especially Lane's, as they concern the role of Jack Ruby. Few men are better equipped than Gertz to engage in such an analysis. It goes far toward confirming a statement that I made at a time, many months ago, when some observers believed that Lane and his caravan had created a stain deeper even than that caused by Oswald's and Ruby's conduct: "History," I then wrote, "and the good sense of equitable men, will accord a fitting place to the 'demonologists' and to their intended victims." Elmer Gertz is an equitable man—and he has good sense. His book supports a double faith: truth can fairly be developed in a properly conducted judicial trial; in a free society it can also be generated in the marketplace.

As I write these concluding lines we are about to place on trial, in courtrooms and in the marketplace, two more men charged with assassination. I hope that the trials of James Earl Ray and Sirhan B. Sirhan, the suspected killers of Dr. Martin Luther King and Senator Robert F. Kennedy, will establish something more than that it is a sometimes dispiriting time in which we live. I hope they demonstrate that we have already learned lessons from the sad case of Jack Ruby, the tormented nonentity who not so very long ago put us all to the test. If, as I anticipate, some of the lessons have been absorbed, the author of this book—one of the few who passed the test—can take a bit of credit.

*Jon R. Waltz*
*Professor of Law, Northwestern*
*University School of Law*

Chicago, Illinois
July 28, 1968

# FOREWORD

THE KILLING OF LEE HARVEY OSWALD by Jack Ruby must be ranked as one of the most astonishing events in history. Never before had a slaying taken place before a nationwide audience. The incredible event of November 24, 1963, was only the beginning of the prolonged, and sometimes incomprehensible, Ruby case.

Since the fact of the killing was never in doubt, nor the identity of the killer, the question for most people over the next months was what punishment would fit the crime. For the legal community, however, the question was different: Given the circumstances and the vast publicity, would Jack Ruby be fairly tried? It was, ultimately, a question of "due process of law." Like many lawyers in the United States, I was concerned as the initial proceedings in the case unfolded, but I never expected to participate in the case.

Then, on March 14, 1964, the verdict was brought in at the original trial. As my wife and I were driving toward downtown Chicago, listening to the car radio, an announcer interrupted to say that the Ruby jury was about to bring in its verdict. I turned to my wife and burst out, "It's a hanging jury!" My wife, startled, believed I was mistaken: no jury could bring in a death verdict in the case.

But experience has taught lawyers that a quick decision, after a long trial involving the presentation of complex psychiatric testimony, means the jury has given little or no or improper consideration to that evidence. And in this instance the jury had considered its verdict for a very short time indeed.

Our conversation was interrupted by the result. Yes, it

was a death sentence. Now I was almost livid with rage. It
was not that I had or have any sympathy for murder, but I
thought I understood the circumstances of the case. It
seemed clear to me that a highly emotional, unstable, perhaps mentally sick Jack Ruby, reacting hysterically to the
assassination of the President, had killed the assassin on
impulse, without premeditating the act. If that was so, then
a sentence of death was wholly unjust.

I did not know on that March day that soon I would be
deeply involved in the case, not simply in an abstract way,
but personally and professionally. The involvement did not
come immediately and directly, but gradually, because of
my concern for Jack Ruby's rights as a human being. He
had been punished excessively. He had been treated merci-
lessly in the city that was his home by those who wished
to dissociate themselves entirely from him. He had been
condemned, at least in part because he was a Jew, and at
least in part because he made his living by catering to the
low, if highly human, tastes of good citizens of Dallas.

Now Jack Ruby is dead; the case is closed. Nothing,
presumably, can be added to the record. But the record
can be clarified.

The law is many things, including human drama. If the
actors in this drama are miscast, if the events are illogical,
if the psychology is faulty, the drama falls apart and becomes meaningless.

The case of Jack Ruby was all these things. What he did
was wrong, but his act was not completely indefensible.
The details of his life make a somewhat sordid tale, but it
is not incomprehensible. The treatment he received was
inexcusable, but not uncorrectable. So long as Ruby lived,
it was the task of his counsel to convert what would have
been a shameful episode into a tribute to the system of
justice in a democracy—the administration of the courts
in a fair and impartial manner.

The story of that many-faceted attempt is told in this

book. It is, to an extent, the story of failure, for Jack Ruby died before the case was finally adjudicated. Technically, however, he died innocent of any crime. It is also a story of partial success, for if our client did not ultimately get the fair trial he deserved, he at least saw in the reversal of the first verdict the promise of a fair trial.

No small part of the Ruby case turned on an achievement of a different sort. The post-trial process proved that it is possible today to assemble a team of lawyers of different backgrounds and beliefs, and from distant geographical regions, who yet may work harmoniously and effectively to achieve a common goal.

Finally, although the case was not "won" for Jack Ruby, it raised for the consideration of the legal profession a number of serious questions about the rights of a criminal defendant and the conduct of the courts. Melvin Belli, chief counsel in the first trial, sought to establish new precedents under Texas law in his leadership of the defense. In this he was unsuccessful. In the appeal new questions were raised, and if we were not wholly successful in the manner we wished at the time, at least the questions would be grappled with and mulled over by other attorneys and the courts.

What appears here is an account, then, of the legal and personal tribulations of Jack Ruby, with primary emphasis on the post-trial and appellate stages. It is, in a sense, a lesson book, of what can be done and of what should not be done. Although I have tried to show the persons involved as they were, and to avoid any misrepresentations of any sort, it is always difficult to reconstruct a case, particularly one that has absorbed so much of one's attention for so long a time, and do complete justice to the whole story. Where there are many complicated strands to unravel, I have had to simplify the narrative.

Throughout the period of my involvement in the case, I was essentially an advocate. But now that Jack Ruby no longer requires an attorney, I am, I hope, a fair historian,

recording an extraordinary case for students who will follow me. Mine is the prayer of the doomed Othello: "nothing extenuate and set down nought in malice." What follows is the truth, so far as I know it.

E. G.
Chicago, Illinois
July, 1968

# ACKNOWLEDGMENTS

IN THE WRITING of this book I have relied to the greatest extent on my files pertaining to the Ruby case: the transcripts of court proceedings, briefs, memoranda, correspondence, autopsy reports, press clippings, and other materials too various to describe. In the organization of this material into usable form I was fortunate to have the inspired and devoted assistance of my talented secretary, Mrs. Gladys Fuller, and my wife Mamie. Additional assistance in the completion of specific portions of research in the archives and the cases was provided by impressive young people from Northwestern University: Karan Huckleberry, David Thompson, Tim L. Harker, James Montana, and Harold Bressler. First and foremost in assistance, however, was Wayne B. Giampietro, my associate, who worked arduously on the case itself. On my son Theodore, himself from Northwestern, I often leaned for guidance and cheer.

My associates and predecessors in the Ruby case—Sol A. Dann, Phil Burleson, William M. Kunstler, Sam Houston Clinton, Jr., Melvin M. Belli, Joe H. Tonahill, Emmett Colvin, Jr., Charles Bellows, Michael Levin, Alan Adelson, and many others—influenced the writing of this book through our association during the case. Most of them also generously granted permission to use portions of their correspondence to describe the day-to-day events in the case.

To Professors Jon R. Waltz and John Kaplan I am indebted both for ideas and for materials. As will be apparent, their book, *The Trial of Jack Ruby*, played a special role in the Ruby case and therefore in this book. Professor Paul F. Rothstein, of the University of Texas Law School, constantly assisted me during the legal proceedings and helped to shape my thinking in connection with the events described here.

Anyone who studies any aspect of the Kennedy assassination and the slaying of Oswald must acknowledge his debt to the monumental work of the President's Commission on the Assassination of President Kennedy. The index prepared by Sylvia Meagher, despite its imperfections, was of great assistance. And the many books, pamphlets, and articles by defenders and critics of the Warren Commission have been consulted; those by Mrs. Meagher, Thomas Buchanan, Mark Lane, Harold Weisberg, Edward Epstein, and others caused me to rethink the Ruby case even when I was unmoved or even angered by what they wrote.

I was fortunate, too, in the assistance I received from distinguished physicians—foremost among them my brother Dr. George Gertz; the psychiatrists Werner Tuteur, Thaddeus L. Kostrubala, David Abrahamsen, and David A. Rothstein; and finally, the dean of medical writers, Dr. Morris Fishbein.

Although I gave assistance to, rather than received it from, Garry Wills and Ovid Demaris, they, too, contributed, if indirectly, to this book. In *Jack Ruby* they have captured Ruby the man; and in the section destroying the myth of a conspiracy involving him, they have produced a small gem of psychological insight.

As I gave help to journalists and writers, so I received help from them. Bernard Gavzer of AP Newsfeatures and Jack Beers of the Dallas *Morning News* were particularly helpful.

Portions of this book were first delivered as addresses to chapters of the Civil War Round Table. The questions and comments of the members of this intriguing historical society helped to sharpen my awareness of the many problems in the case. I am conscious, too, of my very great debt to the late Dr. Otto Eisenschiml for his remarkable research into the assassination of Abraham Lincoln.

Others who have given important assistance are my son-in-law, Henry R. Hechtman, who provided the title and subtitle; my son Jack M. Friedman, who was constantly on the alert for material relating to the case; Rabbi David Graubart; the staff of the Library of Congress; I. Bleckman, one of those who photographed the slaying of Oswald; the Texas State Library; and Burt W. Griffin, who served on the legal staff of the Warren Commission.

Finally, to Dwight W. Follett, who took a profound interest in the Ruby case, I must express my thanks for his encouragement. Had he not prodded me, in his persuasive fashion, to set down these words for the record, I doubt that the book would have been written at this time, if ever.

Although all these people and others have contributed to the book, the responsibility for what appears here must obviously be mine alone.

# CONTENTS

# BEFORE THE TRIAL

# 1

## CLASS

JACK RUBY's manliness has been belittled by many persons, and his stature in the community in which he lived has been ridiculed. At the end of his life, after the trial and the appeal, he was indeed a shrunken shell of the person he had been. But when he was taken into custody on that November day in 1963, he was still the bouncy, buoyant Jack Ruby of the Carousel Club. He had been, in his own terms, something of a success, and he was not without friends. Within a very short time of the shooting of Lee Harvey Oswald, five of his friends and acquaintances called five different attorneys to represent him, and all of these attorneys appeared at the jail prepared to act in his behalf. Perhaps they came in the hope of notoriety; perhaps they saw cash in the venture; but in any event they came.

The arrival (and departure) of these men foretokened much that was to happen in the case, for from first to last, even to death and beyond, the spectacle was provided in scenes by attorneys, and the chief actor was gradually edged offstage. Four of the would-be counsel departed immediately. Tom Howard, who had been called in by Ralph Paul, Ruby's business partner and faithful friend, alone remained—at least for the time being.

Howard, like Ruby himself, was a "little" man of great aspirations. The striking difference between the two was that Howard was highly successful in his small way, whereas Ruby was a spectacular flop in all that he did. Howard's clients were pimps and prostitutes and murderers and unimportant people. He lost no clients to the electric chair, however, and he was reasonably confident that he would not lose Ruby either. Some of his detractors said that he handled "nigger cases," and Ruby himself thought Howard had no "class." It was true that Howard, like Ruby, had been a nightclub operator, and again like Ruby, he had had tax troubles with Uncle Sam. Nevertheless, he had good ideas for the case. In brief, he planned to secure a short sentence for Ruby by pleading that this highly emotional, overwrought little fellow had shot Oswald, the sneak assassin of a beloved President, on impulse. Of course, shooting Oswald was an evil act, but it would be equally evil to punish Ruby excessively.

In retrospect, this plan seems better than the grandiose ideas of Howard's alleged betters. His defense would not have jangled any Dallas nerves, and would have accommodated the sensitive feelings of the community. Howard, however, was soon told that others were going to be brought in to work with him, to give new direction to the case. That was the beginning—and perhaps the cause—of the debacle that followed.

Ruby and his family, having decided that Howard was lacking in legal eminence, nevertheless wanted him to assist them in finding another lawyer to work with him. Howard offered various suggestions, including the famous Houston lawyer, Percy Foreman. But his efforts were fruitless, possibly because he was not wholehearted. The Ruby family grew impatient. There were volunteers, like Jake Ehrlich, but the family thought it inadvisable to hire a Jewish attorney.* Finally, they found what they were look-

---

* Not entirely without reason. Anti-Semitism is often difficult to pin down, as it is not always overt. It certainly existed in Dallas. Jack Ruby was born Jacob Rubenstein, but his name had been lawfully changed to Jack Leon Ruby, and that was the name under which he should have been indicted. But the indictment was against "Jack Rubenstein alias Jack Ruby." Since the Dallas District Attorney's office does nothing by error or inadvertence, one could be sure that they deemed an indictment of Jack Rubenstein as more prejudicial to the defendant.

ing for in a chief counsel, and in wholly unexpected fashion.

The first and most flamboyant chief counsel for Ruby, Melvin Belli, says in his account of the trial that, three days after Jack Ruby shot Oswald, Earl Ruby "slipped unobtrusively into a California courtroom and watched me sum up in a murder case." Earl says he did not go to California to scout one of Belli's trials; he had gone to see Billy Woodfield, who had been recommended as a writer who could handle Jack Ruby's story. The family needed funds for the defense, and selling the story of Jack's life was one of the few means open to them. Woodfield, Earl was told, had worked with Belli on the Caryl Chessman case. Until he mentioned Belli's name, Earl had never heard of him. It was Woodfield who arranged the meeting between Earl Ruby and Belli, on December 1, 1963.

According to Earl, Charles Bellows, of Chicago, a distinguished criminal lawyer, had been his first choice to represent Jack. He had known Bellows personally for many years, and he attempted, immediately after the shooting of Oswald, to retain Bellows for the defense. Nothing came of this.

(These stories, although told in retrospect, are entirely typical of the confusion in the case. From the beginning, as attorneys entered and left, the stories differed. Even usually reliable chroniclers have erred in such details, and the principals, for understandable reasons, often have told stories that scarcely resemble what others have reported to be the facts.)

Whatever the precise sequence of events, Belli was hired. He quickly rounded out the defense with Sam Brody, a Los Angeles associate; Joe Tonahill, of Jasper, Texas; and Phil Burleson, of Dallas.

Opposing the defense, in the name of the people of the state of Texas, was the staff of the Dallas district attorney's office. Any lawyer who underestimates the ability of this prosecuting team courts disaster.

The district attorney himself has a deceptive appearance and constantly underplays his talents. Henry Menasco Wade, Jr., was born to the law. His father had been a judge in nearby Rockwall, Texas, and five of his seven brothers were lawyers. It is a family that believes utterly in the rule of law. Wade attended the University of Texas on a football scholarship, and his attendance there is noteworthy, for the University, and its law school in particular, is *the* institution of higher education in Texas. The law school nurtures the state's politicians, and a degree from the university means more in Texas than any parchment granted by Harvard. Wade had the foresight, as it were, to room with John B. Connally, who was destined to be the governor of Texas. That Connally was seriously wounded when President Kennedy was assassinated was an added incentive to Wade to prosecute the man who had deprived the world of the opportunity to learn more about the man who had almost killed his friend.

Wade was the president of his 1938 law school class, graduating with academic honors. His bent for law enforcement was perhaps strengthened by the years he spent as an agent in the Federal Bureau of Investigation in Boston, Washington, and Baltimore and in anti-Nazi undercover work in South America. In 1951 he became criminal district attorney of Dallas County, and he has been firmly seated in that office ever since. His men have won 93.5 per cent of their cases, statistically the best record of any district attorney's office in the country, and this record has helped to persuade the voters of Dallas that Wade is the man for the job, even if Melvin Belli was unimpressed. Wade, unlike other attorneys in his office, handled both civil and criminal cases, but it was the fanfare around felonies that earned him his reputation. Few felony cases were lost by his office, and an amazing number of those convicted ended up in the electric chair. Wade's record was altogether one to command the respect of opposing defense counsel.

There were eighty people in Wade's office in 1963, forty-two of them lawyers, and it would be hard to find a more dedicated, and indelicate, lieutenant than William F. "Bill" Alexander. In Texas no one seems to be known by any name other than the familiar sobriquet. This is true even on such majestic occasions as addressing a high court or putting one's name forth as a candidate for public office. If Alexander had been elected to the Presidency—God forbid!—he would have signed treaties and public documents as "Bill." He was Bill even to those whose lives he was intent on taking—in a legal way, of course. The gun which he carried was a symbol to him of the strength of the law. Whereas Ruby's pistol sulked in his pants pocket, Alexander's was worn in a place of honor.

For years Ruby had regarded Alexander as his friend; Alexander did not deny it, but friendship did not deter him in the least from his grim task. He was determined to "fry" his friend, and to that end he would devote his shrewd, resourceful, and remorseless mind. When told that the psychiatrists were going to examine Ruby, he replied, with his usual tasteless humor, "They want to examine Ruby's brain? We'll be glad to deliver it to them from Huntsville [the state penitentiary] after we fry him." Whether or not Alexander mourned the assassination of the President, he could not resist a typical crack when a St. Patrick's Day parade was held in 1964 on the street of the President's death: "Don't you think we're pushing our luck a little having another parade for an Irishman around here?" In the same manner, he described his political philosophy as being "just to the left of Little Orphan Annie and just to the right of the John Birchers." He was, in short, a true rightist denizen of Dallas.

To himself and to the press, Alexander was the man next to Wade in authority, but in truth A. D. Jim Bowie was Wade's first assistant. The antithesis of Alexander in demeanor, he was more effective, for he could beguile his opponents. All, including Ruby, spoke of him with respect and affection. This sophisticated, learned man of the law was a gentleman, even when his work toward securing a death sentence was most devastating.

Why Belli should have been so disdainful of the Dallas prosecutors, one will never know. His attitude was evidenced toward the very beginning when he edged the Dallas man, Tom Howard, out of the case. Howard was small-time to Belli, but his clients did not "fry," and this was a distinction that the "King of Torts" never learned. Howard could sympathize with Jack Ruby; Belli could only patronize him. It is said that Ruby, who could wangle favors in the most unexpected places, once called Belli from the jail early one morning, declaiming desperately, "Mel, I must see you before court opens." The preoccupied prima donna replied, "Jack, take a cab and come to the hotel." And Ruby, distraught, responded, "Mel, don't you know where I am?"

Tom Howard would have known all the time. That was why he analyzed the case more realistically than Belli. After having built up an emotional defense that would have drawn, rather than antagonized, the community, he would have thrown Ruby upon the mercy of the court. In this way, he reasoned, the sentence would be a short one, easily served, and certainly not the death penalty. But Belli would not accept this strategy, and Ruby, looking for the "class" which Howard supposedly lacked, was willing to see Howard, his best bet, withdraw from the case. Belli was left in firm control, with Joe Tonahill a step behind him, and young Phil Burleson almost disdainfully relegated to the books and forms and technicalities.

Belli, who has tremendous legal talents at his best, is disdainful of lesser people, among them his opponents, his associates, the judiciary, and the Establishment. The very amiability of Judge Joe B. Brown could only disgust him, for he respects the strong.

Belli was born of wealthy parents. His banker-investor father had seen his fortune slip away during the Depression, and Mel was thereafter on his own. The experience was good for him. He learned from life as well as from books; and he may even be a legal genius, as some of his admirers say. Certainly the outsized awards he has won his clients in personal injury cases, his skill in playing with demonstrative evidence, his knowledge of applied medicine, his love of the esoteric in law, attire, and conduct, have made him the terror of the insurance companies and the envy of his colleagues. He exudes confidence, and he easily persuaded himself that he could not lose the Ruby case. He delighted in the frenzied opportunities for acclaim that it afforded him. Always good copy for the press, he was at his best before the cameras and microphones.

Phil Burleson, the junior member of Belli's team, seemed a typical Texan in vocal twang, diction, taste, and bearing, but he was actually born and educated in the East. He had quickly adapted himself to the life of "Big D" and the great state of Texas, and although subdued in manner, he had fierce, ungratified ambitions. For a time he had served as staff attorney in the Texas Court of Criminal Appeals and had been a highly successful appellate man in Henry Wade's office, winning almost every criminal appeal with which he had been associated, including the affirmation of several death sentences. An expert in the law books, he was now determined to make himself as adept at criminal trial work. Big and strong, he could put in long hours at the office, at the country club, on the golf course, or with a Bible class at church. He could receive rebuff, suspicion, and discontent with outward calm.

Joe Halbert Tonahill was the one true son of Texas on the defense team. Born in Hughes Springs of a mother who had local fame as an author, he became a lawyer in 1941 and was immediately appointed an assistant district attorney in Beaumont. Later he became an assistant United States attorney and then took up the private practice of law in Jasper. Like Belli, he specialized in negligence, or personal injury, cases. Unlike Belli, he sought official position with his colleagues. He was a director of the International Academy of Trial Lawyers for two years, and chairman of its executive committee for one year, and director of the Texas State Bar for several years. He was close to judges, bankers, and many powerful persons. Just as Belli had his offices in the Belli Building, Tonahill's were in the Tonahill Building. Physically, he towered over Belli; he towered over most men. You noticed him, you remembered him, not because of any physical or intellectual attraction, but because of his very ungainliness. There was something misshapen and grotesque about him. There was no polish in his speech. Where he thought he had a country manner, others thought he was rude, for there was nothing that he hesitated to say. Yet he and Belli seemed to get along perfectly. They were a team to drive other teams wild, but their measure had been taken by Wade, Bowie, and Alexander.

## THE LAW

In every criminal case, and not merely in a sensational murder case such as Ruby's, there is a sequence of events that follows a definite pattern. These events are well understood by practitioners of the criminal law, but the citizen is often bewildered by the intricacies of the legal maneuvers in and out of the courtroom. The trial itself is the focus of newspaper and television reports, but it is in reality the culmination, and only a part, of a sometimes complicated pattern that begins with the arrest or indictment of the alleged wrongdoer.

Fundamentally, the sequence of events in a criminal trial is the same no matter the difference in detail from jurisdiction to jurisdiction. The defendant must, first of all, choose an attorney and consult with him; a defense must be prepared. The defense counsel, once selected, must then decide on a plea in answer to the indictment—guilty or not guilty, whether because of insanity or for any other

legal or factual reason. There may be a series of pretrial
hearings before the trial begins, but once started, the legal
process moves inexorably toward the moment when the
defendant either will be free to walk again among his fellow citizens or will be consigned to prison where the sentence of the court will be executed.

The federal Constitution, and the state constitutions as
well, guarantee to every defendant in a criminal case the
right to a speedy trial by jury, so that the defendant, if not
guilty, will not suffer unduly from the law itself. That
right, however, must be offset against the equal guarantee of "due process," whereby the defendant is assured that
he shall have every consideration that the law can afford.
As a consequence, a trial at law is more than the appearance of the defendant in court. It is a series of moves by the
defense to insure that no opportunity to protect the defendant has been lost, and by the prosecution to insure
that the People shall not be at the mercy of lawbreakers.

Equally fundamental to the concept of trial by jury is
the law's rigid demand that impartial justice be administered. The jury trial has developed through the centuries
to put an end to star-chamber proceedings, vigilantes, and
lynch law. A man is to be judged by his peers, and the law
demands that these jurors must be free of prejudice about
the defendant's guilt or innocence. To insure justice, the
law provides a means to test the impartiality of those who
will hear the case. In addition, it provides that, in certain
instances, where a fair trial cannot be held in one community, it may be moved to another. It is also fundamental to
the administration of justice in the United States that the
judge shall be impartial and qualified to act in the case.
Thus a judge may be asked to disqualify himself if there
is reason to suspect his impartiality, and if he does not do
so himself, additional means of accomplishing the same
end are available.

In every case, particularly a murder case where the accused's life hangs in the balance, the attorneys on either
side make various motions, offers of proof, objections and

the like, and the court—that is, the presiding judge—rules on them. Sometimes his rulings are right, sometimes wrong, but in either case, the very course of the trial and the life of the defendant may depend on them.

What recourse is there to the victim of an adverse ruling? If the State is the wronged party, it can do nothing about it, generally speaking. Only the defendant can appeal from an adverse judgment. If the defendant is acquitted, however wrongly, that is the end of the matter; he goes free, and the State can do nothing about it. In some circumstances, if, for example, there has been perjured testimony or jury-tampering, there can be a new indictment and trial, but the original case is at an end; it cannot be retried. The defendant, particularly in a capital case, can appeal to higher courts, all the way up to the United States Supreme Court, and there are other legal proceedings that he can utilize.

Except when he is blinded by overconfidence, an attorney envisions this entire judicial process for the benefit of his client. Somewhere along the intricate trail, the path to justice will be found. Thus a lawyer tries his case with the thought of winning it in the first instance before the original judge and jury; but he has in mind the record of the case, for possible reversal on appellate review.

In the Ruby case, planning a defense presented special problems. After the shooting of Oswald, Ruby had been taken into custody immediately, and an indictment was handed down on November 26, two days later. The offense: murder with malice.

Since Ruby had clearly killed Oswald in sight of millions of television viewers, and in the presence of policemen and press representatives, a plea of not guilty to the charge would have to depend upon special circumstances: Had he acted with "malice"? Was he lacking in the mental capacity to commit the murder? And these are two of the most complicated sets of circumstances known to the criminal law.

One does not turn to Webster's dictionary, abridged or

unabridged, to learn the legal meaning of malice. One reads the authorities; in this instance, the authorities are the pertinent Texas statutes and the murder cases that have been reviewed by the appellate court of the state—the Texas Court of Criminal Appeals. What constitutes malice is what the reported cases say it is; and in Texas, or any Southern state, what is said may depend upon whether victim or defendant is white or black. Essentially, however, a sure guide to the meaning—and the complexities of the meaning—is consideration of the related term "premeditated." Had the defendant consciously, "with malice aforethought," planned to kill the victim?

On insanity, Texas holds essentially to the old view: You are sane if you know the difference between right and wrong and can act on such knowledge. You are insane, not if you have a mental illness, however severe, but if you do not know right from wrong and cannot act accordingly. Thus it is possible in Texas, as in England (where this concept of sanity developed), to execute a truly mentally ill person if some technical legal requirements are not met.

Tom Howard's answers to these questions about defense strategy were simple and straightforward. There would be no question of insanity, but merely of "impulse." And the first steps taken by the defense were consistent with that approach. But it was not long before Belli, who deemed himself an expert in forensic medicine, concluded that Jack was actually suffering from a little known (and only recently recognized) neuropsychiatric disturbance, a variant of psychomotor epilepsy. With that, the entire defense strategy was shifted to encompass highly complicated, and largely unexplored, matters on which, as it turned out, even the experts could not agree.

### THE FIRST BAIL HEARING

One of the first actions taken by the Ruby defense was to ask for his release on bail, pending actual trial. If this maneuver succeeded, the legal and psychological effect would be considerable, and it might insure that no death verdict would be returned by a jury. For release on bail is tantamount to a finding by the court that the proof is not evident, to use the constitutional phrase, or the presumption great, as far as guilt of murder with malice is concerned. In Ruby's case, the court would be saying, in effect, that he should be released on bond because it was unlikely that he could be subjected to the death penalty.

Aside from the likely psychological effect on a jury, there are other advantages to having the defendant outside, rather than inside, a jail cell. For one thing, it is much easier for him to cooperate with counsel, since conference rooms may be "bugged" and other impediments to frank conversations in the planning of a defense may be present.

Judge Brown, responding to Tom Howard's motion, set December 23 for a bail hearing. On the appointed day the principals in the drama of the Ruby trial were brought face to face in a courtroom for the first time—defendant, judge, prosecution, defense.

Jack Ruby was delivered to the court under close guard by the Dallas County Sheriff's office, led by Sheriff Bill Decker himself.

"I feel wonderful," Jack said to onlookers as he was led into the courtroom. Wearing a dark blue suit with a white tie, his sparse hair neatly combed, trying as always to look his best, he removed his glasses when he saw the photographers in the hallways leading to the courtroom.

Seating himself at the counsel table between Belli and Tonahill, he inquired, "Where's Tom?" (He was referring to Howard.) He did not want any of his legal entourage to miss this moment of greatness. He shook hands with Belli and Tonahill, and recognizing a photographer whom he knew, he shook hands with him. He thanked one of Sheriff Decker's deputies for his courtesy and greeted an employee of a radio station with a wave.

When the photographers turned their cameras from

Ruby to Sheriff Decker, Ruby did not appear to resent the
loss of the spotlight. If he did, he concealed it well. "Bill
Decker don't want no publicity," he said with a laugh. He
knew that all men love pictures, preferably of themselves.
And Sheriff Decker, who was an especially good model for
photographers, was no exception. His large glasses and
toothy grin and big hat seemed made for display.

"Thanks, Bill," Ruby said, of nothing in particular. He
was supremely confident that in a very short time he would
be free again to move about Dallas. Therefore there was
every reason to be convivial, not solemn. That his life was
at stake seemed scarcely to have crossed his mind.

At this bail hearing the prosecution called only two
witnesses to establish its case that bail should be denied:
Will Fritz, captain in the Homicide Bureau, and Detective
James R. Leavelle, of the Dallas Police Department.

The defense strategy, to show that Ruby's attack on Oswald was unpremeditated, now depended upon the witnesses it could offer, and on the testimony of one witness
in particular, pint-sized, nineteen-year-old, red-haired
(some called it honey-blond) Karen Lynn Bennett, of
nearby Fort Worth. "Little Lynn," a stripper at Ruby's
Carousel Club, turned out to be a great disappointment.
She did less than justice to the truth, because she was
young and inexperienced and lacked guile. And even before the hearing had begun, she found herself in a situation
embarrassing to her and even more embarrassing to the
Ruby defense.

Little Lynn was *the* essential witness for the defense at
the bail hearing because she alone could offer testimony
that would establish the innocent and commendable reason why Ruby was in the neighborhood of the police station on that ill-fated Sunday morning: Ruby was going to
wire money to her, a destitute and pregnant girl, so that
she might pay her landlord, and the only Western Union
office open that day happened to be near the police station.
The rest, including the slaying of Oswald, was mere

chance. The details of Ruby's actual movements would be spelled out by others, but the indispensable capstone of the testimony was what Little Lynn would say.

All this was wrecked, psychologically at least, by the precautions taken by the sheriff's staff: because they did not wish to lose another prisoner, they frisked everyone who entered the courtroom. Court bailiff Nell Tyler's discovery of a gun in Little Lynn's purse as she sought admittance to the courtroom, two days before Christmas, was no holiday gift to Ruby. It was certainly a godsend to the prosecution.

Sheriff Decker immediately charged the young lady with carrying a weapon without a permit, and a misdemeanor complaint was filed with the district attorney's office. The gun was described, with the usual particularity, as a 6.35 caliber Italian model with a pearl handle, not the sort of weapon used by a gangster or even by a gangster's moll, but it was enough to cause trouble.

R. B. Denson, the defense investigator, who was accompanying Little Lynn, said that she did not know the delicate little gun was in her purse. It had apparently been there for a long time, and it had no firing pin and no ammunition. Little Lynn confirmed these statements. Despite this explanation, she was taken into Judge Brown's chambers and questioned by FBI agents and United States Attorney Barefoot Sanders.

Little Lynn spoke with affection of her whilom employer, Jack Ruby. "Jack is the most wonderful fellow I know," she said. "I'd do anything for him."

She was permitted to testify, notwithstanding her mishap and the charge against her, but by the time she took the stand her voice could scarcely be heard. She told the now-familar details of her asking Ruby to wire the money to her, the reason for it, and his compliance with her request. But so far as the public and the court were concerned, the tiny gun in her purse had destroyed the credibility of her testimony.

Later that day, as she was being booked, she wept. Her fingerprints were taken and the usual cold formalities followed. When reporters questioned her, she pleaded with them: "I don't know anything to say. Please leave me alone."

Tom Howard posted a $1000 bond for her, and she was released. Showing obvious signs of pregnancy, she sighed with relief as she left. "I came to help him," she sniffled.

Having heard the witnesses for both sides, Judge Brown decided that, for the present at least, Jack Ruby would not go free on bond. He would accede to a defense request that Jack be examined by psychiatrists.

Ruby, who had been smiling and relaxed at the beginning of the hearing, grew nervous and discouraged as it went on. After Judge Brown had refused to let him leave the jail, Ruby's sister Eva Grant, who had been present throughout, sat in the courtroom and wept. For her benefit, if only for a moment, he managed to smile again as the sheriff's men hurried him off to jail.

It is a part of Yiddish folklore that there are persons who are invariably clumsy, and they are called *schlemihls*. And there are persons who are invariably the victims of misfortune, and they are called *schlamazels*. Or as the words are sometimes defined: the schlemihl spills hot soup on the schlamazel. The day's events had gone far to show that both expressions might be applicable to Jack Ruby. Caught in a process beyond his comprehension, there was to be no surcease. He was to be in the soup from first to last.

### DENSON REPORTS

While Melvin Belli and his burly associate, Joe Tonahill, were still publicly expressing supreme confidence in the result of the upcoming trial, Jack Ruby, his family, and R. B. Denson, the Dallas investigator who had been called in to assist the defense, were greatly worried. They tried desperately to communicate their fears to the irrepressible Belli and his sidekick.

Denson, who had been working on the case since December 10, 1963, had interviewed all employees of the Carousel Club, as well as Jack's friends and acquaintances. He was trying to prepare a roster of potential witnesses to circumvent what the prosecution might bring out in court. On January 8, 1964, he reported in writing to Belli; although Denson often tried to talk with Belli, he sometimes felt that he was being excluded because of Belli's preoccupation with proper press relations.

"Of the persons interviewed at the Carousel Club," Denson said, "only Karen Lynn Bennett [the stripper to whom Jack had wired money on that terrible Sunday morning after the President's assassination] proved to have information of a worthwhile nature. No other employee, with the exception of George Senator [Jack's roommate], had talked with Ruby on the day of the shooting." He had taken notes on all the many interviews and had excerpted them for Belli in a looseleaf notebook, much too thin, he feared, for the heavy demands of the defense. He had also taken detailed statements from Jack's quiet brother Sam and his ever-communicative sister Eva Grant, who had ideas on everything, sometimes provocative ideas, always expressed with her own kind of unlettered fluency.

It became apparent to Denson, as a result of interviewing persons with whom FBI agents had talked, "that the FBI was the only investigative agency doing work for the prosecution in this case; *that their material was being submitted daily to the offices of the District Attorney. . . .*" (Denson's italics.) He thought the FBI was concentrating on:

a. Any possible connection between Ruby and Oswald.
b. Ruby's so-called gangster connections.
c. Ruby's alleged pandering activities, regarding female employees, both present and past.

d. Ruby's alleged homo- and/or bi-sexual activities.

e. Ruby's reputation for bearing concealed weapons.

f. Any of Ruby's activities in detail commencing on the morning of November 22, 1963, until noon, November 24.

g. Any and all affiliations of a political nature by Ruby or any member of his family.

Denson then put down for the benefit of Belli and his associates a series of findings that were to prove prophetic of the dire events to come.

I. During the course of the investigation the undersigned [Denson] went to the local telephone company and got a list of all long distance calls placed by Ruby during the past six months. These calls clearly indicate some very undesirable connections with underworld characters. There are calls of record to unsavory characters. . . . Ruby explains that these were business calls for the purpose of securing entertainers for his clubs, or of discussing "union problems." It is clear that the F.B.I. has thoroughly investigated these telephone calls. Competent sources repeatedly report that the State intends to capitalize on these facts.

II. This investigator is informed that the State expects to be able to prove conclusively that Jack Ruby is a volatile and quick tempered individual, and that numerous witnesses will be paraded to the stand to testify to his acts of violence. I believe that we can best capitalize on this by developing witnesses who will testify that these acts are always spontaneous, as reenforcement for the opinion which I feel certain will be expressed by our psychiatric staff.

Several local medical doctors interviewed by this investigator are of the opinion that Ruby is irrational or bordering on the irrational. One, Dr. Coleman Jacobson, was particularly emphatic in this area. These doctors also reported that examination of Ruby indicated no chronic physical ailment.

Many persons interviewed stated that Ruby carries a pistol very frequently. The State intends to rely upon this fact to partially support its case.

An interesting sidelight became evident several days ago from a close source of information at the District Attorney's office, which reported that Eve Grant will be questioned on the witness stand regarding a fight with her brother some months ago at the Vegas Club. Investigation disclosed that Ruby assaulted his sister, causing her to fall to the floor. She then locked herself in the office of the Vegas Club and summoned the police. She reportedly stated to the investigating officer that "Jack tried to kill me!"

It is also interesting that Eve Grant has had psychiatric attention on at least four occasions, and that Ruby's mother, now deceased, was at one time in a mental institution. Effort should be made to learn what other psychological help has been extended to members of the immediate family. This would be particularly helpful in the event it is desired to raise the issue of heriditary insanity.

Psychologically, it is also interesting to note how many people have commented to this investigator regarding Ruby's emotional, almost fanatical devotion to his dogs.

Denson was ruthlessly thorough in his investigation. Not even the staff of the district attorney's office escaped his scrutiny. What he had discovered bordered on the libelous, however, and was much too dangerous to use or to quote. And he had much to say about public opinion and the press:

Reliable sources report to this investigator that the Dallas Police Department is exceptionally bitter toward Ruby, that the Chief of Police has "passed the word" that any officer giving information or testimony for Ruby in any respect will be either dismissed or severely disciplined. It might be added that the same attitude prevails throughout the city of Dallas.

Sources in the Jewish community also report that most Jewish people are extremely unhappy with Ruby. They feel they have been embarrassed and humiliated, not only by Ruby, but by Bernard Weis[s]man, who caused the article entitled "Welcome Mr. President" to be published in the Dallas Morning News.

Around town, about 50% of the population appear to believe that there must be some tie between Ruby and Oswald. This is due mainly to the fact that the F.B.I. has not released its report regarding the Oswald shooting.

Some consideration might be given to putting pressure on the Bureau through press release from defense counsel. The Bureau is particularly sensitive to adverse publicity, and might be goaded into at least revealing that they have found no connection between Ruby and Oswald. . . . Also, my press contact with the Times Herald has indicated that he will print stories about Ruby's dogs and things of that nature, which might do a little something to soften the opinion of the populace regarding Ruby as an unfeeling vice-lord—which is what a lot of people believe at this time because of the "strip-joint operator" publicity.

The district attorney, Denson learned, was preparing almost life-size blowups of the shooting. Denson himself was keeping a detailed, indexed, daily scrapbook of the growing press coverage of the case.

The motion for a change of venue preoccupied Denson, as it did Belli and his associates. The presiding judge, presumably, was the key to what would ensue. What Denson wrote of him was of peculiar significance in view of what happened later:

Judge Joe B. Brown is extremely sensitive to political pressures, especially from wealthy and influential persons. He is a vacilating [sic] figure whose personality can be capitalized upon through the indirect influence of our Jewish rabbi friends who have expressed willingness to aid—anonimously [sic]—in that direction. Although he could change overnight, it appears at present that Judge Brown will favor change of venue, and may consult us as to where we would like the venue changed.

Where should the case go in the event a change of venue were granted? Tonahill, more familiar with his state than Belli, favored San Antonio—"an excellent choice," according to Denson:

San Antonio, being largely Mexican and Catholic, is a city having some rather strong minority groups. Burlesque operations and coexistence with vice are a part of its accustomed way of life. Because of the prevelent [sic] Latin population, there is a marked tolerance for actions triggered by emotional outbursts. In addition, the San Antonio Light has handled publicity in a more enlightened manner than we have experienced here.

Other good cities, in order of preference, were El Paso, Beaumont, and Midland-Odessa:

Beaumont supports an unusually large prostitute population and open vice has always been the rule there. The populace is still mad at the Attorney General because of some vice raids conducted several years ago. They are also notorious for light murder sentences.

Midland-Odessa has to recommend it the possibility of joining attorney John Watts as local counsel. Watts is very popular among the oil field workers there. It would be hard to pick a jury of people who feel no ties to John Watts. Also, good relationship with newspapers there in the past could be valuable in this case.

Waco and some other central Texas cities of the so-called "Bible Belt" would not be to our advantage. Some of these cities are completely dry. They countenance no tolerance toward vice, and their conservative populations would have no sympathy for a man in Jack Ruby's profession.

Denson thought the prosecution would concentrate on Ruby's possession of pistols, at the time of the shooting of Oswald as well as in the past; and he posed a number of questions that should be answered before the trial. The State, be believed, would also concentrate on Ruby's alleged gangster connections, his reputation for violence, and "premeditation."

The State, Denson thought, anticipated that Ruby would take the stand. This would enable it to stress the "gangster" issue. On the other hand, his propensity to violence might be used to establish temporary insanity.

On the all-important issue of premeditation, he was
brief and troubled:

A detailed interview should be conducted with Ruby with
the purpose of knowing his every move and the names of all
persons with whom he spoke, beginning with the morning of
November 22, 1963, and up to the moment of the shooting of
Lee Oswald. The F.B.I. has traced Ruby's activities during this
period meticulously, and it would be well to know their findings.

In this regard, circumstances have tremendously hampered
any attempt to gain information needed from Ruby himself. I
am not permitted to see him in the counsel room, but must
transmit questions through Eva Grant. Mrs. Grant has done her
best, but she is not well, and when she visits Ruby, she has to
present her questions in writing to assure privacy, then stand
and hold a paper against the glass, then wait for Jack to write
a reply which she has to copy, standing. This is extremely difficult for her, and unsatisfactory from an investigative standpoint when there are so many questions in need of answers, and
time is so short.

Belli and Tonahill should have bestirred themselves in
response to the suggestions of their perceptive and competent private investigator, but neither Denson nor the family felt that they were sufficiently aroused to the perils that
faced Jack Ruby. In the glare of the flashbulbs, they were
blinded to the clearly outlined dangers.


THE SECOND BAIL HEARING

At the bail hearing on December 23, the defense had
had its first opportunity to present its case in a courtroom,
and it had not fared well. Judge Brown had concluded the
hearing, not with an absolute determination, but by stating that he was denying the defense motion for release on
bail "for the present." He would hear more testimony on
the matter on January 10, 1964. Thus the results were

mixed. Ruby's release had not been secured, but testimony had been adduced that might cast a more favorable light on the case. And at the second hearing, perhaps there would be a more favorable ruling from the unpredictable judge.

Melvin Belli's public reaction to Judge Brown's decision, however, was to announce immediately that he would move for a change of venue "because it is impossible to get a fair trial here in Dallas because of statements that have been made and are now being made by the Dallas *News*."

The second bail hearing, set for January 10, was continued to January 20. Belli regarded the delay as providential, because it permitted him to obtain, somewhat belatedly, psychological and psychiatric data on his client from competent and distinguished men. At the hearing itself Belli put this material into the record. He believed that this testimony, showing the unpremeditated nature of the murder and the disordered temperament of his client, would tend to create public sympathy for Ruby and lead to his release pending the trial. He ignored the likelihood that this information would also serve to alert the prosecution to the defense to come. With advance knowledge, they would surely be prepared at the trial to controvert what the defense experts said.

Belli also sought to adduce something from the prosecution. He called Dr. John T. Holbrook, the State's psychiatrist, to testify for the defense and brought out through him that more tests of Ruby had to be made before there could be a definitive diagnosis. These tests, Belli argued, could best be made if Ruby were not confined in the county jail.

Ruby himself showed visible emotion in response to the ebb and flow of the hearing and the questions put to him by reporters. He wept copiously when asked how he had reacted to President Kennedy's death.

The hearing ended abruptly. Judge Brown declared that, by agreement of both sides, Ruby would receive all the neurological tests that were required. These tests were to be supervised by three doctors of his selection—Dr. Robert L. Stubblefield, chairman of the Department of Psychiatry at the University of Texas Southwestern Medical School in Dallas, Dr. Martin L. Towler of the Titus Harris Clinic in Galveston, and Dr. John T. Holbrook, who, it will be recalled, had been chosen as a State psychiatrist. Melvin Belli, proclaiming a defense victory, thereupon withdrew the motion for bail, and Ruby remained in jail. The next act in the drama was set for February 10; it was to be the defense motion for a change of venue.

Much might be said about each of these maneuvers. Most obvious is that Belli was finding the competition much more difficult than he had anticipated. Tom Howard, although nominally a member of the defense, was making no secret of his joy over Belli's discomfiture. Jack Ruby and his family were beginning to feel that perhaps "class" was not enough, or perhaps only that they had obtained the wrong kind. Perhaps they had added to their problems by inviting Melvin Belli, the great enemy of the insurance companies, to the insurance capital of the Southwest. Jack was often joyous in appearance and always garrulous when the reporters were around; but there were moments when even he began to wonder about his public, his legal advocates, his ultimate fate.

# 2

## PUBLICITY

ONE MAY SAFELY SAY that no series of events within the last century attracted so much instantaneous attention and publicity as did the assassination of President Kennedy and the shooting of Lee Harvey Oswald. The communications media were out in force to record the President's visit to Dallas, and when he was gunned down, these reporters and cameramen were quickly augmented by yet another contingent determined to inform America and the world, immediately and in depth, of all that was happening.

If there is to be any villain in this piece, however, it must be the public, or if not the public, then that intangible quirk of the mind that caused Pandora to loose on the world all its woes. For the people's curiosity has been converted by the press into "the right to know," and that has often become "the right to intrude." The press, radio, and television know one and only one objective, and in pursuit of it their representatives flocked to Dallas. The sheer force of their presence is seldom, if ever, felt in most communities, and with it the Dallas authorities were entirely unprepared to cope. The result was pandemonium and disaster. After the arrest of Oswald, newsmen descended on the headquarters of the Dallas police and turned it into a bedlam. And so it was until after Oswald himself was killed.

From the beginning of the Ruby case, the press placed great pressure upon anyone who was connected with it in any way, especially those authorities in charge of the investigation. Unfortunately, few public officials were averse to giving out, not only such information as they had, but their opinions as well.

The flow of information did not stop with the silencing of Oswald. Even District Attorney Henry Wade, who should have known better, was quoted as saying that he would ask for the death penalty with full confidence that a Dallas County jury would return the correct verdict in the case. The relentless Bill Alexander described Ruby's action as "the shooting of a manacled man down in cold blood, and this is a death penalty case." Sheriff Bill Decker said that "it is not inconceivable that the whole plot could have been hatched in Russia." Wade was emphatic: "Nobody deplored the assassination of President Kennedy and the murder of officer J. D. Tippit more than I. They were cold-blooded murder and an assassination. I think this kind of premeditated murder calls for the death penalty and I intend to ask it." And he intended to fill the gap on the trial calendar caused by Oswald's death with the trial of Jack Ruby.

Statements prejudicial to Jack Ruby's case were not directed solely at him. They were aimed at his counsel as well. Immediately upon Belli's arrival in Dallas for the first time, a newspaper printed his picture in the company of another gentleman, stating that Belli was accompanied by a bodyguard! In fact, the "bodyguard" was R. B. Denson, the local investigator hired by the defense. Many such stories were to appear before the trial was over.

In view of the ultimate result of the case, it is ironical that, on December 19, 1963, before the trial began, Judge Brown issued a reassuring statement outlining the ground rules. He warned all and sundry: "Throughout the trial of Jack Ruby, due process of law will prevail in my court, and decorum will be maintained at all times by those participating in the trial, by the press and by the public witnessing the trial. No television equipment, no radio recording equipment and no cameras for still photographs will be permitted in the courtroom while the court is in session."

But the shadow of things to come was evident: the judge's statement was issued by his press spokesman! So it was to be throughout this notorious case, where words and deeds were ever at cross purposes. Indeed, words were in conflict with words! For Judge Brown could not always discern the implications of what he was doing or saying. What was obvious to others was not always clear to him.

Attorneys have long known, and the courts have recognized, that no matter what is said in the newspapers before and during a trial, the notoriety of a case is itself bound to affect those directly involved in it. All the extraneous matter that appears in the newspapers must have some effect upon the jurors even though they make a conscientious attempt to put it out of mind. As Mr. Justice Holmes has said, in *Patterson* v. *Colorado,* "The theory of our system is that the conclusions to be reached in a case will be induced only by evidence and argument in open court, and not by any outside influences, whether of private talk or public print."

The coverage of Ruby, in words and pictures, by all the communications media, was enormous. Much of it was bad to the point of maliciousness, some of it was perhaps written in good faith, but distorted and inaccurate, and all of it was part and parcel of the atmosphere that was to make it impossible to give the unfortunate man a fair trial in Dallas, and possibly elsewhere.

Even so august a newspaper as *The New York Times* was not immune to the desire to print whatever could be learned about Jack Ruby. Three weeks after the shooting of Oswald it spread a headline across seven columns: RUBY'S CHICAGO ACQUAINTANCES DESCRIBE HIM AS THE VICTIM OF A STUNTED YOUTH. Very quickly the *Times* writer, Austin C. Wehrwein, made his point:

Jack (Sparky) Ruby, the fawning small-time quick-buck hustler who made the big time after a fashion by killing the accused assassin of President Kennedy, is being explained by perplexed friends who knew him when as the victim of an underprivileged youth.

"When" means the grimy depression years in the old West Side ghetto area, now a Negro district. Insecure, vain, sensitive to racial slurs, young Ruby lived by his wits but despite a glib tongue those who remember say he didn't have enough of them.

His chief talent was a desire to ingratiate himself with people, and if there is any simple explanation for his murder of Lee H. Oswald to be gained from a reconstruction of his early years it is, his former associates believe, that he wanted, in a tragically mistaken way, to ingratiate himself with society at large.

Then, in the ensuing columns, the now familiar story of Jack Ruby and his family was told. They, and particularly Jack, were made to appear as objects of pity. For obscure people, much seemed to have been known, and told, of them. By now, they and those they knew had been badgered by every reporter and would-be psychologist on both sides of the Atlantic Ocean. In millions of words the section and dissection and resection of Jack Ruby was ushered into millions of homes by millions of television sets and newspapers and magazines. Throughout the case there remained the artificiality of video tapes and tubes and ink and newsprint rather than something smacking and smelling of real life.

As the preliminary sparring in the case went on, men and women all over the country speculated about the result of the trial. Would Ruby go scot-free? Would he be acquitted because of temporary insanity? Would he get only a few years in prison? Would there be a long sentence, even a life term? Was it conceivable that a death sentence would be voted by the jury?

Few people had heard of a similar case in Sioux City, Iowa, growing out of the presidential assassination. There a dental technician, a man in his forties, had stabbed his step-father to death when the latter made disparaging remarks about the murdered Galahad, John F. Kennedy.

Pleading guilty, he was given a suspended prison sentence and fined $1000. Then the judge, after telling him how serious a crime it is to kill a man, wished him the season's best: it was Christmas Eve.

A month later *The Capital Times,* in Madison, Wisconsin, posed as "The Question of the Day," "Do you think Jack Ruby will be freed by a Texas court?"

A housewife answered: "Well, I hope they don't! I think that Ruby committed a crime, and justice should be done down there just like it would be if he had killed him here. I understand that he is going to plead temporary insanity. No matter how bad Oswald was, I don't think he should be acquitted on that plea of temporary insanity."

A meat cutter thought they would free Ruby: "I don't think he should be released on bail. But it's quite probable he might get off at his trial. It seems to me that there are just too many loopholes in the present laws. His plea of temporary insanity just might stand up in court—especially down there in Texas. You never know what will happen in court."

A salesman said: "He committed a horrible crime and should be punished like anyone else. Oswald should have had his day in court, too. This idea of a plea of temporary insanity is a very hard thing to define. Temporary insanity is possible, I guess, but I question sometimes if this should be a reason for acquittal."

Another housewife responded vehemently, yet thoughtfully: "He did kill Lee Oswald! I don't think they'll let him go free. The public may sympathize with Ruby because of Oswald's crime. However, I feel the law will take its normal course. I don't feel that he should be convicted of first degree murder. This is probably because I feel so strong about President Kennedy's assassination. I think Ruby has a better chance of a fair trial than Oswald would ever have had."

This random sampling may, or may not, have been typical of the country at large. Those who shouted "Hurrah!"

when the deed was done, and there were many, even in Dallas, could not have reversed themselves in so short a period of time. Others, knowing the increasing reluctance of juries everywhere to impose a death sentence, felt that the reluctance would be greater in the case of the man who had executed, as it were, the cold-blooded assassin of the beloved young President. A Dallas jury might be different, but it was still part of the human race.

Another article, by a feature writer of the Associated Press, published in many newspapers on Sunday, January 26, 1964, lingered in the memories of the family. It was written by Bernard Gavzer after much contact with the family and friends in Chicago, San Francisco, and Dallas.

Ruby, Gavzer said, "killed more than a man. He killed a secret"—what had caused Oswald to assassinate the President? There were questions, too. Did Ruby act impulsively in his grief? Did he kill for publicity? Was he involved in a plot? Gavzer felt that Ruby himself was puzzled by these questions, rather than by his own fate:

"He talks, oh my, how he talks," says one of Ruby's visitors, "but not once have I heard him ask, 'What will happen to me?' He does ask, 'Do people approve of me?' "

"Just this week, he spoke with me nearly two hours, and over and over he talked about that Sunday morning. It was like hearing a man talking about something that didn't happen to him, as though he was trying to figure out to whom it did happen. He goes over every single detail, over and over, as though he is trying to learn something or find something."

Gavzer told of Ruby's ambivalent attitude toward his sister Eva. He quoted Ruby as saying, according to Eva, "If this was my wife, I'd divorce her, but how can you divorce a sister?" Ruby, he said, would take real joy in the visits of "classy" persons like Rabbi Hillel Silverman; "class" was his great shibboleth, even when he did not know what true quality was.

An old acquaintance of Jack's was quoted: "Ruby is the kind of guy who reads a newspaper and lives it. He reads about a kid getting polio or a dog getting run over, and he cries. The same way in a movie. If the good guy gets double-crossed, Ruby acts like it happens to him." Gavzer concluded that Ruby was deeply, almost obsessively, involved in what people thought of him. He quoted a visitor to Ruby: "When he reads letters from people who tell him he did right, or otherwise compliment him, his spirits go way up. He says he has had no mail from anyone criticizing him. Maybe they only give him the complimentary mail. I don't know." Gavzer also quoted the prosecution: "Ruby is a class-conscious nobody who saw an opportunity to do something that would put him in the public eye and even make him a hero. He wasn't insane. He was rational. But he figured wrong. He's not a hero; he's a heel. Because of fouling up history."

Thus there was destined to be a clash between both sides on this very issue of class that was so dear to Ruby. Gavzer developed this theme in his longish account of the nondescript career of the man in Chicago, San Francisco, Dallas, and other places, while in and out of the armed forces. In a sense, all life was a pitched battle for Ruby. Those who could fight back, like the crowd around Davey Miller's West Side restaurant in Chicago, were the ones he could understand; he was a part of that crowd, whatever the occupation of the moment. "He wanted to be liked, and he was," said Joe Cavagnero, a hotel executive in Dallas. "He'd do anything for you if he liked you. He could be in the hole to someone but he'd still loan you money if you needed it."

Gavzer's conclusion provided a clue to Ruby's troubled character: "Recently a visitor asked about his ambition in life. Ruby thought about it a while. Then he said. 'A success.'"

He was now a success: the eyes of the world were upon him.

## FOR A CHANGE OF VENUE

Belli professed outrage at the publicity accorded his client. On January 28, he spelled out the reasons why he believed a fair trial could not be held in Dallas. He, Sam Brody, and Tonahill joined in a printed brief in support of Ruby's motion for a change of venue. "Prejudice," they urged, "is a combination and blending of many ingredients." To answer those who argued that such prejudice as may have existed was rampant everywhere, and not only in Dallas County, they asserted that the "extensive combination of prejudicial factors" was present in Dallas County "alone." They listed the factors that "so simmered" these as "to preclude the probability of a fair trial":

1. Assassination of President Kennedy on Dallas street;

2. Assassination site close to the courthouse where Jack Ruby will be tried;

3. Assassination site still visited and flowers are still placed near by;

4. Assassination and shooting of Oswald are conceptually intertwined;

5. Dallas blamed directly and indirectly for the assassination of the President;

6. Dallas blamed for allowing the shooting of Oswald;

7. Dallas representatives have expressed feelings of recrimination publicly;

8. Dallas County's deprivation of prosecuting Oswald could find atonement in the persecution of Ruby;

9. Revulsion over Stevenson spitting and efforts to blame Dallas for such incidents;

10. Dallas blamed for promoting extremism;

11. Dallas County cannot judge Ruby fairly, while State, Nation and World judge Dallas;

12. Publicity regarding fear of political and economic reprisals against Dallas;

13. Subliminal effect on Dallas jury of the publicity against the Dallas community;

14. Dallas District Attorney published pre-trial demand for

the death of a citizen who is charged with killing the vicious assassin of the President;

15. Adverse publicity concerning Ruby's legal counsel and clearance by Grievance Committee of District Attorney's press releases;

16. Such extreme pressure and publicity that trial judge needed services of public relations expert;

17. Necessity of taking extreme security precautions for transfer of Ruby to County Jail, undisclosed location of jail cell, newspaper's own security precautions, and protection of courtroom for bail bond hearing;

18. Adverse local press stories carrying innuendos of conspiracy between Ruby, Oswald, and Communists;

19. Threats of physical violence against other citizens of Dallas after assassination of President and shooting of Oswald;

20. Adverse local press referring to Ruby as "tough guy, Chicago mobster and strip joint owner";

21. Anti-Semitism against Ruby sparked by publicity that name had been changed from Rubenstein;

22. Such strong local prejudice that Parkland Hospital, which treated the avowed Marxist, Oswald, initially refused to permit Ruby to undergo tests that were to be made available to defendant's counsel, the State and the Warren Commission.

To prove their point, they closed their brief with a lengthy appendix of excerpts from the Dallas press, illustrating the censure and defense of Dallas in connection with the presidential assassination and its aftermath, the comments and innuendos linking Ruby with Oswald and suggesting a Communist conspiracy, the adverse and prejudicial publicity against Ruby and his attorneys, and, finally, miscellaneous statements affecting an impartial trial.

The Texas statute and the leading cases with respect to change of venue were analyzed, including a number of Texas authorities and *Irvin* v. *Dowd* from Indiana and the *Rideau* case of Louisiana.

In the *Dowd* case Justice Frankfurter, in a concurring

opinion, had dealt with the heart of the matter, with an eloquence that is still memorable:

More than one student of society has expressed the view that not the least significant test of the quality of a civilization is its treatment of those charged with crime, particularly with offenses which arouse the passions of a community. One of the rightful boasts of Western civilization is that the State has the burden of establishing guilt solely on the basis of evidence produced in court and under circumstances assuring an accused all the safeguards of a fair procedure. These rudimentary conditions for determining guilt are inevitably wanting if the jury which is to sit in judgment on a fellow human being comes to its task with its mind ineradicably poisoned against him. How can fallible men and women reach a disinterested verdict based exclusively on what they heard in court when, before they entered the jury box, their minds were saturated by press and radio for months preceding by matter designed to establish the guilt of the accused. A conviction so secured obviously constitutes a denial of due process of law in its most rudimentary conception.

On February 10, an extended hearing on the motion for a change of venue began. The record of this hearing alone was to run to 788 pages (and the documentation to many more). The defense called the only witnesses, while the prosecution contented itself with placing into the record several affidavits to the effect that Ruby could in fact obtain a fair trial in Dallas.

Witness after witness testified that he had doubts that Ruby could be tried fairly. Clayton Fowler, president of the Dallas County Criminal Bar Association, testified that most of the people he talked to were highly opinionated, that it would be most difficult to find a fair jury in Dallas. Costine A. Droby, an attorney, testified that he thought the consensus to be that the only way Dallas could vindicate itself was to convict Jack Ruby. Earle Cabell, a former mayor of Dallas, testified that there could be a civic resentment against Ruby and that this might make a difference in his getting a fair trial. Barefoot Sanders, United States attorney for the Northern District of Texas, said that he felt it would take more time and effort to get a jury in Dallas than elsewhere.

R. S. Walker, news director for WFAA-TV in Dallas, declared that the people in Dallas had been "saturated with information." Stanley Kaufman, another attorney, testified that there was a better chance of getting a fair jury where there was less consciousness of the event and that the farther the trial was from Dallas the better for Jack Ruby. Robert O'Donnell, yet another attorney, said that almost everyone he had spoken to about the case had an opinion on it. A. C. Green, editorial page editor of the Dallas *Times Herald*, while of the opinion that Ruby could get a fair trial in Dallas, stated that it would be impossible to say that the case was not on their minds, as it was one of the most talked about subjects in the community. And one of the most respected members of the Dallas community, the merchant Stanley Marcus, stated that he had great reservations about whether a fair trial could be held in Dallas.

Despite all this testimony, Judge Brown was not convinced that a change of venue was necessary. He refused to believe what should have been amply evident without a long hearing. Even District Attorney Henry Wade had been quoted as saying, on December 3, 1963, "I think it is highly unlikely that the inflamed public feeling will permit such a trial until about mid-February." His belief was that by then the atmosphere in Dallas would have become normal enough to permit a fair trial. But there is nothing in the transcript of the entire venue hearing that leads to the conclusion that matters had returned to normal. In fact, evidence was given that newspaper coverage had become even more prejudicial to the defendant. Far from returning to "normal," the public was given more and more information and misinformation, which could only make it more difficult, if not impossible, for a jury to reach a verdict derived only from evidence presented in court.

Later the district attorney was quoted as saying that "with the tremendous amount of coverage, I think he can get as fair a trial here as anywhere." This being the case, Judge Brown should have waited until the furor had died down. A defendant is not entitled to "as fair a trial as anywhere," but a trial that is fair to him in all respects. If the publicity is so bad, then the only possible thing to do is wait.

Judge Brown, however, "was getting a little impatient to get on with the trial." After much argument, he announced that he would postpone a decision until after an attempt had been made to empanel a jury. If unprejudiced jurors could not be found, then it would be necessary to move the trial to another city. He did not believe, however, that it would be impossible to find an impartial jury in Dallas.

## SELECTING THE JURY

The selection of a jury in a criminal case lends itself to great drama and is a test of the skills of competing counsel. The legend of Clarence Darrow derives in large part from his supposed genius in choosing jurors and inculcating in them his compassionate and skeptical viewpoint even before the offering of evidence. In fact, Darrow looked for Jews, Negroes, Italians, and drinking men, indulgent men, of all ethnic groups; he fought against the selection of dour Scandinavians, Anglo-Saxons, and northern strains generally. He wanted jurors in whom charity was inbred, jurors who would understand sinners.

Belli, too, had great skill in selecting jurors who were generous and sympathetic enough to enrich his clients and himself in personal injury cases. But where, and how, was he to find such warmhearted jurors in Dallas, the Baptist citadel, the financial center of the Southwest, the epitome of "Establishment America," the enemy of social revolution, where "undesirable types" and advanced ideas were systematically excluded?

Now, with the judge's decision on change of venue in

abeyance, waiting the test of actual inability to empanel an
impartial jury, Belli was confronted with two conflicting
tasks at one and the same time. In selecting the jurors he
would have to show that Ruby could not receive a fair trial
in Dallas, but if he could not do that, he had still to choose
men and women who would try the case. Since Belli was
convinced that acceptable jurors could not be found in the
first place, he would have no reason to avoid antagonizing
prospective jurors, the exact opposite course to what would
be his usual practice in finding sympathetic jurors.

In addition, Belli had to operate within the normal
framework of the law on the challenging of prospective
jurors. Jurors may be rejected "for cause" or "peremptorily" (without cause). Cause may include a juror's
relation to the parties in the case or to the attorneys; his
having witnessed the events; his demonstrable prejudices;
his insanity; his conviction of a felony. Disqualifications
"for cause" are unlimited in number; as many as are tainted
may be excused. Peremptory challenges may result from no
more than the attorney's dislike for the manner in which
the venireman folds his hands; there need be no reason
whatsoever offered for the rejection of the prospective
juror. Peremptory challenges are not unlimited in number;
they are set by the court in accordance with established
rules and precedents. Thus every attorney uses them with
caution, never forgetting that he may have good use for
every one of them.

Belli was not concerned. He believed he had the ultimate
question, one that would dispose of nearly every prospective juror. He immediately challenged, "for cause," the first
venireman who said that she had seen the shooting of
Oswald on television. She was a "witness," Belli said.

To Belli's despair, Judge Brown did not agree. If he
accepted Belli's challenge, then very few of the prospective
jurors would not be excused; for if they had not seen the
shooting "live," they had had innumerable opportunities to
see it rerun after the event. But Judge Brown did not

believe that television viewers were witnesses in the sense intended by the law, and he rejected such challenges for cause. Belli then had to make the most of what he regarded as an improper ruling; he would have to cajole prospective jurors whom he really distrusted.

The State was not without its own secret weapon, one unrecognized by most citizens. At the time of the trial the precedents held that if a juror was opposed, in principle, to capital punishment when that might be the penalty for a crime, then the State could excuse him for cause. The effect was to exclude from a jury exactly those sympathetic human beings who would most likely temper justice with mercy, exactly the sort of persons whom Belli wanted on the jury. Since it has been shown that those who favor capital punishment are more likely to convict and to pronounce stiff penalties than are those who oppose, the State had inherent advantages in bringing into the case severe and settled jurors who would stand for no nonsense about the possibility of a person's acting on uncontrolled impulse or as the result of a mental disturbance. (In the *Witherspoon* case, decided by the United States Supreme Court in 1968, this precedent was overturned. Then the court held that jurors may not be disqualified because of scruples against capital punishment, unless it is shown that they would not convict the defendant or impose the death penalty in any circumstances.)

When at last Belli realized that he was not going to get his change of venue, that he was not going to be allowed to challenge those who had seen the slaying on television, that he was going to have to "live with" the situation, he decided, by obverse logic, that because of the highly technical evidence that would be offered by the defense, he wanted intelligent men and women who could understand it. This was a sure recipe for disaster; for such Dallas citizens would be utterly unsympathetic to Jack Ruby, his occupation, his derivation, his crime. It is remarkable how even an essentially shrewd man such as Belli could deceive himself. The prosecution team, less learned than Belli, was nevertheless wiser in the ways of the world of Dallas.

Slowly, day by day, the wrangling over the jury diminished, and slowly the panel filled. Belli used up his peremptory challenges; he was granted more. Then, in a rush, during one day while Judge Brown was ill and another, less lenient judge sat in his place, the last juror was selected. In all, 162 prospective jurors had been examined. Of these, 121 were dismissed for cause, 68 by the prosecution and 58 by the defense, and 1 for illness. The defense used all 18 of its peremptory challenges, and the prosecution used 11 of its 15. This alone should have convinced Judge Brown that a change of venue was warranted.

Certainly the experience in choosing the jury must have made it clear, after all the testimony at the change of venue hearing, that while it may not have been impossible to select a fair jury, it was certainly improbable. The life of a human being ought not to have depended on such a gamble.

Now Ruby was to be tried by a group of tough-minded Texans who did not like his kind of man, who had no use for his action.

# THE TRIAL

# 3

## THE TRIAL

I DO NOT WANT to repeat here what has already been written about the trial in the excellent account by Professors John Kaplan and Jon R. Waltz.* My aim is to cover material not generally known, to deal with those matters I know at first hand, and to examine information that became available after the trial. But it will be helpful to make a quick survey here of all the testimony at the trial of Jack Ruby.

It should be realized that this recital of the testimony is foreshortened. No effort is made to give the testimony in full, and thus all the drama and tension implicit in the actual event is missing. Except in so-called opening statements at the beginning of a trial—and there was none in this case—lawyers do not give advance information to the jury about precisely what they hope to prove as they parade the witnesses before it. They insinuate by their bearing, their questions, their tone, what they think they are demonstrating. These nuances, which cannot be captured in a transcript, sometimes penetrate deeper and remain longer in the memory of a juror than a witness's factual utterances.

Drama is always implicit in any trial, for there are bound to be conflicts in testimony. Witnesses do not always stand up as well as anticipated by the attorneys; no matter how assured the witness is, he can always be taken by surprise. And this applies equally to the attorney. Witnesses are sometimes better, and sometimes worse, than anticipated.

* *The Trial of Jack Ruby*, Macmillan, 1965

Unconsidered trifles become mighty portents of things to come.

This trial was no exception in that respect. If the trial was exceptional in any way, it was in decorum. From beginning to end there were constant displays of bad manners, bad tempers, shouting matches, interruptions, rudeness, by attorneys on both sides. The courtroom was never the serene and calm forum it should have been.

All this lay in the future, however, and was not to be anticipated from the outset. Attorneys do not undertake a defense, however complicated, in the expectation that they will lose. They begin confidently, or at least hopefully, but even they cannot be unaffected by the course of the testimony. Both the prosecution and the defense were certain each would win. Only the jurors could decide.

The first witness called by the prosecution on the morning of March 4, 1964, was *Don Campbell,* an advertising salesman for the Dallas *Morning News.* Campbell said that he was with Ruby in the newspaper offices until about ten minutes before President Kennedy's assassination. (The purpose of this testimony obviously was to show that Ruby did not go to see the presidential parade, that his protestations of love for Kennedy were exaggerated.)

On cross-examination Campbell was led to admit that Ruby was a volatile individual and that he was not at the parade because he was working.

*John Newman,* another member of the advertising staff of the *Morning News,* testified that he had returned to the office at 12:40, without knowing that Kennedy had been assassinated. Then the news of the assassination came in, and although Ruby appeared stunned, he was no more so than anyone else. Newman testified that Ruby usually wrote his own advertisements and was competent in this phase of his business.

On cross-examination he testified that Ruby at times became "hysterical" and "excited," and that Ruby had complained very bitterly about an advertisement in the newspaper attacking Kennedy. Ruby, he said, would get into very strong emotional states from time to time.

*Georgia Mayer,* a secretary in the advertising department of the *Morning News,* was present in the office with Ruby. She did not talk to him or remember whether he had watched television with the rest of those present.

On cross-examination she said that Ruby had been sitting in the newspaper office in a dazed condition, with a fixed stare, and that this was something remarkable. She saw only this stare, for she had looked at him only for a moment.

*William Glenn Duncan,* a newsman for radio station KLIF in Dallas, remembered that Ruby had called him around midnight of Friday, about twelve hours after the assassination, and asked if he wanted to interview Henry Wade, the district attorney. When Duncan said yes, Ruby put Wade on the telephone. About 1:30 or 1:45 A.M., Ruby appeared at the radio station with sandwiches and soda for the newsmen. Ruby had stated that he had been in city hall when Oswald was brought out and had found himself standing close to Oswald. Ruby left the station about 2:00 A.M.

On cross-examination the witness said that he hardly knew Ruby and could not comment on his character.

*Richard M. Sims,* a detective in the Homicide and Robbery Bureau of the Dallas Police Department, said that on Friday night he was in the bureau office when Oswald was being questioned. At that time Ruby telephoned, asking whether the officers would like some sandwiches. (This was groundwork for the prosecution argument that Ruby was looking for excuses to get close to Oswald as often as possible.)

Sims admitted, on cross-examination, that he had heard that Ruby was a highly emotional and excitable individual, a sort of character around town. Ruby, he said, was friendly with various Dallas police officers.

*T. B. Leonard,* a lieutenant in the Burglary and Theft

Bureau, was present when District Attorney Wade was holding a press conference on Friday night at city hall, and Ruby was there, saying to him, "I'm a reporter tonight."

*Wesley A. Wise,* a newsman for Dallas radio station KLRD, testified that on Saturday, November 23, at about 3:00 P.M., he was in a mobile television unit near the Texas School Book Depository when Ruby appeared and rapped on the window. Ruby suggested that Wise take the pictures of two Dallas policemen who had been assigned to investigate the Kennedy assassination.

*Sgt. D. V. Harkness,* of the Dallas Police Traffic Division, recalled that at about 3:00 P.M. that Saturday he was clearing the crowd from the entrance to the jail in preparation for the transfer of Oswald, which was scheduled at 4:00 P.M. He had seen Ruby in the crowd.

*John Rutledge,* a reporter on the night police beat for the Dallas *Morning News,* was in the Homicide and Burglary Bureau office about 7:00 P.M., Friday evening. Ruby had appeared there, identifying Dallas officials, in a knowing way, to the out-of-state press. Ruby, he said, was acting essentially as an "information man" to those around.

On cross-examination the witness stated that he considered Ruby to be "mean." He also stated that he did not think Ruby was normal.

*Garnett Claud Hallmark,* general manager of the parking lot where Ruby usually left his car, was present when Ruby attempted to call Wesley Wise of radio station KLRD at 2:50 P.M. Saturday. Ruby, he said, had told someone on the other end of the telephone that many people were strewing flowers at the assassination scene and that this would probably cause Oswald's transfer to be postponed.

*Doyle Lane,* a Western Union employee, took the stand. He said that Ruby was in the Western Union office only four minutes before he shot Oswald. The Western Union records with the decisive time stamp were introduced into evidence.

The cross-examination emphasized the time. (Lane's

testimony could be decisive in showing whether or not there had been premeditation or malice in the shooting of Oswald. While intent to kill can be formed in a moment, it is psychologically unlikely if there is necessarily haste and little time for premeditation.)

*Ray Brantly,* owner of a Dallas hardware and sporting-goods store, testified that he had sold Ruby a snub-nose Colt Cobra pistol, serial number 2744, on January 19, 1960. The gun, which had been used to shoot Oswald, was admitted into evidence.

*James R. Leavelle,* a detective in the Homicide and Robbery Bureau, testified that he was handcuffed to Oswald for the transfer from the City Jail. He, Oswald, and Detective Graves, who held Oswald's left arm, walked into the basement behind Captain Fritz. The basement was brilliantly illuminated for television and movie cameras. He saw a man rush out of the crowd, raising a pistol in preparation for shooting. It looked as if he took two quick steps. Then the man fired the gun, and Oswald grunted and fell to the floor. The witness and another officer took Oswald back into the jail office. As they were examining Oswald, Ruby was brought in and said, "I hope the son of a bitch dies!" Shortly after this, Leavelle rode in the ambulance with Oswald to Parkland Hospital.

On cross-examination Leavelle could not remember how Ruby was holding the pistol at the time of the shooting. He did state, however, that Ruby had a calm expression on his face at the time. (Photographs show that neither Leavelle nor anyone else actually saw Ruby step forward and shoot Oswald.)

*Dr. Earl Forest Rose,* the Dallas County Medical Examiner, testified that he examined Oswald's body and determined that the cause of death was "hemorrhage, secondary to gunshot wound of the chest." (This was another way of stating that Ruby's act had resulted in the death of Oswald. The question still was whether or not the act was premeditated or unpremeditated, murder with or without malice, with the penalty ranging from death to a short term of imprisonment or even acquittal.)

*A. C. Graves,* a detective in the Homicide and Robbery Bureau, was holding Oswald's left arm as he was brought into the basement. The lights were shining directly on them. He did not see the man—Ruby—come out of the crowd. He saw the pistol and the person at the time the shot was being fired. He seized the weapon from Ruby; it was a revolver. As he was trying to get the gun, Ruby was still trying to shoot.

The witness could not remember, on cross-examination, which finger Ruby had on the trigger. The witness did not hear Ruby say, "I hope the S.O.B. dies." He did not know whether there was any connection between Ruby and someone on the police force.

*D. R. Archer,* a detective in the Auto Theft Bureau of the Criminal Investigation Division, was standing, he said, by the door of the jail office when Oswald and the others went past, and after they had gone about six steps behind him, he had seen a figure move from the crowd and then he had heard a shot. He had heard Ruby say something, including the words "son of a bitch." When Ruby was brought into the jail office, Archer said that he had heard him exclaim, "I hope I killed the son of a bitch." As Ruby was being taken upstairs, Archer had said to Ruby, "Jack, I think you killed him," to which Ruby, he said, replied, "I intended to shoot him three times." Archer testified that Ruby had said, when he was hauled to the ground, "You all know me. I'm Jack Ruby." He said that Ruby had been arrested previously.

When the defense asked for the production of the reports that Archer had filed with the police department, Judge Brown refused to give them access to these telltale documents. This precluded full disclosure of the truth, but it troubled Judge Brown, ignorant of the legal implications on review, less than it bothered the more astute prosecution.

*Thomas Don McMillon,* the partner of officer Archer,

had been a few paces behind Oswald when he was shot. He
heard Ruby say, "You rat son of a bitch, you shot the President." He then heard the shot, helped subdue Ruby, and
marched him into the jail office. According to McMillon,
when Ruby was taken to the office he kept yelling, "I hope
I killed the son of a bitch." And when Ruby was being taken
upstairs he stated that he had meant to kill Oswald, that
he had meant to shoot him three times, but that the police
moved too fast and prevented this.

The witness said on cross-examination that he knew that
Ruby had been arrested several times and that he ran some
taverns.

Judge Brown refused to order the production of the
report of the shooting made by the witness, just as he had
refused to order the production of the report by Archer. It
was a graver blow to the defense than Ruby's attorneys
realized at the time.

McMillon testified that Ruby had said he had to kill
Oswald because the police could not do it, and that he
hoped he had killed "the S.O.B." Ruby shouted, according
to McMillon, when the police pounced on him, "Don't you
know who I am, don't you know who I am? I'm Jack Ruby!
I'm Jack Ruby!" McMillon said Ruby had told the police
later in the day that he had left his dog in his car across
the street.

On redirect examination, Henry Wade, for reasons of
his own, clear neither to Judge Brown nor to Melvin Belli,
introduced the reports made by the witness which the judge
previously had refused to let Belli see. The jury could be
favorably impressed by Wade's benevolence.

McMillon now said that Ruby told the police that he had
walked into the basement without any impediment.

On re-cross-examination, Belli established that there
were inconsistencies in the two reports made by McMillon
—the quotation of Ruby's alleged remarks was set forth
in the second statement, but not in the first, where, logically,
it should have appeared. Had the memory of the witness
been encouraged in some way?

At this point, the film clips of the shooting of Oswald were introduced by the prosecution and shown to the jury. (Why Belli did not contest this most vigorously is incomprehensible. He had opposed the qualifying of jurors who had seen the shooting on television. Now he was sanctioning the use of that very television tape. It was difficult to see how it could help the defense, for it must have seemed like a confession of guilt in the eyes of the jury.)

*Captain Glen D. King,* of the Dallas police, said that he went into the jail office shortly after Ruby was taken there, and he heard Ruby say, "You didn't think I was going to let him get by with it, did you?" He said that $124.80 had been found at one place in Ruby's apartment and $131.41 at another. When Ruby was searched, he had $2,015.33 in money and $60.00 in traveler's checks on him. (To the defense, this explained why Ruby was carrying a gun. The prosecution, of course, did not agree.)

The most important witness of the case now took the stand. *Sergeant Patrick T. Dean,* of the Patrol Division of the Dallas Police, said that he had been stationed outside the jail. About ten minutes after the shooting of Oswald he had accompanied Secret Service agent Forrest Sorrels to the fifth floor of the building, where Ruby was questioned. According to Dean, Ruby said he came down the ramp into the basement as a car was pulling out, and that he had thought about killing Oswald two nights earlier, when he had seen Oswald on the show-up stand. Ruby said, according to Dean, that he saw no reason for a lengthy trial or to subject Mrs. Kennedy to being brought to Dallas for it. When he saw the sarcastic sneer on Oswald's face, Ruby thought, as Dean reported it, that he would kill him if he got the chance. He guessed that he wanted the world to know that Jews do have guts.

District Attorney Wade offered into evidence two reports made by Dean. After reading the statements, Belli attacked them because of contradictions, one report declaring that the interrogation of Ruby took place about noon, whereas Dean had testified in court that it took place about 11:30

A.M., a half hour earlier. (Belli was attacking Dean on an extremely crucial issue, for the time of the interrogation would determine whether or not Dean's testimony about statements allegedly made by Ruby were admissible in evidence. Such testimony could be admitted only if the statements were a spontaneous and integral part of the act of shooting Oswald.)

Here, on a crescendo of damning testimony, the prosecution rested. Everything that preceded had led irresistibly to Sergeant Dean's declaration of Ruby's confession of premeditation. If Dean were believed, the defense was in desperate straits. Could his attorneys somehow repair the damage, or would Belli be content to "make a record," as lawyers say, for appeal after an adverse verdict? (We shall have more to say about the testimony of Dean and the other officers.)

The defense naturally wanted to begin as forcefully as the State had closed, through a witness who would highlight the essence of Ruby's defense. As the first witness, they called *Mrs. Karen Lynn Bennett Carlin*—Little Lynn —the stripper at the Carousel Club for whose sake Jack had gone to the neighborhood of destiny, the city jail. Calling Ruby on Saturday, she had asked why the night club was not open and complained that she did not have enough money to return to Fort Worth, where she lived. On Sunday, between 10:00 and 10:30 A.M., she called Ruby again, to ask him for $25. Ruby, who had sounded as if he were crying, said that he would drop the money off at the Western Union office downtown, as he was going there anyway. (Would the jury believe this testimony? Would it persuade them of Ruby's lack of premeditation?)

*William G. Serur*, a salesman, testified to Ruby's unusual love of dogs, Ruby referring to them as his "children." (Everyone who had worked on the preparation of the defense had been troubled by this. Did it indicate a mental illness?)

On cross-examination, Wade brought out that the witness

was a married man who spent much of his time in Ruby's night clubs and strip joints. This admission, although having nothing to do with the merits, was a telling reduction of the weight of the testimony.

*William E. Howard,* a Dallas oilman who had known Ruby for about thirteen years and had visited his clubs, testified to Ruby's sudden and violent temper. He told of one episode in which Ruby had beaten a man. Often, according to the witness, as he was eating dinner with Ruby, Ruby would get up suddenly and leave, saying that he had some unfinished business to take care of.

*Dr. Fred Bieberdorf,* an employee of the Dallas Health Department, said that at the time of the shooting he was a fourth-year medical student on duty at the jail. At about 2:00 or 2:05 P.M. on Sunday he had gone to the fourth floor of the jail to examine Ruby. At this time Ruby had his street clothes on. (This testimony bore upon the time element in police testimony about when Ruby had talked to Sergeant Dean. The later these events occurred, the less likely it was that Dean's testimony about Ruby's alleged statement was admissible, even if it were believed, even if it were true. Could it be shown that Ruby was allowed to dress after being stripped and questioned and that it was then that Bieberdorf saw him? The State would probably have to explain the possible discrepancy to the jury, and in the process might weaken Dean's testimony.)

*Barney Ross,* a former welterweight boxing champion and a war hero, testified that he had been a boyhood friend of Ruby's. Often Ruby would go into tantrums, he said, about trivial matters. Almost anything might arouse him. (Belli and the Ruby family, to whom notables of the fighting world were important people, thought Ross would make a favorable impression on the jury. Twelve stiff-necked churchgoers from Dallas County, Texas, might not agree.)

*George Senator,* Ruby's roommate, should have been a persuasive witness. He testified that Ruby had appeared broken up by the assassination. Ruby had seen the "Im-

peach Earl Warren" sign in a conspicuous place in Dallas
and had tried to trace the sponsors of it, as well as the
sponsors of the venomous "Welcome Mr. Kennedy" advertisement in the Dallas *Morning News* on the day of the
assassination. Senator said that when Ruby left to telegraph
the money to Little Lynn, he had a faraway look in his eyes
and was in a strange state, not at all normal.

On cross-examination, Senator said that Ruby was always willing to fight, that he acted as his own bouncer at
the night club. The prosecution tried to create the impression that there was a homosexual relationship between the
witness and Ruby. (Such an insinuation was characteristic
of Bill Alexander. Unless it boomeranged, it could not be
helpful to the sorely pressed defendant.)

*Patricia Ann Burge Kohs,* a former stripper for Ruby,
admitted from the stand that she was being held for trial on
a narcotics charge. (This was brought out by Belli, who did
not want the State to adduce it on cross-examination, where
it would do more damage.) Ruby, she said, picked a fight
with a man without any apparent provocation. Jack was
beating the man's head on the sidewalk. Suddenly he
stopped and said, "Did I do this? Did I do this?" He acted
as if he didn't know that he had done it. (This would appear
to be very favorable testimony for the defense, if it were
believed by the jury, for it would indicate that Ruby was
not always aware of what he was doing, and that he could
have shot Oswald in the same unknowing state. This was
a hint of the plea of psychomotor epilepsy variant, the so-
called fugue state in which a man could commit an act, a
crime even, without being responsible for it, in a legal
sense.)

*Roy Pryor,* a printer at the Dallas *Times Herald,* who
had worked for Ruby at one of his night clubs, testified that
Ruby had at one time taken some presents to children
residing at a Catholic orphanage. He described the increasing emotional stress which Ruby showed after the assassination. Pryor had run into Ruby at about 4:00 A.M. on

Saturday, and Ruby had talked of the great loss to the nation and the Kennedy family and mentioned that he had "scooped" his nightclub competitors by changing his advertisement to a memorial to Kennedy. He said that Ruby had overheard District Attorney Wade talking on the telephone and had corrected him. "Jack was happy about being able to feel like he could assist the district attorney in making that correction, and told me, he said that he knew Mr. Wade and that he knew influential people."

On cross-examination, Pryor said that Ruby had been pleased by the privilege, not accorded many others, of seeing Oswald at the press conference, the Friday night of the Kennedy slaying, and referred to him as a "little weasel of a guy."

After this testimony the defense introduced a tape recording of an on-the-spot radio broadcast of the shooting to show that the remarks claimed by the police officers had not, in fact, been made.

*Ike Pappas,* a newsman for New York radio station WNEW, authenticated the tape of the shooting of Oswald. The tape showed mass confusion. Neither did the witness hear, nor did the tape pick up, Ruby saying anything. Both the microphone and the reporter had been closer to Ruby at the time of the slaying of Oswald than had any police officer who testified to Ruby's alleged statements at the time.

*Robert Walker,* news director of station WFAA-TV in Dallas, authenticated a news film of the shooting. He also testified that the transfer of Oswald had been announced for ten o'clock Sunday morning. On numerous occasions, he said, his station and others had broadcast that Oswald would be transferred at that time. (This coincided with the defense theory of lack of premeditation.)

*James R. Davidson,* a free-lance movie cameraman, had been standing next to the jail office door when Ruby was brought in from the main basement. He had not heard Ruby make any of the remarks attributed to him by the prosecution witnesses. But, he admitted, so far as he knew, all the reported remarks could have been made without his having heard them. (This testimony, which had started out well, fizzled out; the defense was getting few breaks.)

*Michael Hardin*, the ambulance driver who took the dying Oswald to Parkland Hospital, testified that he received the call to pick up Oswald at 11:21 and that he arrived at the jail within two minutes. He delivered Oswald to the hospital by 11:30. (This testimony conforms to what Hardin stated before the Warren Commission, but some unusually careful chroniclers of the events have unexpectedly given a later timing for both the initial call and the arrival at the hospital.)

In a sense, all the witnesses so far presented by the defense were supernumeraries as far as Belli was concerned. He was counting on the psychiatric testimony to win for him. Now it was presented.

*Dr. Roy Schafer*, of Yale University, the first of the superb group of expert witnesses that Belli had assembled, himself an expert in clinical psychology, had tested Ruby in his cell during the last three days of December, 1963, spending a total of nine and one-half hours with him. The witness had only now seen the results of electroencephalograms taken on January 27, 28, and 29, 1964, and had concluded that Ruby had organic brain damage and that it was most likely psychomotor epilepsy. He had given Ruby ten different psychological tests, and he described them.

Dr. Shafer explained that the appearance presented by a psychomotor epileptic in a fugue state varies. Such a state could last from a second or two up to a day or two; the facial expression of a person in such a state is no different from that of a normal person. (If the jury grasped what Dr. Schafer was saying, any testimony about Ruby's appearance would be discounted.)

The witness testified that the tests given to Ruby showed him to be a person of great emotional instability, becoming greatly elated and then despondent. (Some of the other witnesses had already said this; now an expert confirmed it.)

On cross-examination, the prosecution tried to show that Ruby may have been coached to answer on the tests given by the witness. Dr. Schafer again conceded that he had no opinion on whether Ruby knew right from wrong at the time he shot Oswald.

On redirect, the witness testified that he did not think Ruby was a malingerer.

(The obvious effort of Dr. Schafter to tell the exact truth should have impressed the jury. He would not say things, however helpful to the defense, that he did not actually know.)

*Dr. Martin Towler*, a member of the panel that had examined Ruby after the second bail-bond hearing, had given Ruby the electroencephalograms (EEG's) to which Dr. Schafer had referred. Dr. Towler gave Ruby's medical history, which included many fights and brawls and a number of head injuries. Ruby had told him that he experienced spells during which he felt an intense sense of uneasiness, the feeling that his head was cracking up. These spells were infrequent, coming about once every nine months. Dr. Towler stated that he thought Ruby had an abnormal condition. He felt that Ruby was suffering from a "seizure disorder," which falls within the category of "psychomotor variant." He testified that when having one of these seizures a person is "behaving as an automaton" and does not know what he is doing. A person in such a state would show no visible or detectable change in his personality. The EEG's, he said, showed abnormal patterns.

On cross-examination the witness reiterated that he thought Ruby had a kind of seizure referred to as a psychomotor variant, in which the person would have no control over himself. However, he had no opinion of Ruby's condition at the time of the shooting of Oswald.

(Dr. Towler, like Dr. Schafer, was so guarded in his statements, saying no more than he could truthfully testify to, that he should have impressed the jury. He had been selected as Judge Brown's own witness for the purposes of the tests, but the judge, at the prodding of the State, hedged on his commitment. He would not concede that he had designated Dr. Towler as the court's representative on the psychiatric panel.)

*Dr. Manfred S. Guttmacher,* a psychiatrist of world-wide reputation and the last witness to testify for Ruby at this stage of the case, had examined the defendant and had formed the opinion that Ruby was not capable of distinguishing right from wrong or of realizing the nature and consequences of his act at the time of the slaying of Oswald. In his diagnosis he placed great emphasis upon heredity. He thought Ruby had a very abnormal personality structure. Among other things, he thought that "there's a very definite paranoid flavor to his thinking."

Ruby had told Dr. Guttmacher that he was led to the jail by his curiosity. He said that he was suddenly confronted by Oswald, who looked "cunning and vicious, like an animal, like a Communist. I felt like I was looking at a rat."

Dr. Guttmacher said that often such people show an unusual degree of calmness, and this is often a sign of their abnormality. Ruby did not seem to have any guilt feeling about the killing, but felt, at a deep level, that he was an exterminator. He thought Ruby was unable to tolerate anxiety and was a very unstable person. All the lights and commotion in the basement of the police station triggered his actions. (The witness did *not* say that Ruby had psychomotor epilepsy, but what he said was not inconsistent with the other psychiatric testimony.)

"My best diagnosis," he said, on cross-examination, "is that this man is a mental cripple and was carrying on his shoulders an insufferable emotional load and, to use the vernacular, he cracked under it momentarily."

Here the defense rested for the moment.

The prosecution's rebuttal began with *Ira N. Walker,* a technician in the engineering department of station WBAT-

TV of Fort Worth. On November 24, Walker had been in a mobile unit in front of the Police and Courts Building, waiting for Oswald's transfer. He said that Ruby had been waiting in the vicinity of the building for some time and that twice after 10:30 A.M. he had come to the unit and asked if Oswald had been brought down yet. (This testimony was inconsistent with other evidence that had all the indicia of objective truth.)

*Frank Johnston,* a photographer with United Press International News Pictures, was in the crowd of newsmen when the shooting occurred. He generally corroborated the story told by detectives Archer and McMillon.

On cross-examination he admitted that he was not looking at Ruby at the time; all he knew was that the sound came from Ruby's general area. The words could have been spoken by others around him.

*Dr. Sheff Olinger,* a physician on the staff of the Dallas Neurological Clinic, where Ruby had been examined, testified that all of Ruby's tests, with the possible exception of the EEG's, had turned out normal. He had been present at a portion of Ruby's examination. He stated that the nature of the EEG brain waves did not positively indicate any particular clinical diagnosis. The tracings were "insignificant." A diagnosis of psychomotor epilepsy could not be made on the basis of EEG readings alone, he said. He thought it unlikely that Ruby could have his first seizure at the age of fifty-two, and that his behavior in such a seizure would be silly and appear unusual to an observer.

*Dr. Robert L. Stubblefield,* chief of psychiatry at Parkland Memorial Hospital and a member of the panel appointed by Judge Brown to examine Ruby, did not consider himself a qualified expert in EEG. To the hypothetical question put by the prosecution he answered that, in the circumstances stated, Ruby would know the difference between right and wrong and would know the nature and quality of his act.

On cross-examination he conceded that the hypothetical

question and answer were based on the assumption that Ruby was conscious at the time of the shooting. He conceded that Ruby was an emotionally unstable person, and in the face of certain kinds of stresses he had a breaking point lower than normal.

*Dr. John T. Holbrook*, a psychiatrist and the third member of the court-appointed medical panel, had seen Ruby for about two hours on the day after the shooting of Oswald. He had gone to the jail again, on December 4, to perform a neurological and physical examination, but Ruby, on the advice of his attorneys, had refused to cooperate. He had seen Ruby on January 27, 28, and 29, 1964, in the company of Drs. Towler and Stubblefield. At that time he had ruled out all functional psychoses as well as any form of epilepsy. He was of the opinion that Ruby was sane at the time of the shooting. He felt that the tests of Dr. Schafer's were not accurate since they were taken too long after the act. He admitted, on cross-examination, that epileptics can perform antisocial acts while in a seizure, but he did not think it possible for Ruby to commit his act while in a fugue state. (Now the jury had another opportunity to select that psychiatric testimony which they would choose to believe.)

*Alfred Breninger*, a retired lieutenant colonel in the U.S. Army and an expert in small arms, said that Ruby's possible use of the middle finger to pull the trigger of his pistol when he shot Oswald was a common method of firing and the preferred method for quick shooting at short distances. (This, again, was intended to show premeditation by Ruby.)

*Dr. Peter Kellaway*, an experienced specialist in EEG's, from Houston, stated that the EEG never provides a diagnosis of itself. Ruby's EEG's showed an abnormality, but there was no way of knowing the origin of this abnormality. Psychomotor variant, he said, is not a disease, but a name given by Dr. Frederick A. Gibbs to a particular pattern in EEG's.

*Dr. A. Earl Walker*, a professor of neurological surgery

at Johns Hopkins University, stated that the brain waves shown in Ruby's EEG's were not necessarily abnormal. He said that there was a multiplicity of possible causes for the phenomenon. He said, further, that there was no basis for a diagnosis of epilepsy. The EEG alone could not show brain damage. A clinical psychologist such as Dr. Schafer, however, "might" be able to detect brain damage through a sequence of psychological tests.

On balance, these witnesses were better for the defense than the prosecution had bargained for. The rebuttal was somewhat feebler than might have been anticipated. Now the defense could put on its rejoinder.

*Lieutenant Jack Revill,* of the Dallas police, identified pictures of the shooting which showed that the prosecution witnesses were not looking at Ruby when he shot Oswald. How, then, could they know what he was doing or what he had said?

*Mrs. Elnora Pitts* had telephoned Ruby on Sunday, at which time he sounded strange to her. He arranged for her to call back later that afternoon. (This evidence was obviously intended to show that Jack was in an abnormal state when he shot Oswald. It also indicated that he expected to be back at his apartment that day, which would preclude a premeditated killing.)

*E. H. Combest,* a detective in the Vice Section of the Dallas Police Department, testified that he was in the police building at the time of the shooting and was standing about three feet from officer Leavelle, who was handcuffed to Oswald. He was looking at Ruby when the shot was fired. Ruby's lips were moving, but he was not close enough to make out any words, but he—the witness—had shouted, as Ruby lunged forward, "Jack, you son of a bitch, don't!" (This testimony could cast doubt on what other police officers had said, if the jury chose to interpret it so.)

*Dr. Walter Bromberg,* director of a private psychiatric hospital at Mount Kisco, New York, said that he had seen Ruby on December 21 and 22, 1963, with Dr. Guttmacher and had interviewed him again on January 20 and 21, 1964, spending a total of about eighteen hours with him. In his opinion Ruby was mentally ill and did not know the nature and quality of his acts at the time of the shooting. Dr. Bromberg said Ruby's "acts were in a state of suspended consciousness, based on a complicated mental illness." He thought Ruby was emotionally unstable, and had an epileptic personality. His emotional instability was severe and expressed itself in impulsive actions, triggered by emotional stimuli of intense type. Ruby's actions were of an automatic nature, not voluntarily controlled.

(Again it was demonstrated how readily experts could differ, depending on their professional prejudices as well as on their opportunities and competence to pass judgment. In such cases some cynical persons believe the answer depends on who is the paymaster. Thus, in the opinion of many lawyers and laymen, any eye-witness is more credible than any expert.)

*Dr. Hillel E. Silverman,* rabbi of Ruby's congregation, said that at a memorial service on Friday night, after the President's assassination, Ruby seemed to be in a trance. About two months before the assassination Ruby had had a fight with his sister, Eva Grant, because she would not attend the High Holy Day religious services, and Ruby had struck her. Ruby did not remember this. The rabbi testified to Ruby's unusual love of dogs. He was of the opinion that at the time of the shooting, and even at the time of the trial, Ruby did not know the difference between right and wrong.

*Curtis L. Crafard* had accompanied Ruby and George Senator to take the picture of the "Impeach Earl Warren" sign in the wee hours of the Saturday morning after the Kennedy assassination. He corroborated the story told by Senator.

*Sam Mack Pate,* a furniture salesman and also a news reporter for a local radio station at the time, described the Friday night press conference. (The testimony was probably meant to show that Ruby could have killed Oswald more easily then than on Sunday.)

*Kenneth Dowe,* a disk jockey at station KLIF, said that Ruby had called the radio station, offering his services, as he thought Wade could help him get a story.

*Arnold C. Gadash,* a printer at the Dallas *Times Herald,* said that he saw Ruby at the paper's offices at about 4:00 A.M. Saturday. Ruby had stopped to deliver a "twist board" which he was promoting. When Ruby spoke of the assassination, tears came to his eyes. He had also talked about the anti-Kennedy advertisement in the Dallas *Morning News.*

*Frank Bellocchio,* a jewelry designer, had seen Ruby at a bar on Saturday, and Ruby was not coherent.

*Mrs. Ingrid Carter,* a teller at Ruby's bank, said that Ruby had told her that he had to take Preludin pills to keep going and stated that he was very lonely. Ruby had withdrawn a large sum of money from the bank before the President's assassination.

*T. R. Apple,* a pilot for American Airlines, had been at the bar with Bellocchio and corroborated his testimony. Ruby had referred to the picture he had taken of the "Impeach Earl Warren" sign as a scoop.

*Stanley Kaufman,* a Dallas attorney and Ruby's lawyer in civil matters, said that Ruby had called him the day after the assassination in a state of alarm.

*Dr. Herman Ulevitch,* an internist who had treated Ruby for bronchitis, said that his examination of Ruby was so cursory it was impossible for him to evaluate Ruby's personality.

*Dr. Coleman Jacobson,* a dermatologist who had known Ruby for several years as a casual friend, said that Ruby had called him a few hours after the assassination and was very upset. He said that Ruby was emotional and volatile.

*Russell Lee Moore* (Russ Knight, the "Weird Beard"), a radio announcer at station KLIF, testified that Ruby was present at the beginning of an interview with District Attorney Wade at the press conference on Friday night. (This testimony, too, was probably intended to indicate that Ruby had a better opportunity to shoot Oswald then than on Sunday, if that had been his intention.)

The prosecution now had a chance to reply again—the so-called surrebuttal.

*Dr. Robert Schwab*, a neurologist and EEG expert at the Harvard Medical School, had read Ruby's EEG's and Dr. Towler's report, which, he felt, suggested a mild non-specific abnormality that could be caused by many things, such as taking drugs regularly and prolonged lack of sleep. He disagreed with Dr. Towler's diagnosis from the EEG's.

*Dr. Francis Michael Forster*, chairman of the Neurology Department at the University of Wisconsin School of Medicine, was a qualified EEG expert who had examined Ruby's EEG tracings without knowing whose they were. He felt that they would not support a diagnosis of psychomotor epilepsy. He also disagreed that they reflected organic brain damage, although he conceded that this was a possible interpretation.

*Dr. Roland MacKay*, a professor of neurology at Northwestern University Medical School, thought the EEG's were within the limits of normal, except that they seemed to be of a sleepy person. They did not suggest psychomotor epilepsy to him. He stated that a person in a psychomotor-seizure state could not pick a moving target out of a crowd, move in on it, shoot from close range, and yet recall it.

On this strong note, the prosecution closed again. The defense had another round—and needed it.

*Alice Nichols* testified that she had known Ruby since 1949, and they had talked of marriage. She had spoken to Ruby on the day of the assassination, and he sounded upset. She said that Ruby was very emotional and high-tempered, but she did not think he was insane.

Then, in an extraordinary sequence of events, the EEG expert whose name had been constantly mentioned by the medical witnesses on both sides flew in from Chicago and testified for Ruby. *Dr. Frederick A. Gibbs* had studied the EEG's and concluded that they clearly showed Ruby had a rare type of epilepsy. The only way this kind of epilepsy could be detected was through EEG's. Dr. Gibbs stated that it was not necessarily true that one in such a seizure would not remember what had happened.

And so the testimony in the case came to an end.

As I was to learn later, in criminal cases Texas has rules and procedures of its own. It is at once more lax and more technical. Most states permit the attorneys for the prosecution and the defense alternately to argue the merits of the case as soon as all the evidence has been introduced, and only then does the court give its legal instructions to the jury. Texas requires that the presiding judge instruct the jury before the arguments are presented. In either event, the jury then retires to deliberate over its verdict, which must be unanimous.

There is much merit to the Texas procedure, handled properly. "Handled properly" means that the instructions are arrived at by careful deliberation of court and counsel together and that such instructions and the closing arguments are delivered at reasonable hours, so that neither court, counsel, nor jury is fatigued. In ancient Israel, the court first prayed and fasted and then slept before deciding a case. There was an understanding of the preciousness of human life; speed in arriving at a judgment was looked upon askance. Not so before Judge Brown. By March 13, 1964, he wanted to finish the case, regardless of how tired anyone might be.

In many jurisdictions the instructions to the jury are agreed upon, or at least prepared, before the trial has begun, so that court and counsel know how to direct the testimony and argument. It is not unusual for the prosecution to draw up the proposed instructions for the court and then to submit them to the defense. Wade's men had done their work early, but Belli and his associates did not see the material until after the last witness had left the stand. The instructions, they declared, amounted to a directed verdict of guilt. Wade countered: "We don't care what's in the charge as long as there's room at the bottom for the jury to write a verdict of guilty." Wade knew his jury; Belli did not.

Judge Brown, increasingly impatient with these altercations, wanted to avoid an overnight recess or—worst of all —adjournment for the weekend. Reluctantly, he allowed the defense time to look over the instructions and prepare objections or substitute language.

Phil Burleson, learned in Texas law, prepared thirty-six pages of objections in the short time available; but his efforts, and those of three tireless secretaries, were in vain. Judge Brown made only a few slight corrections in the instructions as prepared by the prosecution and at 8:04 P.M. on that ominous Friday the thirteenth of March, 1964, he droned the instructions to the jury. The twelve men and women were supposed to bear these words in mind as they listened to the arguments of the attorneys and deliberated on a verdict.

The instructions defined the difference between malice and absence of malice and dwelt upon mental condition and passion. They told what constituted knowledge of right and wrong and the consequences thereof. All the cautions and shibboleths of the law were explained—in words that really did not explain. In effect, the jurors were on their own.

At 8:22 P.M. the attorneys began to present their arguments. At 1:06 A.M., an extraordinary hour, they were finished, and the case was in the hands of the jury.

It was clear from the beginning of the argument that Wade and his men were in excellent shape and the defense in a state of near collapse. Four lawyers—Bill Alexander, Frank Watts, Jim Bowie, and Henry Wade—took turns in presenting the case for the State, and the three defense lawyers—Burleson, Tonahill, and Belli—were sandwiched in between. The State opened and closed and had the advantage of position, as well as the greater skill as it turned out.

Bill Alexander opened with his customary triphammer summation of the facts. Few excel Alexander in the ability to draw the attention of jurors to the worst in a situation. Ruby, he said, was a seeker of notoriety and money who mocked American justice, and he should die for his offense. In superior fashion, he poked fun at the psychiatric testimony and invited the jury to make light of it.

Burleson, the antithesis of Alexander, tried to reason through the evidence. He became somewhat emotional only when he dealt with the suspicious failure of the police to include in their first reports what they had testified to in court.

Frank Watts, for the prosecution, analyzed the evidence to show the logic of Ruby's guilt. He threw in enough invective to stir the fires of passion. But by this time one of the jurors was asleep. Judge Brown should have realized then, if he had not earlier, that he had worked a terrible injustice by forcing the summations to be given at so late an hour.

Tonahill was the lengthiest and most histrionic of the attorneys. His theme was that Ruby was a GI patriot who had killed a rat in heat and passion. On the other hand, he said, Wade, the prosecutor, was "uncouth, unsavory, ungentlemanly, undignified and un-Texan." Tonahill, big and brusque, might have been effective at another hour, in another courtroom. When he completed his oration, near 11:20 P.M., everyone tried to stretch, talk, and yawn away his tiredness.

It became clear that the rising and stretching and yawning had been to no avail when the usually wise and self-possessed Jim Bowie resumed argument for the prosecution. Bowie was not at his best, but it was he who gave the jury a compelling reason why they should convict Ruby: "to write out a verdict that will show this state, this country, this land and this world that this is a law-abiding community, that we do not allow murder to occur here of a shackled man!" This imagery—the shooting of the handcuffed Oswald—was one that the jurors would surely carry into their deliberations.

It was now up to Belli to save the situation. He talked of

himself and of his love for the law; he talked of his bumbling client, the village clown, who, because of his psychomotor epilepsy seizures and other elements in his sick psyche, had just happened to kill Oswald. The great weakness of his argument was that he attempted too much—the acquittal of Ruby because of insanity—when he should have held the door open for a sentence less than death. Perhaps the jury would have slammed the door shut even then, but they were given little opportunity to show compassion. Belli closed with an all-or-nothing plea.

Wade closed for the prosecution. He took only sixteen minutes; perhaps he sensed that no more time was necessary. Ruby, he said, "was the judge, the jury and the executioner!" He was entitled only to "the same compassion and the same sympathy that he showed . . . Oswald in your police department and mine"—death.

The press and public, with near unanimity, had concluded that Ruby's conviction was likely; but they had concluded, too, that there would be no death sentence. The next morning they found that the jury was of a different mind.

After about ten minutes of discussion on Saturday morning, they decided that Ruby was sane; after another fifteen minutes that he was guilty of murder with malice; and after a few more minutes of discussion that the verdict was death. The principal circumstance influencing their judgment, apparently, was that Ruby had killed a manacled, defenseless man: the argument of the tired Jim Bowie had been magical.

Judge Brown had promised to permit the televising of his charge, the arguments of counsel, and the verdict, but had cancelled all television arrangements except for the hearing of the verdict. So posterity was permitted to hear the hasty decision of twelve good and true men and women who had concluded that Jack Ruby should die in the electric chair.

For an instant there was a shocked silence in the court-

room. Belli was the first to comment: "May I thank the
jury," he shouted, "for a verdict for bigotry and injustice!"
Then, remembering his often forgotten client, he yelled,
"Don't worry, Jack, we'll appeal this to a court outside
Dallas where there is justice and due process of law!" And
he added, for all to hear, "I hope the people of Dallas are
proud of this jury!"

# 4

## THE TESTIMONY OF THE

## DALLAS POLICE OFFICERS

IT IS NECESSARY now to dwell at some length on the testimony that contributed most to bringing about the death verdict. To understand why this testimony is so important one must recall the surprisingly enlightened provisions of the Texas Code of Criminal Procedure with respect to "confessions," "admissions," and "statements" of accused persons. The statute says:

A confession shall not be used if, at the time it was made, the defendant was in jail or other place of confinement, nor while he is in the custody of an officer, unless made in the voluntary statement of accused taken before an examining court in accordance with law, or be made in writing and signed by him, which written statement shall show that he has been warned by the person to whom same is made: First, that he does not have to make any statement at all, second that any statement made may be used in evidence against him on his trial for the offense concerning which the confession is therein made; or, unless in connection with such confession he makes statements of facts or circumstances that are found to be true, which conduce to establish guilt, such as the finding of secreted or stolen property, or the instrument with which he states the offense was committed.

Another provision of the code spells this out in unmistakable terms:

No evidence obtained by an officer or other person in violation of any provision of the Constitution or laws of the United States or of this State shall be admitted in evidence against the accused on the trial of any criminal case.

These are wise provisions, consistent with the letter and spirit of the Fifth Amendment safeguards against self-incrimination. In theory, Texas is one of the more enlightened states. Unfortunately, the statutory protections have been diminished by the courts, in their usual way, by the theory of *res gestae*, a Latin phrase meaning literally "things done." Phrased in understandable terms, *res gestae* means that if what the defendant is quoted as saying was the spontaneous, or automatic, result of his act, then his statement may be received in evidence. Thus if a person, in shooting another, yells, "Now I am giving you what's coming to you!" or if, immediately after the act and while in an emotional state engendered by it, he shouts, "I've planned this for a long while," then testimony on the making of the statement may be received in evidence. For it is construed to be part of the very act, the thing done.

An extremely crucial problem that had faced Belli and his associates as they prepared the Ruby defense for the trial was that they knew Jack may have made statements, highly damaging statements, to the police after the shooting of Oswald, and these could be interpreted as self-incriminating. They also knew that policemen, eager to secure a conviction in a sensational case, particularly if there is some culpability of their own, are sometimes given to embellishing the truth or even to concocting stories. The challenge was to keep all such statements—true, false, dubious, or mixed—from being heard by the jury.

The reader may ask, Why should a jury not hear everything if the ends of justice will be served? The answer is that by dint of tragic experiences of the past, including the Inquisition of the Mother Church and the Star Chamber of English kings, we have learned that, unless accused persons are fully protected, they will be compelled to give witness against themselves, through torture, the third degree, deception, and other questionable methods familiar to the lawless protectors of the law. Out of this sad knowledge on the part of the Founding Fathers came the Fifth Amendment to the Constitution of the United States, which declares that an accused person cannot be compelled to testify against himself. This should mean that no statement by a defendant ought to be admissible in evidence, regardless of where and when it was uttered and regardless of the circumstances in which it was made.

In the Ruby case the State wanted to show that he had planned to kill Oswald, that the act was premeditated, that there was "malice." Any statement by Ruby himself that he had planned to kill Oswald would be extremely persuasive to a jury, and the State would certainly try to produce it. The defense, on the other hand, would strive just as hard to keep the jury from hearing anything of the sort.

It was Belli's theory that a statement made by Ruby even a few minutes, and surely any statement several minutes, after the shooting was inadmissible unless the statutory requirements were met. And certainly no statement made after the act could be admitted under the theory of *res gestae*.

Belli's understanding of the situation was quite correct, and in normal circumstances the defense would have encountered no difficulties. But he evidently refused to believe that the State's contention would be accepted by a judge who perversely refused to interpret the law as Belli interpreted it. The State would contend that one could be talking under the influence of the act even a half hour or more after it was done. So far as the prosecutors were concerned, it was the revolving of the hour hand on the clock, not the minute hand, that was to mean the difference between life and death for Jack Ruby.

At the very core of the Ruby case were just such considerations as these, and justice for Jack Ruby depended largely on how closely the court would follow the letter of the law.

The only showing of malice in the case came from the lips of Dallas police officers—Dean, McMillon, Archer, and Leavelle. Their testimony was admitted into evidence by the court under the theory of *res gestae.*

### SERGEANT PATRICK DEAN

Sergeant Patrick Dean was the final witness in the case in chief for the prosecution, on March 6, 1964. Dean had been charged with the security in the basement of the Dallas Police and Courts Building during the moving of Oswald. He and other officers had searched the basement thoroughly, and it was Dean who placed the guards at the various entrances to the basement. He gave the men their orders: they were not to let anyone pass unless he could produce a valid press identification card.

Henry Wade lost no time in getting to the crux of Dean's testimony. Led by Wade's questioning, Dean told this story:

About ten minutes after the shooting, on the instructions of Police Chief Curry, Dean had accompanied Forrest Sorrels of the Secret Service to the fifth floor of the jail, where Ruby was being held. When they arrived, Ruby was already stripped to his shorts, and detectives McMillon, Archer, and Clardy, as well as several jailers, were with him. In Dean's presence Ruby and Sorrels then had a conversation that lasted four or five minutes. After Sorrels left, Dean asked Ruby how he had got into the basement. Over objections from the defense, Dean was allowed to state that Ruby told them that he came in through the Main Street ramp.

Wade's next question was hardly subtle: "All right, what

else did he tell you, Sergeant Dean, about—that you can recall at this time, with reference to when he planned to kill him?"

The defense immediately objected, on several grounds, and demanded a mistrial. The histrionics were wonderful to behold. Wade then withdrew the so-called leading part of the statement, and the jury was instructed to disregard it. After more attempts (with attendant objections, which were overruled) the question and answer came to this:

Q. [By Mr. Wade] Tell the Jury what else you recall Jack Ruby saying on that occasion.

A. He said that—after he had explained to me how he got in the basement or told me how he got in, I asked him how long he had been there, and he said just a few minutes, maybe two or three minutes, he said something to that effect, that he had thought about this two nights prior, when he had seen Harvey Oswald on the show-up stand.

Belli again asked for a mistrial, and this was overruled. Wade continued:

Q. Go ahead, tell us, Sergeant, what else he said with reference to the matter of Friday, seeing him Friday night at the show-up.

After another objection, Dean replied:

A. He said that he believe [sic] in due process of law that he was so torn up over this situation, and on the event that had happened, he and his sister both; he said something about his sister had just gotten out of the hospital, and she was very emotional also; and because this man had not only killed the President but had also shot Officer Tippit, and him being so emotionally torn up and he knew that the outcome of a trial, it would be inevitable that he would receive the death penalty that he didn't see any sense for a long and lengthy trial or to subject Mrs. Kennedy to be brought here to Dallas for it.

Again Belli asked for a mistrial on the basis of a violation of Jack Ruby's constitutional rights through the admission of statements allegedly made by him after he was under arrest and before he had been advised of his legal rights.

By his next question Wade was going to make sure that Dean remembered what his answer was to be:

Q.   Now, going back to Friday night, what are the facts with reference to whether or not he told you anything about deciding what to do when he saw him there in the line-up?

Another objection, again overruled.

A.   He said that when he noticed the sarcastic sneer on Oswald's face—
Q.   On what night now?
A.   That was two nights prior when he was in this show-up room.

Belli wanted to know which conversation this was, and he was assured that it was the same one.

Q.   Go ahead and tell what he said about that Friday night.
A.   Well, he said that is when he first thought that if he got the chance he would kill him. And also that he guessed that he wanted the world to know that Jews do have guts.

Again objections by Belli, after which Dean reaffirmed, under prompting by Wade, that this conversation had occurred some ten or twelve minutes after the shooting.

Wade was finished with the direct examination of Dean, and the trial was recessed for lunch. The defense attorneys must not have enjoyed their repast.

When the court resumed, the cross-examination began. Dean amended his earlier testimony slightly, saying that Ruby's statement about Friday night had been made when both he and Sorrels were questioning him. Dean reaffirmed that Ruby had said that the thought of killing Oswald had come to him Friday night. He elaborated: "As well as I can remember it, he said that the night that he saw him on the show-up stand and observed the sarcastic sneer on his face, this was when he decided to do it, or to kill him if he got the chance."

Belli kept trying to make Dean admit that Ruby had made other statements contradictory to these:

Q. Did he also tell you, "I couldn't have had it planned, because I couldn't have timed it so perfectly"?

A. He did not tell me that.

Q. Did he tell you, "Just as I happened to get there, Oswald was coming out"?

A. He did not tell me this.

Belli then discovered Dean's two reports to his superiors. After much wrangling, Belli used both reports to cross-examine Dean. In his first report, Dean had written that at approximately noon he had been contacted by Chief Curry and asked to escort Sorrels to see Ruby. When asked by Belli about the discrepancy between the report and his prior testimony, Dean replied that the time in the report was wrong. He said that he was interviewed by the television reporters in the basement just after the ambulance left the basement. He said that this was two or three minutes after the shooting. Belli suggested that the ambulance did not pull out of the basement until seven to ten minutes after the shooting.

Dean said he realized the time in his report was wrong after he had seen the tape of his interview and determined how long this took, for he went to the third floor immediately after the interview.

Dean admitted that he had made no notes of the conversations, but that Sorrels had. Dean did not put this conversation into writing until February 18, almost three months after it occurred.

Sorrels had asked Ruby why he did it, and Dean had asked him how he had gotten into the basement. After this conversation, they both had left.

Dean said that Ruby had made the statement (with regard to thinking about killing Oswald two nights before) in reply to questions by Sorrels. (In Dean's testimony on direct examination, it had been implied that Ruby had told Dean this himself, in reply to Dean's questions.) Shortly after this exchange, Belli concluded his questioning and the State rested its case for the time being. After the defense was presented, the prosecution would have another opportunity to offer evidence.

Belli was certain that Dean was not telling the truth, yet he had not been able to prove it through the witness's answers. Although Belli had made some telling points, it was clear that Sergeant Dean had made a strong impression on the jury.

It was unfortunate for Belli, and tragic for Jack Ruby, that at the time of the trial and the immediate post-trial actions the attorneys did not have access to the subsequent testimony of the various Dallas police officers before the Warren Commission.* Nor had they been permitted to see the various reports given by these officers to the Dallas Police Department, the FBI, and other agencies. Whether or not the sometimes blatant contradictions that were to appear would have had any effect on Judge Brown or the jury cannot be known, of course, but to a student of the case, able now to look at all the facts dispassionately, the contrasts in the testimony and statements offered at different times, to different audiences, are disturbing.

One of the basic issues in the case was whether Ruby had shot Oswald "with malice" or "without malice," the difference being literally a matter of life or death under Texas law.

The testimony adduced by the State was admirably constructed to prove that Ruby had acted with malice. Presented chronologically, it followed Jack Ruby's move-

---

* Not through any failing of defense counsel. Recently declassified Warren Commission files reveal that the Commission's chief counsel feared that if members of the Commission went to Dallas before the trial was concluded, they would be subpoenaed by Ruby's counsel. So Allen Dulles canceled a speech he was supposed to make in Dallas.

ments from the hour immediately preceding the assassination of the President to the hour immediately after the
slaying of Oswald. The capstone of this elaborate edifice
was Dean's testimony. The essence of the testimony is
simply summarized: on Friday night Jack Ruby made up
his mind to kill Oswald if he got the chance; that chance
came on Sunday morning; Ruby was in the basement long
enough that he had to wait for Oswald to appear; he shot
Oswald; he declared to his captors that he had planned to
kill Oswald.

All this depended, of course, on Ruby's own statement of
premeditation. And the only person who could testify to
Ruby's statements was Dean. Over the frantic objections
of Melvin Belli, the damning testimony of Sergeant Dean
was admitted into evidence.

But if Belli had had access to all the information, he could
seriously have impugned the credibility of the State's most
important witness. Let us see how.

On March 24, 1964, after the trial, Sergeant Dean was
interviewed, and roundly rebuked, by Burt Griffin of the
Warren Commission staff. In his deposition[1] Dean first testified about the preparations that had been made to secure
the basement for the moving of Oswald.

After Oswald was shot, Dean went to the pile-up of bod-
ies on the basement floor, and when he had seen to it that
Ruby was subdued in the office, he went to where Oswald
was lying. He remained there about a minute. After that he
went back to the basement. A few minutes later he was interviewed by news and television reporters. Then he went
to the third floor where he was met by Police Chief Curry
and Secret Service agent Sorrels. Curry asked Dean to take
Sorrels to the fifth floor. When Sorrels and Dean got to the
fifth floor, detectives Archer, McMillon, and Clardy were
with Ruby. Several jailers were around, but not necessarily
near Ruby. The detectives stood nearby during the conversation that followed. According to Dean,

[Sorrels] asked [Ruby] what possessed him to do it. Of course, I have testified to all this in court. And he said that he was—had been despondent over the assassination of the President, also Officer Tippitt, and that he was a very emotional man, and that out of grief for both these people, was one of the motivations, and that he couldn't see any reason for a long and lengthy trial, even though he believed in due process of law. . . .

After Sorrels finished, I said, "Ruby, I want to ask you a couple of questions myself." And he said, "All right." I said, "How did you get in the basement?" and he said, "I just walked in the Main Street ramp." And he told me, he said, "I have just been to the Western Union to mail a money order to Fort Worth." And he said, "I saw Sam Pierce"—and he referred to him as Sam Pierce—"drive out of the basement. At that time, at the time the car drove out is when I walked in." [At the trial Belli had asked Dean, "Did he say anything about the Western Union Station?", to which Dean had replied, "No, sir."]

After he answered that question, I said, "How long had you been in the basement when Oswald came into your view?" And he said, "I just walked in. I just walked to the bottom of the ramp when he came in." [On this same subject at the trial, Dean had testified that Ruby said he had been there "just a few minutes, maybe two or three minutes." And on cross-examination, he was asked, "Did he tell you, 'Just as I happened to get there, Oswald was coming out'?" and his reply was, "He did not tell me this."]

It appears that either Dean had a very poor memory or was misstating the truth. A mere two weeks had elapsed between Dean's testimony at the trial and the taking of his deposition, and in that very short time he remembered something that he had previously said had not happened. Of course, at the trial he was trying to prove something, whereas this was not necessarily the case before the Warren Commission. In any case, the two basic contradictions are important.

In addition to the testimony at the trial and the deposition, Dean had prepared two reports about what had happened on November 24, 1963. The first report, on November 26, describes the incident.[2]

At approximately 12:00 Noon Chief Curry contacted me just outside his office and instructed me to escort Mr. Forrest V. Sorrels, Agent in charge of the local Secret Service, to the Fifth Floor Jail for Mr. Sorrels to interview Mr. Ruby.

After Mr. Sorrels interrogated the subject I questioned Ruby as to how he had entered the basement and the length of time he had been there. Ruby then stated to me in the presence of Sorrels that he had entered the basement through the ramp entering on Main Street. He further stated that he would estimate his total time as about three minutes before the detectives brought Oswald into view, then he immediately shot him [Oswald].

This report dealt primarily with his security assignment, and the only notes Dean had taken on November 24 were about the assignments he made of officers to guard various entrances to the basement.

On February 18, 1964, almost three months later, Dean was asked by Chief M. W. Stevenson if he had been present at the entire interview between Ruby and Sorrels. Dean replied affirmatively, and upon stating that he thought he could remember all that had happened, he was ordered to write a report, which he did. The pertinent parts of that report[3] are:

Sorrels asked Ruby if he had thought or planned to kill Oswald and Ruby stated he first thought of killing him when he observed Oswald in the showup room two nights prior. He stated the thought came to him when he observed the sarcastic sneer on Oswald's face when he was on the showup stage. He stated that when he saw Oswald on that night he thought it would be ridiculous to have a trial for him when he knew the results would be the death penalty, since Oswald had killed the President and Officer Tippit.

Ruby also stated that he and his sister were very emotional people and that his sister had just gotten out of the hospital and she also was taking this hard, and that with the facts of the incident already known to him was the motivation for his shooting Oswald. Ruby then stated some words to the effect, "I also want the world to know that *Jews do have guts.*" . . .

This interview was conducted in the outside corridor of the jail cells on the fifth floor city jail approximately five to ten minutes after the shooting of Oswald.

It is important to note that Dean had changed his story about the time of the interview by the time he wrote his second report in the middle of February. When interviewed by the FBI on December 2, 1963, he was vague about the time —"a few minutes." According to his testimony, he had spoken to no one in particular about this incident before he wrote this second report. If this is true, that he had changed the time before he spoke to anyone from the district attorney's office, it might tend to show that his second thoughts on the matter were in good faith.

In fact, Dean was more nearly right about the time in the first report, and wrong on every occasion thereafter.

Station KRLD-TV televised the exit of Oswald from the city jail. It showed the shooting of Oswald and viewed the basement continuously after the shooting for approximately eighteen minutes and one second. Dean was seen on television intermittently during this entire period, never being off camera for longer than two minutes and forty-six seconds at any one time. (This means it was impossible for Dean to have talked to Ruby during an absence from the screen; he could not have left the basement to go to Ruby during the continuous filming by KLRD-TV.)

In addition, the film of Station WBAP-TV showed Dean in the basement for an additional four minutes and fifty seconds, immediately and continuously after the KRLD-TV filming. In sum, there was physical proof that Dean remained in the basement of the building for twenty-two minutes and fifty-one seconds, *before*, according to his own testimony, he rode the elevator to the third floor, went to the Chief's office, talked with him, went with agent Sorrels to the fifth floor, found Ruby, and started questioning him.

Since the shooting occurred at 11:20 or 11:21 A.M., it was at least 11:43 A.M. before Dean left the basement. Allowing approximately ten minutes for Dean's subsequent actions, the time of the conversation with Ruby was very near 11:55 A.M. or "approximately noon," just as Dean said in his first report. Thereafter, Dean fitted the time to the needs of the situation.

Dean's statements also deserve careful examination on what Ruby said about the length of time he had been in the basement before Oswald was brought out. At the trial, in his first report, and when interviewed by the FBI, Dean stated that Ruby said he had been in the basement for two or three minutes before Oswald appeared. But when interviewed by Griffin for the Warren Commission, Dean said that Ruby told him that Oswald was brought out just as he came to the bottom of the ramp. And Dean had denied exactly that at the trial. Why should he have changed his story for Griffin when he had been consistent up until then? Did Dean suddenly speak the truth on a vital point, one that precluded premeditation on Ruby's part? Why, then, did he not tell the truth on all points?

### FORREST SORRELS

The person best able to contradict or corroborate Dean's version of the interview was Forrest Sorrels. He was actually doing the questioning at the time of Ruby's alleged statements concerning premeditation. In preparing his report, Sorrels had the advantage, too, of notes taken during the interview. (Dean had taken no notes.) Sorrels' report, then, should be the more accurate, even though it was not written until February 4, 1964. (Normally, such a report would be written within a day or two of the event, but Sorrels was extremely busy at this time.)

Sorrels was interviewed for the Warren Commission by Leon D. Hubert, on May 6, 1964.[4] Much of what he says in this interview is relevant to the time of the transfer of Oswald, since he was the last person to question Oswald before he was taken to the basement. After Oswald was taken downstairs from the office of Captain Will Fritz, Sorrels went about a hundred feet down the hall to Chief Charles Batchelor's office with Inspector Kelley. About ten minutes after Sorrels had left Captain Fritz's office, he was informed by a police officer that Oswald had been shot. Sorrels immediately rushed down to the basement and went to the office where Oswald was lying on the floor. He then went to a public telephone and put in a collect call to Secret Service headquarters in Washington, D.C., at which time he was told to get as much information as he could. This telephone call went through before Oswald was taken out of the basement; and when the call was finished, Oswald had been taken out. After this, Sorrels went immediately to Captain Fritz's office. At this point, Dean appeared and was instructed to take Sorrels to the fifth floor where Ruby was being held.

Sorrels states that there were uniformed men present with Ruby and that possibly some others came in later. He questioned Ruby with two words: "Jack—why?" Ruby then went into a monologue about being in the newspaper office placing an advertisement, which he canceled when he learned of the assassination. He said he had been grieving for three days and had heard a eulogy of the President on Friday, that his sister had been hysterical and had been recently operated on, and that when he saw that Mrs. Kennedy was going to have to appear for the trial, he thought to himself, why should she have to go through this ordeal for this no-good son-of-a-bitch. Sorrels continued with Ruby's statement:

That he had heard about the letter to little Caroline, as I recall he mentioned. That he had been to the Western Union office to send a telegram, and that he guessed he had worked himself into a state of insanity to where he had to do it. And to use his words after that, "I guess I just had to show the world that a Jew has guts."

This statement contradicts Dean's testimony at the trial that Ruby had said nothing about the Western Union office, which he subsequently changed before the Warren Commission. Sorrels's testimony would indicate that someone had been coaching Dean before his appearance in court. Though Wade stated that he had not spoken to Dean until the day before his testimony, he did state that Alexander had been talking to the witnesses while he, Wade, was picking the jury. Of course, any mention of the Western Union office would tend to discredit the idea of any planning on Ruby's part to kill Oswald. It would appear that someone had carefully explained to Dean the importance and consequence of his testimony on this vital point.

Above all, it should be remembered that the references to the letter to Caroline appeared in the Sunday newspapers, which were read by Ruby for the first time on the morning that he shot Oswald. Copies of the newspapers were found strewn about Ruby's apartment after the shooting. This would indicate that he could not have thought of shooting Oswald for such reason at the time alleged by Dean.

Sorrels further stated that Ruby told him no one else was involved with him in killing Oswald. Hubert was intent upon finding out about the possible premeditation of Ruby.

*Mr. Hubert.* Do you remember him saying then anything about that he had intended to shoot Oswald and had formed that intent as early as Friday?

*Mr. Sorrels.* No; I did not.

*Mr. Hubert.* He did not comment at all about his intent?

*Mr. Sorrels.* No; nothing except his response to my question as to "Jack, why?", and then his relating as I have told you there a moment ago.

In other words, after I got—

*Mr. Hubert.* Did he mention anything about he intended to shoot him three times?

*Mr. Sorrels.* No; I did not hear that statement.

*Mr. Hubert.* In other words, the only comments that you heard him state which bear upon intent are those you have already made—that is to say, somebody had to do it, and also that he wanted to show the world that a Jew had guts?

*Mr. Sorrels.* No; I did not hear him say that somebody had to do it. I heard him say that he guessed he had worked himself into a state of insanity to where he had to do it, felt he had to do it.

*Mr. Hubert.* But he did make the report saying he felt he had to show the world that a Jew had guts?

*Mr. Sorrels.* Yes; that was very plain.

Sorrels went on to state that he left Ruby after this, and that he left alone. (Dean had recalled that he and Sorrels left together.)

From Sorrels' testimony it is clear that Ruby did not say that on Friday he had formed an intent to kill Oswald. Sorrels was making notes, and he certainly would not have failed to notice such a statement.

Sorrels also testified to a subsequent interview with Ruby held later that day, with the questioning being done by Captain Fritz. During this later interview, Ruby's statements were consistent with his earlier ones. He said that he came in off the Main Street ramp; that he felt Oswald was a Red; that he had acted alone; that he had seen Oswald in the showup room; that he knew whom he was going for; that he had never seen Oswald before; that he guessed that there was a moment of insanity; that he had read about the letter to Caroline. Sorrels did not remember Ruby's saying anything at that time about intending to shoot Oswald three times or that he was glad Oswald was dead.

Sorrels' written report[5] is fully consistent with his testimony before the Commission. It is vague, however, about the time of the interview. Though it states that Sorrels and Inspector Kelley were in Chief Batchelor's office shortly after 11 A.M., and about twenty or thirty minutes later heard that Oswald had been shot, after this it refers to time only in terms of "then."

The report also elaborates the statements attributed to Ruby. Ruby "also stated that he was afraid that he [Oswald] might not get just punishment as he had known instances where just punishment had not been given." Although this statement differs somewhat from the other reports of what Ruby said (that he wanted to save the trouble of a trial because he knew Oswald would get the death penalty), it is more damning appearing in Sorrels' report. The statement appears in Sorrels' notes of the interview, and there would appear to be no reason for him to fabricate it.

Near the beginning of Ruby's trial, Sorrels spoke to Chief Curry about the interview with Ruby and told him that some police officers had been present. He told Curry that he did not know if he would be able to testify because he had not warned Ruby of his constitutional rights. Before the trial, Sorrels had seen Wade at the Dallas airport. He mentioned his interview with Ruby, and Wade said he wanted to talk to him; but Wade did not follow up on this until after the trial had begun. Wade then called Sorrels into his office and they discussed the interview with Ruby. Wade told Sorrels that if he needed him he would contact him. He also told Sorrels that the defense might subpoena him. (The defense did in fact get in touch with him, and after he told them over the telephone what was said at the interview, they decided not to call him. Although much that Sorrels could have said would have been helpful to the defense, some would have been harmful. The defense, of course, would have been bound by both, and so it had to decide where the balance of value lay.)

Sorrels, at his interview with Wade, told him, in Dean's presence, that he had not heard Ruby make any statements about having planned the killing of Oswald for three days. Nor did Sorrels hear Ruby make any statements about coming down the ramp.

*Mr. Hubert.* Do you remember any comment that Dean made in Wade's office?

*Mr. Sorrels.* The only comment that I can remember that he made is when Mr. Wade asked me if certain things were said by Ruby when I was talking to him in the jail on the morning of November 24, when Dean was there, and I told him no, that that statement was not made in my presence, I did not recall any statement like that. And Dean said, "Well, maybe it was after you left." And I said, "Well, if it was—if the statement was made, it would have had to be after I left, because I don't recall any statement like that."

But by Dean's own testimony, such a statement about the planning of the killing could not have been made after Sorrels left: after the interview Dean had gone down in the elevator with Sorrels.

The following conclusion must be drawn from the conflicting testimony: Without a doubt, Dean was on the spot. He had been charged with the security of the jail, and he was at fault in Ruby's having got into the basement. Adding to the pressure was a newspaper story in which Dean was quoted as saying he saw Ruby coming down the ramp. In such a fix, Dean would naturally want to do everything possible to atone for the slipup. Whether consciously or subconsciously, he would be most anxious to get himself back into the good graces of his superiors. What better way to do this than to put the clincher on the State's case against Jack Ruby?

One does not have to go far for corroborative evidence. Dean had testified at the trial, and for the Warren Commis-

sion, that he had spoken to no one in particular about the
incident before he wrote the second report (on February
18, 1964). District Attorney Wade contends that he did not
speak to Dean until the day before Dean testified at the
trial, on March 6, and that he knew nothing of what Dean
knew until that time. On March 5, Wade talked to both
Dean and Sorrels, and their descriptions of the incidents
were consistent, except on the one all-important point: Did
Ruby state that on Friday he had determined to kill
Oswald?

Dean, according to Wade's theory, left the incident out
of his first report because he was not asked about it and
because that report dealt only with the matter of security.

Wade testified for the Commission that he formed the
impression that Ruby had thought about killing Oswald on
Friday night; he had seen Ruby's "excited demeanor" on
Friday. Wade also said he thought it was Ruby who had
killed Oswald as soon as he heard that Oswald was shot.

Dean's testimony clearly accords with Wade's theory of
the case. It is most probable that a suggestion was made to
Dean that possibly Ruby might have said such a thing;
Dean then remembered that Ruby had in fact made such
a statement. I think it most likely that Dean did not con-
coct the statement by himself. It was most certainly planted
in his mind by someone. It is not strange, in such a case,
that a person, once committed to a story, should grow
stubbornly attached to it.


## T. D. McMillon

Other officers had given testimony at the trial that helped
to persuade the jury that Ruby had acted with malice and
so deserved death. They, too, were questioned by counsel
for the Warren Commission, and a comparison of their testimony raises troublesome questions.

At the trial, T. D. McMillon immediately preceded Sergeant Dean to the stand.

McMillon, stationed just outside the jail office doors, saw a man come out of the crowd in a crouch, but could not see exactly where he came from. After the shooting he and several other officers wrestled Ruby to the floor and took him to the jail office. Wade asked whether Ruby had said anything at the time. The defense objected, on the grounds of the Texas statute and the Fifth Amendment. The objection was summarily overruled.

McMillon then testified that, as they were taking Ruby to the jail office, Ruby said: "I hope I killed the son of a bitch. I hope I killed the son of a bitch," and that he said this more than once. Ruby kept hollering, "You know me, you know me, I'm Jack Ruby."

McMillon accompanied Ruby to the fifth floor. When they got there, Ruby said, "I meant to shoot three times." Again the defense objected, to no avail. Wade asked McMillon for Ruby's exact words, to which McMillon replied: "Well, he made this statement, sir. Detective Archer had told him, 'Jack, I believe you killed him.' And he said that he meant to kill him, that he meant to shoot the man three times, but that we moved too fast for him and had prevented him from doing so." This was an even fuller and more damaging statement than had been testified to by Archer, who had allegedly begun the conversation.

Having obtained the desired testimony, Wade turned McMillon over to the defense for cross-examination.

McMillon did know Ruby around town before the shooting, but not very well. He certainly did not know him well enough to describe him as a "peculiar character," as Belli suggested. The extent of officer McMillon's knowledge? "Well, the things I had heard about him, I knew he had had some trouble with the police before, had been arrested several different times, and that he did run some taverns. And that's about my extent of knowledge. I don't know him real well." McMillon did not know what Ruby had been arrested for. The mere statement of arrests was irreparably damaging.

Belli went over the testimony with McMillon persistently, asking him how many times he had spoken with the district attorney's office about the testimony, and trying to break him down or cast suspicion upon his statements.

It appeared that McMillon had prepared a written statement[6] of what occurred at the time of the shooting of Oswald. Belli was not allowed to see this statement.

McMillon said that everything to which he had testified on the stand was contained in his written statement.

Belli went back to showing that Ruby had been calm throughout the entire occurrence. McMillon agreed that Ruby had looked about the same when he was shooting Oswald as he looked sitting in court.

Like the other officers, McMillon could not recall anyone having said anything to Ruby before he made his claimed admissions.

Belli kept testing McMillon's memory, and it got better as time went along. During cross-examination, McMillon remembered that somewhere along the line, when Ruby and the officers were either waiting for the elevator or in it, Captain King asked Ruby why he had done it, to which Ruby replied that somebody had to do it, because the police could not do it. McMillon admitted that he had not put this conversation in his report.

Later, McMillon remembered what it was that Ruby had said as he shot Oswald: "You rat son of a bitch, you shot the president."

On December 5, 1963, McMillon was interviewed by the FBI. He told them that he had heard Ruby holler at Oswald, "You rat S— of B—, you shot the President," as he fired the shot. McMillon also told the FBI that while they were struggling with Ruby, he kept hollering, "I hope I killed the S— of B—." McMillon also told the FBI that when Ruby was taken to the fifth floor, he was talking freely and said that Oswald did not deserve a trial for what he had done, and that he, Ruby, thought he would save the taxpayers time, trouble, and money. Ruby also said that he was not trying to be a hero and that he did it on his own as a spur-of-the-moment thing. (This evidence of lack of premeditation on Ruby's part was lost, unfortunately, in the flood of more damaging statements.) Ruby also said, according to McMillon, that his shooting of Oswald could not have been more perfect in timing because just as he arrived in the basement they were bringing Oswald out of the jail door. (This, too, shows the happenstance nature of Ruby's act.) McMillon told the FBI that Ruby said he was surprised he got off only one shot and that he thought he could fire at least three.

McMillon's report to his superior, written immediately after the events, does contain the statement about what he heard Ruby shout as he shot Oswald, but this is the only statement allegedly made by Ruby which McMillon included in his report. He did say that he recognized the assailant as Jack Ruby at the time he was taken into the jail office. There was no mention of Ruby's shouting his name.

On November 25, 1963, McMillon was interviewed by the FBI yet another time. In this interview, he recounted Ruby's statement when he shot Oswald, his repeated shouting of who he was, and the statement that he hoped he had killed the son-of-a-bitch. He also said that when interviewed on the fifth floor Ruby said he could not have timed it better. (This was more evidence that the event was fortuitous.)

In addition to his written reports and FBI interviews, Detective McMillon was interviewed by Burt W. Griffin, assistant counsel of the Warren Commission, on March 25, 1964.[7]

Asked why he had not put all the information about what he had heard Ruby say into the report which he wrote on that same day, McMillon replied that he simply could not have mentioned everything at that time. He said he did not think it important at the time. He said he gave the information a short time later, and this is substantially true.

Of all the police officers who testified, McMillon is the

only one who included in his early reports, made shortly after the occurrence, any of the statements allegedly made by Jack Ruby at the time of Oswald's shooting. Even he did not include all of them in his original report, nor did he include them in his first statement to the FBI. He did, however, include all of these alleged statements in his second interview with the FBI less than two weeks after the shooting.

### D. R. ARCHER

Officer D. R. Archer, a very effective witness at the trial, in effect backed up much that Sergeant Dean said and was instrumental in persuading the jury to decide upon the extreme verdict.

Archer was standing by the jail office door when Oswald was brought out. Oswald and his escorts walked right past him. As they got about six paces past him, he saw a figure move from the crowd and shoot Oswald. This figure was no farther than one pace from Oswald when Archer first saw him, and he saw no gun before the shot was fired. Ruby was in a crouch as he fired the shot.

At that moment, Archer heard Ruby utter a phrase, part of which was "son-of-a-bitch." This is the only part of the phrase he heard. He could see Ruby's lips moving at the time. (This is remarkable: Archer saw Ruby's face only for a split second before the shot was fired and at the time the shot was fired Ruby was out of his line of sight, since he was crouching. How was it possible for Archer to see Ruby's lips through Oswald and his guards, who were between him and Ruby?)

When the shot was fired, Archer and several other officers immediately converged upon Ruby, subdued him, and took him into the jail office. At this point, Wade asked Archer if he had heard Ruby say anything. The defense objected that, since Ruby was in custody at the time, nothing he said was admissible in evidence. Wade countered that this was a part of the *res gestae*. Judge Brown allowed Archer to answer.

In reply to Wade's questions laying further groundwork for his *res gestae* contention, Archer estimated that it took them ten or twelve seconds to get Ruby into the jail office from the time the shot was fired. As the police got Ruby down on the floor in the jail office, Ruby said, according to Archer, "I hope I killed the son-of-a-bitch."

Archer then testified that he, detectives McMillon and Clardy, and Captain King took Ruby by elevator to the fifth floor. Again Wade asked what Ruby said, and again the defense objected that the testimony was inadmissible. Again Judge Brown allowed the witness to answer.

Archer said that, to his statement, "I think you killed him," Ruby had replied, "I intended to shoot him three times." According to Archer, Ruby said this from three to five minutes after the shot had been fired. Wade concluded his direct examination by eliciting from Archer a statement that Ruby had seemed coherent.

In response to Belli's cross-examination, Archer stated that he was certain that Ruby had said "son-of-a-bitch" and that he had said it loudly with a "straight face." It was Archer's opinion that Ruby was unusually calm for having killed a man. He also stated that when Ruby was first wrestled to the ground he had said, "You know me, I'm Jack Ruby." All through this, Ruby was calm.

(Later, when he testified before the Warren Commission, under questioning by Leon Hubert, Archer said: "I had been watching Oswald and the detectives, and more to my right, and then I caught the movement of a man, and my first thought was, as I started moving—well, my first thought was that somebody jumped out of the crowd, maybe to take a sock at him. Someone got emotionally upset and jumped out to take a sock at him and I started to move forward, and as I moved forward I saw the man reach Oswald, raise up, and then the shot was fired." Had this testimony been known to Belli, he cauld have made much of it to indicate that the slaying of Oswald was the result not of premeditation or malice, but of emotion.)

Archer was positive about what he had heard Ruby say, but he seemed unaware of what anyone else said. He testified that he did not hear anyone shouting that Oswald had been shot. All he could recall was that there had been much confusion and a lot of shouting. He seemed to have been tuned to Ruby exclusively. As a matter of fact, he could hear nothing else that was coherent.

At the time that Ruby said he intended to shoot Oswald three times, Detectives McMillon and Clardy were also present.

Archer testified that he did not know Ruby, and had never seen him before. Seizing upon this, Belli asked Archer how he could have addressed him as "Jack," when he informed him that he had killed Oswald. In reply, Belli got more than he had bargained for.

Q. You got the name "Jack" from where?

A. He told me his name down there, and I was familiar with him name since our department had arrested him previously.

Of course, Archer was not familiar with just what it was that he had been arrested for. He did know that it had been in connection with his club and that as far as he knew it had nothing to do with moral turpitude.

It also came out that Archer had prepared a written statement of the day's events on the very same day, but the district attorney's office knew nothing of the statement. Judge Brown, characteristically, refused the defense's request for a copy.

After Ruby had been taken upstairs, according to Archer, Sorrels of the Secret Service and Dean of the Dallas Police came to talk to him. Although Archer was present at the time, he could recall nothing of what was said.

After Archer's testimony was concluded, the defense served a subpoena upon Archer's superior requiring him to produce the written statement that Archer had made;

but Judge Brown would not let the defense see it, and would not even listen to the defense arguments about why they were entitled to see it, for possible impeachment purposes.

Detective Archer's elusive statement was produced for the Warren Commission.[8] What does appear in the statement coincides largely with Archer's testimony at the Ruby trial (except for the all-important observation as to how Ruby's act impressed Archer), but the statement does not contain everything to which Archer testified at the trial.

The report, dated November 27, 1963, does corroborate Archer's statement that he heard Ruby shout "son-of-a-bitch" just before he shot Oswald. It also corroborates Archer's testimony that he asked who it was, to which Ruby replied, "You know me, I'm Jack Ruby."

What is most interesting is that there is nothing at all concerning Archer's alleged conversation with Ruby later, at which Ruby is supposed to have said that he had intended to shoot Oswald three times and that he hoped he had killed the son-of-a-bitch. This is particularly significant, since the statement says that Archer "stayed with him until 3:30 P.M., when Homicide officers came to the jail and asked us to assist in escorting him to the Homicide Bureau. . . ." The statement also makes no mention of the interview with Ruby by Dean and Sorrels, although there is no doubt that this interview did take place.

Archer's deposition for the Warren Commission was taken by Leon D. Hubert, on March 25, 1964.[9] In this deposition, Archer's testimony was consistent with his testimony at the trial, except for the observation already mentioned.

Hubert was concerned that Archer had not included in his written report Ruby's statement that he had intended to shoot Oswald three times. Archer's explanation is less than satisfactory:

Well, I didn't go into every detail. There are several statements that I didn't include in this report, and of some of the conversation that took place in the jail during the time that I was with Ruby, and then some of the statements that were made downstairs. By this, I mean when this investigation was made, I didn't have in mind of any testimony being involved, that it was—more or less an investigation as to how Ruby got into the basement, and what the security breakdown was. That my—that was my impression.

*Mr. Hubert.* I think you are relating to the fact that both of those statements [his report to his superior officer and the oral statement he gave to the FBI] omit any statement as to what Ruby told you concerning his intent to kill. . . .

*Mr. Archer.* Well, at the time, I just didn't consider them pertinent to the investigation that was in progress, and I just didn't recall them as important information at the time. And as I explained, it was in my mind that it was an inquiry, more or less, as to where I was and what I was doing, and of an inquiry as to whether there was any negligent [sic] on my part in regards to this security breakdown.

*Mr. Hubert.* Do you think that the inclusion in these two statements of his statement of his phrase "son-of-a-bitch," was more important than his statement of his intent?

*Mr. Archer.* Sir, at the time, it is like I say, whenever I gave the statements I had in mind as to what I saw at the time of the shooting, and that did take place at the time of the shooting, and I didn't go into great detail as to what took place after we took him into custody, took him upstairs and searched him and all. In other words, I had in mind that if anyone wanted to know about it, well, they would be afforded a chance for me to relate that.

It turns out that Archer made yet another report to his superiors, on November 30, 1963, which he interpreted as a part of the "continuing inquiry as to how Ruby got into the basement of the city hall." Again, Archer did not include in this report anything about Ruby's intent.

When did Archer finally get around to telling someone about these incriminating admissions by Ruby? Archer could not remember exactly. The closest he could come to

remembering was that it was about three weeks before the
trial began, but that was just a guess, because he "just didn't
recall the time." When he did come forward with this information, it was in response to a general inquiry by Bill
Alexander as to what they heard "that might be pertinent."

Mr. Hubert did not appear to be convinced by this explanation:

*Mr. Hubert.* Well, I gather from your testimony that you
didn't convey this information to anybody at all until you were
asked to do so in an interview with Mr. Alexander, which, from
your testimony, I judge to be approximately the middle of
January or afterwards, which is to say, 2 months after the event.

Now I ask you if you did not think that that information was
extremely valuable information in a pending prosecution for
first-degree murder?

*Mr. Archer.* I didn't, at the time, give it a thought in the way
of prosecution, because in my own mind I didn't feel that a lot
of the statements would be admissible. I don't know what would
be admissible and what wouldn't.

*Mr. Hubert.* It never occurred to you that it was your duty to
tell your superior officer, or somebody that you had heard that
this man said, "I meant to kill him?"

*Mr. Archer.* No, sir; it didn't. Had they inquired about it, I
certainly would have told them.

This concluded Archer's testimony before the Warren
Commission. It appears to be singularly unsatisfactory. At
first he thought that it was not pertinent to the inquiry
being made, as the inquiry concerned only the security
breakdown. Then, he did not think it was admissible evidence (indicating, at least, that he had a better understanding of the situation than Judge Brown), and anyway
he didn't think that it was important to the prosecution.

## L. C. GRAVES

L. C. Graves was the officer on the left side of Oswald as
he was taken down the corridor to the ramp. As they ad-

vanced along the corridor, the lights were shining directly
in their eyes. A man sprang out of the crowd and shot Oswald. Graves did not see the man until the shot was fired.
Immediately, Graves grabbed Ruby's arm and the pistol.
While he was attempting to take the pistol away, Ruby was
still trying to squeeze the trigger.

Graves got the gun away from Ruby, and by the time he
had straightened up and put it in his pocket, the other officers had taken Ruby to the jail office. Graves then accompanied Oswald to the hospital.

On cross-examination, Graves testified that when the shot
was fired, he was the man closest to Ruby and that he did
not hear Ruby say anything. He did not hear Ruby say anything at any time before he was taken into the jail office.

Belli attempted to elicit from the witness that he knew
Ruby as a character around town. Graves admitted that he
knew who Ruby was, but he refused to characterize him.

Graves testified that the moving of Oswald had been
postponed about an hour and fifteen minutes from the time
that had been announced to the press. He refused to speculate about why it had been postponed.

Graves's statements in his deposition[10] before the Warren Commission, on March 24, 1964, follow his testimony at
the trial, although he goes into slightly more detail.

Graves was asked if he heard Jack Ruby say anything
when he came forward with the gun in his hand. "I heard
noise. There was a racing of a motor and noises, talking
going on. As I say, my attention had been directed to that
car, and we had already turned, looked in that direction
and something could have been said, but as I said, I heard
noises but just exactly what was said I wasn't able to determine."

On April 6, 1964, Graves's deposition was taken again, in
Dallas, Texas.[11] This deposition deals solely with Graves's
part in the investigation of the assassination of President
Kennedy and the events prior to the day on which Oswald
was shot.

In all, Graves seems to have been an honest and truthful witness. He did not hear much, and his value to the prosecution was minimal, as far as showing Jack Ruby's motives and intentions are concerned. His greatest value in this respect is probably his statement that as he took the gun away from Ruby, he was still attempting to squeeze the trigger. The defense attempted to show that this action indicated that Ruby was acting in some kind of fugue state as an automaton.

There is no reason to suppose that Graves was any less alert than his fellow officers. If they had heard Ruby say the things they reported, he should have heard them, too. He told why he did not hear anything. The loud noises to which he testified should have prevented them, too, from hearing Ruby. Judged objectively, Graves's testimony was more believable than that of his associates and should have raised doubts about their credibility. The difficulty was that there was only one Graves but several of the others. They were more willing to say what he could not honestly attest.

### J. R. LEAVELLE

J. R. Leavelle was the only officer handcuffed to Lee Harvey Oswald for the transfer to the Dallas County Jail. It is interesting to note that Leavelle was not given his instructions about the moving of Oswald until about 11:00 A.M. on the morning of the move, when he was called into Captain Fritz's office.

As they reached the basement, they waited in the jail office while Captain Fritz preceded them into the hallway to check on security. As they waited, Leavelle could see that the area was lit up, but he could not see the lights themselves. As they moved through the door of the jail office, a number of floodlights shone directly on them.

As they advanced down the hall, a man came up from the opposite side, took two quick steps and raised a gun. Leavelle reached out and caught the man by his left shoulder at about the time the gun fired. Oswald grunted and hollered, "Oh," and slumped to the floor, still handcuffed to Leavelle.

Leavelle was pulled to the floor with Oswald, and Graves, the officer on the other side of Oswald, grabbed Ruby's gun hand and wrestled him to the floor. As Ruby was brought down, his hand was still contracting "as though he was attempting to fire another shot." By this time Leavelle had swung Oswald back so that he was between Ruby and Oswald.

Leavelle had known Ruby for about eight or ten years, but at the time he could not recall his name. All he knew was that he looked familiar.

Leavelle helped carry Oswald back to the jail office, and after he had taken the handcuffs off Oswald, and was standing up and placing them on his belt, he observed Ruby standing by the elevator in the custody of other officers, waiting to go upstairs to the jail.

At this point, Wade asked if Leavelle had heard Ruby say anything. The defense objected strenuously, on the ground that Ruby "was under arrest, and this is a violation of his constitutional rights." Wade again tried to prove that this was *res gestae*, eliciting from the witness that this was not more than a minute from the time the shot was fired. By then it was clear that Leavelle had heard Ruby say something, but he did not know whether or not it was in response to a question. Judge Brown held that this was in the nature of *res gestae* and allowed the witness to answer.

Ruby, Leavelle testified, had said, "I hope the son of a bitch dies."

After hearing this, Leavelle went back to tending to Oswald. (It certainly was fortuitous that Leavelle had picked this very minute to look up from his charge, the mortally stricken Oswald, to hear the incriminating statement by Ruby. It is interesting, too, that Detective Archer also testified to this statement; but he said it had been made while

Ruby was on the floor in the jail office. Since "son-of-a-bitch" is not an unusual epithet among men, and certainly not where police and criminals are intermingled, how could anyone know to a certainty by whom or where it was uttered?)

Leavelle then accompanied Oswald to the hospital in the ambulance, along with officers Graves and Daugherty.

On cross-examination, Belli immediately began to attack the testimony that Ruby had said he hoped Oswald would die. Leavelle did not know whether the statement was spontaneous or whether it came as the result of a question.

Belli drew attention to the testimony that after Ruby had been wrestled to the ground and his gun was no longer pointing at Oswald, his hand was still contracting as though attempting to pull the trigger. Later Belli would rely upon this heavily in his insanity defense.

Belli also brought out that the officer was originally informed that the transfer would take place at about 10:00 A.M. Leavelle did not know how the ultimate transfer time was arrived at.

Leavelle, who was much closer to Ruby at the time of the shooting than Archer, testified that Ruby mumbled something just as he fired the shot, but he could not tell what it was. (This is certainly contrary to the shout from Ruby's lips which Archer allegedly heard.)

Again Belli brought out that Ruby's face and voice expressed no discernible emotion.

Detective Leavelle's deposition was taken twice by the Warren Commission, first on March 25, 1964,[12] and again on April 7, 1964.[13] He also prepared a written report[14] to his superiors, in which he omitted any reference to any statements by Jack Ruby.

Leavelle was interviewed twice by the FBI, on November 25 and December 11, 1963. In neither of these interviews did he say anything about Ruby's alleged statements of intent to kill Oswald shortly after the actual shooting. In the latter report, however, he stated that when Ruby was

transferred to the county jail, he remarked to Ruby that
Ruby had really put the Dallas police force on the spot, to
which Ruby replied: "That's the last thing in the world I
wanted to do. I just wanted to be a damned hero and all
I've done is foul things up."[15]

One interesting sidelight of Leavelle's testimony before
the Warren Commission is that he had suggested that Oswald be transferred by a route other than the one announced to the press. This suggestion was turned down because the Chief had made a promise to the press. "I thought
it would be done quicker and easier and I was fed up to my
chin, in a way, with these news people, and they—as soon
as we could get rid of them the better, was my sentiments,
and I didn't have any desire to parade through them with
the prisoner in tow."[16]

At the first interview, nothing was said about Leavelle's
failure to report what he had heard Ruby say immediately
after the shooting of Oswald.

During the second interview the questioners were not
concerned with what had occurred at the time Oswald was
shot, but with various happenings while Oswald was in
custody. One thing which came out clearly was Detective
Leavelle's dislike of the newspaper reporters who swarmed
through the jail during the time of Oswald's custody. Leavelle stated that he was fed up with them, mainly because
of their failure to cooperate.

*Mr. Ball.* On those occasions when you would move Oswald
would the hallway be crowded with reporters, newsmen, and
television cameramen?

*Mr. Leavelle.* Yes; cameramen and television men all over
the place; in fact, I was plumb up to my chin with those people.

*Mr. Stern.* How do you mean?

*Mr. Leavelle.* Well, I was disgusted with them.

*Mr. Stern.* Would they not cooperate with your request to
stand in a particular place?

*Mr. Leavelle.* No; if you ever slopped hogs and thrown down

a pail of slop and saw them rush after it you would understand
what that was like up there—about the same situation.

## SUMMARY

What emerges from a consideration of the various statements of the officers who testified at the trial may be succinctly stated:

Most of the testimony that went to prove malice on the
part of Jack Ruby was inadmissible as evidence. It should
have been excluded by Judge Brown.

What the officers testified to, in different circumstances,
was not always consistent, either between one officer and
another or even the same officer with himself.

Those officers who were closest to the shooting of Oswald
heard least; those who were farthest removed had most to
testify to.

That officer who had most to defend in his own conduct
offered the most damning testimony.

All the officers, with one exception, failed to record in
their first reports of the events of November 24, 1964, the
damning statements they later testified to.

No one in any official position thought to ask the officers
for specific information about any statements Ruby may
have made until shortly before the trial.

The defense was severely handicapped by its inability to
obtain copies of the reports made by the officers.

The defense inexplicably failed to use the one witness,
Forrest Sorrels, who could have impeached the testimony of
Sergeant Dean.

If one were to sum up the meaning of all the conflicting
testimony of the Dallas police officers, one would have to
say that these men acted and spoke in the traditional manner of police officers in every part of the country. Objective
truth was much less important to them than the official story
of what had occurred. This does not mean that they were
prevaricators or completely dishonest. Men in authority,

and men out of authority, too, have the habit of suiting their words to the desired end. They respond to the suggestions of their superiors and mentors; they say what they think is wanted or required by the circumstances. This is unfortunate, but human. It is the basic justification for the guidelines laid down by the courts for the admission or exclusion of statements allegedly made by accused persons. As this narrative proceeds, we shall deal in depth with what the United States Supreme Court said in three historic cases that followed the Ruby death verdict. They will serve to explain and justify the ultimate result of all our maneuvering.

# 5

## WHAT JACK RUBY SAID

JACK RUBY did not take the stand in the trial for his life.
Whether the decision by his attorneys not to permit him
to testify was wise or foolish will never be known to a
certainty. But during the proceedings of the President's
Commission on the Assassination of President Kennedy,
Ruby was examined at length by Chief Justice Warren
himself and was given, through him, the opportunity to
take an extended polygraph test, pronounced at the time
by J. Edgar Hoover and others as inconclusive because
of Ruby's mental and emotional condition. Ruby's statements, as given, have been subjected to extended critical
analysis by some qualified (and many more unqualified)
persons.

On innumerable occasions before, during, and after his
trial, Jack talked with his attorneys, jailers, physicians, and
the press. He talked and talked—nothing seemed more
necessary to him than talk; there seemed no way of stop-
ping him. And he wrote letters, such letters, long and
short. Inevitably some found their way into auction catalogs, newspapers, magazines, and books. He whispered to
his brothers and sisters and to his attorneys. He was reported at the trial and before the Warren Commission by
police officers, reporters, and others as having said, and not
said, many things at the time of the shooting of Oswald
and on other occasions. These reports have the qualities
and defects of time and circumstance.

It seems to me that nothing is more important, in this
context, than what Jack Ruby first said to those who were

preparing his defense—the investigator R. B. Denson, his sister Eva Grant, and the attorneys Belli, Howard, Tonahill, and Burleson. His first-person account, as given at that time, has never been published, so far as I know. Here it is, exactly as it was taken down, unedited, unadorned.

I. 11/22/63

11:00 A.M. FRI. Went to Tony Zoppi office to pick up Weimar brochure.

11:10 Talked to salesman about the owner of the Castaway Club.

12:00 Saw John Newman at the news talked to him for few minutes, and then saw different people running back and forth, and went to watch the television set, and then heard the tragic news.

Called Eva at home and she was hysterical John was standing nearby and knew Eva was crying so put receiver to John's ear. Phones were ringing constantly and people were complaining about ad in paper—Then John Newman comment to someone that they shouldn't have taken the ad, and he said that were his superiors and their was nothing he could do about it, and he said to someone standing nearby "that you saw the fellow the fellow when he paid for part of the ad.—called Chicago spoke to Eileen.

In the same semicoherent telegraphed style, doing violence to verbal niceties, Ruby continued:

II. Then I called Andy at the club and told him I would be there in a little while. Left the news and drove back to the club, told Andy to call everyone that we wouldn't open tonite. Larry was their also.

Called Alice at her office, and left RI2-6189 for her to call back.

Phoned Ralph Paul.

Called Al Druber in Calif. and apologized for not sending dog, and started to cry and had to hang up.

Delivery boy from Gibson's came by and I paid for some

records and also gave him some cards to take back with him.

2:30 P.M. Went to Rita delicattessen and bought quite a few to take to Eve. (foodstuff)

Arrived at Eves house and received a call from Andy to call Don Safran, I called Don and he asked me if we were going to close, that the Cabena & Century Rooms were closing, and that he asked the other two clubs and didn't know yet, and I answered that I've made up my mind to close, and I didn't have to ask if anyone else was closing. That I already had decided to close by about 1:30 P.M. and then he asked me about Sat. and I said I didn't know yet, he said he would be there for another 45 min. that I can phone him back, and I hung up, and I said to her that were going to close, and I called Don back immediately and told him we were going to close Fri. & Sat. & Sun. and that it didn't take me long to make up my mind to decide. Then I called back again and spoke to Mr. Porter and to told him to tell Don that I wish he wouldn't tell the other clubs what I was going to do, that let them decide for themselves whether or not they should close.

I called the Morning news twice and the composing room, and them to change my ad.

I called Dr. Jacobson about going to Synogaugue and asked what time services would be, also I called the synogauge to inquire the time of the services.

7:30 Then had gone home to dress and go to the services. Stayed for services and said greetings to Rabbi and talked about Eve.

9:30 P.M. Then went into reception room and had some refreshments and said hello Joe Colman, and Elaine.

11:15 From their went to Phils Delecatteson told counter man to make up sandwiches—called Sims of homicide, if he wanted sandwiches, and he said they were winding everything up and was going to tell the boys about my thoughts for them.

11:30 Then wanted to find phone number for K.L.I.F., because I wanted to bring sandwiches there.

Looked through my clothing and every place I could think of but couldn't find Russ's *number.*

Tried to look for Russ Knight's number but couldn't find it, then called information, but somehow couldn't remember Russ's real name. However, I dialed for information and tried anyway, and mentioned his name as Roberts and that he lived on Northwest Highway, but she couldn't help me.

Then I decided to call the Gordon McLendon home, and asked a young lady if anyone else was at home, and told her my name, but she said there wasn't anyone else at home, and I asked her name, and I think she said Christine, and told her I wanted to bring sandwiches to the station and she could get me the number, and she said her mother already had brought some food, then she left and gave me a Riverside number which was discontinued. I had made so many calls that the woman behind the counter asked if I would like to use the business phone, but I told her I was through.

The counter man helped me with the sandwiches, and thanked him for making such wonderful sandwiches for a good cause, and told him if he ever wanted to come down to the club he was welcome.

Drove down to the station to look for Joe Long to try to find the number so I could get into the radio station, parked car with dog on corner of Harvard & Commerce, and thought I would run up for a minute just to get number.

12:00 MID. Taken the elevator to 2nd or 3rd fl. and asked policeman if he knew Joe Long from K.L.I.F., and he let me go by.

Ran into some officers I knew, and even had asked a police-officer if he could help me, and he called out quite loudly throught the hall, but no answer to the page.

At different intervals I would spot check and ask someone if they were Joe Long.

Then as I was standing in the hallway they brought the prisoner [Oswald] out, that was the first time I had ever seen him, I don't recall if he was with Capt. Fritz or Chief Curry or both.

Then the reporters shouted if there was a better place they could gather so as to have room for all the reporters.

The authorities said they would go down to the assembly room in the basement, and that is where I had gone too.

They brought the prisoner out and he mumbled something unintelligable and it wasn't before they had taken him back again.

Then Henry Wade started to answer many questions whether or not he was the man.

Then everyone left the room, and two fellows walked by as I was walking out of the room, one I had recognized who had worked at a service station across from the Vegas Club., but I asked the other fellow if he was Joe Long, and he asked why, and I said I had some sandwiches to bring to K.L.I.F. and I couldn't get in, unless I had the right phone number and he said we are from K.B.O.X. what about them, and I said next time, and he did give me the number, and I spoke to the other fellow for a minute and was surprised he was working for radio, I believe his name is Sam.

I went around the desk and dialed the number, and spoke to some disk jockey by name of Ken, and I told him I had sandwiches for the boys, and he was very about it, but then I suddenly said you would like to talk to Henry Wade and to have his tape ready, and he became very excited and said definitely yes. Wade was on the phone talking to New York I believe, to another radio station so I surely though[t] he wouldn't object to talking to this other disk-jockey, and I shouted to Mr. Wade just as he was about to hang up the receiver, or perhaps they were waiting for someone to come to the phone, and I did get him to leave and he did talk to this fellow, when they had finished I got on the phone again and he was thrilled and didn't know how to thank me enough, and said if I would leave immediately they would leave the door open for me.

As I was leaving and walked up one flight of stairs, I saw Russ Knight talking to someone and he seemed to be asking for information. What he was asking was where the assembly room was, and then he saw me, and I immediately told him that I got an interview with Henry Wade for his station and replied that is what he come for, and I said follow me, and taken him to

Henry Wade and shouted here is Russ Knight Henry and he answered Oh! The Wierd Beard! ! !

Then I left and drove over to K.L.I.F. but the door was closed, because I had taken too much time getting there. Waited for Rus for about 15 minutes and we both had gone up, he was so happy for what I had done that he definitely was going to tell Gordon McLendon what I had accomplished.

They started to work in splicing the tape in bringing both interviews together somehow. They called the New York and told them they had a story for them.

We all started in on the sandwiches and soft drinks, and they certainly enjoyed them.

We talked about a number of things, and I mentioned how much respect I had for Gordon, that he was the only one who came out with an editorial after the incident with Adlai Stevenson. Russ Knight had agreed with me. Mentioned that the prisoner [Oswald] resembled a very popular movie actor. Also that he had a scratch on his forehead and a little discoloring around his eye.

2:00 Russ had made the 2:00 A.M. news bulletin and put the Henry Wade interview on the air.

Russ and I had left and we spoke on the way to my car, and I mentioned I had some literature I picked up at the H. L. Hunt's exhibit at the Texas States Invention at Market Hall. Told him he could have some, that I was certain that I had copy for myself. Also mentioned the way Hunt was told he could pull out of the New York's World Fair.

Said good nite to Russ and drove on. . . .

Went to the Times Herald to bring a twist board I had promised to Pat Godosh for some time. Went to composing room and demonstrated board, a few of printers gathered around and they enjoyed my agile way of doing it.

2:30 Then the subject came with a woman who works in a little anteroom about the big ad the news had taken, and I remarked don't worry, the phones were ringing off the desks, and people were cancelling subscriptions, and ads from all over the United States.

(Told Pat to put my ad in that I was closing.)

I had taken the elevator down and spoke to the nite watchman at the door for a few minutes, and got in my car and drove home, and then awakened George, and he said he had seen my ads in the newspaper that I was closing for three days, and we talked about the tragedy, and he was heartbroken too!

3:30 A.M. I made him get out of bed, and told him I wanted him to go with me, and called Larry at the club got him out of bed and asked him if he knew how to work a polaroid camera, and he said yes, I told him to be down in the garage in ten minutes with the camera and bring plenty of film and bulbs. George and I got to the garage and he wasn't there, and I became impatient thinking he may have gone back to bed again, and had nite man call him, and he said he would be right down.

4:00 A.M. We drove to E. Ross and Expressway and took photos of a billboard that read

IMPEACH EARL WARREN
WRITE TO BELTHAM
BOX 1757 MASS.

The above sign was above another sign that read POTTER'S WROUGHT IRON, Located somewhere on Expressway.

We had taken three snapshots of same, then stopped at post-office asked man how does it happen that they have given a box to person placing an ad of that sort in the newspaper. He said he didn't have a thing to do with it. He went and checked again and said their was a person and that is all he could answer me. I went to look at the amount of mail that Box 1792, and tried to make certain I would remember if the contents would be removed the next time I'd stop by. George was with me, and Larry was sitting in the car.

From there we had gone to Habb's Coffee Shop in the Southland Hotel, they had some coffee and I had some juice. I spoke to the owner for about a minute. I don't recall what I had said to him, perhaps about hunting?

However, when I got back to the apartment I decided I would go to bed.

It wasn't long before I got a phone call, and it was Larry, and

I asked him what did he want very angrily, and he wanted to know what kind of dog food he should buy, then I asked what time it was, and when said 8:30 A.M. I bawled the heck of him for getting me up at this early hour forgetting that I mentioned that I wasn't going to bed, and then hung up on him. 8:30 A.M. SAT.

11:00 A.M. That same morning I phoned Andy or he may have called me and he said that Larry had left, that he gave the key to Mac at the garage and to tell me thanks for everything, and later Andy said he took seven dollars from the register, and I felt quite sad and guilty, because was a wonderful person.

That same morning I think George also had stayed in the apartment and watched television, and we watched all of the dignitaries pull up in their limousines to go and pay their last respects, and my heart was just broke, because of all these wonderful people. And how they grieved for their friend and beloved president.

Then I watched on television a memorial given by some synogague and a Rabbi Saligman of New York for Sabbath services in honor of the late President Kennedy, and it just tore me apart when he said to think that our president had untold courage to combat anything and everywhere and then to be struck down by some enemy from behind.

I really don't know what time I left the apartment, and Andy said that he phoned me or I phoned him.

I drove towards town and either had gone to the club first or had gone to look at the wreaths?

I pulled my car north on Houston St. past Elm St. to park my car, their was a policeman on that intersection guiding the heavy traffic, and I walked down Elm St. toward the underpass and saw officer Chaney their, I've known him for many years, and had asked him which one of the windows was used and he pointed or described it to me. We talked for a few minutes and then I couldn't talk anymore and had to walk off because I was choking and holding my tears back.

Walked up on the north bank of Elm to look at the wreaths and started to cry when I read the car[d] on one that read "We Greive for You."

Then I said to myself that I was going to send flowers.

Walked a little further down Elm closer to the underpass and started to make it across the other side where the Plaza is located so as to see the rest of the wreaths, but the traffic was bearing down to[o] fast and had to wait a minute. However, I was determined to get across regardless of what would happen to me, and I finally dashed across recklessly, and people driving thought I must have been crazy, because the cars were speeding very fast at that point.

Saw the wreaths on the Plaza and started to cry again. Crossed over the other side of Houston St., and walked north to cross over Elm.

As a reached the other side of Elm and about 50 ft. from the corner, I ran into Wes Wise parked in a K.R.L.D. News car, and stopped to talk and he mentioned that I get a scoop for K.L.I.F. and I said it was just a little something that happened, and didn't talk more about it.

3:00 P.M.? Got into my car and must have circled back either to the club first or had gone to Sol's Turf Lounge, I had gone their to look up my accountant Abe Kleinman went in and heard a lot of comment about the big ad in the news, and they were complaining why a newspaper would take such an ad. Mr. Kleinman was their and jewelry designer by name of Belochio. It became quite a discussion, and then heard Belochio say that he is leaving Dallas and was very emphatic about it, that his mind was made. I jumped all over him telling him that Dallas was good enough for him when he was making his living here, and now he wants to quit and run. I kept repeating don't say that because you will start something we won't be able to stop.

Then I had taken out my three photos of impeach Earl Warren, and he could not believe that it could happen here, and he became very belligerent that he wanted one and I practically had to fight him off from taking one from me. I said I've got a special purpose for these. I'm going to give them to Gordon McClendon so he can run an editorial on soon. He insisted that I show the picture to a fellow sitting at the bar, because he knew the Potter's and surely they wouldn't allow something like that. Abe Kleinman was witness to all this. *SAT. 3:30 P.M.*

From there went to sister Val's [Eva's] apartment, and told her I wanted to send some flowers to the Plaza, but she said not to have the same place when I ordered for her when she was at Caston Hosp. The nurse told her one of plants or flowers were stale.

Then I told Eve I was tired after watching television for awhile and took the phone with me to her bedroom and called Russ Knight and told him I had more pictures and he said that was swell to hold them for awhile, that this wasn't the time for it. That he would tell Gordon about it. Their was also something about Leonard Woods and (1000) Eve and I spoke about my visiting Chicago 3 days.

Then I must have called Stanley Kaufman and also told him about the photos, and he thought that was wonderful as to what I was going to do with them. I believe he told me that some persons checked about the person that placed the ad. Didn't have any residence in Dallas that their wasn't any such person in this area. I told him how I checked the box number etc.

SAT. Then I think I had taken a nap, and awakened and then had gone down to the club, and Andy was cleaning, and he thought he was going to get off early, and I insisted that he will have to stay until 9:00 P.M. and gave him an ultimatum that it would have to be that way. I may have called Ralph Paul and told him we were closing.

I called the Adolphus Hotel and asked for Joe Petersen, they said he left town for three days, they gave me the phone number in Galveston and I called and talked to Joe or Breck? and told them I had closed for three days and they said they also wanted to get away.

SAT. 8:00 P.M. Had gone back to my apartment and showered and shaved. Phoned Andy and told him about the new girl and to go over and catch the show over at the Colony Club, and to see about the audition show and I would give them their money back.

10:20 SAT. Phoned Eve and asked her if she was watching television.

10:30 P.M. Drove to town and drove out to Bob Horton at

the Pogo Club, and a girl came over and asked me what I would like and I ordered a coke but didn't feel like drinking it, I sat for about 15 or 20 minutes, and didn't want anyone to recognize me, because I didn't want to explain to anyone why, if I didn't want to dance or to have a drink. I sort sat in a shell and didn't want to be recognized. Bob Horton came over and apologized saying he didn't know I was there or he would have been there sooner. 11:00 P.M.

We talked and he started to explain why he remained open etc. I stopped him and didn't want to hear any of it. That was his business.

Told him that my type of entertainment was different than his, my was burlesque, and I wouldn't want the performers to put on our type of show at a time like this. Anyway, I liked Bob too much as a friend to make him feel uneasy in my presence. SAT.

He gave me $25.00 and I asked him for what, and he explained and I refused to take it, but he insisted. Said good-nite and drove downtown and pulled into the garage asked the attendant something and then drove to my apartment. SAT.

12:40 A.M. Phoned Eve and told her something asked why she didn't go to bed. SUN.

SUN. 10:00 A.M. Received call from Lynn, said she had to have some money, told her I don't have to let her draw money, that all I'm obligated to do was to pay her salary, but she said she had to pay her rent, and then it dawned on me that we were going to be closed tonite, and thought she may desperately need some money and then I said how can I get the money to you, and I think she said she will come to my apartment but I certainly didn't want that because of her supposed to be husband, and that is all I would need for them to know where I live. I took time to ask her how to send it, because all I know her by was Little Lynn, I think I wrote her name out and spelled it Karren Bennett, and asked her if she knew where the Western Union was in Ft. Worth. (By the way she said she was broke, and didn't have a penny, and I asked her if she get it somewhere else, and she could return it the next day, and then I think I

asked her where husband was and that I thought he would let
her have the money but I think she said he was out of town.
—Anyway I told her it will be in care of Will Call Western
($25.00) George Senator was there during all this. SUN. A.M.

Then left the apartment and spoke to a neighbor for a minute
(Curtiss?) about some fences I promised him then left to go to
Western Union to send money to Lynn. 10:45 A.M.

Was always in the habit of taking the freeway straight down
Commerce St., but since the tragedy have been going by to see
the wreaths, and remember their would be more traffic on Main
St., because it is where their is more activity going on than
Commerce St., and if I was in hurry to get anywhere I certainly
would have stayed on Commerce, especially Sunday, the street
is dead. 10:45 A.M.

Anyway I passed the intersection where I was to turn left and
then right on Industrial, so that I could pass where the wreaths
were and at the same time drive towards the Western Union.
I backed up in reverse, so as to make correct turn.

10:50 Did pass where all of wreaths were and then passed
the County Jail on the left and saw the largest crowd I had ever
seen there, and thought to myself that they already have transferred the prisoner, and continued to drive on the Western
Union,* and pulled in to a parking lot on the left. Waited my
turn, because the clerk was waiting on someone else, and I
filled out a form to send money. *(When I passed by the station,
I looked down the ramp to my right and saw a lot of people
down in the basement so when I finished with the Western, I
had walked west and down the ramp just out of curiosity. When
I walked by to go down the ramp I saw this officer guide a car
out of the upper portions of the ramp, and thought the officer
was there only to guide the cars coming out.

I continued *walking* down the ramp and just hit the *bottom*
part of the ramp. That is all I remember. . . .

The memorandum closed with a few minor notes, here
omitted. There was enough to indicate Ruby's highly
charged and obsessed state of mind, after the Kennedy

assassination, his incessant moving around, talking, telephoning, dwelling on what had happened and what he could do to help. His going down to the Western Union office that fatal Sunday morning appears to be the merest chance, with no inkling of what was to come until it actually happened. The most significant of Ruby's statements is that he did not remember what happened after he reached the bottom of the ramp. It is completely consistent with Belli's theory that Ruby killed while in a fugue, or epileptic, state.

# 6

## WHAT MIGHT HAVE BEEN

FOR BOTH good reasons and bad Belli refrained from using the members of the Ruby family as witnesses at the trial. The single exception was a brief technical bit by the youngest sister, Eileen. With after-knowledge of the jury's verdict, one may well ask if he could have done better by using their testimony.

There is much that they could have said.

For the purpose of structuring the material, we will assume that a new trial is pending and that Ruby's attorney wishes to make the fullest possible effective use of the members of the family as witnesses.

Barney Ross's testimony at the trial concerning Jack's youth in Chicago appears to have been worthwhile. From a witness whose name was well known and who was himself popular as a ring champion and war hero the jurors were assured that (1) Jack's boyhood was spent in a grim environment, and (2) despite such surroundings, Jack was known to be honest and reputable.

Having demonstrated the bleakness of Jack's early years, an attorney who then established that Jack had never been convicted of a felony, as Belli did through Eileen Kaminsky, would have made a good start toward showing the jury that his client was "poor but honest," in short, a good man. Since suggestions were being made that Ruby was (1) a gangster, (2) a homosexual, and (3) a political extremist, it would seem that character testimony that gave the jury an undistorted glimpse of the facts would be valuable evidence.

Perhaps witnesses who could testify to Jack's good reputation in Dallas would have been worthwhile. These will not be considered here because (1) such testimony might open the way on cross-examination to a discussion of Jack's numerous arrests in Dallas, and (2) in any event, a member of the accused's family would probably not be used for this purpose.

Sam Ruby told the Warren Commission that Jack was hospitalized because he received a blow on the head when he was ticket-scalping in the 1930's. A large bandage was required to cover the wound. Testimony on this point might be helpful to counsel planning to use an organic insanity defense based upon brain damage.

Sam's deposition provides the information that Fannie Rubenstein and Earl Ruby, Jack's mother and his brother, had suffered from mental illness. Fannie was confined to Elgin Hospital in Illinois for several months in the 1930's, and Earl spent time in a VA hospital's psychiatric ward in the early 1960's because of a nervous breakdown.

Finally, Sam told the Commission that he "found out" that Eileen "was treated by a doctor . . . following a nervous breakdown some years ago," and that she had "had somewhat of a nervous breakdown since she came here to visit during the trial."

On the topic of Jack's mental condition the defense's professional testimony was extensive, if not conclusive. On the other hand, the lay testimony was incomplete and inadequate, and certain family members could have contributed significantly.

Jack's background was punctuated by unpredictable conduct, often violent in nature. Barney Ross mentioned Jack's outrage over matters that were objectively trivial.

Hyman Rubenstein, the oldest brother, described Jack's quick temper to the Commission. He noted that any person who made an anti-Semitic remark in Jack's presence risked being "knocked flat." Jack was also known to "disrupt" Chicago meetings of Nazi Bundists in the late 1930's.

Most of Hyman's testimony appears to be hearsay, but perhaps some of it could be salvaged.

Earl Ruby likewise reported Jack's violence in regard to the Bundists. Earl stated that on several occasions Jack returned home from downtown Chicago with his "suit full of blood." When he was asked the reason for his appearance, Jack said that someone had called him "a dirty Jew or something like that."

Eva Grant testified to Jack's moodiness in general, and to their argument, in early summer, 1963, when Jack pushed her, causing her to fall back, injuring her arm and shoulder.

There were two persons who saw Jack for extended periods during the critical weekend. One of these was George Senator, who testified at the trial that Jack acted moody and depressed. Senator also told the story of Jack's picture-taking expedition during Saturday morning's wee hours.

The other person who was in close contact with Jack at the time was Eva Grant. Her testimony could be presented to the jury as evidence of the progressive deterioration of Jack's mental capabilities as the weekend wore on.

On Friday, at 1:25 P.M., shortly after Jack learned of the assassination, he called Eva from the offices of the Dallas *Morning News.* "His mind was wandering," Eva said.

At 3 P.M. Friday, Jack stopped at Eva's apartment for a few minutes and agreed to buy some food at the delicatessen and to return after a stop at the Carousel Club. He called her from the club at about 4 P.M., promising to "come right over." He arrived more than an hour later. Perhaps Jack was experiencing difficulty in functioning effectively even at this point.

When Jack did return (with "enough groceries for 20 people"), he stayed till 7:30 P.M. Jack spent $22 for the food, a sum so high that Eva was annoyed, but no serious skirmish ensued because, as Eva told the Commission, "he didn't know what he was doing then."

While the two watched television that Friday evening, Eva was directing a steady torrent of abusive and vindictive language toward Oswald while Jack sat quietly, occasionally crying. Although he had eaten sparingly, Jack excused himself at one point to throw up. Jack's only reference to Oswald in those hours was to call him a "creep." "When he was leaving, he looked pretty bad. . . . He looked too broken, a broken man already. He did make the remark, he said, 'I never felt so bad in my life, even when Ma or Pa died.'"

Jack and Eva next saw each other from approximately 4 P.M. to 8 P.M. Saturday. By this time Jack was carrying both the pictures he had taken early that morning and the Weissman advertisement, and he and Eva were speculating about the possibility that Communists or "Birchers" had signed an arguably "Jewish" name to the advertisement in an effort to discredit Jews.

Jack, during this visit, urged Eva to accompany him to Officer Tippit's funeral on Monday. (This would have been *after* the transfer of Oswald.) Eva, physically infirm because of her recent surgery and emotionally upset by the assassination, agreed reluctantly, but privately felt that she would not be capable of fulfilling this commitment. Such testimony from Eva could have a favorable influence on the jury's deliberations concerning premeditation or lack of it.

Saturday evening, Jack called Eva after he had returned to his apartment (about 10 P.M.). "[H]e was droopy depressed." "He was so low, I said, 'Go see somebody.'"

The final communication between the two, before the shooting of Oswald, was Jack's call to Eva at about 10:45 A.M., Sunday. Eva could remember only that Jack asked her how she was.

Eileen Kaminisky was called to the witness stand during the trial, but she was not asked about the long-distance call from Jack after the President's assassination. In his conversation with Eileen, Jack had suggested that he might come to Chicago for three days while his club was closed. This, it would seem, precludes participation in any conspiracy in which Jack might have been designated as the man to get rid of Oswald. He changed his mind about going to Chicago because it was felt, as pointed out to him by Eileen, that someone had to watch over Eva, who was just out of the hospital and still not well.

Finally, Earl might have testified that he had thought of going to Dallas that weekend to attend a meeting or convention of the cleaning industry. (He owned a cleaning business in Detroit.) On impulse, he decided not to go. Had he been in Dallas, it is certain that Jack would have been with him almost constantly. In those circumstances, it is utterly unlikely that Oswald would have been shot by Jack.

In view of what have might been established at the trial by the testimony of Jack Ruby and his brothers and sisters, some may wonder why Belli did not utilize all or some of these witnesses. It is fashionable to attack Belli as if he were a boob in this case. This is somewhat, but not completely, unfair to him. Belli feared that the highly emotional and not always perceptive Rubys might be slaughtered in cross-examination by the callous prosecutors or that the jury might take an unsympathetic view of them. Once a person is on the stand, the side that calls him is bound by what he says, and this can be disastrous. Some have argued that the very emotionality and absence of intellectuality might have done more good than all the psychiatric testimony and that, at the very least, it might have strengthened that testimony.

With hindsight, I feel that Ruby himself should not have been called to the stand. Belli was right; the risks were too great. But Eileen, Earl, Sam, Hy, and even the volatile Eva had important things to say that would have proved the happenstance nature of Ruby's offense, the complete lack of malice, and certainly his highly emotional, if not mentally sick, temperament.

# THE RIGHT TO COUNSEL

# 7

THE RIGHT TO COUNSEL

## FOR A YEAR AFTER THE TRIAL

WHEN JUDGE BROWN promptly entered judgment on the jury's death verdict, on March 14, 1964, those who were attempting to save Ruby's life were confronted by several major tasks. But within only a few days the overriding question was, Who would do the prodigious amount of work that was required? For the Ruby family, outraged by the verdict, wasted no time in firing Melvin Belli and set out again to find a chief counsel.

No less a problem was how and from whom would money be obtained to pay for the appeal, which could be protracted. If Ruby could be declared a pauper by court order, then the State would have to bear the considerable costs and trouble of preparing the record and printing the briefs and other documents, when required, but the family—and this really meant Earl more than the others—would still have to raise money for other expenses. And even more trying were the continuing anguish and uncertainty over the outcome of the case.

Then, too, there was the question of the immediate steps to be taken as the result of the extreme verdict. Defense counsel could ask Judge Brown for a new trial—admittedly unlikely, but it had to be attempted "for the record" and to show good faith. They had to prepare the bills of exception and the statement of facts—what are generally called the transcript of proceedings, or the record of the case—a considerable task in view of the length and complexity of the pretrial, trial, and post-trial proceedings. And something had to be done about Jack's mental condition, either through hospitalization and treatment or through requests for hearings on his sanity. And his sagging morale had to be sustained.

The Ruby family, never wealthy, still had rich taste in lawyers. They wanted nothing but the best, even if they could not afford it. Hoping to solve some of their problems at once, they approached Percy Foreman, of Houston. The negotiations reached the point where he drew up a proposed agreement on undertaking the appeal. It is typical of the arrangements that sometimes must be made in the absence of ready cash.

It is contemplated the second [payment] will be raised from the disposal of assets belonging to the S & R Corporation. . . . If the assets of the Club do not bring as much . . . then you will be responsible for seeing that it is sold and the difference . . . raised among the addressees of this letter [the members of the Ruby family]. . . .

It is understood that I [that is, Foreman] shall have the exclusive right to sign any contracts concerning books, moving pictures; television productions; music; dramatic reproductions or plays; magazine articles; and still pictures; and that I shall receive and retain the first $30,000.00 so produced, if in my opinion such is proper. Any funds over and above that amount shall belong to Jack L. Ruby and/or his estate.

This document, on the letterhead of the attorney who has achieved so many successes and who has boasted that the penance demanded of his lucky clients is the payment of his fees, is representative of what must be done in an age in which the communications media present both opportunities and temptations. This agreement, however, was never implemented.

There were many other problems to be solved, some tangible, like finances and legal representation, some intangible, like public relations.

Certainly Jack and his family could find nothing funny in the almost hopeless predicament they faced on March 20,

1964, but there are those who can make an appalling situation into a humorless joke. The *News Call Bulletin* of San Francisco, Belli's home town, offered an editorial:

Obviously neither Jack Ruby nor his family can possibly be happy over the verdict in Dallas and it is natural that they would take it out on their attorney, Mel Belli, by firing him.

But there is an odd reasoning evident in the statement of Hyman Ruby, Jack's brother: "The opinions this man expressed about Dallas, the jury, Judge Joe B. Brown and District Attorney Henry Wade are not shared by Jack or any member of his family."

If these opinions are not shared, then it follows that the Rubys must hold to the opposite opinion, to wit:

Dallas is a fine city.

The jury was fairly installed and fairly came to a verdict.

Judge Brown conducted the trial impartially and in full judicial decorum.

District Attorney Wade presented a most compelling case for the death penalty.

Ruby set one precedent by committing his crime in the white heat of television. Now he seems to have set another by openly siding with the prosecution against his own defense.

This was, of course, a paltry play on words. It took Jack Ruby days to recover from the shock of facing death by electrocution. The recovery was in reality a retreat into a world of fantasy. He began to hallucinate about conditions in the jail and in the world of which it was actually a tiny, inconsequential part. In his sick world, the jail loomed up as the most important of places. The brothers and sisters faced reality more readily, albeit starkly. Where were they to get the means to save Jack, as save him they were determined to do? Simple, unsubtle in outlook, some of them very early, even before the disastrous trial had begun, had been taken in by strange characters with brash techniques. It cannot be surprising that they sometimes lost their way in the complicated windings of a notorious case.

The prevailing myth is that, from beginning to end, and without exception, there was a never-ceasing succession of attorneys in the Ruby case. Indeed, there were many attorneys who were in the case at one time or another, but there was never the "revolving door" that some claimed. Tom Howard, the first attorney for the defense, was no longer involved in the case when it came to trial, leaving Belli, Tonahill, and Burleson. (Howard, in fact, died of a heart attack early in the protracted proceedings.) Others who had been approached by the family before or after Belli was hired were sometimes identified with the case although they in fact had nothing to do with the legal proceedings. At one time Ruby and his family thought it would be wise to augment the defense team with Charles Tessmer, possibly the best criminal lawyer in Dallas. Jack himself asked Tony Zoppi, a friend even though he worked for the unfriendly Dallas *Morning News*, to make the overtures. Zoppi felt that he had to talk first with Belli, and he and Jack virtually had their heads chewed off by Belli. Thus Tessmer was out of the case for the second time before he was ever in it.

Sam Brody, Belli's associate from Los Angeles, had left the case almost as quickly as had Howard. (If it will provide any comfort to those who believe the bizarre theories of Penn Jones, Jr., Brody was later killed in an automobile accident, as was his companion, Jayne Mansfield.)

Joe Tonahill, who had entered the case with Belli, and who was fired with him, would not leave it—voluntarily or involuntarily. Ultimately, he would be forced to yield.

The third Belli man, Phil Burleson, remained a part of the defense team to the very end. Belli and Tonahill were fired because they had failed in Dallas, and Burleson had participated with them in that failure; but he was not fired, even though Ruby and his family longed to let him go. There was an essential difference between Burleson and the others, however; Burleson was not a party, apparently, to any efforts to exploit Jack Ruby. He did not try to procure pictures of the condemned man to sell to *Life* or other takers, nor did he assist others in similar efforts. He did not form a syndicate for the purpose of making a motion picture of the tragedy. He did not look upon his client as an offering to beasts of prey. And if he was not close to Jack, Earl, Eva, or other members of the family, still he did not patronize them.

For almost a year—from March, 1964, to February, 1965 —there was a bleak period in the legal proceedings. During this time several men entered the case in haste and left it hurriedly—Percy Foreman, leaving because he wanted no intermeddling by anyone; Dr. Hubert Winston-Smith, a lawyer-physician, once medical consultant to Belli, who began with high hopes and ended by yielding to the dictates of his law school; Clayton Fowler, whose tenure, "although not long, was hectic"; Emmett Colvin, Jr., an appellate specialist who weaved in and out and in and out again on his own or as an associate of Tonahill; and Charles A. Bellows. In addition, Stanley Kaufman and other Dallas attorneys were consulted informally; Tonahill employed associates to help him; and Michael Levin of Chicago was asked to assist occasionally.

Foremost among the attorneys who joined the case after the firing of Belli was a tireless gamecock of a lawyer from Detroit, Sol A. Dann. Just after the debacle in Dallas, he translated the general interest he felt in the fate of Jack Ruby into direct action by attempting to take over as quasi general counsel. How he actually got into the case one cannot be sure: the stories differ. One account states that the children of Dann and Earl Ruby knew each other as teacher and students at a Jewish parochial school in Detroit and talked about the case; this aroused a special feeling of sympathy through suffering together over the death penalty, and Dann's children then urged him to volunteer his services in one capacity or another. Earl's memory differs.

Dann entered the case in the spring of 1964, and from that moment his presence was felt by Ruby and his family

—and by opposing counsel. The latter phrase includes those lawyers ostensibly on Ruby's side as well as those who had prosecuted him for the State.

There is high and low comedy as well as tragicomedy in the story of Dann's relations with other attorneys who lacked his staying powers. As a plaintiff's lawyer in negligence actions, Dann had met Melvin Belli and Joe Tonahill, who were well known in this sort of litigation; but mere acquaintance did not create the ties that bind. Dann suspected everyone. He feared that all would fall apart unless he intervened at every turn. True, he was not familiar with the criminal law, but he was devoted, pugnacious, and resourceful—in an unorthodox fashion.

At last, as Ruby's fortunes reached their lowest, Dann, Earl Ruby, and Michael Levin (an old friend of the Ruby family), each in his own manner, brought William Kunstler and me into the case. As a result of Kunstler's connection with the American Civil Liberties Union, Sam Houston Clinton, Jr., the Texas counsel for the A.C.L.U., came into the case. This team of lawyers, consisting of Burleson, Dann, Kunstler, Clinton, and myself, remained intact to the very end. Others would later appear briefly for some special purpose, but the defense team completed in early 1965 was in control, and the credit or the blame for all that followed was ours, and ours alone.

Does a single connecting thread run through this dreary chronicle of changing lawyers? Is there one simple explanation for the ins and outs of counsel? It seems to me that everyone looked upon Jack Ruby, not as a man, not as a human being worthy in himself of dedicated service, but as a source for something else—notoriety or fame; money, if not now, then ultimately; exploitation through books, motion pictures, a dozen different and devious ways. Even Jack's family, consciously or subconsciously, sometimes thought of him as someone to be used.

The terrible truth is that few persons could find Jack Ruby lovable, interesting, emotionally rewarding, nor could

they admire or defend his one mad act—the shooting of
Oswald. We who were in the case in its climactic stages
felt that we were being used, nobly even, in a great cause—
the redemption of American justice after it had been raped
in a courtroom. Immodest as it may seem, we felt that we
were making a notable contribution to jurisprudence, one
that would be remembered. We did not treasure Jack Ruby
as a friend, not even for one moment of beguilement. We
scarcely communicated with him, or he with us, even when
we paid him long visits or sat beside him in a hall of justice;
there was much talk, but no communication. Yet we were
closer to him than our predecessors had been, certainly
closer than Howard, Belli, Tonahill, Foreman, Fowler, and
others.

In maintaining relations with their client, our predecessors had failed notably. They were disinclined to keep Ruby
and his family fully informed of the whys and wherefores
of every move in the case. Since they were contemptuous
of the views of laymen and of those not schooled in their
field of law, they did not solicit the advice or opinion of the
family. In addition, Jack and each of his brothers and sisters
felt, in different degrees, that, because they were Jews,
the lawyers did not like them. This feeling deepened, and
became articulate, when Sol Dann entered the case. Joe
Tonahill, in particular, was the victim of this sensitiveness.
He held on despite, or perhaps because of, the antipathy of
those around him.

Tremendous energy and much time were devoted to
getting Joe Tonahill out of the case. It is legitimate to ask
whether the effort was worthwhile. Could not the same
effort have been devoted to other maneuvers in Ruby's
behalf, without excluding Tonahill? The objective observer
is likely to say that Jack Ruby and his family and their
advisors—and Sol Dann especially—were too carried away
by animosity toward the big man from Jasper. Not having
been the instigator of the struggle against Tonahill, nor a

vigorous protagonist of it, I have no vested interest in clinging to a defense of what was done by my associates and myself. That Tonahill had outlived his usefulness in the case is clear. Professional relations depend upon mutual confidence, and there was none between Tonahill and the Ruby family. Tonahill stood for the tactics which had led to defeat and the death verdict, and Jack and his family wanted nothing more to do with him. Whether they were right or wrong, this was their privilege, and Tonahill should have stepped out at their request, no matter how wronged he may have felt. When he insisted upon remaining, he had to be removed forcibly. The Texas courts, for reasons not always apparent, were reluctant to remove him, and this worsened the situation. Perhaps, with patience and diplomacy, Tonahill and the courts could have been shown that a change was imperative. Dann's method of achieving this end was perhaps wrong; but Tonahill's reaction was indisputably wrong. More suave and subtle methods were just as unsuccessful as Dann's. In the end, only an adamant stand prevailed, as Dann had anticipated. Then, to confound him and us, Tonahill still remained in the case, in one way or another, even after he was formally removed. I know of nothing comparable in the history of litigation in this country, and the full story must become a classic in American law.

Despite the plight of counsel at the time, it must not be inferred that absolutely nothing was happening in a legal way. To the contrary, the official docket of the Ruby case is filled with clerk's entries evidencing the pursuit of all trails and courses by the attorneys of the moment. It will save much time and space—and bewilderment—to list here some of the court entries for the bleak period from March 14, 1964 to November 20—eight dreadful months:

*March 14* Jury verdict: "Death."
*March 14* Judgment of court: "Death."

*March 20* Defendant's motion for a new trial filed.

*April 9* Defendant's first amended motion for a new trial filed.

*April 9* Defendant's motion for an extension of time to file second amended motion for a new trial filed; overruled by Judge Brown.

*April 13* Defendant's supplemental motion for extension of time to file second amended motion for new trial filed; overruled by Judge Brown.

*April 22* Defendant's motion for the hospitalization of Ruby filed; overruled by Judge Brown.

*April 27* Defendant's request for a sanity hearing filed.

*April 29* Judge Brown refuses leave to file defendant's second amended motion for a new trial hearing and refuses to hear witnesses thereon or allow verbal offer of proof.

*April 29* Order overruling defendant's motion for a new trial and notice of appeal to Court of Criminal Appeals.

*June 16* Motion for continuance in sanity hearing.

*July 27* Motion for extension of time to file statement of facts and bills of exception; denied as to bills of exception, and sixty days granted for filing statement of facts.

*July 28* Fifteen formal bills of exception filed.

*August 6* Judge Brown "refused approval" of fifteen formal bills of exceptions.

*August 21* Bystander's bill of exceptions number one filed.

*September 25* Second motion for extension of time to file statement of facts filed.

*September 25* Order by Judge Brown granting thirty days to file statement of facts.

*October 22* Third motion for extension of time to file statement of facts filed.

*November 20* Fourth motion for extension of time to file statement of facts filed.

*November 20* Order by Judge Brown granting ten days to file statement of facts.

*November 20* Statement of facts signed by Judge Brown and filed.

This record, as stated here, is almost cruel in its coldness. The tug-of-war that went on during this period and later is unlike any other that I know.

To the layman who has not experienced "the law's delay," and whose experience in the courts is slight, what happens after a dramatic trial is of little consequence. If he hears of the case again, it is likely to be only when he learns that the verdict has been affirmed or overruled on appeal. He knows, of course, that in some cases the appeal may be taken all the way to the United States Supreme Court, and even, as new tactics are tried, back to that tribunal again and again. (It is not unusual for the Supreme Court to refuse to take a case in the first instance and then to take it at a later time when new tactics are used.) The layman is less apt to know the complicated legal steps that the law itself requires in the process of appeal.

The record of the attorneys' maneuvering in the eight months after the verdict in the Ruby case was merely the beginning of a long process. Most of the motions that were filed—with two important exceptions—had to do with completing and perfecting the record of the proceedings in the original trial. As yet, the other complicated procedures were not under way.

Texas has more technical requirements than many other states with modernized procedures. In Texas the court reporter's transcript of the proceedings is called the "Statement of Facts." This transcript must be signed by the trial judge and forwarded to the Court of Criminal Appeals. It is, once signed, the official record of the case.

Defense counsel, for obvious reasons, is given the opportunity to object to the transcript and to explain why certain exceptions were taken to the judge's rulings during the trial. These are known as "bills of exceptions." The judge in the case has the opportunity to certify these bills of exceptions. If he does not, the defense may enter "bystander's bills of exceptions"—one had been filed by Ruby's counsel

—and these do not need the approval of the trial court.

What was happening in the Ruby case during these eight months was part of the elaborate ritual of the law as both the lawyers and the judge, not always together, sought to get the case into the hands of the Texas Court of Criminal Appeals.

The two important exceptions to this series of maneuvers were the motions of April 22, 1964, for the hospitalization of Ruby, and April 27, for a sanity hearing. The latter motion, in particular, was to assume tremendous importance as time went on.

For some time Sol Dann stood virtually alone in attempting to hold the shattered Ruby forces together. Throughout this period of attorneys entering and leaving the case, Phil Burleson and Joe Tonahill remained, but one could not be sure of just what they were doing. Often enough, although he was not officially "of counsel," Dann was clearly on the right track in his thinking about the various involvements in the case.

Not long after the verdict, Ruby's counsel and his family thought it essential to remind the court of Jack's mental condition and to ask that something be done about it. He was clearly deteriorating, and not simply because he faced the possibility of death in the electric chair. Even the State's psychiatrists began to feel that some action was essential.

Jack had been examined many times before the trial, and after the verdict he was examined again and again, both by those employed by his attorneys and by the State. On May 1, 1964, six weeks after the death verdict, and in response to the motions made by Ruby's attorneys, Dr. R. L. Stubblefield, one of the State's psychiatrists at the trial, examined Jack and reported his findings to Judge Brown.

In my opinion, . . . Mr. Ruby is currently severely emotionally disturbed with major paranoid and depressive features. There is no evidence of organic brain damage. If this behavior pattern persists, it will be necessary, in my opinion, for me to recommend to you the possibility of a hearing to consider a trial by jury on the question of Mr. Ruby's sanity. . . .

Some weeks later, on May 27, Dr. Stubblefield, this time seconded by Dr. John Holbrook and Dr. William R. Beavers, wrote again to Judge Brown:

We are submitting a brief report of the results of our conference regarding Jack Ruby. We recognize that the responsibility for a decision about a sanity hearing is a judicial and not a medical matter. However, in our medical opinion, we believe that Mr. Ruby should be treated properly; accordingly, *we* recommend that you consider seriously a formal sanity hearing for him.

If you decide against a formal hearing, or if a jury declines to call Mr. Ruby insane and thus require that he be transferred to Rusk State Hospital, then we offer our consultation service, if requested, to Dr. J. W. Pickard [the official Dallas County physician]. . . .

Jack's condition was acknowledged with mixed feelings by defense counsel. If Jack were found insane and sent to the state mental hospital at Rusk, not highly regarded by some, his condition might worsen. There was the danger, too, that a jury might not consider Jack insane, and that might create a desperate situation. The dilemma was resolved by not pressing the matter after placing on file the affidavits that could be used to obtain a sanity hearing. Since Judge Brown was given to alternating between sudden—if not abrupt—rulings and procrastination, and could not make up his mind without prompting, it might be assumed that nothing decisive would happen; and that since action on the alleged insanity could be taken at any time, and even after a legal determination of the issue, counsel would play it by ear and simply keep the subject in a state of semisomnolence.

Dann, however, had expressed himself to the family on

the implications of Jack's condition and on what it might mean in the future. If a sanity hearing were held, the defense would have to be prepared. It could not be left to chance. Thus, with the matter temporarily dormant, Dann proceeded to counsel the family wisely on the assembling of information on Jack's early behavior patterns. What he hoped to prove was that Jack could not, at the time of the murder, have been capable of planning out his actions. He firmly believed that Jack had acted without malice or premeditation and that he was of "unsound mind," a state sometimes short of actual insanity.

As he analyzed the matter, the family should proceed to record, in detail, the incidents of abnormality in Jack's behavior, beginning with his childhood. There was, in fact, abundant evidence of Jack's psychiatric makeup, including aberrant responses to quite usual events. With a thorough record available, defense counsel would confer with experts in the exploration of Ruby's entire past. This would then be used in a sanity hearing, if a hearing was held, or it could be used in preparing a new defense for a sceond trial if the appeal was successful.

Ultimately, nothing came of this endeavor, not through any failing of the family or of Dann or other counsel. When, as we shall see, the courts did seize upon the affidavits and order a sanity hearing, counsel decided that a quite different approach was neccessary.

At this time, also, Burleson, "as Jack Ruby's only local attorney of record," requested Sheriff Decker that he "be notified in advance of any visits by any person to see Jack Ruby." He specifically referred to "all doctors, officials, laymen, or other persons who might want to see, visit, or observe him." He excluded the sheriff's staff and those who might be involved in emergency situations. It was, he said, his responsibility to the family, co-counsel, and others to keep current with all phases of the case.

This letter was a none-too-subtle means of excluding Tonahill from the case. Other means were adopted from time to time, some of them having the impact of a ton of bricks being emptied on a quiet morning.

May 30, 1964, was notable as the day on which Tonahill sent Sol Dann one of the few friendly letters that either ever addressed to the other.

"Please forgive me for failing to reply to your letters of recent date sooner," Tonahill began. "I have been somewhat engaged in preparing for the sanity hearing for Jack Ruby. The contents of your submissions have been noted with interest." Reassuringly, he added, "In our Motion for New Trial I believe we touched every point on the compass of substantial error. Naturally we are pleased to have the benefit of your suggestions and advices." He asked to be remembered to Earl, closed "With all good wishes," and subscribed himself "Cordially yours."

This letter is unique in the Ruby saga. Lacking vituperativeness, it was not as readable as the communications that were to follow. And, in retrospect, it suggests that there may have been better ways to handle Tonahill. Perhaps he was too much involved in the disastrous trial to be accepted by the family on any terms.

The conflict with Tonahill was not long in surfacing. Dann, even when out of town, left explicit instructions for those with whom he was presumably working. These well-intended promptings to action were regarded as an intrusion by the Texas attorneys, who felt they understood better the workings of Texas courts.

The storm broke as a consequence of the investigation conducted into the assassination of President Kennedy by the Warren Commission. The Commission did not begin its hearings with respect to Ruby until after the trial was over, and by June, 1964, it was ready to hear Ruby himself. Such a hearing posed substantive legal questions. Since Jack would be testifying under oath, anything he said could be held against him in a second trial. Should he be permitted to testify? And could he, if he was insane, waive his constitutional right to remain silent?

Ultimately, Jack was questioned, by the Chief Justice himself, on June 7, 1964, in the presence of his nominal counsel, Tonahill and Clayton Fowler. During the interview Jack repeatedly asked to take a polygraph (lie detection) test; indeed, he begged for it. Tonahill acquiesced. This led the Chief Justice to assure Ruby that arrangements would be completed. Dann insisted, however, that the test should not be given, and he made dire threats to all who would subject Ruby to examination. It was this difference, more than anything else, that precipitated the struggle between Dann and the world.

Later in July, after the polygraph test had been given to Jack over the objections of Dann, Sol flew to Dallas to confer with Tonahill and Fowler. Both had been enmeshed in the giving of the test, and Sol was furious. Now it was his purpose to get Tonahill out of the case, once and for all, a goal much desired by Jack Ruby and his family.

The conference was a stormy one. The details cannot be known with assurance, because the participants in the conference differ in their accounts. One person has said that he heard Tonahill shout anti-Semitic remarks at Dann. Dann himself has said that his life and limb were threatened. To Dann, who is short and not sturdily built, it must have seemed like a contest between David and Goliath, for Tonahill is tall and powerful, like a primordial Texan of legendary creation. The contest ended in no decision: Tonahill regarded himself as still in the case, and Dann was more fixed than ever in his determination to protect Ruby from his erstwhile counsel as well as from the prosecution.

On July 25, after returning to Detroit, Dann wired to Tonahill and Fowler in capitalized anger and sent copies to both Dallas newspapers:

AM BEGINNING TO BELIEVE THAT IF THERE WERE LESS AND FEWER LAWYERS IN THIS WORLD THERE WOULD BE MORE JUSTICE AND LESS NEED FOR CHARITY.

THEREFORE, REQUEST YOU IMMEDIATELY TO FULLY EXPLAIN TO DALLAS PRESS, PUBLIC AND ME WHY YOU THREATENED ME LAST

WEDNESDAY NIGHT WITH BODILY HARM AND SAFETY OF MY LIFE
IN TEXAS IF I REMAINED THERE OR IN RUBY'S CASE.

ALSO WHAT PROMPTED YOU TO CALL ME KIKE, JEW-BASTARD,
WHITE NIGGER, AND OTHER ANTI-SEMITIC VILE EPITHETS SIMILAR
TO THOSE RESORTED TO BY PROSECUTION AND THEIR WITNESSES
DURING COURT PROCEEDINGS TO INFLAME AND INCITE HATE AND
PREJUDICE OF COURT AND JURY AGAINST JACK RUBY. . . .

ALSO REMIND YOU THAT RUBY FAMILY INTEND TO HOLD YOU
FULLY ACCOUNTABLE FOR ORDINARY AND PUNITIVE DAMAGES FOR
CAUSING THEM UNNECESSARY ANXIETIES AND INJURIES AND BRING
THEM INTO PUBLIC DISRESPECT, DISREPUTE, HUMILIATION AND
PAINFUL EMBARRASSMENT AS RESULT OF YOUR MALICIOUS INTER-
FERENCE, MISCONDUCT AND CONTINUED MEDDLING AND INVASION
OF THEIR RIGHTS, AND REFUSAL TO WITHDRAW AND REMOVE YOUR-
SELVES WITH SOME DEGREE OF DIGNITY FROM ANY AND ALL RUBY
CASES, DIRECTLY OR INDIRECTLY, AS PREVIOUSLY REQUESTED.

IN INTEREST OF LEGAL PROFESSION AND RUBY FAMILY AGAIN
REQUEST YOU TO CEASE AND DESIST FROM MALICIOUS MISCONDUCT
AND INTERFERENCE WITH APPEAL AND REQUEST YOU TO CONSIDER
YOURSELVES COMPLETELY REMOVED, DIRECTLY AND INDIRECTLY,
FROM ANY AND ALL RUBY CASES. . . .

Then, in response to a call from a Dallas columnist, Dann
sent a four-page exegesis on his telegram. It takes little
insight to understand that, however justified they may be,
such communications do not ease relations with the purged
persons.

Dann's was the kind of approach that made Clayton
Fowler squirm. Ultimately he withdrew. In any event, he
continued to harbor misgivings over interference by the
family, and especially by civil attorneys whom he felt to
be ignorant of the craft of criminal law.

It must not be assumed that Dann, during this episode,
was acting in haste or without securing the counsel of more
experienced attorneys. Probably in fact, and certainly by
his lights, the case had reached a crisis, and such stern and
unorthodox methods were indispensable. A judge of the
Common Pleas Court in Detroit, to whom Dann had sent

"excerpts of information," agreed to "act in a consultative capacity to aid and assist you in your battle for securing American Justice for this unfortunately aggrieved individual [Ruby]." His letter could only encourage Dann, for it concluded with passages that seemed to be in marked contrast to what Dann had experienced in his dealings with others:

Regardless of the enormity of one's crime, regardless of the guilt or innocence of an accused, it is basic in American law and good moral conscience that the accused be adequately represented by competent counsel who will insist that each and every right accorded by law be fairly and adequately protected, before, during and even after trial.

The concern for justice and fairness, for human right and human dignity is the duty of everyone—be he a private citizen or a public official. The denial of simple justice to any person has the tendency, and amounts to a denial to all of us.

As a public official, and a human being who is interested in safe guarding the basic rights of every person, you may feel free to call upon me for a full discussion of this, or any case where liberty and justice is involved. However, this must be entirely and distinctly removed from my official position as Judge, and entirely upon my own time and not the Court's, and, of course, entirely without compensation or remuneration (except the satisfaction that may come to one who feels he is doing something that is right and good and beneficial to American law and a sense of justice).

Dann's wrath was not directed solely toward Fowler and Tonahill; he was outraged also that the Warren Commission had conducted the polygraph test. In reply, J. Lee Rankin, general counsel of the Commission, wrote to Dann, on July 30, spelling out the details, verifiable from the record:

In view of Mr. Jack Ruby's repeated requests for a polygraph examination, the commitment of the Commission to afford him an opportunity to take such an examination and the absence of

an adjudication of insanity or incompetency, the Commission
concluded that it would make the polygraph examination available to Mr. Jack Ruby so that he could accept it or reject it. . . .

In the proceedings in the Dallas jail on July 18, Mr. Specter
made it clear to Messrs. Clayton Fowler and Joe H. Tonahill
that the Commission was not insisting on or even requesting the
polygraph examination, but merely stood ready to have it administered if Mr. Ruby wanted it. Mr. Fowler then conferred
with Mr. Ruby, and Mr. Fowler advised Mr. Specter that Mr.
Ruby still wanted the examination even though Mr. Fowler had
opposed it. When Mr. Ruby was brought into the examination
room, Mr. Specter carefully advised him of his rights and of the
fact that the Commission was not requesting the examination
but merely wanted to fulfill the offer which was made on June 7
when Mr. Ruby testified before the Commission. At that time,
Mr. Ruby insisted on going forward, and the Commission ful-
filled its commitment by having the polygraph examination administered to him. . . .

Dann was not satisfied with this explanation, and he said
so. He wrote and talked to many persons about this and
other aspects of the case. His private law practice was often
disrupted or neglected because of his preoccupation with
the case. Increasingly, as Dann encountered the opposition
of Tonahill, he began to see himself surrounded by all sorts
of dark forces.

While Dann was trying to dislodge Tonahill from the
case, Belli was himself making the same effort in a more
subtle and graceful manner; but even Belli's best polish
was bound to give added offense to Sol Dann and the
Rubys. On August 17, 1964, Belli wrote to Tonahill. Since
Belli was "out" of this case, "fired" by the Rubys, some of
his words are nothing less than startling:

DEAR JOE:

I met with Phil [Burleson] and Clayton [Fowler] yesterday
in Dallas to go over some of the points on Jack's appeal. . . .

Whether I am one of Jack's lawyers or not, I am going to file a brief and no one can stop me from doing that, because this man is my friend and he is being horribly mistreated and this case will be reversed. But, by the last above statement, I do not mean that I have any desire to reenter the case.

I am satisfied we can reverse it if things take an even course and we don't go into a lot of extemporaneous and irrelevant matter. . . .

Now I come to the most important conclusion and this is my sincere conclusion, solely for the good of Jack Ruby and your own personal welfare:

Joe, you should get out of this case and forthwith. You have done a herculean job. You have driven yourself to physical exhaustion and you have done more than any human being or lawyer could do for Jack Ruby, but unfortunately now, and because of his mental condition, he definitely wants you out and is definitely unhappy with you. You know I have your welfare at heart as much as you have mine and I do feel that if you would get out of the case, then just the Dallas lawyers could and should handle it, with you and me doing a brief because of our friendship with Jack. Indeed, you can do a brief as amicus curiae and sign it. Mine, I don't want signed by my name.

I definitely feel that Sol Dann should not be in this case. I think, as a Jewish lawyer, he is injecting the Jewish issue and he will irreparably hurt the case. I think Dallas lawyers should handle it from here on out, with Sol's advice and our briefs.

Of course, the above might be entirely disregarded by you, by Sol Dann and by anyone and everyone else. I only speak my piece because of my loyalty and friendship to Jack Ruby and my long and deep loyalty and friendship with you.

I hope you will all call me if you have any questions and I hope that there won't be "releases" handed to any press by anyone and I want to say for the record right now that I strongly resent the insinuations made against me by Sol Dann. Sol professed a great friendship and admiration for me, my handling of this case and originally so wrote me. I was shocked when I read some of his statements. . . .

In conclusion, I am not going to say, "I'm sorry I got you into this case," because you and I both know if we had it to do all over again, even knowing the insults that would be heaped on us, we would take it on and try it in the same way *and* see it reversed in the same way. The only tragedy is that Jack is now in jail, but as to that, Phil and Clayton should move immediately to have him hospitalized and declared incompetent. . . .

Belli may have been content to be "out" of the case except for the writing of a brief. But, in truth, he was also engaged in the writing of a book with a collaborator. He was determined to set the record straight and preserve his reputation while putting Dallas in its place. Ruby would be the ostensible center of attention, but the real battle would be between Belli and Dallas.

As published reports of Belli's book, *Dallas Justice*, took tangible form, Dann felt compelled to take action. Reams of copy had been prepared by writers of every competence from the instant of the killing of Oswald, and the family could not begin to halt the publishing of what was written, even though they much desired to do so. Now that the trial was over, however, they wanted to put a stop to what they regarded as harmful.

Belli's was certainly not the first account to which Dann objected for the family. The *Saturday Evening Post* had published "The Untold Story of Jack Ruby," and the family was offended by it. Dorothy Kilgallen, who had covered the trial for the *New York Journal American*, had also been a target of the family's wrath.

Dann's motives, to the extent they are known, seem to have been a mixture of laudable intent and firm misapprehension of the law. He felt that the stories might jeopardize Jack's rights before the courts, since they were based on hearsay and gossip or were simply inaccurate. He also felt that what Jack Ruby said and did was "private property." For this there was no legal basis. Jack, by killing Oswald, had thrust himself into the limelight, and to the extent that he was now a public figure, he was "fair game"—whether or not what was written about him or his case was fair or accurate. Dann simply refused to accept this interpretation of the law.

In any event, it would be difficult to see how Belli could do more damage in his book than he had already done. And trying to stop Belli could only exasperate him. Nevertheless, Dann tried. He advised Belli that unless he withheld publication of the book, he would hold him and his publisher responsible for any violation or invasion of Jack's rights. Then, to add chaos to confusion, he informed Belli that any future communications with the Ruby family should be addressed to him in Detroit.

Belli did not reply directly to Dann. He wrote instead to Eva:

I have no intention of being embroiled in any controversy with Mr. Dan [sic]. However, if Mr. Dan mis-states the record, or in any way defames me as he has the other lawyers in this case I shall act accordingly. I send no copy of this letter to Mr. Dan since I see no need of communicating with him as far as my interests are concerned with Jack.

I had intended to write a brief for Jack and, indeed, I have had two of my top men . . . working on this brief presently. I have always felt it was the obligation of the trial lawyer to work on the appellate brief. I had intended that this brief be filed amicus curiae or that it be sent to the appellate lawyer for inclusion. I have no desire to have my name on this brief, but that is immaterial.

I have gone as far as I can go without the transcript but I have no intention of embroiling myself with Dr. Dan and other lawyers in order to get a transcript. . . .

My only interest presently is to do everything humanly and legally possible to secure a reversal of Jack's conviction and I am satisfied . . . that I can write a brief that will reverse this most unfair and hideous conviction. I feel very badly about some of the unfactual and very bitter things you people have said about me in the newspapers but I would prefer to make my reply in my attempts to help Jack rather than engage in any recriminations with you. . . .

I should like to know from you just who are the lawyers for Jack, who is handling the appeal, so that I may synchronize my efforts and in these regards I do hope that you will keep Clayton Fowler and Phil Burleson as your Dallas lawyers, regardless of whoever else is on the appeal. I think it is essential that these two lawyers remain.

Dann, rebuffed by Belli, wrote to the David McKay Company, demanding that Belli's publisher refrain from publishing or distributing his book, but they, like the *Saturday Evening Post*, which had published articles about the case, chose to do otherwise.

Belli would write about the case, and he could not cease to think about it. Whether Dann was willing to accept Belli's proffer of help as sincere, Belli was concerned about Jack Ruby. Later, in November, he wrote a letter to Judge Brown that did him much credit.

DEAR JUDGE BROWN:

We both know I have no further official connection with Jack Ruby or the Ruby case. I have, however, been given permission by the Texas Court of Criminal Appeals to file an amicus curiae brief. . . .

What I write about now is the condition we both know Jack Ruby presently is in. He is psychotic, he does need medical attention badly. His family won't ask for medical attention and apparently his present lawyers, whoever they may be, won't ask for it. I don't know what are their reasons but I do know that if this boy isn't given some medical psychiatric attention directly we're not going to have this tragic figure alive by the time his case gets through the Appellate Courts and neither you nor I want this to happen. . . .

I know everyone has Jack's interests at heart as far as giving him proper treatment. . . . But I also know that we all "leave it to others" and thus evade our own individual Christian responsibilities. I don't say that you're the only one who should move to do something for this tragic man, but I do say, and you know in your heart, Judge, you can do something for him and fully within the law. This has nothing to do with his case or his appeal. This has only to do with his treatment as a human being. I'm just talking about getting a sick man into a hospital.

If this man were anyone but Jack Ruby I believe he'd have been moved to a mental institution a long time ago. If we leave him as he is and in the County Jail, he's going to deteriorate so badly we'll all be ashamed of what we have done, or he will have succeeded in his avowed purpose to commit suicide and then we'll all say "Why didn't we do something about it?"

It may be too late even now to do anything for Jack Ruby medically, but I just can't let this Christmas season of good will to men come upon me and think of Christ's teachings without asking you to do something for this forlorn person who was caught in the tragic events of that tragic weekend. . . .

Perhaps Belli was "out" of the case. He had sincerely urged Tonahill to get out, and he meant it. But he could never get the case out of his own mind. Whether formally a part of the proceedings or not, he was irretrievably bound to the case by his own consciousness. It would remain forever his case. He could not disown it; it could not disown him. The press and the people would think of Belli when they referred to Ruby, just as they associate Clarence Darrow with Nathan Leopold. Ironically, the counsel who succeeded Belli were often ignored, while Belli was treated as if he were still a part of the case.

My own entrance into the case was gradual, a result of the forces that impel each of us, when we believe in the rightness of a cause, to follow as truly as possible the dictates of conscience. What happens in consequence is never fully foreseen, or foreseeable. I never anticipated that my indignation at the jury's verdict of death on Jack Ruby would lead ultimately to my participation in the case.

I had been outraged by the death verdict in March, 1964, and when Michael Levin, an old friend, came to my office one day shortly thereafter to ask my help, I was of a mind to do so. Mike explained that day that he had been a boyhood friend of the Rubys, and particularly of the oldest brother Hyman. He was still close to the family and wanted to do something to help set aside the death sentence. The family had no more money; they had been impoverished by the case, and it was now necessary to raise money for the appeal. People had given money to the widow of Officer Tippit and to Marina Oswald as well. Why should they not give it to assure justice for Jack Ruby? A small committee could be formed to appeal for financial help. Mike would act as chairman and do all the work. Barney Ross, the prize fighter, and like Mike a boyhood friend of the Rubys, had agreed to lend his name. Would I? Remembering my reaction to the death verdict, I said Yes.

On April 30, 1964, a letter listing the committee members was sent out over Mike's signature in an appeal for funds. It brought little cash, but many letters in response. An advertisement by the committee in *The New York Times* was just as unsuccessful. The appeal, all in all, was a failure.

In September, Michael Levin approached me again. Hy and other members of the family had shown him correspondence between Dann and themselves, and he, in turn, came to me for consultation, in particular, about the publication of material about Jack to which the family objected. Since I was known as an attorney who specialized in suits involving questions of censorship, libel, plagiarism, freedom of the press, and the right to publish, the family evidently did not object to having the benefit of free counsel in these areas.

At this time, of course, I had nothing officially to do with the case, and I did not expect to become involved beyond informal consultation. Without my realizing or intending it, by donating my services I was contributing to the difficulties of Charles Bellows, the chief counsel whom the

Ruby family had settled upon after the uproar over the polygraph test.

Of all the attorneys who entered and left the Ruby case, there were special circumstances with respect to Charles Bellows. Although he was the first choice of Earl to defend the case, he was not selected. He had wanted about $20,000 for his fees and, in addition, his living expenses, an amount beyond what the family felt it could afford. But in the spring of 1964 the family again turned to Bellows, paying him a retainer of only $2500. Later he wanted an additional sum, but by then the family believed he was overpaid for what they, typically, regarded as insufficient services. The difficulty, in the eyes of the family, was that Bellows did not really take complete command of the case. He seemed content to let Tonahill and Burleson maintain dominant working positions. They complained also that he did not keep them sufficiently informed and that he did not go along with them in their determination to be rid of Tonahill. Whether they would have felt that way if Sol Dann were not prodding Bellows and prompting them, one cannot say. Certainly Dann had ideas, expectations, and above all, suspicions; he felt that Bellows was doing little or nothing to advance Jack's defense.

All through the fall of 1964, Sol Dann urged me to take a more active role in the case, especially in the peripheral matters, such as Belli's book, the *Saturday Evening Post* article, the Dorothy Kilgallen pieces. As I read reports on the situation, I was puzzled. Finally, I wrote to Dann, on October 26, 1964: "It is only fair that I know, as quickly as possible, whether your consultations with me are authorized by the family (specifically with whom), . . . I do not want to find myself barging in without full authorization and without full knowledge of the exact arrangements to be made."

Dann had wanted me to go to Detroit to visit with him and Jack's younger brother Earl and to work out some arrangement while there, but I could not go at the time, since

I had become a grandfather for the first time and wished to see my daughter and granddaughter. At last the visit was arranged. In the civil proceedings my role was clear: I was to be in complete charge. In the criminal appeal there were problems. It had been suggested that I participate in the appeal, but this meant that Dann and Earl Ruby would have to speak frankly to Burleson and Bellows.

On December 1, Dann bore witness to the partnership that had been sealed in Detroit: "I sincerely hope your 'role' will be that of an equal member of a team where all of us will work together toward a common goal in the criminal appeal, but in the civil matters also concerning Belli's book, the *Saturday Evening Post*, the *New York Journal American*, etc., it will necessarily be only your firm and ours to pursue those remedies we discussed." He would, he said, see to it that the file of Charles Bellows should be made available to me along with the medical reports and other material. Nothing would be withheld.

In mid-December, Earl Ruby wrote to confirm that my role in the civil suits would be chief counsel, with Sol Dann of counsel. He had not yet heard from Bellows on the appeal, but he expected an answer within a few days.

At this time a warm letter from the oldest member of the Ruby family, Hy, who alone carried the original name Rubenstein, made it apparent that what was needed, as much as anything else, was communication in the true sense. Earl and Hy and the others constantly wanted to know what was going on and the reasons for it. They did not want to be treated as infants or ignoramuses. They wanted a friend as well as a counselor, and as this is the relationship that I prefer with clients, I was prepared to extend it to them.

Matters, it may truly be said, were in disarray. At this time, as I then thought, Sol Dann was the one attorney who had the confidence of Ruby and his family. Phil Burleson was still in the case, bloody and somewhat bowed, badgered by all and accused of not doing what had to be done in connection with the pending appeal and the various post-trial proceedings. Charles Bellows was still of counsel, but when the family asked him to agree to my presence in the case as an informal consultant, he insisted, with some forcefulness and justification, that there was no need for additional counsel; the various attorneys were getting into each other's way. Joe Tonahill had been fired at around the time that Melvin Belli had been pushed out of the case; but, unlike Belli, he refused to stay fired. Bellows, a natural mediator, tried to placate Tonahill by assigning him a small role in the forthcoming oral argument before the Texas Court of Criminal Appeals. Sol Dann and the family would have none of this—Tonahill had to be out completely, and if Bellows would not acquiesce, then he could go, too.

Thus, in early 1965, Earl Ruby and Sol Dann began to discuss with me the possibility of enlisting the help of William M. Kunstler, a New York attorney who has been in the forefront of the civil rights struggle as one of the best "Freedom Lawyers" in the Deep South. At the time I knew Kunstler only by name and reputation. He was on the national board of the American Civil Liberties Union, a true mark of distinction, and on the national advisory body of the Commission on Law and Social Action of the American Jewish Congress, a dynamic group in which I had long been active.

Kunstler, we were to learn, was as unfettered a fighter for the rights of man as one was ever likely to meet. We did not know then that early on Sunday morning, November 24, 1963, he was preparing to go to Dallas as a representative of the American Civil Liberties Union to see what could be done to protect the constitutional rights of one Lee Harvey Oswald, said to be the assassin of the President. A shot by Jack Ruby, a person completely unknown to him, interrupted his trip. Now, on behalf of the same Jack Ruby, Kunstler, Sol Dann, and I were arranging to meet at the International Airport in New York City, so that we might plan our participation in the struggle to set aside the death sentence.

On February 6, Earl and Sol flew to O'Hare Field in Chicago to meet me, and together the three of us went on to New York. We spent several hours there with Kunstler, who had to leave to do battle somewhere in the South. Earl and Sol returned to Detroit and I to my home in Chicago almost before anyone knew that we had been gone. But in those few hours we forged a relationship that endured to the end of the case. One of the things I enjoyed most in that relationship was observing Kunstler, my kind of man and lawyer, although there were basic differences between us.

Kunstler was highly articulate. This was evidenced by his innumerable appearances before trial and reviewing courts, legislative committees, and administrative boards all over the country. He was always coming from or going to some out-of-the-way spot and seemed to live out of suitcases and duffle bags. He was constantly making speeches before boards, committees, live audiences of every kind, and he was heard frequently on television and radio. He could easily have become an actor—he was a performer. He would tell indiscreet stories at his own expense and that of others. His articles and reviews appeared in leading newspapers and magazines, and he wrote books, highly readable ones. In fact, *The Minister and the Choir Girl*, which dealt with the Hall-Mills murder case of a generation ago, was a best-seller. His first publication had been a volume of poetry, and he had taught writing at Columbia University and law at Pace College. He had been a major in the Signal Corps during the war and had been decorated. Everything filled Kunstler with zeal and zest. When he could not be present for an important hearing in Dallas, he sent a charming letter of excuse in which he referred briefly to what had befallen him: "My trip home was uneventful except for the fact that I was incarcerated on a plane with 103 new divorcees en route to New York from Juarez. This Freedom Flight was more exciting than any plane ride I've ever had."

In *Deep in My Heart* he tells of his battles in countless

Dixie courtrooms. In it there is a priceless account of a
night when he was literally in bed with Dick Gregory, the
comedian, and Wyatt Walker, executive assistant to Dr.
Martin Luther King. "Gregory, who monopolized the
center of the bed, kept up a steady stream of chatter
throughout the night. Whenever Wyatt and I dozed off, he
would shake us back into consciousness. 'Wake up, baby,'
he said, 'I've got a new story for you.'"

I became annoyed at Kunstler only when he showed
tolerance for Mark Lane, expressing the conviction that
*Rush to Judgment,* which he had read in proof, was a good
book. This was the nearest I ever came to quarreling with
him.

He could do sweet and thoughtful things, such as including the names of all his colleagues in the Ruby case in the
dedication of his book. We were, according to him, "civil
rights workers [devoted] to democratic principles." (That
may have puzzled Phil Burleson, a conservative Democrat
from Dallas, who was a friend of Congressman Joe Pool,
who later threw Kunstler and his partner, Arthur Kinoy,
out of a meeting of the House Committee on Un-American
Activities, when they protested against his arbitrariness.)

During the same period in which I met Kunstler I
learned that two law school professors had received a grant
from an education foundation to prepare a study of the
Jack Ruby trial. Jon Waltz, a successful trial lawyer who
had resigned from his prestigious law firm at the age of
thirty-five to become a teacher of law, I had observed
when I audited one of his Northwestern Law School classes
for the legal education committee of the Chicago Bar
Association. Extraordinarily articulate, sharp and unorthodox in his approach, Waltz showed exceptional promise in
his new role as educator and legal scholar.

Of John Kaplan I first learned through a letter that he
sent to Dann on February 8, 1965. At the time, my involvement in the criminal appeal was not definite. I had, and
have, great respect for Charles Bellows, the distinguished

Chicago criminal lawyer. I regard him as a close acquaintance, if not an intimate friend, and it was certainly not my ambition to supplant him in the case, for I wanted to work with him. But Bellows desired no additional counsel in the case, not even myself, and in normal circumstances he would have been in a position to make his desires prevail.

Reports of the conflict over counsel had reached Kaplan, who through his research and study was thoroughly knowledgeable on the case. He wrote to Dann, and Dann sent a copy of the letter to me:

I am writing . . . to tell you of a disquieting report . . . that Charles Bellows is thinking very seriously of withdrawing from the case. . . .

First of all, bringing in a new counsel at this time would obviously necessitate a request to the Court of Criminal Appeals for a postponement in the appeal. The chances are that this would delay the decision beyond the summer term postponing any final resolution of this case and what may very well be a new trial for Jack until after the summer recess period—at least three months. I do not need to tell you just how adversely this will affect Jack. In addition, even if the case is affirmed, the sooner the better for Jack since I then feel confident that the Governor will commute his sentence from death.

Second, the substitution of another attorney for Charles Bellows would deprive you of one of the very best and most honorable criminal lawyers in the country. Not only that, but what with the previous changes in counsel in this case, it would make it just that much more likely that the Texas Court of Criminal Appeals would laugh the entire thing off. I do not know whether you appreciate just what a laughingstock the post-conviction (and I suppose pre-conviction) antics of the Ruby defense have become in Texas, but this is not a mood to have the Court in when they have to decide a question of life or death for Jack.

I do not know whether anything can be done at this late date to repair the situation with Charles Bellows. I do not even know why he is contemplating withdrawing the case. I can tell you

this, though, that if it is a dispute between him and any other
person I think that the chances are very, very good that Charles
Bellows is right—and even if he isn't, this is not a time to change
horses again. . . .

Kaplan's intercession on behalf of Bellows came too late.
On the same day, Kunstler wrote to Bellows, Burleson,
Tonahill, and the Honorable K. K. Woodley, at that time
the presiding judge of the Court of Criminal Appeals of
Texas, that his office had been retained as chief counsel on
the Ruby appeal and requested the substitution of attorneys as asked by the Ruby family. "Naturally," Kunstler
wrote, "we would appreciate any help and guidance that
you may wish to offer, but we have accepted full responsibility for the case." Of Judge Woodley, Kunstler requested
"a reasonable continuance of the argument on the appeal
[then scheduled for March 10] and sufficient time in which
to file and serve our brief." Copies of the letters were sent
to Dann and myself and to Earl Ruby and, in the instance
of the Woodley letter, to Burleson, Tonahill, and Bellows.

I was deeply impressed and encouraged by the manner
in which Kunstler was attacking the case. He seemed to
have exactly the attitude that was required. Everything
had come to a standstill, and a crisis situation had developed. Dann had tried, unsuccessfully, to organize a campaign to set aside the death verdict, but because of
temperamental difficulties or a lack of knowledge in a
highly complicated field of law, he was running in circles
and getting nowhere.

Instinctively, as Kunstler and I entered the case officially,
we realized that matters had to be taken in hand and put
in good order before we could work out an intelligent
strategy. Tonahill, because he hindered other counsel and
was so hated by Ruby, his family, and Dann, had to go.
And time had to be gained to file a brief and prepare for the
argument before the Court of Criminal Appeals. Kunstler
had acted promptly in the effort to gain these ends.

The reaction was not long in coming. Joe Tonahill immediately made clear, beyond a doubt, his attitude toward the attempted substitution of attorneys. He wrote to Kunstler's firm, in a letter notable for vigor and clarity, if not for legal knowledge or acumen:

Your letter and enclosures of February 8, 1965, duly received and noted in which you rather boorishly assert that you have taken over as appellate counsel in the Jack Ruby appeal, and you ask that I, Phil Burleson, and Charles Bellows, "the present attorneys of record for appellant, Jack Ruby," accept you as substitute counsel and relieve ourselves of all responsibilities in the appeal.

As to yourselves, Sol Dann of Detroit, Earl Ruby of Detroit, and Madam Eva Grant of Dallas, allow me to enclose for the interest, guidance, and serious consideration of each of you precise photocopies of Article 430 of the Penal Code of Texas and Article 16, Section 29 of the Constitution of Texas.

Further, for your information, I shall present written briefs and oral argument to the Court of Criminal Appeals of Texas in behalf of my client, Jack Ruby, under the present and future orders of that Court.

Further, as an officer of that Court and the longest remaining attorney of record for the appellant, Jack Ruby, I shall take all steps necessary before the Court and the State Bar of Texas and inferior courts to preserve the status quo of my contractual relationship with Jack Ruby in addition to effecting prosecution and enforcement of Article 430 of the Penal Code as to yourselves, Sol Dann, Earl Ruby, and Madam Eva Grant. . . .

Allow me to respectfully say that I have never quit a client or fight in my life and can't and won't quit this one until all necessary appellate efforts in Jack Ruby's behalf have been exhausted. This position is consistent with my contractual duty to my client, Texas law, and is in full faith with my oath as a lawyer, my duty to my client, my profession, and to a due administration of justice in my past, present, and future efforts to obtain a reversal of the illegal death verdict assessed Jack Ruby in Dallas, March 14, 1964.

Finally, be advised that in rejecting your current interferences with this appeal and the effort of yourselves and the above-named co-instigators to impair my contractual relationship and duties with my client, the Court, and law of Texas, will be fully met and seriously dealt with at the proper time in a Texas court.

Characteristically, as it turned out in the months and years that followed, Tonahill did not refer to me in this letter. He would assail Dann and Kunstler, but he seldom referred to me by name. Whether this was a mark of respect or contempt, or a deliberate ignoring of my presence, I never learned.

What is notable in the letter is that Tonahill based his persistance in remaining in the case upon a purported contract with Jack Ruby. Tonahill was a well-known personal injury lawyer, a field in which contracts with clients once amounted to a great deal. Clients in negligence actions used to be bound by such contracts; such contracts have never bound clients in criminal cases.

Tonahill was no politer—if briefer—in his communication to Earl:

For God's sake will you, Sol Dann, and Eva stop acting like buzzards. You are hurting Jack's public image and all the money that you, Dann, and Eva hope to make off of Jack's legal problems won't help either of you.

There's nothing that either of you can do to prevent Jack from having his rights protected properly despite your efforts to the contrary.

Don't you know that the alleged power-of-attorney the New Yorkers got you to sign February 9th is invalid? Don't you know that the alleged power-of-attorney Eva has is invalid?

Sol Dann was delighted by the new activity in the case. He hastened to give Kunstler and me the benefit of all the thinking he had done during the lonesome months when he had fought alone in his defense of Ruby and in defiance of those who stood in his way.

In an impassioned letter to Kunstler Dann expressed his

deep concern, not only for Jack Ruby as an individual, but also for justice and human rights for all. To him the legal profession itself was on trial, both for the manner in which Jack had been represented (or misrepresented, as Dann saw it) and for the way in which the district attorney's office had conducted itself. (This was a recurrent theme in Dann's approach to many legal issues in the case. The sentiment was shared by many members of the bar, and some felt that a verdict of incompetence had already been returned.

"I cannot express how happy I am to be working with men like you and Elmer, who are not afraid of difficulties," he wrote. His summation was succinct: "We may be trying to crawl thru keyholes of locked doors against Jack, but this represents a great challenge."

Dann's ire had been aroused particularly by the actions and statements of the district attorney's office. To Dann it seemed that they were trying to dictate who should represent Jack and scheming to execute him as a scapegoat for Dallas attitudes that had resulted in the assassination of President Kennedy. Now Dann's "compass" led him to believe that the Dallas attitude toward Jack Ruby would not prevail.

Sol was the one attorney in the Ruby case whom I found most difficult to understand. I saw more of him than any of the others, and we generally worked in harmony. We met often, talked by telephone, and exchanged frequent letters. I knew and liked his wife, an accomplished artist, and his children, the one a school teacher, and the other a social worker, and both deeply interested in the civil rights revolution.

Sol and I were both critical of the Establishment, in our profession and in our communities. But temperamentally we were worlds apart. When provoked, when driven by derision, Sol could threaten to leave this country and go to live in Israel. I could never conceive of such an action, no matter what the provocation. Sol saw dirty work everywhere, conspiracies, double-dealing, whereas I saw mistakes, differences of opinion, deficiencies in character and intelligence, but little that was dastardly in its implications. He was inclined to seek punishment of those whom he distrusted—action by the bar associations, by the courts, by the press. I wanted to concentrate on a single objective —the reversal of the death sentence. I was not concerned with vengeance.

Sol too often voiced his personal opinions as if they were shared by all his associates—not only in personal conversations with his colleagues, which was perhaps his privilege, but also in the press and over radio and television. I—and I was not alone—resented this. It is not wisdom to threaten disciplinary action against lawyers and judges. Indeed, the counsel for Jack Ruby should speak as with one voice, one sane and balanced voice. On one occasion—after our first appearance together in Judge Brown's court—after Dann had indiscreetly and indiscriminately announced in a radio interview his self-conceived plans for the case, I expressed myself unmistakably. Sam Clinton was present at the time—speechless but observant. It was our first meeting, but I don't think that Sam ever forgot the episode.

At times Sol was shrewd and perceptive, but he was not always charming, and one could understand why he did not always wear well. He was not as well informed about the criminal law as other counsel in the case, but his diligence, persistence, doggedness, were deserving of admiration; his mind was always in a ferment, although he sometimes spoke in soft, measured tones. An early riser myself, I was aghast at Sol's hours. He would have risen and had his first breakfast while I was only beginning to think of the possibility of getting up, and when Kunstler and Clinton, night owls, were not aware that morning had arrived. His assortment of suggestions did not always wear well in the morning air.

Sometimes those who knew I was in the Ruby case would ask, "How do you like working with Sol Dann?" or "What is Sol Dann doing in the Ruby case?" Generally they would remain silent as I praised him. The questions

asked were an outgrowth, I now believe, of how Dann
had expressed himself, on occasion, on American foreign
policy or, more likely, the result of his role as gadfly to
certain large American corporations, particularly the
Chrysler Corporation.

Unexpectedly, just as it seemed our new team was well
started on the appeal, the Court of Criminal Appeals
rebuffed Kunstler's efforts to enter our appearances in
behalf of Ruby. Judge Woodley rejected the requested
substitution of attorneys because it was not done in a document personally signed by Ruby. It looked very much as
if the situation there was hopeless, that the court could
scarcely wait until it had the opportunity to affirm the
death sentence, without admitting Jack's right to counsel
of his choice.

We were shocked and bewildered by this apparent arbitrariness and, at the same time, determined to find some
way to rectify the situation. After Ruby personally had
subscribed to his desire to remove Tonahill and to substitute us as his counsel in the case, the court suddenly
entered an order, on February 24, 1965, that opened new
opportunities.

The case, the order recited, had "heretofore been set for
submission on March 10, 1965, briefs to be filed by March
3, 1965." Now a postponement was requested to allow new
counsel time for preparation. The next paragraph had
ironic, if not ominous overtones:

Though the appellant Jack Ruby occupies before this Court
the position of an indigent, controversy has arisen as to which
of several lawyers—none of them court appointed and some
non-residents of Texas—should be recognized by this Court as
his counsel on appeal entitled to use the time allowed for oral
argument in his behalf.

What did the court mean when it coupled the indigence
of Ruby with his desire for counsel of his own choice? Did
not the poor have the right to proper representation?

And what did the court intend by the references to nonresidents of Texas? Was this merely another expression of the suspicion of "foreigners" that seemed to trouble so many people in the state? .

The court then indicated that it was going to resolve the dilemma with which it was confronted by bringing up the motion challenging Ruby's sanity, a motion entered nearly a year earlier that had lain dormant before Judge Brown. The choice of attorneys would depend upon whether or not Ruby was sane. The court repeated the disturbing references: "This is true because we have before us an affidavit of the appellant asking that one of his trial counsel be dismissed . . . and further requesting that an out-of-state firm . . . be permitted to participate. . . ."

The court cited the Texas law applicable in cases of death sentences: If there were a question of sanity, a jury was to be impaneled; if the defendant were by them found insane, he was to be committed to a state mental hospital and all proceedings stayed until return of sanity, unless defense counsel chose to proceed with the appeal.

The court thereupon concluded that the submission of the appeal and decision as to choice of counsel should be postponed to allow Judge Brown to determine Ruby's sanity or insanity in the manner provided by law.

This was our first victory, although only a partial one at that. But even before we had time to reflect on the questions raised by the appellate court, Judge Brown revealed a studied determination to proceed—and in such haste as to indicate that he was fully prepared to rule on the questions without benefit of argument. He was quoted to that effect. How, then, could Ruby's counsel counter any further attempt at judicial precipitousness?

Alerted by Burleson, Kunstler immediately sent off a night letter to Judge Brown:

WE HAVE JUST BEEN INFORMED BY MR. BURLESON THAT YOU
HAVE SCHEDULED A LAWYERS' CONFERENCE FOR MONDAY, MARCH 1,

1965, IN ORDER TO DISCUSS FUTURE PROCEEDINGS IN STATE V. RUBY PURSUANT TO RECENT ORDER OF COURT OF CRIMINAL APPEALS.

SOL A. DANN, OF DETROIT, MICHIGAN, ELMER GERTZ OF CHICAGO, ILLINOIS AND THE MEMBERS OF THIS FIRM HAVE BEEN RETAINED BY RUBY FAMILY INCLUDING DEFENDANT TO REPRESENT HIM IN ALL PROCEEDINGS INVOLVING HIM. WE WOULD LIKE TO BE PRESENT AT ANY SUCH CONFERENCE. HOWEVER IN VIEW OF THE SHORT NOTICE, WE RESPECTFULLY REQUEST MONDAY MEETING BE ADJOURNED FOR AT LEAST ONE WEEK SO THAT WE WOULD BE ABLE TO MAKE APPRO-PRIATE ARRANGEMENTS TO COME TO DALLAS.

AT THAT TIME, WE EXPECT TO BE INTRODUCED TO YOU BY MR. BURLESON AND OUR ADMISSION FOR PURPOSES OF THIS OR ANY SUB-SEQUENT PROCEEDINGS BEFORE YOU IN THIS MATTER NOTED ON THE RECORD. MR. BURLESON WILL CALL YOU TOMORROW TO ASCERTAIN YOUR PLEASURE IN THIS MATTER.

Reluctantly, Judge Brown continued the matter for one week. It was apparent, however, that he was still determined to get rid of us in a hurry.

Necessarily, we had to accept the edict of the Court of Criminal Appeals about the holding of a sanity hearing, ostensibly for the purpose of the selection of counsel of Ruby's choice. At the time, we even welcomed the holding of such a hearing, for we deeply felt that our client was mentally ill, and our psychiatrists had warned us against the continuing decay in his mental processes. The trend might become irreversible. But we knew that it might be disastrous to try the matter before Judge Brown, whom we regarded as utterly unfit, and we could not permit Tonahill to remain in the case, frustrating and impeding us constantly. Besides, we needed more time for preparation. This reasoning led us inevitably to decide on the particular strategy that we were to follow. We had to present appropriate motions to Judge Brown to obtain what we were after, and if, as anticipated, we failed in our efforts, then we would have to go to a federal court to correct the errors made by him.

So, in March, 1965, for the first time, I flew to Dallas. Kunstler and Dann had preceded me by several hours, and Kunstler was gone by the time I arrived. He and Sol had worked with the at first unwilling Burleson in the drafting of the documents intended to get Judge Brown and Joe Tonahill out of the case, ourselves in it, and the sanity hearing postponed until we could be better prepared for it. The documents were forcefully worded, and I could understand why Burleson, who, unlike us, practiced—and would continue to practice—in Dallas, had to be pressured—as Sol told me—into signing his name to them.

The Ruby family had wanted to make a clean sweep of their old attorneys after Kunstler and I got into the case, excepting only Dann, whom they wanted to remain. They had gone through every kind of grief and agitation during the months since the verdict, and anyone who reminded them of the past had to go. They were still contending with Tonahill, still smarting from the blows they had received, and were suspicious even of the one who much deserved their gratitude—Phil Burleson.

Even a nonlawyer knows, instinctively, that there has to be some link from what has happened in the past to what happens in the present. Burleson was now the one person who could supply that link for the Ruby appeal. Even though I had not known him, even by reputation, I knew that the Ruby family needed him. Slowly Earl and Eva and the others were persuaded that they should mask their suspicions and misgivings and retain Phil Burleson. However reluctantly they went along with my arguments, there was never any reason to regret the decision, and the family soon was almost wholeheartedly supporting him. And though his situation in Dallas was sometimes difficult, he did not fail them.

Phil was not at hand when I arrived in Dallas that March day—I did not see him until the next day—and I got my first impressions of the situation from Sol Dann, who whispered hoarsely of dark deeds and vast uncertainties.

I was eager to view Dealey Plaza, Elm Street, the Texas School Book Depository, and the other sights evoking memories of the tragic events of November 22–24, 1963. What struck me most forcibly was the shocking realization that from the sixth-floor corner window of that accursed building, the assassin could have had no special difficulty in drawing a bead on the President. The distance seemed shorter, the view clearer, than I had been led to believe. The railroad overpass seemed out of the question as a spot from which to assassinate anyone. A killer, be he no taller than a cockroach, would be visible to all from there, including those in the presidential procession. The grassy knoll seemed just as impossible a lair, and I quickly dismissed it as a source of the shots. I realized anew, as often in the past, that there is no substitute for first-hand information. I felt as I had when I first viewed the battlefields of the Civil War: no verbal description can be as helpful to the student as an on-the-spot visit.

As Sol and I neared the Dallas County Jail that pleasant March night, we saw the familiar face of Bill Decker, Sheriff of Dallas County. We introduced ourselves, and Decker, ever obliging, invited us, then and there, to visit his famous prisoner, our client Jack Ruby. The temptation to do so was great, but we assured Decker that we would be around in the morning to avail ourselves of his hospitality.

Every case should have at least once character like Sheriff Bill Decker. Once seen, once talked to, he is never forgotten. He is an ideal subject for the caricaturist's pen— his face weather-beaten and scarred; his thick framed glasses calling further attention to the strong lines of the face; and all topped by a big and ancient hat. I never saw Bill Decker without his hat on his head, whether he was inside or outside, whether it was warm or cold, sunshining or drizzling—except in a courtroom when the judge had rapped for order. I sometimes suspected that Bill Decker slept in that hat. It was the trademark of a strong man of the law, a Dallas institution, one known by everyone, and feared and liked by all. One can hardly conceive of a time when he will not be around the Dallas courthouse and jail and general environs. He has been there, in his old haunts, in one capacity or another, for almost fifty years. He started as a courthouse elevator operator in 1919, and, as the wits would have it, he has always been going up. He became a county clerk in 1922, a deputy constable in 1923, chief deputy in 1933 and sheriff in 1949. Already in 1959 all Dallas turned out for "Bill Decker Day in Dallas," and, after the Ruby case was over, the Press Club of Dallas named him the All-Time Headliner. He made news even when he ostensibly sought to avoid it. He was the ideal sheriff for a sensational case. He stood out even in the company of luminaries like Melvin Belli and hams like Jack Ruby. The case belonged as much to Bill Decker as it did to Henry Wade or to us.

Periodically the press reported on the prison life of Jack Ruby, and almost invariably the source of the information doled out was the keeper of the Dallas County Jail. Just as one would not expect J. Edgar Hoover, director of the FBI, to suffer in an inspired account of his agency, one would not expect Bill Decker to suffer in an account of his jail.

Jim Lehrer could not have disappointed Decker in his account of Ruby's life in jail. He suggested, amazingly, that it would cost Ruby $18 a day for the same accommodations at a downtown hotel! (Perhaps this was why the article was printed on the comics page of the Dallas *Times Herald*.) Ruby, the article related, had a private pastel-green room, his own toilet facilities. "His meals are brought to him. Both daily papers are delivered to his door. His sheets are changed every day. The management even furnishes his clothes. 'Don't worry about Jack Ruby,' says Sheriff Bill Decker. 'The boy's doing fine.'"

The article told of Ruby's eating habits, his card-playing, reading, correspondence, telephoning, visits. Ruby's concern over his diminishing hair was treated in depth and concluded with Sheriff Decker's comment: "But I am happy to report that he still has the three hairs across the top of his head he had when he came in." According to the same authority, Ruby was physically healthy. "Outside of an aspirin maybe, he's never been given any medicine, nor asked for a doctor," he said. "The county and assistant county medical officers are in the jail daily, if anything is needed." Ruby thought primarily about himself, said the sheriff. "We'll usually talk about some new developments in his case. I remember some conversation about the Warren Report." The uncertainty of Ruby's future was considered. "But no matter how long it is, nobody has to worry about him," said Decker. "We're taking good care of Jack Ruby."

# 8

MARCH 8, 1965

As Sol Dann and I, with the assistance of Burleson, Kunstler, and Clinton, and on the insistence of Jack Ruby and his family, sought to have Joe Tonahill removed from any role as Ruby's attorney, we learned that this was merely a "trick." Bill Alexander told reporters, with an air of assurance, that his office had had information for months of an effort to create so-called legal errors. He said, in characteristic fashion: "All this lawyer trouble appears to be a trick of the defense to manufacture claimed error in an area which the state has no control over, in an effort to trap the trial judge and the Texas Court of Criminal Appeals into a constitutional question."

That Ruby himself had made it clear he would have nothing to do with Tonahill meant little to Alexander. Over and over again, whenever Ruby was in a courtroom or on the way to or from one, he would say to the persistent Tonahill: "You are not my lawyer." This was meaningless to Alexander; nor would he draw a proper inference from Judge Brown's refusal to recognize Dann or me as Ruby's attorneys. Neither of us tried to engage the unengaging Alexander in conversation on the subject, but it would have been interesting to learn his ideas, as a really competent attorney, on what constitutes "a lawyer of one's choice." The Constitution of the United States clearly guarantees defendants in capital cases the lawyers of their choice. Why should Ruby, who most needed such attorneys, be deprived of them? Perhaps Alexander had the answer. We did not.

For the hearing to be held before Judge Brown on March 8, 1965, to determine the handling of the sanity hearing, we had prepared four motions, to be filed in the Criminal District Court No. 3 of Dallas County, Judge Brown's court.

We felt, at the time, that these motions marked the most important steps taken in the Ruby case since the pronouncement of the death sentence. More than three years have gone by since the preparation of the motions, and I, for one, feel more certain than ever that they marked a turning point in the case, regardless of how we fared at the time. In any case there comes a moment when the tide of combat flows one way or the other. Sometimes one does not sense that the time of decision is at hand. This time Sol Dann and I, if not all our associates, felt that we were on the right path, that we were finally on the road to setting aside the unjust death sentence.

The pivotal motion sought the disqualification of Judge Brown. It set forth that Judge Brown, who had presided at the trial, had ruled against Ruby's motion for a change of venue—a matter involving "judicial discretion" which could affect his judgment in the matters now before him. We claimed, "upon information and belief," that Judge Brown "is presently engaged in or under contract to a firm of publishers" to write a book on Ruby's murder trial and the subsequent proceedings. Again, "upon information and belief," we claimed that he had received a "down payment thereon and expects to receive further payments and royalties in the future." We said that "the preparation, publication and sale" of the book would be directly affected by the court's decision on our various motions and the other proceedings, and that these matters "could serve as an additional chapter" in the book. This "pecuniary and personal interest" in the book, we said, disqualified Judge Brown from acting as a judge in any proceedings involving Ruby, and we cited in support of our contention a provision of the Texas Constitution, a

Texas case, and another legal authority. We claimed, moreover, that Judge Brown's refusal to remove Joe Tonahill as one of the attorneys for Ruby disqualified him to determine that issue again or to act in any proceeding affecting it. Growing bolder, we referred to Judge Brown's "questionable judicial conduct . . . before, during and after the trial"—"his reading in the presence of the jury a cartoon book . . . ; his poses for photographs . . . converted a serious capital case . . . into . . . a 'circus' that prejudiced Defendant and made it impossible . . . to receive the fair and impartial trial" assured by the Constitution. We feared, we said, "a repetition of such prejudiced conduct." We referred to the judge's improper use of a public relations agency during the trial proceedings, and we expressed the fear that this continuing desire to maintain a "personal image" for the financial exploitation of the book could influence his decisions. Again, "upon information and belief," we said that Judge Brown had shopped around, at the time of the original proceedings, to determine whether he would go with the case and preside if he granted a change of venue to another county, and, when this could not be done, he decided not to grant the change, and he was still predisposed against the motion for that reason. All of these and other reasons, we said, called for the judge to disqualify himself from all pending and future proceedings involving Ruby. This motion Jack's brother Sam signed in his behalf.

Then there was a motion for a change of venue. It asked that all further proceedings whatsoever be transferred "to some County, far removed from . . . Dallas, that is free from all of the objections" alleged. In the original motion for a change of venue, filed before the murder trial, twenty-two reasons for such change were set forth. We asked that that motion and the evidence introduced in support of it be considered as part of our renewed motion for a change of venue. We charged that since the trial Ruby had been subjected to "further prejudicial and damaging publicity," including comments concerning the Warren Report which aroused prejudices and ill-feeling in Dallas, so that Ruby could not receive fair and equal treatment before any tribunal there. The motion to disqualify Judge Brown, we said, might have the effect of further prejudice to Ruby in Dallas County. The more the activity in the case, we said, the greater the difficulty in securing justice for Ruby in Dallas.

A third motion sought to establish Ruby's right to counsel of his own choice. Judge Brown had indicated that the only attorneys he would recognize to speak for Ruby were Phil Burleson and Joe H. Tonahill; the latter was unacceptable to Ruby. Tonahill had been discharged as an attorney in the case on or about July 21, 1964, we said, and had been repeatedly requested to refrain from acting as attorney for Ruby and from interfering with the attorneys of Ruby's choice. In October, 1964, the court had been requested to remove him. Phil Burleson, we said, "is in need of, and is authorized to act only with the assistance of other and additional counsel of Defendant's choice." We attached to our motion both the motion previously made in the Court of Criminal Appeals to exclude Tonahill and the supporting affidavits, which had been served upon him. We repeated the desire of Ruby and all members of his family to exclude Tonahill completely from the case and to have Burleson act with other attorneys designated by Ruby and his family, whether or not such attorneys were members of the Bar of Texas. We declared that the denial of Ruby's right to be represented by counsel of his own choice at all times and the imposition of Tonahill upon him would be in violation of the Sixth and Fourteenth Amendments to the Constitution of the United States, and we cited a good deal of law in support of our viewpoint. Finally, we said, since Tonahill purported to be acting pursuant to a contract with Ruby and yet claimed that Ruby was insane, his alleged contract was either void because of the insanity or, if Ruby was sane—as the law presumes prior to an adjudication of insanity—then Ruby clearly had the right to discharge Tonahill, and this he had done. The attached exhibits included the designation of Kunstler, Gertz, Dann, and Burleson as attorneys by Ruby through himself and the members of his family, the detailed motion to exclude Tonahill already discussed by us, Eva Grant's power of attorney and an affidavit by Earl Ruby to which Ruby and his family subscribed. We felt that we had not omitted one argument against the further participation by Tonahill in the case and our being recognized as Ruby's only attorneys in all further proceedings.

Finally, there was a motion for extension of time to prepare for the pretrial conference and sanity hearing. In it we referred to the order of the Court of Criminal Appeals remanding the case for a determination of Ruby's present sanity or insanity and his mental capacity to employ counsel, including the undecided motions that we had filed in the higher court. We referred to the hastily scheduled pretrial conference that Judge Brown had called for March 1, 1965, which had been postponed for only one week. We reminded the court of the importance of such pretrial conference and of the several vital outstanding problems, requiring "an enormous amount of previous planning and preparation." The requisite proofs of Ruby's mental capacity entailed extensive and thorough pyschiatric and psychological examinations of Ruby and interviews with members of his family and others; these would take a minimum of sixty days in the first instance and the employment of additional counsel and no less than thirty more days to utilize the reports. We reminded the court that Ruby's emotional instability extended back to his tenth year, that his mother had been confined to a mental institution, that he and various members of his family had been treated at various times for mental disturbances, that the available reports were more than seven months old and inadequate for our purposes. We said that the refusal to grant the necessary time for the pretrial and sanity hearing would be prejudicial and deprive Ruby of his fundamental constitutional rights.

As we were preparing for the hearing before Judge Brown on March 8, it became increasingly clear that Burleson was distinctly uneasy about the situation that was developing. Dann and I were outsiders in the closed community of Dallas, and although Burleson was willing to accept our counsel and assistance, he was unwilling to have us appear in court and publicly participate in the proceedings. Because of our awareness of his sensitivity, we compromised: we would appear in the courtroom and sit at the counsel table with Jack Ruby and Burleson, but we would permit Burleson to do all the talking for the defense. On the day of the hearing, we were introduced to Judge Brown before the formal opening of the session. He merely grunted by way of acknowledgment. Later, in the hearing itself, Tonahill asked that we be excluded from the counsel table. Judge Brown did not accede. Thus our position in the case was left unresolved. Although, in time, Burleson raised no objections to our open participation and we became genuine collaborators, publicly as well as privately, the initial compromise on asking formal recognition of the court was to badly affect the course of the case.

Court reporting is a difficult art. Because of acoustical and personal eccentricities, no reporter understands or hears all that is said in the court, and even if the words are taken down fairly accurately, they are not transcribed with the same fidelity. Good court reporters are too busy to do their own typing, so they dictate their notes to subordinates who do not have the same skills and who lack first-hand knowledge of what was actually said in the courtroom.

Experienced lawyers and the reviewing courts look upon these so-called transcripts of proceedings with a good deal of sympathy. No attorney ever feels sure that the stenographer's transcript of any case in which he participates is wholly accurate. Everyone winces as he reads what he is supposed to have said. His perfect diction is mangled, he is sure, by even the best court reporter, and the best is seldom at hand.

Even an abundance of charity could not account for or excuse what was done with the March 8, 1965, hearing before Judge Brown. My first shocked reaction to that transcript was put down in an affidavit, and is not obscured, I hope, by the somewhat legalistic language:

I sat at the counsel table directly facing Judge Brown, listened attentively to all that was said and have a clear recollection thereof. In addition, I had read and was familiar with the four motions in behalf of Jack Ruby, presented that morning by Mr. Phil Burleson, so that I was able to follow the proceedings in court with understanding.

Mr. Phil Burleson presented each of the said four motions to the court and the court immediately overruled each of them without argument and without affording opportunity for argument. In each instance, Mr. Burleson noted an exception to the overruling of the motion and asked for a hearing thereon, which hearing in each instance was denied and an exception to such ruling was taken by Mr. Burleson. In each instance, Mr. Burleson then asked to make an offer of proof as to what he would show at such hearing, and in each instance this was denied by the court and Mr. Burleson took exception thereto.

With respect to the motions presented under the heading "Defendant's Motion for the Right to Counsel of His Choice at Both the Pre-Trial Conference and the Sanity Hearing," Judge Brown expressly ruled as follows: "I deny defendant's motion for the right to counsel of his choice at both the pre-trial conference and the sanity hearing." This stood out in my memory, because of the anomaly of his expressly denying a defendant in a capital case counsel of his choice.

The defendant, Jack Ruby, sat between Mr. Sol A. Dann and myself throughout the course of the hearing before Judge

Brown at the said time and place and audibly expressed dissatis-
faction and disagreement with the court's rulings with respect
to the various motions presented to the court, and particularly
the motion for the right of counsel of his choice. He was particularly vigorous in dissenting to the selection of Mr. Joe M.
Tonahill as his attorney. None of Mr. Ruby's remarks appear
in the transcript, although I am informed that representatives
of the press and other communications media, who were there
in large numbers, caught some of his remarks and repeated
them in their reports of the proceedings.

I have read the purported transcript of the proceedings, prepared by the Official Court Reporter, Mr. L. B. Bailey, Jr., and
it is inaccurate in various respects, and particularly in the
failure to report correctly the proceedings with respect to
defendant's motion for the right to counsel of his choice.

Because Kunstler, as our expert on federal procedures,
was to have the primary responsibility for guiding us in
our efforts to get into the federal courts, Dann, too, had
sent him an affidavit on what had happened in the Alice-
in-Wonderland appearance before Judge Brown.

What Sol said in his affidavit was substantially true. But
he apparently missed certain contradictory remarks of
Judge Brown. At one point, after having denied the various motions, Judge Brown went on to say that, whether or
not Tonahill could hire Emmett Colvin as an assistant
depended upon Ruby! This was characteristic of the judge's
whole bearing at the hearing. There was no consideration
of any motion, no effort to reach the proper legal conclusions, no willingness to tolerate any argument or delay. He
had apparently made up his mind in advance, and he was
going to brook nothing which interfered with this program.

The intention of the affidavits was to remove the matter
to the federal court to assure Jack Ruby both the right of
counsel of his choice and a fair hearing. However, unless
we concluded that the affidavits and other efforts were
essential for the removal of the case, I was disinclined to

indulge in them. My inclination was to get there without
delay, attempting to remove the case completely from the
jurisdiction of Judge Brown. It seemed clear that if the
records in the Criminal District Court showed the filing of
the motions by Phil Burleson and the denial of them by the
court, that would suffice for the purpose of getting the
matter into the federal court.

Since Burleson was still in the case, he could not complain about Judge Brown's ruling to the same degree that
we and Ruby could complain. Therefore we selected Clinton, who was physically closest to the scene, to file the
necessary papers in the United States District Court in
Dallas for the purpose of removing the case from the state
court. This automatically gave the federal court sole jurisdiction, until and unless the court of its own motion or as
the result of a hearing decided the case did not belong
there and sent it back—"remanded" is the legal phrase—
to the state court. We hoped the matter would come before
Judge Sarah Hughes, whom we regarded as enlightened
and sympathetic, but it was assigned, instead, to Judge T.
Whitfield Davidson, an ancient and old-fashioned gentleman who, in the distant days of 1948, had nearly deprived
one Lyndon B. Johnson of his first election to the United
States Senate.

# 9

## IN FEDERAL COURTS

I HAD NOT KNOWN with any particularity that Sam Houston
Clinton, Jr., was going to be associated in the case with us.
I knew that he had been brought in for consultation be-
cause he was general counsel for the Texas Civil Liberties
Union, and it was obvious to us that Ruby's constitutional
rights were being violated in Texas.

My first meeting with him occurred during my initial
devastating run-in with Sol Dann. As I sailed into Dann
for his ill-timed remarks, I glanced occasionally at Clinton
to learn his reaction, if any, to my assault on our colleague.
His strong, handsome face remained composed. Neither
then nor later could I be sure what Clinton was really
thinking.

Clinton enjoyed all the appetites of a strong man and
had a droll sense of humor, but he was essentially serious.
It took a man with philosophy and gumption to espouse
the causes of labor and civil liberties in Texas. Clinton was
unflustered, unhurried, thoughtful. He carried himself
with assurance, and he was not intimidated by what anyone said. He had his own views, and he expressed them
when he felt it necessary; at other times he would be silent,
simply absorbing without comment what others were saying. He and Kunstler were two of a kind, it sometimes
seemed to me, but with a difference or two. Kunstler was
the New Yorker and the Jew, expressing himself easily,
and with his heart on his sleeve; Clinton the sometimes
reserved Texan, who was distrustful of the overt expression
of thought and feeling. Yet both were in essential agree-

ment on all that mattered—an American's right to the constitutional guarantees and a full-bodied person's appetites for the gifts of life.

On the morning of March 18, 1965, Clinton appeared in the United States District Court, in Dallas. Judge T. Whitfield Davidson invited him to "be heard briefly as to the proceedings to take place here this afternoon." The court clearly intended to move on with the proceedings as quickly as possible. It was our position, as Clinton stated, "that by reason of the removal petition the matter now is in the jurisdiction of this Court. We have sought a writ of habeas corpus in order to make sure that this Court's control over the petitioner is not interfered with by anyone else." He was careful to explain:

"Now, Your Honor, in seeking a writ we are not asking that the physical presence of Mr. Ruby be modified in any way, we don't think that is necessary. The Dallas County Jail, as I understand it, is also the place of commitment used by the Federal Marshal."

"That is true," the court assured him.

Clinton continued: "We are only saying that the Court should grant the writ so that the custody of Jack Ruby will be in the hands of the marshal and the marshal will be responsible for his whereabouts, for his presence, and the defendant, or petitioner in this case, could not be moved about except on orders of the marshal and under the orders of this Court."

Judge Davidson immediately asserted: "We have some mighty good marshals in Dallas County, and we have a good Sheriff, too."

"I don't deny that," the suave Sam Clinton responded, "but in the answer to our petition, I don't know whether it is before you or not, in their answer they say to the Court that tomorrow morning Judge Brown intends to have some sort of hearing. We don't think he has jurisdiction to have a hearing. I am told that Judge Brown intends to bring the defendant into court and ask him some questions and we don't think the judge has that right, and we don't think that the judge should have such a hearing and subject the defendant to possible examination in the State Court. . . ."

At this point, a loud and resounding voice was heard: "My name is Bill Alexander. I feel that the issue has been joined in the pleading and that this can be determined by your Honor this afternoon."

He went on to affirm the State's contention that our petition was legally unfounded. "The cases uniformly hold that there must be a constitutional provision to be construed, or a State Statute to be construed. There is nothing in the petition which would bring it within those rules, which your Honor very well knows." He asked that the judge remand the case to the Criminal District Court No. 3 of Dallas County, Judge Brown's court.

Jim Bowie reaffirmed Bill Alexander's view of the law, adding "that Judge Brown had previously had a hearing set for tomorrow morning for the purpose of removing Joe Tonahill from the case as a court-appointed attorney. That case was set prior to the pleading filed in this court. Judge Brown can no longer have a hearing tomorrow on that question or any other question in this case so long as there is a petition before your Honor's court, not only as a matter of law, but as a matter of courtesy. . . ."

Judge Davidson inquired whether the United States attorney had anything to say. Mr. B. H. Timmins, the assistant United States attorney, a new man so far as Jack Ruby was concerned, responded: "We are not parties to this case, we are only here after being notified by the Court of the setting. I do not feel we could take a position in regard to the merit or lack of merit of the motion, but certainly I think Mr. Alexander's and Mr. Bowie's statement to the Court of what the provisions of the law are is correct. . . ." This was a special kind of neutrality.

Clinton assured the court that opposing counsel were in error as to their legal contentions, but he did not have the cases with him. One of his associates, not available at the time, would have these authorities and argue them to the court. He asked for the opportunity for such argument by his associate.

*The Court:* Who is your co-counsel?

*Mr. Clinton:* Mr. William Kunstler is the main co-counsel, and we would like to have a hearing on the answer, if it is construed as a motion to remand. At least, we want to demonstrate to the Court just what our situation is and how this man [Jack Ruby] is being denied rights, and cannot enforce his rights under the Constitution of the United States.

*The Court:* Will your co-counsel be here in the morning? Is he in town now?

*Mr. Clinton:* Judge Homer Thornberry in Austin is setting me up in this court on a matter which has been set at least two and a half or three months. If we can have until Monday of next week my co-counsel will be here. . . .

*The Court:* Will your co-counsel be down there?

*Mr. Clinton:* No, sir, not in that case.

*The Court:* I have already heard you, why not let him come here and take over in the morning? [The judge's belief that he had heard Clinton revealed a peculiar notion about how to hold a hearing.]

*Mr. Clinton:* I will try to get him here in the morning.

*Mr. Alexander:* Is he in New York?

*Mr. Clinton:* No, he is not, but I cannot assure the Court he can get here.

*The Court:* I don't like to enter an order on short notice. Mr. Tonahill phoned me and said he was concerned about the matter and he asked me to give him a chance to come here in the morning and I told him to come on. I have cases set to run for weeks following this and I'm very much inclined to either rule on this case this evening or do so in the morning. I think I will not rule on the case, but will adjourn this hearing over until ten o'clock tomorrow morning and let your co-counsel take over, and I will consider you have already presented your side of it. [Clinton actually had spoken in only the most cursory manner, but the judge persisted in regarding his few words as a full argument.]

*Mr. Clinton:* Because of time could we make it at 2:00 o'clock tomorrow afternoon, and in that way I can be sure to get somebody here.

*The Court:* I don't think it will take but a few hours to get here. How does it suit the other parties to be here at two o'clock tomorrow afternoon?

*Mr. Alexander:* Whatever is agreeable, your Honor, we will be here.

*The Court:* How about the Government?

*Mr. Timmins:* We can be here at any time.

*The Court:* I have a motion set tomorrow that I don't think will take very long and I will get it out of the way and I think everybody will be in shape to present this tomorrow at two o'clock. So this hearing will be without prejudice to anybody's right, and it will be adjourned over until two o'clock tomorrow.

The next afternoon, however, the matter came up for hearing before Judge Davidson in the absence of Ruby's attorneys. None of us could be present. Judge Davidson insisted upon going ahead. Jack Ruby himself was present in open court, as required by the writ, and the judge apparently deemed that sufficient.

"Gentlemen, we have before us a petition for writ of habeas corpus," the judge intoned. "That petition was followed by a motion to remand to the State Court. It was the purpose of this Court to pass upon the bill at the same time, because the jurisdiction of this Court is linked with the petition of habeas corpus. I have read both papers, and I will ask if counsel is present who filed the petition for a writ of habeas corpus."

Bill Alexander advised him that Clinton was not there. Jack Ruby, ever willing to be heard, blurted out: "Your Honor, may I say something? I don't have any counsel here, your Honor, and I wish the courtesy of the Court to give me a chance to take the stand and back up my statement. . . ."

"I see no objection," said Judge Davidson. "Is there any objection on the part of opposing counsel?"

Joe Tonahill, as willing as Jack Ruby to talk, got up and declared: "I am the attorney of record for Jack Ruby, and the longest remaining attorney of record for him, and when the Court is ready for me to proceed in answer to any question he may have, I will point out some matters that might bear upon your Honor's consideration with reference to the testimony."

The court responded: "In view of the fact that your relationship as an attorney is attacked in the matter, I can't recognize you as being an attorney for the defendant, but since you are made a defendant in the same proceeding, you are entitled to be heard, and I will hear you for fifteen or twenty minutes."

The court was mistaken in believing Tonahill to be a defendant; but the latter did not correct him. Instead, he began by reading an excerpt from what Judge Brown had said on that strange occasion on March 8, 1965, when he had overruled our motions without reading them and without granting us a hearing: "Mr. Tonahill, the reason that I appointed you and Mr. Burleson to represent the defendant is because you . . . did participate in the trial of the case, and therefore, you would be very valuable to the defendant in handling his appeal. . . ."

Tonahill then told of Dr. L. J. West, an eminent psychiatrist, who had given his affidavit "that Jack Ruby was insane, and highly susceptible to delusions and suspicions, and a complete paranoid." Dr. West demonstrated, he said, that Ruby could act only through an attorney in these proceedings affecting his life.

He then told of his claimed contract with Ruby.

He presented the contract, the affidavit of Dr. West, the order of Judge Brown, and "the Congressional Record with reference to the other attorneys" (in which a scurrilous attack had been made upon William Kunstler, largely because of his participation in the ongoing fight for civil rights).

He declared that he had been with Jack Ruby throughout the proceedings "and have visited with him and worked with him and have constantly stayed on the job undertaking to be his attorney." He failed, however, to stress to the court that these things had occurred in the earlier stages of the case and that Ruby would have nothing to do with him now.

"The record will show that I participated in most of the hearings, in the 6,800 page transcript, and I raised somewhere in excess of 1200 points of error; that I participated in challenging, and seeking to protect this defendant's rights.

"Having been with him on the hearing and knowing the state of the record that exists, particularly with reference to his mental history and the examination of the doctors and psychiatrists, and the development of this case, and understanding all of that, Judge Brown, when he made the appointment, which I did not consider necessary, by virtue of a contract that compels me to complete my task, it impels me to go forward and finish the job I started and not abandon a sick man who is under a death sentence.

"There are a lot of things I could be doing, and it would be better for my family and my income, but I couldn't quit Jack Ruby. I couldn't respect myself and continue to practice law."

He said that there had been "in the neighborhood of eighteen lawyers" who had been in and out of the case. But he had remained.

"Now, these attorneys from New York and Chicago and Detroit say that Jack Ruby doesn't have counsel of his choice. . . . Why do they want me out of the case? The man who has the most complete knowledge of the case? The man that is familiar with the scene that went on at

the time of the errors, and knows how to find them. Why
do they want me out? . . . They are seeking to commercial-
ize on Jack Ruby, and to degrade the legal profession, and
I refuse to tolerate it and I would not permit it, and they
cannot get me out of the case."

He accused us of wanting "to incorporate Jack Ruby,"
of employing public relations people to handle the appeal.
He said that we were trying to sell the suit Ruby had
worn when he had shot Oswald, that we were making
various arrangements with a publisher in Michigan. He
was too angry to be clear, too involved to state the truth.

"And when the Warren Commission took Ruby's polygraph examination in July, Mr. Dann got on the phone and
said, 'You are fired. You are no longer in the case.' That
was just a day or two after we had this big blow up. He
says, 'You are fired,' he said, 'I am going to sue you and
Bill Decker and the Warren Commission for assault.' Jack
got what he wanted. . . . Whether there was any connection between him and Oswald, he wanted to disprove that,
and the Warren Commission gave it to him. So Mr. Dann
uses that as an excuse, and there has been nothing but constant harassment.

"Mr. Dann is aware that if Jack Ruby dies in the electric
chair, he will be the first Jew to be electrocuted in the
State of Texas.

"Why does he want me out? Why have they undermined
Jack Ruby's confidence in me? He has been visited in his
cell by the district attorney without my knowledge or con-
sent or my presence.

"Now, with reference to disqualifying Judge Brown—"

Judge Davidson interjected: "I believe we will not go
into that. I might say to you, if we rule on this case it will
be on the question of jurisdiction . . . and on that you are
entitled to be heard."

Tonahill went on to explain that when Ruby said he did
not want him to remain as his attorney, he did not know
what he was doing. He was mentally sick and could not

act for himself. The prosecution, too, wanted to get rid of him, for Mr. Wade's own reasons. ". . . But I have a job to do for the defendant and as long as the courts of this State, or anyone will permit me to do it, I am going to continue to defend him, and I couldn't do other than that, so long as I live."

Judge Davidson, desirous of hearing Ruby, said that he did not need to be sworn, "I will permit him to stand where he is and he may give the Court any statement he may care to give."

Jack was eager to be heard. "This is the most tragic thing in the history of the world," he began. "One of the most tragic conspiracies in the world.

"I will get on the stand and speak with tears in my heart because of such a terrible conspiracy which is combined against me.

"It is not a question of more time. I am the person who is speaking, who doesn't care if he goes to the chair.

"What Mr. Tonahill has said has been a total lie. That goes from the contract I signed, I never did sign a contract with him. It has been a conspiracy between him and the District Attorney, Phil Burleson and Joe Tonahill, to convince the public that Jack Ruby is insane.

"Now, your Honor, you have had many a person appear before you pleading their case. If I am a person who sounds insane at this time, then the rest of the world is crazy. I say this with choking in my heart and tears in my eyes.

"The most tragic thing happened that Sunday morning when I went down that ramp. I happened to be there for a purpose which is going to be the most tragic thing that ever happened in this world.

"I wish you would give me a chance to tell you everything that occurred from the time Joe Tonahill came in the case and Phil Burleson came in the case, and when I knew Percy Foreman.

"When Percy Foreman came up, it seems they didn't want Percy Foreman to come into the case, and I'd heard a great deal of him. My civil attorney was Stanley Kaufman. He said, 'Stanley, I know Jack, he has done me many favors and I feel heartbroken and sick because he requested I come in in the first place.' He said, 'Stanley, I want to know when I can see Jack.' I wanted Fred from the start. The result is my younger brother, Earl, and my sister, they go to Fred Bruner's home, they had discussed it with him. And they made an agreement, but they didn't want any publicity or anything in the newspapers. So they came back and visited me at the County Jail and they said, 'We have Fred Bruner, the person you have always wanted.'

"But when you are incarcerated you are at a loss to tell who you want. And Fred Bruner said, 'I owe Jack Ruby so much.' I said, 'Earl, I can't understand it.' And in the meantime, in the Morning News, and after nothing was supposed to be placed in the newspaper, here is a 10-inch, one column put out, 'Fred Bruner is going to be legal counsel for Jack Ruby.' So my brother, Earl, went down to Houston to engage Percy Foreman, and he came back and said that the fee was too large. Percy Foreman came to Dallas, and we were enthused about him because of his great reputation.

"Naturally, I am a little unnerved after receiving a death sentence, but I am used to it now, after being incarcerated so long and Percy was in my room and he requested I come down to have some pictures made by the photographers.

"I have one person, Stanley Kaufman, who is a Silver Star winner in World War II, he was reluctant to have Percy make any exhibition of me. Percy resented that, but Stanley felt Percy was trying to gain a little publicity.

"Then comes along Phil Burleson and Joe Tonahill, puts his arm around my shoulders and said, 'Jack, I will go all the way to the Supreme Court with you.' And then when Mr. Belli came he said, 'Jack, I will endorse it.'

"I thought he was a great guy.

"They stayed in the hotel with Percy Foreman, for a

minimum of eight hours and Percy Foreman didn't know who was doing what. Tonahill and Burleson, they were going to tell him what to do. My good friend, Stanley, knew the situation. Well, I lost Percy Foreman because he knew of my start with Phil Burleson and Joe Tonahill, plus the fact Fred Bruner comes up to visit me. He said, 'You don't want Percy Foreman. I don't know a judge in Texas that likes him.'

"Now, for a person to recall of this, I think I'm doing pretty well for an insane man.

"This is the most tragic thing that ever will happen. I am going to die and I don't care.

"During the time of my incarceration Phil Burleson knew all my witnesses, and knew what upset me. He knew of certain things that happened in the jail. I have never been easy in that jail, certain things that scare me in jail, and he knew the breaking point at a certain time for Jack Ruby. In the meantime, unbeknowings to me. I didn't know there were tricks to get verbal statements from persons that will be used against them at an opportune time. Maybe I didn't know—"

"Yes," interjected the judge.

Jack resumed: "I never had any defense. . . . I never had any defense. Anything that was said in court went back to the District Attorney from Phil Burleson. Right now there is a good policeman and a bad policeman, between Phil Burleson and Joe Tonahill, and here is Henry Wade, when he states that Henry Wade wants to get a habeas corpus, he uses the names of his dear friends to talk against him—

"Getting back to the incarceration. This particular guard of mine, works on the Bible with me, as a matter of fact, he has taught me various phases of the Bible in which I am not well learned. He said, 'Jack,—' and I became enthused—"

Judge Davidson interrupted, saying: "I might say to you, you have no right to feel ashamed of Abraham or

Moses or any of those men, so just move along." Jack had not said he was ashamed of any person or thing Jewish.

As the judge commanded, Jack moved along: "This was an ulterior motive, the question of my confidence, and I became very close to this particular person because he told me he studied for the ministry, and during that time, there were so many things in my past, one little item that will come out later on about me being involved in sending four guns to a friend of mine in 1959, during peacetime, and my association with Cuba, and this particular man, Mr. McWillie—incidentally, I notice in reading the Warren Report, that because of Jack Ruby not knowing the difference between reality and rights, we will not release the result of the polygraph. There is a reason for that, because I know what happened and what took place in jail. Certain evidence that is going to be submitted, that I did know Oswald. So when this was over, Mr. McWillie called me on the phone and said, 'You know Ran Hart who has a hardware store?' This is in early 1959, and not realizing what would happen later I called Ray Brantley and said, 'Ray, wants you to send him something—' Mac was a prominent gambler around this country. That is all I had to do with it, and all I had to do anything in the future, from that date on. When the FBI picked me up I forgot to mention the fact that I called Ray Brantley and sent four guns to McWillie. I asked someone to check Ray Brantley about that call—and that particular night Phil Burleson knew I was unnerved, and he has part of the itinerary of what happened from the time I reached the News Building, and everything until I went down to the station. And I called Mr. Gordon McClendon's number to find a party to get to KLIF, and I recall the radio broadcast disc jockey was at the station house, so my purpose in going to the station, I came down and tried to get the phone number, but prior to that I called Gordon McClendon, I had to get this number.

"All these things were coincidental with what happened. It couldn't have happened in a million times. How I criminally indicted myself in a conspiracy that will be proven later.

"At 10:15, I left my apartment, and the story was out that this particular person [his oblique way of referring to Oswald] was supposed to leave the jail at ten (10:00) A.M. I received a call from a young girl who wanted some money. I went to the Western Union, which was coincidental, and prior to that, I will admit a letter was to Caroline which broke my heart. I was emotional, and I closed the club for three days. This letter was written to Caroline telling her how awfully sorry I was for her. And another situation, there was said something about a trial. Don't ask me what took place, and that triggered me off that Sunday morning.

"I accepted the call at 10:15 and went down to the Western Union and parked my car across the street, and took off to transact my business. . . . At 11:17 I walked, I don't say it was premeditated, but never prior to Sunday morning, I never had made up my mind what to do.

"From 11:17 until later, I was guilty of a homicide. Which must be the most perfect conspiracy in the history of the world that a man was going to accept a call and came from his apartment down to the Western Union. If it had been three seconds later I would have missed this particular person. I guess God was against me. I left the Western Union and it took about three and a half minutes to go to the bottom ramp. I didn't conspire or sneak in to do these things, I am telling you. If they had said, 'Jack, are you going down now?' that would make some conspiracy on me. I left the Western Union and it was a fraction of a second until that tragic act happened.

"Now, it seems that all these circumstances were against me. I had a great emotional feeling for our beloved President and Mrs. Kennedy, or I never would have been involved in this tragic crime, that was completely reverse from what my emotional feeling was.

"From the moment that Tom Howard came in Phil Burleson didn't care whether he got any money or not to work on the case. So I said to my sister, 'Eve,' I didn't pay them anything, and that is not good, and I didn't think he was willing to do anything that was not good.

"And Joe Tonahill was a very charitable person. Well, I am sorry to say this, it is strange that a person like Harvey Oswald, who never worked a day in his life, and I have reason to think of these things because I know all the things that are going on, a man has never worked in his life is able to secure a job in a book store weeks prior to the anticipated arrival of our beloved President. Who else could know that our President was coming to Dallas? I couldn't know. And I am speaking of what I anticipated to happen.

"Now, I am standing in front of a court of law, and I am as competent as Joe Tonahill when he looked at you in the eye, and he knew how to tell a lie, and Mr. Tonahill is trained for these things. He can look at you and tell you certain things from his construction of various types.

"May my soul never rest, this man sitting here has lied to you, everything he stated right here at this moment, when he made that speech."

Here Judge Davidson spoke up again: "I will ask you not to deal too much in personalities, when you use the word 'lie.'"

"All right, Your Honor," Ruby conceded.

"Mr. Wade, some time back, I requested a polygraph test because I could sense certain things, I can't prove them, but I can sense certain things; so Mr. Bill Decker said, 'Jack, if you want a polygraph why don't you send a letter to Henry Wade stating what you want?'

"I first wrote a letter in longhand and somebody said, 'Why don't you let somebody do it on the typewriter?' And they typed this letter off, my desire to want a polygraph. And there was no conspiracy in my mind. Nothing in my heart, from the moment I left that Sunday morning, and any questions put before me, I won't hesitate to answer.

"And after I signed this letter, then it dawned on me that there was a half-inch margin between each paragraph. . . .

"Now, unfortunately, the time I was arrested, the Federal Bureau of Investigation came to interrogate me and they said they would like to ask me questions, and the Chief suggested, I had better not have any breakfast, I was going to have the lie detector test or truth serum.

"I went into the reception room and asked what about the polygraph, and they said evidently the FBI didn't want it.

"Now, getting back to Mr. Tonahill . . . whether Mr. Tonahill is in the case or Mr. Burleson is in the case or not, that is not the main issue.

"The important issue is this: I didn't believe there was a God, on account of the things that happened. Now, I believe there is because of having a chance to be heard before you. And I want to say you are hearing the most fantastic story, greater than even Emile Zola who defended his client, because from the moment Tom Howard came into the case, from the moment I was indicted, I didn't have any incrimination against Tom Howard. From the time I was indicted, from the time Bill Alexander received a courtesy pass from me, he said, 'Jack, I have been your friend 13 years.' On that particular evening, he came up to visit me, the prosecuting attorney, and minutes later, he met a newspaper man and said he was going to ask for the death penalty for Jack Ruby. From that moment, I didn't have an attorney.

"Mr. Belli was sincere, but only judging from the time the wire was sent, because the wire was sent at 11:17, and I said I wanted to get on the stand and tell the truth, and I will tell you why I haven't got on the stand; this particular incident of sending four guns to Cuba, and Phil Burleson unnerved me and makes me blurt out. I came out openly and stated, 'Oh, my God, we killed the President.' And the criminal minded man don't make that mistake. That evening I was shook up and I cried, and the guard came to me and said, 'Jack, what is the matter, aren't you going to talk to me tonight?' And I came out as if he were my Savior and I said, 'Steve, I sent guns to Cuba.' I magnified something in my mind which incriminated myself innocently. This letter come out later and I went on to tell the story of how I left the apartment. I was so emotional because of the loss of our beloved President, and not wanting Mrs. Kennedy to come back to this trial.

"Then when I left the Western Union I walked down that ramp and I said to this guard, I said, 'I saw it.' He knew what to ask, and he said, 'Jack, your lawyer said you blacked out.' He was able to divulge a weak spot in my testimony. So like a little boy that tells a lie to his teacher, I said 'You promised you wouldn't tell because we are biblical buddies now.' Not knowing it, but he had this little microphone in his pocket. He made the greatest scapegoat in the history of this world, which will be proven later, that I was a party of a conspiracy in the assassination of our beloved President.

"The only way I can be vindicated is for unbiased people to give me a lie detector test, and not some doctor, because Dr. Beavers said I had an unsound mind—I wish I could think of all the other things regarding my status, but—

"As far as Joe Tonahill is concerned, he doesn't care what happens to me, nor does Phil Burleson, and I am not saying this just to make the headlines, I am not remembering this from rehearsal, I am speaking word-for-word, that I know what took place. And I am like the stupid idiot, that loved this country so much, and loved the President so much, and I felt so sorry for Mrs. Kennedy when she was standing on that plane with blood on her dress, and they were bringing the casket back with our beloved President, and now I am going to [go] down in history as the most despisable person that ever lived.

"If I am able to use this little oratory on you, as I am doing, if I have that capability, looking at you and telling this courtroom a slight fraction of a lie then I am a genius.

"Thank you."

The pathetic oration was at an end. Even without the aid of the court reporter's errors of transcription. Ruby wandered from point to point. What was possibly clear to him was blurred in the telling.

"You have had several lawyers, I believe," the court asked him. "Tom Howard was your first?"

*Mr. Ruby:* Yes, sir.

*The Court:* You had no difficulty with Tom?

*Mr. Ruby:* Let me explain what happened.

*The Court:* Since then you have had 16 or 18 haven't you?

*Mr. Ruby:* No, sir, that is exaggerated.

*The Court:* How many have you had?

*Mr. Ruby:* It is exaggerated. Tom Howard had the opportunity to push himself in the case and I didn't want him to start with, I tried to get someone like Percy Foreman and I could never get them.

*The Court:* I am not concerned, Mr. Ruby, with their names, I don't want to consume the time. I want to ask you if you had trouble. Those lawyers, did you fire them, or did they fall out among themselves?

*Mr. Ruby:* May I answer intelligently?

*The Court:* Yes.

*Mr. Ruby:* Belli, we felt, created a bad impression, naturally we fired Belli because we felt he was unjust in making that speech at the time of the trial. . . .

I don't want to be vicious in explaining these things, but if you could take a telescope and look at the various conspiracies I can answer these things. I didn't want Dr. Smith, he was put in to push out Percy Foreman, so I don't know how to answer your question.

After the Warren Report came out that vindicated me supposedly, but it didn't, these various attorneys, like Choulos and

others, they came into the case when I resented it, so I don't
know how to answer this question.

*The Court:* Did you employ your lawyer—

*Mr. Ruby:* No, I didn't fire them. This is the circus they are
putting on. Mr. Tonahill is putting on a show, Sol Dann making
certain statements about the press which I have not confirmed.
Here is my attorney, I insist on taking a polygraph, and he
states, 'Jack Ruby's mind is deteriorating more and more.'

*The Court:* I think this is a matter that will come up on the
trial.

*Mr. Ruby:* You were asking about Mr. Tonahill and Phil
Burleson.

*The Court:* I will ask Mr. Burleson if he is in this case. You
may be seated.

Are you in this case?

*Mr. Burleson:* In the Federal case?

*The Court:* Yes.

*Mr. Burleson:* No, sir.

*The Court:* How long have you been in this matter?

*Mr. Burleson:* Since the first part of December, 1963.

*The Court:* You say you are not employed in this present
hearing?

*Mr. Burleson:* No, sir.

*The Court:* If you had been approached, would there have
been any reason why you couldn't have accepted employment?

*Mr. Burleson:* No, your Honor.

*The Court:* All right. Be seated.


The court had been in session for some time, with Tonahill and Ruby as the principal participants, when suddenly
Judge Davidson thought of a matter that would ordinarily
be the first item under consideration—the continuance
that had been requested by Clinton on behalf of all of us.
"I believe I will ask the Government to give me about five
minutes on that," Judge Davidson said, "just why this motion for continuance should be granted."

Bill Alexander responded. The issue, he said, was joined

on the pleadings. The court, he said, knew everything that it needed to know. Ruby's counsel had said that they would be present, he declared; Tonahill was present. He offered in evidence "the docket sheet of Judge Brown's court showing the appointment and release of lawyers in the case" and supporting documents, including the affidavit of Judge Brown himself. Alexander gave Judge Brown's version of the chronology of events, commencing with the affidavit, filed on April 27, 1964, asking for a sanity hearing with respect to Ruby.

Accordingly [Alexander went on with Judge Brown's version of the facts] hearing was set on March 1st, 1965, to determine in a pre-trial hearing whether the defendant Ruby desired to go forward with his previous trial motion for a sanity trial or withdraw it. This hearing was postponed at the request of William A. Kunstler until March 8th, 1965.

On March 8th, 1965, on preliminary hearing, Mr. Sol A. Dann and Mr. Elmer Gertz were present at counsel table, along with Mr. Joe H. Tonahill and Mr. Phil Burleson. Mr. Dann and Mr. Gertz were not presented to me nor request made for them to be admitted to practice. At this hearing a number of motions were untimely and prematurely presented for my consideration and immediate ruling demanded. These untimely and premature motions were by me overruled, but would have been considered by me as they became timely and full hearing with evidence allowed at proper time and in proper order. As regards the motion for my disqualification, I was and am prepared to give full hearing to said motion at a proper time after due notice to all parties allowing time for the preparation and production of evidence on all issues. . . .

In an effort to adequately protect the rights of this indigent person, I appointed both Mr. Burleson and Mr. Tonahill to prosecute the appeal, basing this upon the fact that both are duly licensed, competent attorneys of the State of Texas, and the Federal courts, and both appeared throughout the trial on the merits for defendant, and should one be removed by death

or disability, that the other could proceed, having full personal
knowledge of all the proceedings theretofore.

On March 8th, 1965, it was brought to my attention that
members of the Ruby family and the foreign lawyers objected
to Mr. Tonahill being in the case. Therefore, I personally visited
Jack Ruby in jail to determine his preference. He informed me
he wished Mr. Tonahill released, whereupon I contacted Mr.
Tonahill and informed him I set this matter for hearing on
Friday, March 19th, at 9:00 A.M., this being prior to the filing
of petition for removal to Federal Court of the Ruby matter by
the Texas Civil Liberties Union attorney Mr. Sam Houston
Clinton.

As a matter of courtesy, if not of law, to the most Honorable
T. Whitfield Davidson, Judge of the United States District Court
of this Northern District of Texas, I have continued the hearing
on all matters until Judge Davidson may review the records of
this case.

"And that"—Alexander concluded—"is subscribed and
sworn to before a notary by Judge Joe B. Brown, and we
have copies of all of these items of evidence to furnish to
defense counsel."

Tonahill observed at once: "Now, Judge Brown didn't
visit Jack Ruby in jail until March 17th, after Mr. Wade
returned to duty on March 15th and stated publicly I
should not be in the case. I want the record to be complete
on that."

"The petition for writ of habeas corpus is now before the
Court," Judge Davidson said. "Also the motion for a continuance.

"Counsel stated that if I would continue the case or
postpone the hearing until two o'clock today, he would
either be present or have his co-counsel here. His co-counsel was from New York, and was temporarily hearing a
case in Montgomery, Alabama.

"In his motion for a continuance, he says he is unable to
contact his co-counsel in Alabama because he is busy. In

his motion this morning he says he is unable to be present because he is in the trial of a case in Austin.

"This case is just as important as the Austin case, and at the time he filed his petition here he should have associated some counsel in Dallas and not depended on someone in New York to get here at that time. There are some 1200 able lawyers in Dallas. You heard one say a minute ago that he was open to employment on this very issue if he had been approached. Any of the lawyers that has served him in the past would have done so. . . .

"I don't think it was fair to the Court or fair to counsel to file that case, under the circumstances, and walk away. I see no reason why the motion for postponement should be granted, particularly so, that the decision we intend to render will not likely be contingent on the facts, but on the law.

"In the first place, when the petition for habeas corpus was presented, the question came to my mind, 'Why should not this State prisoner have had the benefit of the great writ of habeas corpus in the State Court of Dallas?' Dallas has capable judges. It has a Court of Appeals that, in my mind, is the peer to any court anywhere. . . . Why should it not be heard at Dallas instead of being brought here?

"Maybe I flatter myself that somebody wanted to try this case before me, and I would not mind hearing the case, I would not shrink from the trial of any case, but when the law of the land, of the State of Texas and the United States of America places the jurisdiction of this question in the State Court it doesn't lie within me to say that the State doesn't have jurisdiction. . . .

"Now, what is the law that pertains to the writ of habeas corpus?

"The United States Statute, Title 28, Section 2254, an application for a writ of habeas corpus on behalf of any person in custody pursuant to a judgment of a State Court shall not be granted unless it appears that the applicant has exhausted all remedies available in the States. And the State has authority over it.

"I would have to hold that the facilities of the State Court of Dallas, and the Court of Appeals were not capable of protecting the right this man has in order to grant the writ."

He then expounded learnedly on various cases that had been decided by the Supreme Court, and went on:

"They tell us that the Civil Rights Law alters that. The Civil Rights Law does not repeal this law, it gives certain rights and privileges, but this law still remains in effect. . . ."

He reverted to the various cases, including a recent New York one which he did not like. He said it was exceptional.

"There is relief to be had in Dallas, no showing to the contrary," he declared with finality.

"Judge Brown has been attacked, and I shall not either condemn or exonerate Judge Brown, because that is not within my power. Neither will I pass upon the question of the attorneys in the case, or the right of any man to appear as attorney.

"This case remains on the docket of the Dallas Criminal Court.

"I shall remand this case to the Dallas Court, and in order that no thought may be left that Judge Brown is unfair, or that he has let this long litigation make him partial, or cause him to form an opinion that would be unfair to this man, there is a way that some of these other judges can hear it, and I will remand this case back to the State Court, subject to the orders of the Administrative Judge of that district, I believe that is Judge Blankenship.

"So this case will not be continued—and the writ of habeas corpus will not be granted, but the petition will be returned to the Dallas Court without prejudice, and the Dallas judge who is selected to hear it will hear it without prejudice to any ruling of this Court."

Thus, while denying our petition in our absence, Judge

Davidson still sought to circumvent Judge Brown by returning the case to the administrative judge of the district.

After Judge Davidson remanded the case to the Texas court, it became imperative that defense counsel decide on the next steps to be taken. My own feeling was that an appeal ought to be taken from the order of remandment. Even if we should get rid of Judge Brown and Tonahill without the appeal, there was still the unsettled, and unsettling, question of who would hear the case in the state courts. Moreover, it still seemed essential that the case be removed from Dallas County, that counsel of Ruby's choice be allowed to represent him, and that a continuance should be afforded us to prepare for the still expected sanity hearing. In addition, the record showed that just as Judge Brown had acted without due consideration, the United States District Court judge had acted in the same fashion.

Finally it was decided: we would appeal to the United States Court of Appeals for the Fifth Circuit, and in due course we would take the requisite steps in connection with the appeal. In the meantime we would ask the Court of Appeals for a stay of the remandment order.

At this point, despite ostensible setbacks, we had made several gains since entering the case in February, less than two months before. Although the Texas Court of Criminal Appeals had said it would not delay the hearing on the appeal or permit new counsel of Ruby's choice, it had, in fact, sent the case back for a sanity hearing and a determination of the matter of representation. When Judge Brown refused to consider our motions, we removed the case to the federal court. And while the federal court had remanded the case, it had sent it to the chief judge of the Texas district court, recommending, in effect, that a judge other than Judge Brown hear the matter. And we were hearing rumors that the court would remove Tonahill as counsel. Meanwhile, too, Ruby had been heard in open

court, and his pathetic words and bearing only confirmed
his mental illness.

We were not the only ones to respond to the actions
of the court. On March 23, the Dallas *Morning News* reported that Judge Brown had said "he would like to have
a conference with attorneys for Ruby and the State before
further legal action." It was clear that the judge was troubled because we were determined to get him and Tonahill
out of the case. What he would have suggested at the
meeting will never be known, but it is likely that at this
point he would have done anything to appease defense
counsel that would not have offended the State.

Clinton wrote to Judge Brown at once "that I shall be
happy to attend any such conference that you may arrange. You have only to give me reasonable notice." When
I learned of this letter, I was upset. It was not like Clinton
to proceed unilaterally. Our motion to stay the proceedings
was still pending before the United States Court of Appeals, and we had the right to hope for success there. In
those circumstances, I thought it unwise to confer with
Judge Brown, and I told Clinton so:

From what I can judge, Tonahill will probably be removed
and Judge Brown may voluntarily withdraw. If the case is kept
in Dallas, and particularly if it is turned over to Judge Wilson,
we really have gained nothing and, perhaps, have lost something. I think that, above all, we need to get the case out of
Dallas and to get for Jack Ruby attorneys of his choice; namely,
ourselves, with the assistance of Phil Burleson. We also need
a good deal of additional time in order to prepare for the sanity
hearing. If, as we believe, Jack Ruby is insane, then it will
become increasingly obvious that he is, and the prosecution
may be inclined to go along with the placing of Ruby in a
hospital for the mentally sick. . . .

From what I can gather, Alexander and, perhaps, Wade
presently believe that Ruby is feigning. They also think that
this battle over counsel is a phony one. We, of course, know

that such thinking is sheer nonsense. Maybe they know it also.

Our experience thus far has been that, when we press for what we want hard enough, we get part of it, even while the opposition pretends otherwise. That is one reason for holding out on the conference with the judge. Assume now that the judge calls a conference. Who will be invited to it? The chances are that at this time Tonahill and Burleson from our side will be the only invitees. This is something in which we ought not to acquiesce. If we do, it will be a virtual admission that our various motions and court proceedings are not in good faith.

To sum up, I think it would be salutary to make Judge Brown realize that we are in earnest and that, if the matter is carried all the way, we are likely to prevail.

The conference did not take place. (At a subsequent time, however, there was a secret meeting between representatives of the State and the defense in Judge Brown's apartment. For this important occasion, the judge baked a cake, a very good cake—the one success in the meeting. Then the conversation dealt with an agreement to commute the death sentence, but, as on other occasions, the stumbling block was the number of years Ruby should have to serve. The State thought there should be a life sentence, and we felt that a lesser term was called for. The meeting ended on an indecisive note. It was the last time that we met privately with Judge Brown.)

Nearly a month passed before we—that is, everyone but Burleson—appeared in the Court of Appeals in Jacksonville, Florida, to argue for a stay of Judge Davidson's order remanding the case to the State court. We were fortunate enough to argue our motion before three extremely good judges, Chief Judge Tuttle and Judge Wisdom of the Fifth Circuit and Judge Orie Phillips of Denver. The judges, particularly Judge Tuttle and Judge Wisdom, asked perceptive questions, and it was clear that they were fascinated by the case.

Judge Wisdom posed an interesting problem. He said

that, while recognizing that ordinarily in Texas there cannot be an appeal in a sanity trial, we might have special circumstances, since the Texas Court of Criminal Appeals in an unprecedented manner had ordered Judge Brown to consider the matter of a sanity trial. He suggested that, having made such order, the court might have supervisory power to compel a proper trial. We knew of no Texas statute, court rule, or precedent to justify Judge Wisdom, and yet the idea was intriguing.

Chief Judge Tuttle was concerned, in particular, as well he might be, by the consequences of permitting removal to a federal court in a case other than a racial one. He asked whether the removal provisions actually applied to a situation such as ours, but gave no indication of his answer.

Although the court ordinarily allows each side a half hour for argument, it had given us over two hours, and would have given us more time if we had sought it. The court then took our motion under advisement. It would hand down its ruling later—as it turned out, in a few days.

The question raised by Judge Wisdom was one to ponder. It seemed that there was a simple answer to it. The Texas Court of Criminal Appeals had already been asked to remove Tonahill and to substitute Kunstler and other counsel to act in behalf of Jack Ruby, and it had denied these requests, without consideration, and only then had it sent the matter back to Judge Brown. These actions could be pointed to as additional reason why the case should be removed.

On April 23, the Court of Appeals ruled on our motion for a stay. It entered a Per Curiam order (an order for the entire panel, signed by none of the three judges) that followed the lines indicated by Judge Wisdom's interrogation at the hearing. Although in form a denial of our motion, it actually encouraged us.

Jack Ruby (Rubenstein), in reliance on 28 U.S.C. §1443 and habeas corpus *cum causa,* and acting through one of the two

groups of attorneys claiming the right to represent him, removed to the United States District Court for the Northern
District of Texas a sanity hearing the Texas Court of Criminal
Appeals had ordered to be held for Ruby in the Criminal District Court of Dallas County, Texas, incident to Ruby's appeal
of his murder conviction. The district court remanded the
proceeding to the state court. Ruby appealed the remand order
and filed a motion for a stay of the sanity hearing pending
determination of the appeal.

On the record before us and on the showing made to this
Court, it appears that the sanity hearing is either an integral
part of Ruby's appeal now pending in the Texas Court of
Criminal Appeals or is so closely related to it as to be under
the supervision of that court. In the circumstances, we decline
to issue an order staying the sanity hearing. This ruling is not to
be considered as deciding or even touching upon the question
of Ruby's right to remove under Section 1443 or any of the
other issues in the case.

The motion is DENIED.

We regarded the next-to-last sentence as fraught with
great hope for Ruby's future. Acting upon the suggestion in
the order, Clinton, for all of us, filed a motion for relief in
the Court of Criminal Appeals on Wednesday, April 28. It
was returned to him less than twenty-four hours later with
the notation "Permission to file denied," signed by Presiding Judge W. T. McDonald. There was no opinion or order
entered. Once again the Court of Criminal Appeals seemed
determined to frustrate our efforts, and so, on May 4, we
filed a second motion to stay with the clerk of the Court
of Appeals.

# 10

## JUDGE HOLLAND REMOVES TONAHILL

ALL DURING OUR MANEUVERS in the federal courts reports
had been circulating in Dallas that Judge Brown was contemplating the holding of the long-postponed hearing to
determine whether Joe Tonahill would remain as Ruby's
lawyer. "It might be a pretty good idea," he said. The
judge professed uncertainty about the next steps in the
case in view of the activity in the federal appeals court. We
let it be known that we would oppose his holding any hearing for such purpose, since Ruby had the right to select his
own attorneys and should not be saddled with Tonahill.
Then, after repeating that he did not intend to remove
himself from the case, the judge hied himself off to California to speak before several bar and news groups. There
he would not be hounded by us.

Tonahill had a few opinions on the matter himself. He
wrote a letter to the judge asking that he bar out-of-state
attorneys—meaning Dann, Kunstler, and myself—from
further participation in the case. "I wish you would consider this letter," Tonahill wrote, "as a motion to do one of
two things—note your disqualification upon the docket, or
set the matter of your disqualification for a hearing." Having learned what we had learned, Tonahill contended that
Judge Brown was disqualified because he was writing a
book about the case. No judge should sit in on a case in
which he is interested, Tonahill said. Judge Brown was not
available for comment.

Suddenly, on May 6, Judge Brown entered an elaborate
order under an elaborate heading:

COURT'S REQUEST THAT THE PRESIDING JUDGE OF THE
FIRST ADMINISTRATIVE JUDICIAL DISTRICT OF THE
STATE OF TEXAS ASSIGN A JUDGE TO THE CRIMINAL
DISTRICT COURT NO. THREE OF DALLAS COUNTY, TEXAS,
FOR THE PURPOSES OF DETERMINING WHAT ATTORNEYS
SHOULD REPRESENT JACK RUBY IN CONNECTION WITH
HIS MOTION FOR A POST-TRIAL SANITY HEARING

After reciting the history of the case since the Criminal Court of Appeals had entered its order in February requiring the holding of a sanity hearing, the order concluded:

THEREFORE, PREMISES CONSIDERED, this Court does respectfully request the Honorable Dallas A. Blankenship, Presiding Judge of the First Administrative Judicial District of the State of Texas to assign a Judge to the Criminal District Court No. 3, of Dallas County, Texas, to sit as Judge of said Court for the purposes of determining the question of counsel for the Defendant in connection with his Motion for Sanity Hearing, and the Court does further request that the Honorable Dallas A. Blankenship make such assignment effective beginning May 17, 1965, and as long thereafter as may be necessary to dispose of the said Motions now pending and any other Motions that may be filed prior to that time.

Thus, under relentless pressure, Judge Brown was forced to yield ground and was part way out of the case. Technically, however, he was still in it.

Without delay, Judge Louis Holland, a judge of good reputation, from Montague, Texas, was designated to conduct the hearing on choice of counsel. It was believed that he would limit the hearing to the choice of counsel, but Tonahill, joining with us in this goal, announced that he would seek the disqualification of Judge Brown as well. Judge Holland immediately set the hearing for May 24, at 9 A.M., and then, as if to indicate a completely open mind, he instructed Bill Shaw, the District Clerk, to notify every attorney concerned—Kunstler, Clinton, Dann, Burleson, and myself, as well as Tonahill—of the hearing. Individual letters were sent to each of us—a novelty in the case and a confirmation of all that we had heard about Judge Holland's ability and fairness.

The press now began to speculate increasingly about the book Judge Brown was supposed to be writing, but the ineffable judge said publicly, "I haven't written a word." (He did seem to admit that he had written a song, "The Great Society," dedicated to Mrs. Lyndon B. Johnson.)

If the judge would not admit publicly what there was good reason to believe was true, then we would use every legitimate means to find out the truth. Therefore we decided to propound interrogatories with respect to the book and to ask Judge Holland to consider the motions that we had filed with Judge Brown in the March 8 hearing—for a change of venue, for defendant's right to counsel of his choice, and the rest. In fact, Judge Holland seemed to be withdrawing from his previous intention to consider only the matter of counsel. He was quoted as saying that he might consider the motion for a change of venue. "But I certainly think," he said, "the first order of business should be this: Who should be counsel for Mr. Ruby?" The lawyers he appointed, he said, would handle Ruby's case in the sanity hearing. After that, "the Court of Criminal Appeals could most likely assign counsel from there on, depending on its outcome."

When word got out that we were going to take depositions in New York about Judge Brown's unacknowledged book, Judge Brown began to change his tune. "Sure, I'm writing a book," he said. "But I'm not even sure of the name of it yet."

Our determination to proceed with the taking of depositions was reinforced by information, privately given, by those who professed to know the facts. Needless to say, we were elated by the revelations, however undocumented. If true, we felt, they would put Judge Brown to flight. He would be out of the case permanently and, better yet, the verdict of the jury might be made invalid.

The district attorney, whistling in the dark, said he did not regard the writing of a book as sufficient grounds for disqualification. "Unless he took sides," Wade said, "I don't see how he could be disqualified." This was contrary to all that we regarded as good law.

As the hearing approached, Tonahill continued to express complete confidence that he would remain as Ruby's attorney. "The law is with me 100 per cent," he said. We thought it was against him 100 per cent.

On May 24, as scheduled, Judge Holland convened the court for the hearing on counsel. Earl Ruby was the first witness. In response to Tonahill's questioning, he gave his opinion that his brother Jack was insane. Neither Jack nor his family had employed Tonahill; he was brought in by Belli. When Belli was fired, Tonahill went with him. He charged that Belli and Tonahill neglected Ruby while preparing a movie.

"What kind of movie was this?" District Attorney Henry Wade asked.

"Well, we first found out about it when they asked permission to make some pictures in Jack Ruby's old Carousel Club," Earl Ruby replied. "My sister, Eva Grant, refused to let them make the picture.

"Sam Gallu was the producer. They received a large sum of money—$65,000, we think—as an advance."

Tonahill characterized this as an "absolute lie" and demanded proof. He admitted an educational film was made, but it was a "complete failure."

Earl then charged that Belli and Tonahill, secretly and without permission, took pictures of Ruby in his cell and tried to sell them to *Life*.

Tonahill questioned Judge Brown himself about the circumstances in which the latter had named him, together with Burleson, as Ruby's attorney, on March 8.

Q. (By Mr. Tonahill) Now, Judge Brown, just one more question: On March 8, 1965, you appointed me to represent Jack Ruby because you considered from my experience in

appearing in your Court throughout the entire trial, you thought
that I would be effective as attorney on his appeal.

A. If you will, let me answer that question, Mr. Tonahill,
with another statement.

Q. Yes, go ahead, Judge.

A. Yes, sir, I did appoint you for those reasons, but at the
same time there was an affidavit from Mr. Ruby and his family
asking that you be relieved that I did not see.

Had I seen it, I would not have appointed you to represent
him and you would have been relieved of your duties as attorney of record, relying upon the affidavit filed by Mr. Burleson
and signed by the Ruby family.

Q. Well, Judge Brown, here is the Motion that was filed
that morning and overruled by you.

A. Yes, I considered it, but I didn't go into it far enough.

Q. And attached to that motion is the affidavit asking that
I be removed and signed by Jack Ruby and his family, is that
correct?

A. Yes, that is correct.

Q. And did you consider the Motion and appoint me for
those reasons?

A. I would say very lightly considered the Motion. I didn't
appoint you for that reason.

*Mr. Tonahill:* Thank you, Judge, that's all.

Jack himself got into the act, as usual, when he insisted
upon expressing himself. He said that he had taken thirty
antibiotic pills and some other pills (Preludin) shortly
before he shot Oswald. These had stimulated him and
caused him to commit the act. The American people, he
declared emotionally, were going to brand him a part of a
conspiracy with Oswald and forget how he felt about President Kennedy. "I know that I am a lost cause as far as
saving my life," he said. "Don't believe Joe Tonahill. . . ."

He told of waking up that Sunday morning, November
24, 1963, and brooding about the fatherless Kennedy children. "What quirked me after that I don't know. As God

is my judge, that is the truth. I walked into a trap when I walked down that ramp. I know I am going to die a horrible death."

He said that he would have been better off had he discharged his attorneys at the original trial and thrown himself on the mercy of the court. "If I am insane, the whole world is crazy," he said.

Ruby dwelt on the pictures to which his brother had referred. "They were sneaking pictures of me. I was in a delirious mood . . . being just received an electric chair sentence."

After Jack had finished, a letter sent to Tonahill and Belli was received in evidence. The writer said "all of the major distributors have turned us down for the same reason. They are frightened to death about the Texas business, and the possible boycott of their future films in Texas."

"The film should be opened at one of the art houses in New York. If we get a good critique, we can write our own ticket from there on in. If we bomb, then we'll have to make the best of it somehow." The letter went on: "The film should definitely have a controversial and provocative ring to it. Critics will like this, so will the box office, even if they do not agree with it. If it's bland, who cares?"

Tonahill protested that he and the writer of the letter had two different things in mind. He would not agree to a sensational film.

In another letter to Tonahill, the writer said he had found "a party who will put up the monies necessary to finish the film, as well as to promote it. This will be in excess of $65,000. For this we will have to give up 35 per cent. This is the best I can do."

Earl Ruby then admitted that he, too, had been paid for a story appearing in a Houston newspaper and that he had considered hiring a public relations man to improve his brother's "image." He denied that Dann had wanted to incorporate Ruby. Clayton Fowler, who had once been in the case, insisted that such, indeed, had been Dann's intention and that he had had "violent arguments" with Dann as a result. (Sol Dann regretted and resented that he was not permitted to answer these charges made by Fowler, since he felt they placed him in a false light. We decided that having Dann on the stand would only confuse a relatively simple issue, the removal of Tonahill.) Earl denied, too, that he knew anything about a coin that had President Kennedy's image on one side and Ruby's on the other.

And there the testimony and argument ended. Judge Holland announced that he would remove Tonahill as Ruby's counsel and that he would soon hold a hearing on the disqualification of Judge Brown.

We could scarcely have asked for more.

The formal order, entered May 28, 1965, decreed that "Joe H. Tonahill is hereby removed as attorney of record for Defendant Jack Ruby and relieved of all duties and responsibilities attendant thereto."

Thus, after months of nerve-wracking maneuvering, journeys to all the courts in the judicial hierarchy and many setbacks, we had succeeded in removing our relentless opponent, Joe Tonahill, as an attorney of record for Jack Ruby. We congratulated each other and were felicitated by our client's family. We and they felt, for the moment, as if a mighty result had been achieved.

What, in fact, had been accomplished? For one thing, we assured the case sympathetic and concerted consideration by counsel; there was an end to working at cross-purposes. The courts now had to acknowledge that we were in the case; we could not be ignored. This lifted our spirits and gave a feeling of accomplishment. Since morale is always important, this was a very considerable gain. But it was by no means the end of the case. It was simply the beginning of new maneuvering to set aside the death verdict. We could not take a direct course through the appeal from the death sentence or through a trial to test our client's sanity.

For reasons that will become apparent, we decided that we could accomplish more through the indirect approach. If we could secure an adjudication that Judge Brown was disqualified, despite or in addition to his withdrawal, then the original trial might be so contaminated as to be invalid. Thus the death sentence would fall, without our going through the formal appeal proceedings. This was not a decision to be made lightly, on impulse, without careful study of the law and the facts.

# TO DISQUALIFY JUDGE BROWN

# 11

## "WE ARE COMING ALONG NICELY"

No SOONER had we learned from informed members of the press, who were sometimes friendly to us or eager to stir the pots, that Judge Brown, despite his denials, was writing a book about the Ruby case and had been engaged in the project for some time, than we did two necessary things simultaneously and in earnest. On June 1, 1965, we filed an amended motion for the disqualification of Judge Brown for hearing before Judge Holland, and on the same day we served notice that we were going to file the written deposition of Samuel Stewart, the managing editor at Holt, Rinehart and Winston, to be taken in New York. Our March 8 motion had been based on hints given to us rather than on complete knowledge. Now we wanted to supply all the requisite details in damning completeness. In our amended motion, we made allegations in a more confident tone with respect to the judge's disqualification, although we were not yet in full possession of the facts that we hoped to adduce through our deposition.

We had already propounded forty-six interrogatories (or questions), with many subinterrogatories, to Mr. Stewart. Most of them had produced little in the way of helpful answers. A few responses delighted us. In our eleventh interrogatory we asked if any person was employed to compose the book denominated *Dallas, Ruby and the Law*, and we inquired about the pertinent details. We learned that "Holt, Rinehart and Winston, Inc., offered a contract to Judge Brown for the book in question after negotiations with him in the Spring of 1964. Mr. [Paul] Crume was suggested by the witness [Stewart] as the writer." The phrase "the Spring of 1964," was to become increasingly significant as our case unfolded. At the moment, it was a good portent. The employment was entered into in New York on July 21, 1964, we were told. They were to "write a book on Judge Brown's life with particular emphasis on the trial of Jack Ruby." We were also told that the author was an "independent contractor," having "all control over writing of book except for editorial supervision."

Judge Brown "first suggested the project" to the publisher, Stewart said. As to the date and place the idea was conceived, he had "no knowledge"—a disappointment to us. He had "no knowledge" whether the idea was discussed with any person or organization—again a disappointment to us. Representatives of the publisher met with Judge Brown in the "middle of July, 1964, in New York" and with Crume in Dallas on August 10, 1964, we were told. Little else was added by way of answer to our interrogatories. We had to rest upon the documents, and as to them we could rest very well.

Our June 1 motion dealt with the book, the "circus" atmosphere of the original trial, the judge's dubious conduct during the trial (including his posing for pictures), his use of a public relations agent, his arbitrary denial of motions without a hearing, and the like. These things, we concluded, made the original trial and jury verdict void.

In the motion to take the Stewart deposition, we asked for the production of all letters, notes, contracts, checks, manuscripts, and memoranda and the like received from, or sent to, Judge Brown, Paul Crume, the publisher, and others in connection with the book. Through the publisher's catalogue, we knew that the book was entitled *Dallas, Ruby and the Law;* and we propounded about fifty relevant questions for Stewart to answer. Burleson's office sent

Kunstler a long letter giving him minute instructions so that the deposition could properly be taken and its results filed in the Dallas court. Nothing was left to chance.

Finally, we filed a brief for the benefit of Judge Holland in which the relevant law as to judicial disqualification in Texas was set forth. We hoped to present an irresistible case against an inferior judge for the consideration of a jurist whom we regarded as a superior one. If we succeeded, we would topple the whole structure and our client would face a second trial in which the odds might well be in his favor. We had gotten rid of Joe Tonahill, we had succeeded in obtaining time for more careful consideration, we were in the case officially as lawyers, and we had gotten Judge Brown out temporarily. Now we wanted to get him out permanently and simultaneously to obtain an adjudication of his disqualification. This was a unique tactic, and we were delighted with it.

When we took their deposition in New York City on May 20, 1965, we succeeded in getting from Holt, Rinehart and Winston their complete file with respect to Judge Brown's book, except for the incomplete manuscript. An extraordinary tale was unfolded.

The first document, dated July 21, 1964, was an agreement between the publisher and Judge Brown, in the usual form, requiring him to write a book then entitled *The Ruby Trial*. The manuscript was to be delivered on or before November 1, 1964, and the author was to be paid the usual sliding scale of royalties, and, in addition, other royalties and compensation for Canadian editions, exports elsewhere than Canada, reprints, book club editions, anthologies, and the like. If the book sold well, it could be profitable indeed. As an advance against all moneys that might accrue to him, Judge Brown was to be paid $5000 on signing of the contract and $5000 on receipt and acceptance of a satisfactory final manuscript.

In a supplementary document, prepared a few days later, it was stated:

It is now agreed that the second installment of the advance, namely the Five Thousand Dollars ($5,000.00) payable on receipt and delivery of a complete manuscript shall be paid in full to your co-author of THE RUBY TRIAL, Paul Crume.

Although this co-author agreement reduced his advance to $5000, Judge Brown was glad to subscribe his approval to the modification, because, obviously, he did not have the skill or training to write his own book. Crume had been, for years, a front-page columnist on the Dallas *Morning News*.

To complete the arrangement, the publisher offered Crume a letter-agreement, which he signed. The letter stated, among other things: "You agree to undertake the writing as soon as possible and to deliver the complete manuscript to us on or before November 1, 1964."

It was clear that the publisher was in a hurry, as well it might be. Who could foretell the course of the case—or of its presiding judge?

On July 27, Holt sent Judge Brown a check for $288.32 to cover his trip to New York City from July 20 to July 22, 1964. The judge had stayed at the fashionable Plaza Hotel and taken first-class plane accommodations. (He noted, somewhat apologetically, on the statement he rendered that coach accommodations were not available; he did not explain why he had not selected a less luxurious hotel than the Plaza.)

On July 31, Stewart sent Judge Brown copies of the supplemental and Paul Crume agreements. The letter ended: "I hope to see you shortly in Dallas." An almost identical letter was sent that same day to Crume. On August 4, Judge Brown was sent his $5000 advance, and the next day Stewart advised him: "I shall see you Monday evening. I arrive in Dallas at 5:30 P.M. . . ."

The next communication, dated August 10, was from Crume to Stewart. It was on the letterhead of the Dallas *Morning News* and made clear certain things that were to be of prime importance in view of later developments.

I take it that we all want the book out as soon as possible, and there will be minor changes to make right up to publication date, probably.

I expect, of course, to do any rewriting and reshaping necessary after the manuscript is in. I will help with the galleys and pages if desired. Also, I will be glad to do anything I can to help promote the book in this area.

We are to meet within a day or two, I hear. I shall look forward to it.

On August 25, Stewart wrote to Judge Brown at the Del Charro Hotel, in La Jolla, California, his letter indicating that certain arrangements had been made to facilitate the production of the book:

I received your cable, but it looks as though I will not be able to get down to southern California when you and Paul are there. Actually, I don't think I will be in southern California until about the second week in September.

I do hope that everything is just right for you and Paul at the Del Charro.

On August 28, Stewart again wrote to Judge Brown, still in La Jolla, enclosing an article by Dr. Guttmacher on the Ruby case. The famous psychiatrist had been one of Belli's mainstays at the ill-fated trial. On September 2, Stewart's secretary sent to Judge Brown, now returned to Dallas, a copy of an article that had appeared in the Canadian magazine *Macleans*, which had printed in its April 18, 1964, issue some unflattering items of interest to the judge.

At this point the publisher's file revealed some peculiarities. A letter dated September 3, from A. C. Edwards, president of Holt, was addressed to Murchison Brothers in Dallas and enclosed a "check in the amount of $740.31 in payment of Judge Joe B. Brown's stay at Del Charro, La Jolla, California." The bill from Del Charro was also directed to Murchison Brothers. The Murchisons were

Texas millionaires and with H. L. Hunt were supposed to wield much control over men and matters in the Panhandle State. Our curiosity was much aroused, but we would have to wait for an explanation.

On September 28, Stewart wrote to Judge Brown:

I thought you would be interested to learn that the David McKay Company has announced publication of Melvin Belli's book, DALLAS JUSTICE, for October 1964. I am enclosing the ad from *Publisher's Weekly*. Through secret sources I am trying to get hold of set of galleys of Belli's book which I will send down for you and Paul Crume to look at.

There is then a lapse in the correspondence until January 4, 1965, when Stewart wrote to Judge Brown:

How are we coming? The book, as it is now, is very late and we cannot make Spring publication. It looks as if we are not going to have it in time for Summer either. Unfortunately this will harm sales. The further we get from trial, the harder it's going to be.

With the letter was sent the dust jacket of the book, now called *Dallas, Ruby & the Law*, and the authorship given as "Joseph B. Brown the presiding judge at the trial." The catalog of the publisher announced the book for July publication at $4.95. It gave an appetizing epitome of the as yet unwritten book.

Joseph B. Brown is the judge who tried Jack Ruby for the murder of Lee Harvey Oswald in what has since been termed the "Murder Capital of the world." In this insider's view of the most publicized trial of the century, Judge Brown perceptively examines the Dallas community and provides a fascinating exploration into the peculiarities of the Texas laws that played a part in the much-disputed final verdict.

Focusing first on the change-of-venue hearing, the author investigates the public temper outside the courtroom, specifically that of the Citizens' Council, the self-appointed city fathers. Turning to the selection of jurors, which seemed interminable, he tells how the defense agreed on the final twelve. While he cites Melvin Belli's brilliance as a trial lawyer, he nevertheless questions deeply the wisdom of his tying the case solely to the psychiatric notion that Ruby suffered from psychomotor epilepsy. Knowing that Ruby's counsel would call for psychiatric testimony to show the defendant insane and that the state would endeavor to prove the opposite, the bench asked for the opinion of a third impartial psychiatrist. Judge Brown explains here, why, under Texas law, a defendant judged sane at the moment of the crime, despite a history of mental instability, can be given the death penalty by the jury. He also reveals that his unprecedented admission of television to the courtroom was a mistake in that it allowed Belli to turn to the cameras and denounce both the city of Dallas and the verdict.

Should Dallas feel guilty? Illuminating Texas' view of the world, Judge Brown discusses why Dallas has the highest homicide rate in the country and why so many people carry firearms for "protection." His forthright and compelling examination throws new insights on the topic which deeply concerns all Americans.

The letter of January 4, 1965, was not answered by Judge Brown, but Paul Crume wrote to Stewart on February 7. His letter could not have given the editor much comfort:

We have more complications down here, minor I hope.

I turned over to Judge Brown the first ninety or so pages of the manuscript for him to check. I think I told you that he had had some objections to the first chapter, which is devoted mostly to him and to his career. I had mentioned, for instance, that he had spent his youthful summers hoboing around the country, a detail he seems to feel is undignified. At any rate, he is supposed to be at this moment in his apartment dictating a revise to his court reporter.

Confidentially, I'm a little dubious about this, but perhaps we'd better wait and see. Maybe this will start the stream of recall that I tried with indifferent success to tap during the fall. At any rate, we still have a copy of the original material.

His stenographer is supposed to start copying this material in the morning, and I should think that some of it will be on the way to you in the next two or three days.

I would guess that I am about half through. . . . I'm afraid to set a finishing date, but I have hopes of winding up by the end of the month.

Judge Brown remaining silent, Stewart wrote to him again on March 3:

Can you give me any word on your book? It is now overdue by four months. I know that when we spoke together you were as anxious as we to get it out quickly. Not having any answer to my last letter of January 4, you can understand my concern.

On March 12, 1965 the judge, signing himself "Joe," responded to "Dear Sam," in the letter that is certain to find its way into many anthologies of judicial ineptitude and indiscretion.

In your letter of March 3rd, you mentioned not having had an answer to your letter of January 4th. I have moved and my new address is 5924 Dublin apartment 2108. I moved during the Christmas holidays and did not receive your letter.

About the book—it perhaps is a good thing that it is not finished, because they have filed a Motion to disqualify me on the grounds of having a pecuniary interest in the case. I can refute that by stating that there has been no book published or that I have not begun to write a book.

We are coming along nicely. We have approximately 190 pages complete. I have been on Paul, trying to hurry him, have called him, gone to see him and everything else I could do to hurry it, but Paul has been sick and has not been able to do as much as he wanted to on it.

As you probably read in the papers, the Court of Criminal Appeals tossed the case back to me to determine Jack Ruby's sanity and I have set the Sanity Hearing for March 29th, and don't know the outcome, but it is my opinion that they will never prove Ruby insane, but the case is far from being over. Therefore, I ask your indulgence and patience as actually we may have a much, much better book than we had anticipated; but I do not want to put myself in the position of being disqualified.

I think that you will find that the work that Paul and I have done will be very interesting. My sister, who is a book-reviewer has read it and commented that it was one of the most interesting things she had read in a long time. . . .

When we read this letter, we felt that we had achieved our purpose. Now Judge Brown had to be found disqualified. All that followed had to be an anticlimax. We could scarcely believe that we would still have a long road ahead of us; but it was an illuminated road. When we despaired, the words of this letter would appear in bright letters ahead of us.

Stewart could reply to Judge Brown on April 13 with a kind of resigned despair:

I was glad to have your letter giving some word on where the writing of your book now stands. I do really and truly hope we will have a manuscript before too long. As I'm sure you realize, the whole Ruby business is getting further and further away from the fact. So, let us proceed with absolute haste.

A little later, on April 21, a secretary wrote to the judge:

In Mr. Stewart's temporary absence from the office, I am sending you a copy of our Author's Questionnaire which should be returned to the Publicity Department. I do hope that you can spare a few moments to fill it out.

To our very great regret, this was the last communication. What deathless words might have followed we do not know. Somehow, we felt that we had cramped the styles of the judge, the ghost writer, and the editor.

By June 9, 1965, Kunstler had sent on to the Dallas court the material he had obtained, everything except the completed portions of the manuscript. The omission of the manuscript was surprising, but the lapse was corrected later.

"If you don't have enough to disqualify Brown," Kunstler commented, "I don't think anyone can ever be disqualified. In any event, you've got a lot of bargaining material here." When asked by the press, which soon learned of the filing of the material in court, about the letter that Judge Brown sent to his editor on March 12, 1965, a letter that soon was to become famous, Kunstler, who knows the uses of understatement, said: "That is a pretty strong letter."

Burleson and Jim Bowie, of the district attorney's office, agreed tentatively on July 8 as the date for the hearing before Judge Holland on the disqualification of Judge Brown. But before that date could arrive, Judge Brown took action which he thought would relieve him of the embarrassment of disqualification.

Weary of our constant and unrelenting pummeling of him, of our many incursions into the courts, and of the reports in the press or—more likely—persuaded that it was best to retreat from the battlefield while he could depart with a semblance of dignity, Judge Joe B. Brown gave up the case. On June 21, 1965, he wrote to his judicial superior:

*Hon. Dallas A. Blankenship, Judge*
*First Administrative Judicial District*
*Record Building*
*Dallas, Texas*

DEAR JUDGE BLANKENSHIP:
I would like to recuse myself from any further duty in the case styled The State of Texas vs. Jack Ruby.
Therefore, I request that you appoint another Judge to handle all future proceedings.
Yours very truly,
JOE B. BROWN

The significant word was "recuse." Perhaps we were unfair to Judge Brown, but we felt that such an unusual word was not of his own choosing. Even at Harvard and Yale they do not use such language; their legal pig-Latin is of another quality. We ourselves, we must confess, had to look up the meaning of "recuse," and it satisfied us. He was withdrawing from the case as disqualified. Possibly he did not himself know that such was the meaning of the words chosen.

Asked to clarify his sudden decision, Judge Brown for once was reduced to near silence. He refused to comment. He also refused to have his picture taken by cameramen. Some said his official reason for withdrawing from the case was his heavy case load. Most felt that he was "recusing" himself in order to avoid a disqualification hearing. But Judge Brown would not elaborate, saying: "I don't think a judge has to give reasons for personal decisions he reaches." This was not in accordance with the law cases we had read. These required the giving of reasons for withdrawal, it being a judge's duty to remain unless there is good cause for his stepping out. We were so relieved to be rid of him, however, that we did not press for "reasons."

Judge Blankenship, charged with the responsibility of assigning judges to various cases in his namesake city, could now appoint any district judge, civil or criminal, in the thirty-four-county area administered by him. It was said that he was planning to confer with his colleagues before making a choice. It was rumored that two other Dallas judges—Henry King and J. Frank Wilson—had rejected overtures to take over the case. (Judge Wilson had presided in Judge Brown's stead during one contested day of the Ruby trial.)

In a succinct order that projected us a great distance on the way to our objective, Judge Blankenship appointed Judge Louis Holland, of Montague, Texas, to sit for Judge Brown in further hearings in the case. Judge Holland had presided over the one-day hearing in which Joe Tonahill had been removed as defense counsel. It was pointed out by Judge Blankenship that Judge Holland had a lighter docket than other judges who might have been considered, and he was available for assignment. All knew that the reasons went beyond the publicly stated ones.

At last we were rid of Judge Joe B. Brown and his bumbling ineptitude, his inexcusable haste, his lack of judicial decorum and wisdom. We could rejoice for the moment, but we could not really pause. Judge Brown was out of the case so far as presiding over future proceedings was concerned; but this was little comfort to us, or to the man under sentence of death, if what had been previously determined under the aegis of Judge Brown still remained in full and devastating legal effect. What we desperately needed to accomplish was something more basic—an adjudication that Judge Brown had been disqualified, or recused, from a time sufficiently far back to render the death sentence void. We could not trust to the uncertain results of the pending review in the Texas Court of Criminal Appeals. After all, the judges there had not been overkind to us or to our client.

Some short-cut techniques for nullifying the disastrous murder trial had to be found.

# 12

## A GUARDIAN FOR JACK RUBY

A GOOD PART of a lawyer's job is extrinsic to the law itself. He must concern himself not only with the volumes on the law, with what the courts have said, and with the preparation of briefs and documents, but also with the people who are engaged in the legal process. Maintaining proper relations with a client or his family can consume much of a lawyer's time and energy.

The Ruby family had been accused, even before I came into the case, of being difficult to work with and for. I was willing to grant that this might be true, if for no other reason than the complexity of the case and the emotionally trying experiences the family had already undergone. A client legitimately wants to know what counsel is doing; lawyers, just as legitimately, feel that they are not obligated to give minute-by-minute accounts and explanations of every action. This often produces a strain in lawyer-client relations. My feeling, from the beginning, was that if the family was continually informed of what was happening in the case, amicable relations would be preserved until Jack ultimately was freed. To a great extent, that is what happened.

Of the members of the Ruby family, two were particularly to be considered and informed, Eva because she was closest to Jack, and Earl because he was the guiding spirit in the attempt to save Jack's life.

Whenever we appeared in court, either in Dallas or Austin, Eva Grant was also there. She would arrive early and ensconce herself where she could see and hear everything, even the whisperings not intended for our ears.

Sometimes she would pick up wild rumors and, rarely, information of great value. As ebullient as Jack, she was in some respects less predictable. Deeply devoted to him, she did not always act with the calm and restraint that we would have preferred. Some of her rages were calculated, intended for specific purposes. On occasion, we agreed with her objectives if not always with their form. Frank to the point of embarrassment, she did wonders with the English language, for she did not always observe the niceties of grammar and diction. She was eloquent, sometimes devastating, and certainly never dull. One might wince or writhe at the timing of one of her outbursts, but one invariably recalled her with interest and a kind of affection.

Most of the time I tried to keep Eva informed by letters to her, or by copies of letters to others, of what was happening so that she would not think she was low person on the totem pole. In return she would send to me clippings from the Dallas press, relevant and irrelevant, heavily annotated in her own hand. Sometimes they would be accompanied by typewritten letters in which the keys seemed to have jumped madly, spontaneously over the sheet in bizarre designs. These illegible notes contrasted surprisingly with Eva's own clearly readable handwriting.

When we were not around, and even when we were, Eva gladly submitted to press interviews, and what she said was usually quotable. In that respect, as in others, she was much like Jack.

In contrast to his sister Eva or brother Jack, Earl Ruby was almost taciturn. He listened attentively to everything, seemed to grasp what was said to him, and answered questions intelligently, sometimes wisely, and never verbosely. Although he had not been able to attend college—he had refused an athletic scholarship to one—he displayed in his writing and speaking a sensitivity to the English language that was, if not literary, at least ample for the purposes at hand. And he constantly jotted memoranda in a small pad. In an almost formal way, he was polite and cordial. And he wore a steady little grin at the corners of his mouth.

Unlike Eva and Jack, Earl did not seem to be eager to appear before reporters. He was anxious to refrain from any rash word or deed. He deferred to counsel and sought advice. When he formed impressions, even strong ones, he kept them to himself and bided his time.

Earl was the organizer of the family, the businessman, the strategist. His brothers and sisters turned to him for advice, encouragement, and, sometimes, cash. In a reserved way, he could be critical of them, but seldom harshly. The district attorney's staff winced when confronted by Eva, but seemed to respect Earl. Eva we might ignore at times, but Earl we always took seriously.

Just when I was beginning to feel that the charge that the family was difficult to deal with was an unkind myth, I learned from Dann that Earl, without consulting us, had attempted, through another, rather young attorney, Alan Adelson, to open up an estate for Jack in Detroit. Aside from serious doubts about the Detroit court's jurisdiction to deal with any of his assets, we resented so important and potentially prejudicial a step being taken without consultation with us. Surely our devotion to the interests of Jack and his family merited our being taken into their full confidence at all times.

Earl appeared contrite when I talked to him about the matter, and on June 11, 1965, I wrote to him:

I am relying upon your word that nothing, literally nothing, more will be done in Detroit without the prior approval of Sol Dann and myself. Sol and I want the proceeding instituted by the attorney you hired to be dismissed at once and the attorney discharged, this as quietly as possible. . . . Let me repeat what I have told you over and over again. There must be a consensus between your present attorneys. None of us has the right to do anything without the prior knowledge and approval of the others. This is an arrangement that helps Jack and his family even more than it helps us, and it should be adhered to religiously.

For the moment everything appeared to be going well again. When I talked with Earl, I learned that possibly the best way to handle the situation was to keep the probate proceeding pending but to assume full control over it. Dann and I were in full agreement that what we wanted was an immediate substitution of ourselves for Alan Adelson. After we had received this substitution and had an order entered based upon it, Sol and I would consider the next steps after consultation with our colleagues Clinton, Kunstler, and Burleson.

What troubled us, among other things, was the representation of counsel that Jack had an estate of $25,000. If that was true, then why were the Texas proceedings being carried on by Jack as a pauper, with the state bearing the expenses of transcripts of the record and the like? In truth, there were no means, no property, nothing but a potential, to administer.

The truce was short-lived. On June 28 I received a disquieting letter from Earl: "After many conversations with my brothers and sisters, we have come to the conclusion that even though I have a letter of substitution from Mr. Adelson, we want him to remain as my attorney in the guardianship. . . ."

Earl then listed the reasons for retaining Adelson in the guardianship proceeding. It was, first of all, because the family did not want Dann at the helm! Earl said that they did not want to appear any longer in the position of hiring and firing so many lawyers. Besides, they wanted something to be done about the $3000 that Jack had had on his person when he was arrested, as they were heavily indebted because of the expenses they had incurred. And there were tax problems arising out of the moneys originally collected through Jack's ghost-written autobiography at the time of the trial. To appease me, Earl added: "We hope you will agree with our thinking and we also would like for you to join Adelson in the guardianship. Adelson has assured me that he will abide by your instructions as he is only interested in protecting me from any tax problems."

Immediately, I responded:

I appreciate your expressions of confidence, but I am part of a group of attorneys, all of whom are trying their utmost in behalf of Jack and the family. It is just as if we had not had a conversation the other day. You have ignored all that I have said.

Regardless as to your feelings with respect to Sol Dann or anyone else, I think it would be utterly mischievous to bring in another person. . . .

You say that you have complete confidence in all that I have done and you deeply appreciate it. It is all the more surprising that you don't realize that, while you think you are hurting only Dann (which is bad enough), you are, in effect, hurting all of us.

Eva, not notable for diplomacy, supported Earl: the other attorney was going to "donate his time and energy; without any legal fees or expenses whatsoever." (We were doing this very thing ourselves.) She, of all people, objected that Dann acted "on emotions, rather than on sound judgment and proper analysis." But she acknowledged the extent of his labors and was "very grateful."

Since Earl insisted that both Burleson and Clinton were agreeable to the arrangements he had made and that he could not understand why I would not go along with the family's views, I asked my Texas associates for a frank expression of their views. Clinton, with his usual sober good sense, offered a way to resolve the matter:

When I first learned that the guardianship matter had been filed I wrote everyone concerned of my opposition. The reasons were two: First, it injected a new factor into the overall picture which, of necessity, had to be taken into account in planning any move. Second, it alleged that Jack Ruby had property valued in excess of $25,000 although the appeal in the State court is in forma pauperis and it had been suggested that the appeal in Federal Court be prosecuted in the same way.

When Earl spoke to me on long distance Saturday, July 3, he did not ask my opinion as to the filing and prosecution of the guardianship matter but merely whether it should be handled by an attorney other than one on the defense team. I agreed that if it were pursued, such other attorney should handle it.

Now that the guardianship has been filed, however, I see no advantage in discontinuing it. Whatever damage was done by the allegation regarding the $25,000 has already been done and cannot be erased. But I do believe, and I think Phil Burleson agrees with me, that before any further papers are filed in the guardianship matter drafts of them should be submitted to us for perusal to determine whether any statements in the papers will have an adverse effect on the Texas proceedings.

On the other hand, . . . there may be some advantages to be derived. . . . Whatever assets there are in Jack's name and whatever monies come in to his estate by contributions or otherwise will presumably be channeled through the guardianship and expended for Jack's benefit, including his defense. Moreover, decisions made by the guardian regarding attorneys and the like ought to be more authoritative than the power of attorney which has been under attack and expressions of desire by "the family."

In sum, since it has been initiated I see no advantage to discontinuing the guardianship proceeding but do believe strongly that papers to be filed therein should be reviewed by us with an eye to the Texas proceedings.

Ultimately, it was found that nothing could be gained by the appointment of a guardian for Jack in Detroit. The matter was left in mid-air until Jack died, long afterwards. Then the same fruitless maneuvering to create an estate in Michigan started all over again, but was once more abandoned.

The incident, however, served to keep us on guard against similar small but irritating excursions and caused us to make greater efforts in our communications with the family.

# 13

## JUDGE HOLLAND GRANTS A WRIT

No TWO JUDGES could be less alike than Joe Brown and
Louis Holland. The one is, in a sense, an affront to the
other. Where the one was touseled in hair, attire, and general appearance, the other is immaculate, well-groomed,
completely master of himself, off and on the bench. Judge
Holland is Texan in size; six feet tall, he appears to tower
beyond that height. He looks like a successful rancher, and,
indeed, he raises Black Angus cattle on his nine-hundred-
acre ranch and lives in a ranch-style home at the edge of
town. At the time of the Ruby proceedings, Judge Brown
was separated from his wife. It would be hard to think of
the Hollands, faithful members of the First Baptist Church
of Montague, as having any domestic difficulties.

The judge is a big man in his little community of less
than three hundred souls. He is interested in all the people,
young and old. He is part of every charity drive in his
county and helps the youngsters with Little League baseball. He encourages everyone to serve on juries; only
"sickness and death" are excuses, and he is dubious about
both. Through his example, they know that a judge must
be knowledgeable, fair, just, decorous, and firm. He would
never fraternize with a strip artist, but he could send a
friend to prison if his duty required it. He would not
temporize or trust to the luck of those who lack diligence
or courage. Trials in his courtroom take place when they
are scheduled; decisions are promptly delivered. He stands
for no nonsense from anyone, be he lawyer, witness, or
spectator, no matter how exalted he may feel himself to be.
His highest ambition is to be a good judge, or, as he would

phrase it, "a better judge." Yet during the war he had resigned as county judge and enlisted as a private in the Army. For months he had guarded prisoners of war before he was upgraded to military intelligence. Then, after the war, in 1947, he became a district judge and he has served on the bench since then. His regular court stretches over three counties. In addition, he presides over the state's Eighth Administrative District. And so it was that he came into the Ruby case.

After his assignment to the case Judge Holland, in his usual expeditious manner, announced that he was going to make certain that the case moved along. "I realize both sides need a little time to prepare," he said, in the reasonable tone that was characteristic of him, "but I think we should get in court within a short time."

Reflecting a bit, he added: "I realize it is a very important case and a great deal of responsibility rests on trying it. However, I have assumed that responsibility several times, perhaps not in a case so notorious as this one."

Judge Blankenship thought that the matter of disqualifying Judge Brown was moot and that Judge Holland could proceed to other aspects of the case, such as the sanity hearing. But Burleson was quick to indicate our belief that Judge Brown's withdrawal did not preclude the disqualification hearing that we had sought. "There are cases that indicate we are entitled to proceed on the motion for disqualification," Burleson said. "We are looking into that possibility." He added: "A disqualification could affect the [original] trial."

Losing little time, he wrote to Judge Holland, on June 25, first congratulating him on his assignment, and then going immediately to the matters that concerned us:

There has been some talk that the withdrawal of Judge Brown automatically terminates the motion for disqualification that was set on July 8, 1965, and I do not know what you think about this, but felt I should write to you.

I would appreciate hearing from you as to whether or not

you intend to proceed with the motion on the 8th as previously scheduled, or if you intend to reschedule the motion to disqualify for a later date.

If you are going to be in Dallas for the next few days, we might have a conference at that time or I may be able to see you at the Bar Convention in Fort Worth next week.

During the state bar convention, Burleson continued to voice his views on the subject. "This goes deeper than determining which judge will preside during future proceedings," Burleson said. "We want an opportunity to develop evidence about Judge Brown's role. It could have an important bearing on other phases of this case."

He called attention to the hearing that had been scheduled on July 8: "As far as we are concerned, the hearing has not been canceled by Judge Brown's statement," Burleson said. "Unless he [Judge Brown] states in writing that he is disqualifying himself—and not merely withdrawing—we will insist upon the hearing."

His attention called to these remarks, District Attorney Wade declared, "It doesn't make any difference to us one way or the other whether they have a hearing."

On July 6, Burleson, growing increasingly confident and resourceful as new responsibilities devolved upon him, had a conference with Judge Holland that lasted about an hour. During the conference he told Judge Holland that we wanted to proceed with the motion to disqualify Judge Brown because we felt the disqualification might well extend back to the time of the trial. It would definitely extend back to the time of the refusal of the bills of exception in August, 1964. He showed Judge Holland a copy of Judge Brown's letter to Stewart, the managing editor of Holt, Rinehart and Winston. Holland was disturbed by the contents, but said little. It was obvious to Burleson that Holland was disgusted by the letter.

We were seeking the hearing to develop the facts on the disqualification and to have a ruling from Judge Holland.

If he ruled that Judge Brown was disqualified, then the
ruling would be certified on to the Court of Criminal
Appeals. If, on the other hand, he held that Judge Brown
was not disqualified, then the Appellate Court would have
the facts before it to determine if Judge Holland had made
a mistake and the Court of Criminal Appeals then could
consider the evidence and determine the matter of
disqualification.

Judge Holland responded to Burleson with a story of one
of his experiences. He had prosecuted a man for an offense
several years before, and subsequently, after Judge Holland had become the district judge, the man came before
him again on another and different charge and was tried
and sentenced to the penitentiary. The prisoner had filed a
writ of habeas corpus and a hearing was held to determine
Judge Holland's qualifications to sit.

This story was significant to Burleson because it showed
that Judge Holland was aware that disqualification could
be made by collateral attack. Our motion was comparable,
although it was not habeas corpus.

Judge Holland, who had a case set for July 6, said he
would call Burleson later to discuss the matter of the
hearing. Burleson repeated that we felt the motion was still
pending and were entitled to at least a hearing on the
matter. If he did not give us a hearing, where all the facts
could be properly developed, then we might have to file a
writ of error coram nobis (a common-law writ to correct a
judgment, in the same court in which it was rendered, on
the ground of error of fact), which we preferred not to
have to do.

Burleson also informed Judge Holland that we wished to
set a date for the sanity hearing, but that other matters had
greater priority. In his letter reporting on this conversation,
Burleson gave us a bit of chit-chat which showed that we
were not the only persons working behind the scenes:

One very important ex-Judge and close friend of Senator

Dorsey Hardeman told me that Tonahill had come up to him
at the [State Bar] convention and requested that he, the ex-
Judge, talk to Senator Hardeman about getting in the Ruby
case and to encourage Hardeman to do so at all costs. Therefore, it appears that Hardeman is being pushed to get in the
case and the only logical reason I can assume that Tonahill
wants him in is so that Senator Hardeman can turn around and
bring Tonahill back into the case. We must remember that it
was the Texas Senate that passed the resolution endorsing
Tonahill and his actions in connection with the Ruby matter
and complimenting him upon the fine manner in which he handled it.

By July 9 Burleson was able to tell Judge Holland that
he had talked with Jim Bowie, Wade's first assistant, about
agreeable dates for the disqualification hearing and then
for the sanity hearing. He informed the judge, too, of the
renewed efforts in Joe Tonahill's behalf so that the big
fellow might somehow remain in the appellate part of the
case. Of course, we were opposed to this. The same day
Burleson gave us the benefit, in a long communication, of
his considerable amount of thought on the kind of evidence
that should be presented at the disqualification hearing
and legal consequences of our either failing or prevailing.

Delay being a characteristic of all legal proceedings—
and of the Ruby case especially—the disqualification hearing scheduled for July 8, 1965, did not take place. The
press continued to hound the hapless Judge Brown. "I
wish they'd quit asking me questions," he said, plaintively.

A new schedule was worked out: the disqualification
hearing would take place on July 22 or as soon as another
scheduled trial presided over by Judge Holland would be
out of the way, and the sanity hearing would be held on
October 18, 1965.

The preparation for both matters proceeded feverishly,
each of us making his suggestions and contributions. We
learned of a case in New York, involving some juvenile

offenders, in which the presiding judge had written a book and was criticized for it. Perhaps the case would be of help to us. We looked into the matter—and found that Mark Lane was one of several defense counsel in the case.

We continued to give thought to a possible deal with the state for a commutation of the death sentence.

We continued to explore the wisdom of dropping the request for a sanity hearing.

"Although I anticipate Judge Holland is going to give us a full hearing [on Judge Brown's disqualification]," Burleson wrote us on July 9, "I am sure we will not know as a matter of fact until this morning that the hearing is set. The State may oppose the hearing. . . ."

Wade was quoted on both sides of the matter. One report said that he regarded the question as "moot," since Judge Brown had "recused" himself. Another report quoted Wade as saying that he would not contest the request for a full hearing. "It's up to the judge," he said, sagely.

At last, on July 23, Burleson and Clinton had the opportunity to urge our arguments for a hearing on the motion to disqualify Judge Brown.

The State took the position that the question was moot, since Judge Brown was out of the case, and that Judge Holland did not have jurisdiction to hear the motion. They were relying upon Article 828 of the Code of Criminal Procedure which states that after notice of appeal is given and the term in which it is given has expired, the appellate court has exclusive jurisdiction of the case. This is a sensible rule of procedure that prevails in most states. While generally it should be followed, there are special circumstances that call for special consideration.

Clinton and Burleson argued that the State had waived any objection to jurisdiction and had really told the federal court, both trial and appellate, that if the federal court would stay out of the matter, they would handle the motion to disqualify in the state court. Based upon those representations, the federal court had sent it back to the state court. Now the State was taking an inconsistent position in saying that they did not have jurisdiction.

They also argued that the court did have jurisdiction, as it had jurisdiction to dispose of the Tonahill motion and change of venue. They further stated that the State's position that the question was moot was inconsistent with the position of no jurisdiction.

After the court had refused the right to have a hearing, Burleson requested that we be allowed to call the witnesses for the purpose of perfecting the bill of exception and the court declined to allow him to do so. Then he requested that he be allowed to make a verbal offer of proof of what the witnesses would testify, and again he was denied this right.

After the hearing, Clinton and Burleson went back to the office and began to research. The result was put into a letter to other counsel quoted here with explanatory interpolations:

I think that we need to immediately file a writ of habeas corpus in the state trial court, before Judge Holland, upon the following grounds and theory.

We should allege that Jack is illegally confined because his conviction is void. It is void because of Joe Brown's disqualification and the fact that he became disqualified at least as far back as July 24, 1964, prior to the time that he had concluded all of his judicial functions in connection with the Ruby case. In this regard, he refused the filing of the 15 bills of exception [necessary in connection with the appeal] and entered two orders extending the time for filing the statement of facts [the transcript of the evidence, also necessary for the appeal] and actually signed the statement of facts after that period of time and on or about November 20, 1964. In addition thereto, and alternatively, we should take the position that because of the act of disqualification of Judge Brown, Jack Ruby has been deprived of a right to a statement of facts in the appellate court. The reason for this is that the act of extending the period of time by Judge Brown was null and void. The statute in Texas is mandatory and requires that the statement of facts be filed within 90 days. There are two exceptions to this. One exception is if there is an extension of time properly entered. The other exception is if the judge signs the statement of facts after the 90 days, and prior to the record being sent to and considered by the appellate court, then good cause is presumed for the late filing. Since Judge Brown was disqualified at the time that he entered the order extending the time, then no proper extension was had and we can not qualify under that exception. Also, since he was disqualified at the time that he signed the statement of facts, then his signature is null and void and we do not fall under the second exception either. Therefore, the statement of facts is not properly before the Court of Criminal Appeals and can not be considered by them if Judge Brown is disqualified and I am sure that he is under the law. Also, his disqualification should knock out the refusal of the 15 formal bills of exception and therefore the only thing pending before the appellate court for their consideration will be the 15 bills of exception, standing unqualified and as I prepared them.

These bills reflect that error was committed by the trial court and that Jack Ruby was not given a fair and impartial trial and that his conviction was in violation of various statutes and the Constitution of the United States. With just the formal bills before the Court of Criminal Appeals, they have to reverse the case. I can see no way that they can get around that. [Burleson was being overly optimistic, as of this time; but his enthusiasm for the proposed course was persuasive.]

It may seem that we are attempting to get the statement of facts thrown out and that it would be to our advantage to keep the statement of facts there. However, we must keep in mind that anything that Judge Brown did while disqualified is null and void, and that it is conceivable that the State could come forward and also prove Judge Brown's disqualification. As an example, if we were to obtain a reversal on an informal bill of exception contained in the statement of facts in the Court of Criminal Appeals, on motion for rehearing, the State could file a

writ of error coram nobis or some similar proceeding, showing
that Judge Brown was disqualified and that the statement of
facts should not be considered. Then, if the Court of Criminal
Appeals went along with their motion for rehearing, they would
have to back up and not consider the statement of facts. I do
not think that this would happen, but it is immaterial as to who
raises the error, as it can be raised at any time by anyone.
[Here, highly technical matters were under discussion, and the
lay person is likely to become impatient and lose interest; but
it is important to note that even in a sensational case like the
Ruby case, the attorneys must act on the basis of a close study
of the law, and not, as in Perry Mason shows, on the basis of
inspiration and histrionics.]

Further, with the statement of facts knocked out, then we fall
within the recent line of cases by the Supreme Court of the
United States wherein they have held that it is a violation of
due process to deny an indigent accused a statement of facts
for purposes of appellate review.

It may seem that we are seeking to knock out our own statement of facts, which we feel will be beneficial to us, but again
I emphasize that it is not legally before the Court of Criminal
Appeals if our theory of disqualification of Judge Brown is correct. And I hasten to add, I am sure that Judge Brown is disqualified under the facts known to us at this time.

I am not hopeful that Judge Holland will grant the writ of
habeas corpus, but on the other hand, feel that we can make a
tremendous argument under the law as I have briefed it so far.

Then, if we are unsuccessful with Judge Holland . . . I think
we should file a writ of habeas corpus in the Court of Criminal
Appeals asking that they send the writ to Judge Holland to
develop the facts and certify the facts back to the Court of
Criminal Appeals so that they can make a decision in light of
the facts so developed.

In regard to the Court of Criminal Appeals, we have a problem in that they are in a constitutional vacation until the first
Monday in October. [Here, again, what laymen call a techni-
cality was of primary concern. If the court did not have the

constitutional right to act during its recess, we had to get everything to them before that time or else wait until they could
constitutionally resume their deliberations.]

Then, if we are unsuccessful in getting a hearing by virtue
of an order of the Court of Criminal Appeals, we need to think
very seriously about getting a writ of habeas corpus granted in
the federal district court upon the same matter, to-wit: that the
judgment of death is void because of Judge Brown's disqualification and there try to obtain a full hearing and a certification
of the facts.

[This process of court-hopping, while maddening to the uninformed, is essential when one is attempting to exhaust every
conceivable remedy in order to save a human life.]

I know that the federal court was not very receptive to us in
the past, but I think that the nature of this complaint, especially
in view of the background of Joe Brown and the propensity to
be criticized by fellow judges, and the common belief that
Judge Brown is disqualified for writing the book, coupled with
the fact that he has gotten out of the case, leaves us in much
better position for a federal writ.

I do not think we should file our amended motion for a new
trial, as I have found numerous cases saying that the trial court
does not have jurisdiction of same. We would be in about the
same position as we were with the motion to disqualify Judge
Brown. If we do anything along this line, it should be filed in
the Court of Criminal Appeals asking the Court of Criminal
Appeals to broaden the jurisdiction of the trial court for consideration of an amended motion for new trial.

Therefore, I would appreciate hearing from each of you immediately as to your thoughts along the line of filing a writ of
habeas corpus. . . .

This was a long letter, and an optimistic one. It was good
to see the usually phlegmatic Phil in a great sweat and
eager to proceed. As often happened, I first talked with
Dann and then wrote to my colleagues:

Sol and I both feel that we ought to petition the Texas Court

of Criminal Appeals immediately for an order enlarging the
jurisdiction of Judge Holland to include (a) his right to pass
upon a motion to disqualify Judge Brown; and (b) his right to
pass upon an amended motion for a new trial. Our petition to
the Texas Court of Criminal Appeals should incorporate the
text of such motions, so that, even if they are denied out of hand
by the court, they will be part of the record which we might
refer to in connection with the appeal or in the United States
Supreme Court.

Sol and I both feel that, while a petition for habeas corpus
may be a good idea, it should await a ruling by the court on the
first suggested petition. . . .

Of course, too, we must consider where we stand with respect to the pending matters in the United States Court of Appeals. This has been largely the responsibility of Bill Kunstler
and we ought to hear from him on that point.

With respect to the hearing on sanity, Sol and I both feel
more strongly than ever that we must go through with the hearing, that we have everything to gain and little to lose by proceeding. We hope that Bill is now in agreement with us and
Sam on this point.

Although Burleson had once written of the possibility of
enlarging Judge Holland's jurisdiction, his immediate reply
to my letter disapproved of the idea:

. . . I would appreciate very much having any citations of authority that may be known to each of you that gives the Court
of Criminal Appeals that power. The Rules of Criminal Procedure in Texas and the rules of the Court of Criminal Appeals
do not entail such a matter and I feel that they will turn it
down flat. This is especially true as to our right to pass upon
the amended motion for new trial. There are numerous cases
in Texas stating that the time limits for the filing and hearing
of the amended motion are mandatory and that time has already passed.

Another and important reason that I disagree with proceeding at this time in the Court of Criminal Appeals is that the
Court of Criminal Appeals is on a constitutional vacation. . . .

He pointed out that habeas corpus would lie in those situations in which new matters, not coverable in the pending appeal, were set forth. "I want to emphasize," he wrote, "that just because you have good ideas that sound good, that unless we on this end have some type of authority to back us up, it is useless to file any paper with any court."

He felt that the courts would regard us as frivolous unless what we filed was consistent with the authorities and precedents: "I have been doing some research on the writ of habeas corpus and think that we have a better than 60% chance of having a hearing on same."

It was his opinion that we ought to reactivate our proceeding in the United States Court of Appeals so that the state courts might "loosen up the reins" and do something in our behalf. As to the sanity hearing, he thought that we should stay flexible and perhaps take the depositions I had suggested, so that the State would know we were in earnest.

"To summarize," he said, "I definitely think we need to proceed with the writ of habeas corpus in the State trial court and then follow up generally in the Court of Criminal Appeals if we are unsuccessful."

On receiving Burleson's letter, on July 30, I replied immediately:

Frankly, I don't much care what a particular proceeding is labeled or the forum in which it is filed, as long as it is likely to produce a result. If you, Phil, feel that we can produce the result we seek through a habeas corpus proceeding and not through my recommendation, then I will acquiesce in your judgment. I just want to make certain that we do not leave anything unexplored. We know that courts differ in their interpretation of situations that are novel. We have already had the experience of the United States Court of Appeals feeling that the Texas Court of Criminal Appeals has supervisory jurisdiction and that court rejecting the advice of the federal tribunal.

It seems to me that we are in a situation in which we are

probing for weak points, and we ought to continue to do so until something gives in our favor. Obviously, you know more about the Texas precedents than we do and, while our case is, in some respects, unprecedented, we cannot completely ignore what the courts have heretofore said. In short, if you, Phil, Sam and the others feel that what is called for is a habeas corpus proceeding, so far as I am concerned it can be that, as long as it is done as quickly as possible.

I am encouraged by your feeling that we have better than a 60% chance of having a hearing on habeas corpus. That is a much better percentage than would justify such action.

I agree with you that something has to be done with respect to the United States Court of Appeals. I want to repeat my suggestion that Bill . . . should immediately prepare the kind of motion that may reactivate the federal court.

In the same spirit, I discussed other pending matters so that there would be no doubt of my desire to act rather than to talk.

Kunstler, too, was persuaded by Burleson that the habeas corpus route was worth exploring.

If no hearing is granted by Judge Holland, then you could proceed with your alternative suggestion of a writ of mandamus. As for the United States Court of Appeals, we can only proceed with this course if the motion for a sanity hearing is not withdrawn. I am not quite sure just how to activate our appeal here because we are not really complaining that the sanity hearing itself will be unfair and our removal is limited to that proceeding. I would appreciate your rationale on this score.

I am still not convinced of the wisdom of the sanity hearing at this stage but I am not prepared to argue vehemently on this score. I think that it is six of one and a half dozen of another as to when such a hearing is held and my only concern was going to the Court of Criminal Appeals with a ruling of sanity haunting us. . . .

I only throw out one thought. Is there any merit in proceeding with everything at once? We are now prepared to go ahead with the appeal, what with Tonahill out, and we can also keep the sanity hearing going but slowed down a pace. We might then have our cake and eat it too.

Dann and I held a telephone conversation and found ourselves in agreement with Kunstler. I wrote, on August 4, 1965:

For the reasons stated by Phil we can see the necessity of filing a habeas corpus petition at this time. This petition would incorporate everything that would be included in a motion for the disqualification of the Judge and for a new trial. Sol and I feel that at the same time a petition ought to be filed before the Texas Court of Criminal Appeals asking leave to file our motions to disqualify Judge Brown and for a new trial and enlarging Judge Holland's jurisdiction. Neither of us see any harm flowing from filing such petition and we think that it may even be beneficial in that it will show Judge Holland and everyone else that we are trying to exhaust every possible remedy in behalf of our client. . . .

With respect to the United States Court of Appeals, my greatest concern is that we remain in court and not subject to a motion to dismiss our appeal. . . .

So Burleson proceeded with the preparation of the petition for a writ of habeas corpus. On August 6, 1965, he filed the application for the writ with the clerk of the Criminal District Court and sent a copy of it to Judge Holland, together with a memorandum of law. In a covering letter to the judge, he said:

After you have had an opportunity to read the application, study the brief and do whatever research, on your own you desire, and before you have totally made up your mind on your position in the matter, I would appreciate very much having the opportunity to talk with you, either in person or on the telephone, about this matter.

Needless to say, if you have any questions that are in your

mind and are unanswered in the brief, I would be most happy
to do the necessary research and give you benefit of such
research.

In the application for the writ, according to the usual
form, we claimed that the petitioner, Jack Ruby, was being
confined and restrained of his liberties, at the Dallas
County Jail, by Sheriff Bill Decker. True, the confinement
was by virtue of a jury verdict and a judgment of death.
But the conviction was void in that Ruby was denied due
process of law as guaranteed by the Fourteenth Amendment of the Constitution of the United States and by the
Constitution of Texas as well. The conviction was void
because the trial judge, Joe B. Brown, became disqualified
from presiding because he had an interest of a pecuniary
nature in the proceeding. He "was contemplating, re-
searching, preparing, and actually writing a book" on the
proceedings then pending before him. These activities,
we said, culminated in a contract between Judge Brown
and the New York publishing firm of Holt, Rinehart and
Winston, Inc., whereby the judge received several thousands of dollars as advance royalties and a contingent
interest in the future royalties resulting from the sale of
the book. This rendered all acts done by him void and of
no effect. Thereby the jury verdict and judgment became
void, and Ruby was deprived of the right of appellate
review of his conviction. Among others things, it was impossible, because of the judge's disqualification, to present
to him a valid statement of facts required for the appeal,
and he could not approve such statement or grant any
valid extensions of time in connection with it. Taking a
long chance on our ability to prove it, we declared that
Judge Brown's disqualification extended back, as well, to
the various judicial acts prior to the trial, involving bail and
change of venue, and during the trial the renewed motion
for change of venue and the merits of the case, and, afterwards, the hearing on the motion for a new trial and with

reference to the bills of exception filed for Ruby. These things, we said, were not known to us until very recently, and not until the time had elapsed for including them on appeal, if indeed there could be a valid appeal encompassing such things. We therefore prayed the court to grant and issue a writ of habeas corpus and to hold an evidentiary hearing thereon, and then to declare the conviction void and the confinement illegal, and to grant a new trial.

This was more than a little to ask after the same highly competent judge had denied our motion in the original proceeding to the same effect. But this time, on August 6, 1965, Judge Holland issued the writ and ordered Sheriff Decker to produce Jack Ruby before the judge on September 9, 1965, at 9:00 A.M., so that cause might be shown why Ruby should be held "in custody and under restraint in his liberty."

This was the traditional form of such writ of habeas corpus. To the layman, it might have seemed like a lot of legal gibberish; to us it meant the possibility that, in one fell swoop, we might nullify the death sentence and try our luck at another trial, with the atmosphere, we felt certain, much less prejudiced and poisoned than before. We were more content to proceed before Judge Louis T. Holland than before Judge Brown or, indeed, any of the sitting judges of Dallas County. Judge Holland impressed us as a man of integrity, decorum, knowledge, and compassion. Neither District Attorney Henry Wade nor his bloodcurdling assistant, Bill Alexander, could intimidate Judge Holland.

Soon after the granting of the writ, Sol Dann confided to us the contents of a letter he had received from Professor John Kaplan. Kaplan, at the request of Dann, had thought over the habeas corpus petition and had, as always, gone to the heart of the matter.

It seems to me that . . . you have two basic problems. The

first involves the time when Judge Brown should have been disqualified from the case. If you can prove that he had agreed either formally or informally to write a book before the trial, I think you have a very good ground for setting aside the entire trial and verdict. . . .

If in fact Judge Brown conceived of the idea of writing a book or decided to write a book on the trial after the trial, I think your position is a great deal weaker. Then all you can show is that he is the type of person who would do this sort of thing, not really that he did it. I am not convinced that is enough. An enquiry into his state of mind will probably be necessary and he of course will be less than completely truthful in the matter.

A complicating factor will be that you probably will be able to show that he had received offers before the trial, but this might not be enough if the issue of his state of mind were resolved against you.

The next basic issue and probably the more troublesome one is what to do at this time—assuming that you have a reversible error in the record. Frankly, on this, you have only one slender way home. Federal courts and appellate courts in general are the most loathe to overturn criminal conviction unless other than by the normal processes of the law which would of course be appeal within the State system and then habeas corpus as we have outlined in our book. A Federal habeas corpus before the State review process is complete is extremely unlikely.

Nonetheless, there are certain conditions under which it is possible. . . .

Unfortunately the thing that will cause you the most trouble is that in theory (though of course not in fact) Ruby has a perfectly adequate remedy. All he has to do is appeal through the State system and then bring a habeas corpus [proceeding]. The complaints about the disqualification of Judge Brown are of exactly the type that habeas corpus is intended for, and either in the State or the Federal Court you could then hold a complete hearing on the issue. More states, however, do not look with favor upon the taking of additional evidence of the sort which could be raised in habeas corpus proceedings after the trial but before the appeal is finished.

He then analyzed, point by point, questions proposed by Dann, and went on to more basic matters.

In short, aside from getting out the facts, your big problem is that you want relief now and the Texas courts will in all probability, force you to go through your regular appellate processes first. I honestly don't think there is much you can do about this, though of course you can try, and this may generate a good deal of helpful publicity for Jack.

It will be very hard to get the Supreme Court excited about your case, where the only issue is not whether you have a right to have the Judge disqualified or have the trial set aside, but rather whether you have a right to have it done now as distinguished from after taking your appeal.

He then discussed a side issue that had concerned all of us, and especially Dann.

As far as getting the American Bar Association to intervene, and file a brief amicus, your big problem is proof of the facts. I have little doubt that if it turns out that the Judge did agree to write a book on the case before the trial, you will get a great deal of cooperation. On the other hand, it may be that this cooperation will occur only after you have had your appeal and been able to show the facts. I might add that our book [*The Trial of Jack Ruby*] will be a great deal of help in this respect.

In all, his assessment of the situation was a shrewd one, whether or not it was valid in every respect.

We had also filed a petition before Judge Holland setting forth our beliefs with respect to the book about the Ruby trial that Judge Brown was writing—that it would show Judge Brown's disqualifying pecuniary interest in the case. We asked that he be required to produce "his book or manuscript, either in rough or final form, for inspection prior to the time of the hearing on September 9,

1965," so that we could properly proceed at that time. This petition Judge Holland allowed.

It was Burleson's none-too-pleasant duty to write to Judge Brown, on August 27, 1965, to tell him of the habeas corpus hearing to be held on September 9, a fact he obviously already knew, and to ask him to produce voluntarily and as soon as possible the manuscript of his book.

"I want to make it clear," Burleson said in his letter, "that the contents of the material will be kept highly confidential and will not be made public or shown to anyone not connected with the defense. It is not the purpose of this request to in any way infringe upon your contract or to defeat the purpose of the publishers. Said material will be returned to you prior to the hearing."

This was a promise made in good faith. It was not certain that the promise could be kept. We knew that the press would pry into the book and make as much of it as we were hoping to make of it at the hearing. This was an extraordinary occurrence, a judge writing a book about a case not yet concluded. Still the promise of discretion had to be made.

During this period Clinton had been unusually silent. At the end of August, before we could become too concerned, he wrote to us, explaining the lapse and joining with his usual acumen in the discussion of the path we had chosen.

Since late last month, my office has received what now amounts to a file folder filled with correspondence about this matter. . . . I have now read, studied and given much thought to the questions posed. . . . On matters which appear to be current, the following thoughts are offered.

First, with respect to Judge Brown's disqualification on account of his book, I positively concur in the habeas corpus route outlined by Phil in his several letters. I could hardly do otherwise since, as I recall, he and I hatched the idea while drinking coffee across the street from the Courthouse just after

Holland had denied us a hearing on the motion to disqualify. It appears clear from Phil's correspondence with and reports of conference with Judge Holland and the District Attorney's office that we will be given a full evidentiary hearing. The record made at this hearing may be the most important record made in the whole case thus far. Activities and comments of each of you indicate your awareness that this is so.

At the habeas corpus hearing we should put in evidence every thread we can come up with. As Elmer's August 20, brief indicates, extensive research fails to uncover "any case which even closely resembles the fact situation presented here." My own feeling is that we will have to rely ultimately on the doctrine of "probability of prejudice" followed by the Supreme Court in Estes v. Texas; Mr. Justice Clark's opinion in Section 5, collates pertinent precedents. With this in mind it seems to me that our habeas corpus record must develop every facet of Judge Brown's position vis-a-vis the Ruby Trial. Some of the most significant of these, it seems to me, must include: the tremendous amount of public attention focused on Judge Brown from the outset thereby immediately putting him in the limelight of publicity, any pertinent comments or statements made by Judge Brown from the time he was assigned the case to time of hearing on habeas corpus including utilizing the services of a public relations expert and his revealing correspondence with his publisher, attendant publicity during the trial particularly as related to Judge Brown, his activities on and off the bench during the course of the trial such as taking notes, dictating memoranda, collecting photographs and the like pertaining to his own self-aggrandizement, and considerations which caused him to permit televising receipt of the jury's verdict (wasn't this the most climactic point in the entire trial and wasn't Judge Brown its focal point until Belli started his tirade?). I agree that the draft manuscript is important if only to show its existence and whatever Judge Brown's attitude may be reflected thereby; if we are lucky enough to find passages in the manuscript which reveal his self-interest we are just that much better off. But to me the picture that must be painted is one of a judge seeking to get into the limelight, bask in it and profit from it. This notion, like that of televising Estes' preliminary hearings and trial, must be shown to be inherent prejudice to the rights of the Defendant.

Indeed, like Estes our case must rest, at least in supporting part, on standards of conduct of judges as reflected by various canons of ethics. Phil already has the Judicial Canon of Ethics and I note, for example, Section 3 of Article XIII of the Canon of Ethics of the State Bar of Texas directs that a member of the bar "should protest earnestly and actively against the appointment or election of those who are unsuitable for the bench; and he shall strive to have elevated thereto only those willing to forego other employment, whether of business, political or other character, which may embarrass the free and fair consideration of questions before them for decisions." Canon 24, dealing with direct or indirect solicitation, prohibits indirect advertisements for professional employment such as "furnishing or inspiring newspaper comments about causes in which the member is engaged or the importance of the member's position, and all other like self laudation should be avoided." Canons of ethics have been held to be at least quasi statutory and have the same force and legal effect upon matters to which they relate as do the rules of civil procedure. . . .

Second, with respect to the pending appeal before the Fifth Circuit, it seems to me that it is almost moot. Our two basic points there have really been resolved: Joe Tonahill is no longer acting as counsel in the District Court proceedings and Judge Brown has recused himself from presiding over such proceedings. Evidence developed at the pending habeas corpus hearing must first be considered by Judge Holland and after that an adverse ruling by him may, I agree with Phil, become a part of the pending appeal before the Court of Criminal Appeals. In short, the only real value of keeping the Fifth Circuit matter alive is that it may serve to act as some deterrent on the District Attorney and, to a very small degree I am sure, on Judge Holland. . . . I suggest we await the outcome of the habeas corpus proceeding at which time it will probably be my position that the Fifth Circuit matter be dismissed.

Third, at the present time I do not see much to be gained by preparing some sort of motion to file with the Court of Criminal Appeals. It is in its Constitutional vacation until October and I would prefer to await the outcome of the habeas corpus proceeding.

Finally, it is my view that we should proceed with the sanity trial as presently scheduled.

Each of us had now expressed himself. There was clearly a meeting of minds. We were all awaiting the hearing on the habeas corpus petition with scarcely subdued excitement. Whether we won or lost, in a technical sense, we were bound to win in a practical sense. We would expose to all the world, including the reviewing courts, the nature of the man who, with a jury misguided by him, had passed judgment on Jack Ruby in his first trial. We felt that it was bound to shake the conscience of the community and lead to the setting aside of the death sentence.

# 14

## THE TRIAL OF JACK RUBY

OUR CONCERN for what Judge Brown might have written was matched by an equal concern for other publications that might work mischief with Jack Ruby. In a long career as a lawyer, writer, and public figure, I have made it clear that I believe in the utmost freedom for the individual to express himself. I look upon the First Amendment as perhaps the most important part of the Constitution of the United States. While not in complete agreement with Justice Black in his holding this part of the Bill of Rights to be absolute, I am ready to chance all sorts of imagined ills for the sake of protecting the right of authors, publishers, and the public to have full access to the channels of communication. Ideas ought to compete with ideas. For this reason I have fought against any form of censorship or suppression, any kind of obscenity prosecution except where children may be involved. I am committed to the philosophy that those who are public figures, voluntarily or involuntarily, have to tolerate a large measure of intrusion into their lives.

Like many others, however, I fear that the press, left completely to itself, may interfere with an equal, if not superior, right—the right to a fair trial, fair appeal, and due process. There should be protection against those who knowingly lie about people or subject them to great harm in their reputations, privacy, and dignity as human beings.

From time to time Dann or Earl Ruby would prod me to take action with respect to the unauthorized or adverse writings about Jack. I tried, again and again, to explain to them that freedom of the press includes the right to publish in good faith factual material about matters and persons in the sphere of legitimate public interest. I explained the limitations in the law of libel and the meaning of privacy. At times I thought they understood, but then the same promptings would occur and recur. Neither sent me any material to demonstrate the errors in the publications complained of or other objections to them until months after the subject was first discussed. Even then the material was much too slender and superficial to support an action. I felt, too, that we should not do anything that might tend to jeopardize the efforts to save Jack's life. The setting aside of the death sentence was our true goal.

Although nothing came of most of our discussions, the concern remained. Every word written about Jack and the case could have an effect, however small, upon the ultimate outcome. While we could not compel anyone to agree with us, we had the right to urge our viewpoint on them. We could be persistent, resourceful, eloquent, in such persuasion when the stakes were high. For who was to say that the wrong word uttered at the wrong time might not do irreparable harm, might not cause death even? Judges, even those on the reviewing courts, are influenced by the opinions of other judges, law professors, legal authorities. What might be the effect on the Texas Court of Criminal Appeals of a book on the Ruby trial, written by two brilliant expounders of the law? If the authors found nothing fundamentally wrong in the conduct of the Ruby case, the court might gladly say *"So be it!"* and affirm the death sentence.

Just such a situation confronted us as we prepared for the habeas corpus hearing before Judge Holland. We had learned, early during the pendency of the appeal, that two law school professors were undertaking a study of the Ruby trial. In March, 1965, it became certain that *The Trial of Jack Ruby*, by John Kaplan and Jon R. Waltz, would be published, whether we liked it or not, while the case was still unresolved. We felt that it might affect the outcome of the appeal and other legal maneuverings unless mischievous material were kept out of it. It was our hope that, by reason and importunity, we might persuade the two authors to see our viewpoint and to refrain from doing anything harmful. Dann and I were charged with this responsibility.

Because the book has been received with much enthusiasm in professional and lay circles, and is in fact an excellent chronicle of the case from its origin to the death verdict, our pursuit of the authors and success or lack of it may be enlightening. It is an unusual story, and at the time a frustrating one, but it is revealing of the difficulty of determining truth and assigning motives.

By June, 1965, one of the authors and I were on a first-name basis, and the other author had a similar relation with Dann, but this familiarity sometimes seemed almost ironical in view of the words we exchanged. In a letter to Waltz, on June 18, I complained of the "amazing collection of misinformation" about myself. I was annoyed, too, because the authors had completely misconceived the manner in which I came into the case. Dann was said to be wholly responsible.

As of the moment, I would say that, at least as far as Earl [Ruby] is concerned, my participation does not depend in the least upon Sol Dann, although he and I work together very closely. On one occasion, Earl said to me that the first happy moments he has had since tragedy overtook the family was when Kunstler and I got into the case. Whether or not he still feels so, I don't know, but I suspect that it is still true.

Ten days later, on June 28, I wrote to Waltz again to express misgivings. I had been in Boston and, while there, had talked by telephone with Kaplan about my ideas for improving the book and eliminating what I saw as the possibility of harming Ruby.

While I found much of what he said extremely interesting and true, I was a bit disturbed about his preoccupation with the need for speed. . . . A man's life is at stake and that takes precedence over any publisher's deadline. . . .

I agree with Sol Dann that most of your book is extremely good, and I want to applaud it, but there are some passages that worry me a good deal. . . .

What concerns me more than anything . . . is the concluding section [dealing with the events after the death verdict]. I do not think that there is adequate coverage of what has happened since. . . .

Later I learned from Kaplan why he felt that speedy completion of the manuscript was completely reasonable. It was not a question of waiting until this or that step in the case was completed before publishing the book. A final determination of the case, assuming that defense counsel pursued every legal course open to it, was distant, certainly years away. No author who felt that he had something to offer here and now could be expected to wait that long. When the immediate urgency of the situation no longer existed, I came to accept the reasonableness of Kaplan's position. At the time, however, I could not accept it at all and pressed the co-authors relentlessly.

To Waltz I tried to give the gist of my viewpoint. I felt there was no point to our communications unless I was completely open:

To sum up, I would say that my fear as to a few portions of the book is that, if it got into the hands of the higher courts, as is likely, it might be used as an excuse to hold against us on several basic points. Above all, I regret the last chapter, which has every sign of haste and thoughtlessness. It simply is an inadequate and harmful summary of what has happened since the death verdict. It is rather strange that you would have done such a chapter without consultation with those most involved.

Even as I was prodding Kaplan and Waltz, in a manner intended to provoke changes, I confided to Dann:

They have done an extremely good job, despite their excessive self-assurance. If we can persuade them to adopt some of our suggestions, then the book, as published, can do no harm.

Kaplan now took his turn at trying to persuade me that what he and his collaborator were doing was exactly right:

You must remember however, that, while you are advocates, we are not. The entire value of our work will be lost if the idea comes through in any subtle way that we have an axe to grind one way or the other. I think that the book does far more good for Jack this way than it would if we made all the changes you suggest and thereby lost the appearance of our impartiality.

I tried more persuasion on Kaplan. If I was not influencing him, I was nevertheless clarifying my own thinking.

Let me see if I can express briefly my viewpoint as to premeditation in a murder action in Texas. The state of one's mind is an element not alone in the question of guilt or innocence, but in the degree of guilt and the extent of the punishment—however this is spelled out in the cases. The instructions [to the jury] should have spelled this out more clearly; the evidence should have been sharpened on this point; the closing arguments should have dwelt more upon it. In a capital case like the Ruby one, in which the atmosphere was charged before and after the killings of the President and of Oswald and before, during and after the trial, it is essential, indispensable even, that the courts and the readers of your book (which may include appellate judges) should know precisely what the sequence of events was that negatives premeditation or actual malice—regardless of the technical legal point.

Certainly, you should not appear to be advocates in our behalf. *But* since the case is still pending and a man's life is at stake, you must not *labor* any point that may harm him. You do not have the luxury of writing when it is all over. You are writing here and now. That is why you should not dismiss the points made in the trial and since then, even if you don't agree. That is not to say that you should pretend to beliefs you don't hold. Simply don't try to persuade the public or the courts that this or that major point (psychomotor epilepsy, absence of pre-meditation, etc.) is nonsense or dubious. I say this because the primary concern must be Ruby's life. I say it also because you may be wrong in your viewpoint and should not be cocksure about it at this juncture.

Then, thinking that perhaps Kaplan was dangling the last chapter of the book to hold us in line, I said of it:

I can sympathize with your view that, perhaps, you ought to drop the last chapter—that it is too hard to whip it into shape. But I think that would be a mistake, too. There would be a sense of incompleteness so far as the reader is concerned. He wants to know what then happened? Besides, to understand the trial you must understand its aftermath. . . .

To Dann I reported further progress, on July 9:

The last chapter, which is the most defective and dangerous, will be almost completely rewritten and the revised text will be submitted to us in galley or page form. How much progress we made in connection with the rest of the book I don't know. At least, we know their viewpoint and they know ours, and they are giving careful attention to everything that either of us suggested. Since the book is a factual and fair account of a judicial proceeding, we can scarcely ask for more. I impressed upon Waltz the basic fact that a human life is at stake and that doubts must be resolved in favor of saying the safe thing from the viewpoint of Ruby's defense.

Then, because Dann had wanted the Ruby defense to be compensated for the book written about his case, I advised him that I had "carefully refrained from even hinting" at the subject. I had reached the firm conviction that our motives would be misunderstood and our chances of influencing the authors lessened if we had a financial stake in the book.

I was distressed to learn that Dann was not happy about the decision. Earl wrote to me:

... after my telephone conversation with you during which you told me to tell Dann that it was not necessary for all of us to have a meeting with Prof. Waltz as you could handle it yourself, and would save us the expense of coming to Chicago Dann said, "What does he mean, we don't have to be there, of course we have to be there to see what kind of a deal we can make for royalties." This statement after you and I both told him we did not want to mention royalties definitely convinces me and my family more than ever that he is not the lawyer we want to handle the guardianship. After he made that statement, I again had to emphasize our reasons for not wanting royalties even though we needed money desperately.

Weeks later, after we had read and reread the galley proofs of the book, our worries intensified. Accordingly, on August 10, I wrote to Waltz, with some perturbation.

You and Professor Kaplan are publishing a book which undoubtedly means a lot to you, but my associates and I are trying to save the life of a man, and this means even more. . . . What you say can have a tremendous impact on the result in the sanity hearing and in the appeal itself. Frankly, I am disturbed that despite our discussions, some of this damaging material still remains. . . .

Waltz, with his usual skill, blended with some flattery, tried to placate us:

You are, thank God, a tenacious advocate of Ruby's cause. However, your comments seek to enlist us in a partisan effort and that is not our proper role in this matter. Ruby is entitled to your every effort on his behalf and you will, of course, consistently stress those things which you feel support and emphasize his position. On the other hand, from Kaplan and me the public is entitled to a balanced, objective account of the trial. We believe that the book, as it now stands, is balanced, wholly objective and devoid of bias. In my view, your comments, if followed to any greater extent than they have been already, would induce us to abandon our proper role.

Having worked too hard, he was going away on a vacation: "It is a difficult task to remain objective while being pulled and hauled in several directions but I know that you know that we have scrupulously remained so."

So I turned again to Kaplan:

It is not simply matters of opinion that we are questioning, but matters of fact. . . . Some of these are not merely annoying, but highly prejudicial, as where . . . you state that Phil Burleson was acting "on behalf of the Ruby family and attorney Dann." Clearly, Burleson was, and is, acting for Ruby, at the request of Ruby himself and the Ruby family. And, equally important, Burleson is acting in association with Clinton, Kunstler, Dann and myself. . . . None of us act for Dann—we act for Ruby!

I then hit at the authors' assumed greatest strength:

You and Jon excuse some of your statements on the grounds that you are striving to be objective, and not advocates, as we necessarily are. But you are *not* objective. You presume to dispose of some of the most basic issues. You reach conclusions adverse to Ruby's case, while the matter is still pending in court, without the benefit of our briefs and argument. . . . These are sensitive, delicate points on which reasonable men may differ. A court, and particularly a reviewing court, should consider them in an atmosphere untainted by prejudgment. If your book appears with the offending passages prior to such deliberation, you may make it difficult . . . if not impossible, to save Ruby's life. Do you want to carry your "objectivity" so far that it results in an injustice?

Jon has criticized Belli for publishing his book, which breaks professional confidences, during the pendency of the case. Professors of law have an obligation, too, in this kind of case, and it is no less than Belli's.

So much of your book is so good that you ought not to chance ruining it by a disregard for the rights of others at this critical juncture.

Clearly, I touched Kaplan deeply by this last thrust. He devoted a dozen pages to an answer.

Your letter in effect asks us to convey the impression that the
attorneys for Ruby are working as a team with no-one as the
leader. I admit that this is possible, but frankly, I do not
believe it. Throughout the whole post-trial representation Sol
Dann has been the one who was close to the Rubys and in
whom the Rubys had complete faith. As is obvious, he has done
a very able job for them, if not in the actual planning of specific
moves, then in the procurement of counsel who would take effective steps for them. From knowing Sol Dann and the Ruby
family, I am convinced that he is in a position very different
from that of the other members of the team. I want to make
clear that I do not assert that you or any of the other members
are in any way less vigorous or able than he. I do however
believe that if Sol Dann becomes dissatisfied (as, of course, I am
sure he will not) with you or with Bill Kunstler, you or Bill
Kunstler will leave the case just as have several others with
whom he had previously become dissatisfied (in my opinion,
with one exception quite properly so).

In short, though of course there is always the possibility that
I may be wrong, I adhere to the view that the lawyer with the
best rapport with the client is the most important lawyer—and
in this case I think it is Sol Dann.

Although what Kaplan was arguing was demonstrably
untrue, there was little reason to pursue this minor point
when there were major matters that needed correction.

Kaplan was eloquent in defense of what he and Waltz
had written. His words lingered in my mind and caused
me to ask myself some fundamental questions:

Most important on this issue is the fact that Jon Waltz and I
are either going to be honest about this book or we are not. We
have tried as best we can to be honest; we have rejected many
more changes that the prosecution wanted us to make than we
have of yours. As you of course know, and should be careful
not to forget, they have much more reason to be unhappy
than you do.

Of course it is possible that it is true that we, for some reason, are not objective. No-one has full knowledge of his own under-lying motivations, and it may be that after such a long period of intensive work, both Jon Waltz and I have become too re-luctant to re-think our entire positions. Insofar as I can tell, we have done our best, and I suppose the final judgment on our objectivity, as well as our competence, will be in other hands.

I do wish to point out, though, that you too are in a very difficult position so far as your objectivity and your judging of our objectivity are concerned. The fact of the matter is that while we will be performing well if we are objective, you will be performing badly if you are. This is not to say that you are wrong on this ultimate judgment and we are right. It is merely to point out that you may be wrong and we may be right. I think that is about all I can [say] on this issue. . . .

I am sorry if this letter has had the general sound of a po-lemic. I am, of course, enormously impressed with the job that Ruby's defense attorneys have done lately. I think that comes through in the book, and I respect you all the more, not only for that, but for the way you have been constantly fighting for your client.

I made a last effort to correct Kaplan on the matter of Ruby's representation. I felt that this was necessary for the sake both of the truth and in fairness to a group of men who had labored long and effectively.

Kaplan finally admitted, reluctantly and with qualifica-tions, that he might be wrong on the matter: "the worst that can be said is that we imply that Sol Dann was really running things longer than he was." By way of salutation, Kaplan wrote, with some gallantry:

In any event, I do hope that you like the book. We have, as you know, done as well as we possibly could (though I admit that you have just pointed out a way we could have done bet-ter). I hope, and I honestly feel, that in the short as well as in the long run our book will not only help the administration of justice in the United States, but also give a much-needed assist to Jack Ruby.

In retrospect, with the clarity furnished by the passing of time, I believe that Kaplan and Waltz were fully justified in this hope; they have written what will become a classic study of a controversial case.

Although Dann and I were relatively mild in our criticism of those parts of the Kaplan-Waltz book that troubled us, Melvin Belli was far less restrained, because the book was not restrained in what it had to say about him. The authors made it clear that they did not think highly of Belli himself or of his handling of the case. Belli wrote to the Stanford University Press in thunderous accents that could be heard across the continent. "I regard . . . the 'Trial of Jack Ruby' as deliberately and villainously scurrilous, malicious and defamatory," he began his letter.

It is errant in many particulars, designedly so and for the purpose of "taking me on" and also, and not so incidentally, to make money for the authors over and above their professional salary, their grant from the "Meyer Foundation" and otherwise.

The express malice should not be hard to prove and the factual errancies are easily provable.

I have no choice but to sue these two "Professors" for defamation, along with their agents, and this is advice in the premises.

I am amazed that you would participate in such a book as this without first ascertaining the facts and the bona fides of these two "professors" who seek to make themselves wealthy from salaries, grants and now a deliberately defamatory book.

The next day Belli wired a briefer diatribe to the university press:

KAPLAN'S BOOK MULTITUDINOUSLY UNFACTUAL GROSSLY DEFAMATORY DELIBERATELY MALICIOUS ADVICES FILING SUIT AUTHORS AND YOU DIRECTLY AMAZED RESPONSIBLE PEOPLE DID NOT CHECK IRRESPONSIBLE UNKNOWLEDGEABLE AUTHORS.,

Stanford University Press immediately wrote a one-sentence reply:

Thank you for your letter of October 19 and your telegram received yesterday addressed to Stanford Press, but the book is published by Macmillan, not by us.

That was the last ever heard of Belli's libel action against Kaplan and Waltz. As professor Waltz later said to me, "Melvin Belli is a good enough lawyer to comprehend that truth is a complete defense to a charge of libel."

# 15

## DALLAS, RUBY AND THE LAW

AT THE FIRST HEARING before Judge Holland to disqualify
his predecessor, Judge Brown, we had relied largely upon
the depositions of two people connected with Holt, Rinehart and Winston, Inc., and the files of that firm. We had
offered motions, orders, and documents taken from the
record of the Dallas court, the transcripts of other proceedings in Dallas, Judge Brown's letter "recusing" himself, and
the canons of the American Bar Association and the Texas
State Bar. It was not really a full-scale hearing because of
Judge Holland's doubts about his jurisdiction and our inability to marshal all the facts.

In the habeas corpus proceeding we went farther with
the in-court testimony of various witnesses. And we had,
for our main reliance, the manuscript of Judge Brown's
book, a document for the ages, an interior view of what a
"ghost" had got from an indiscreet judge.

*Dallas, Ruby, and the Law* was an inviting feast spread
unexpectedly before us. We devoured it for proof of our
contentions about its "author," and we found more than
we had prayed for. The first two sentences of the book
clearly show that the book was written as a defense of
Judge Brown and the city of Dallas.

Around the trial of Jack Ruby the press and the TV networks
of the nation have created a myth, perhaps the first folk myth
of the age of rapid communication. In it I am cast as the hanging Judge in a city of hate.

Brown then attempts to destroy this "myth": "The great

crowd which met the President at Dallas Love Field was more than friendly. It was affectionate." But "within hours after President Kennedy died, our brokenhearted city found that it was being blamed for his death."

As for the unjust charges against himself:

At best I was pictured as a character, a crude country judge. It was reported that I chewed tobacco while I was on the bench. I have not had a chew of tobacco since I was 10 years old. . . . One writer reported that I occupied my time on the bench reading a comic book while Defense Attorney Melvin Belli tried to interest the jury in the results of the mental tests given Jack Ruby. I have never read a comic book in my life. I was to be called Necessity Brown, "because necessity knows no law." This motheaten wisecrack is as old in the legal profession as the old saw about "Who was that lady I saw you with last night?"

At the worst, I was portrayed as something a great deal more sinister, as a vengeful judge determined to do Jack Ruby to death. Some implied that I was a hatchet-man for an all-powerful Dallas oligarchy that wanted to crucify Jack Ruby for the damage he had done to the image of our city. . . . I could not criticize or even suggest to the defense how to try this case.

Although "[s]ome of the distorted, warped picture which the national news media drew of the trial was accidental," owing to the "circus" atmosphere outside the courtroom and to the unfamiliarity of reporters with courtroom procedure, "the continuation of the stories vilifying Dallas and my court are not accidental. There are some people who have circulation to gain by repeating them and other persons with the need to vent on a hate object the same kind of mean and warped personality that Lee Harvey Oswald had." A great deal of autobiographical information goes to show that he thinks he is pretty good and has accomplished much against great odds. "There isn't much more to say about Joe B. Brown, except that I think he is a pretty fair judge, country or otherwise."

He deals, ambivalently, with Melvin Belli:

Much of the bitterness that has been heaped upon Dallas and me, I feel, must be blamed on Melvin Belli, the strange fascinating and brilliant San Franciscan who was Jack Ruby's chief of defense. From the beginning Mr. Belli set out to make Dallas the villain of the Ruby trial as well as the Presidential assassination. To defend Jack Ruby he sought to put Dallas on trial in the nation's press before the nation's people. Until the verdict went against him, however, Mr. Belli was my friend. . . . His reputation as an infallible personal injury lawyer, as a brilliant and unpredictable legal tactician, had reached Dallas long before him. I was well aware that on the Ruby case he was capable of doing me in as a judge if I did not watch my step.

This interesting concept of a lawyer "doing in" a judge, not fully explained in the book, raises provocative questions about the judge's frame of mind during the trial.

Brown seems to feel Belli's strategy in relying on the sole defense of psychomotor epilepsy variant was a poor one, and that his worst mistake "may have been in estimating [sic] the court and his opposition."

Brown also deals with the other attorney participants in the trial. Tonahill is an actor who performed for the jury. He does not say this in any derogatory way, but rather as a compliment. District Attorney Wade is highly competent. Jim Bowie is "a student of the law," and Alexander, "tough, sardonic and relentless, . . . has what any good prosecutor has to have, the ability to hate the man he is prosecuting temporarily." Brown suggests that he is not particularly fond of Alexander and relates a couple of incidents in which he and Alexander clashed.

Brown obviously thought highly of the legal skills of the prosecuting team:

These men Belli underestimated, and he chose to contend with them in their own state where the ground rules, the law and the public psychology, differed subtly from his own.

Belli undoubtedly was, as the newspapers called him, the

King of Torts, but at trying a criminal case in Texas, he wasn't even royalty.

Then the judge seeks to refute the charge that he sought the case simply for publicity and acted for that purpose during the trial. Although Brown argues that he "was scared to death" of the trial, the text suggests otherwise:

It was obvious from the beginning that a man could live all his life without the kind of publicity I was going to get. Also, although the Ruby case was not the most difficult murder I ever tried, it raised new legal questions. It broke new ground in the law of insanity in our state; I was the first Texas Judge ever to use a psychiatrist as a personal assistant. The Oswald murder was also the first ever committed while a national TV audience looked on, and this was to raise new questions about the objectivity of jurors and the possibility of a fair trial for Ruby anywhere.

Brown argues that the case fell to him by chance alone. When, as a matter of courtesy, he asked the two senior judges if they wanted the case, both declined. No one, he insists, brought pressure on him to transfer the case to another court or county, although Alexander did remark to him that the case was very complicated and that he would support a transfer to another judge. Why had he taken the case? "A man's self respect, I think, makes him face a thing that he knows he wants to dodge. I tried Jack Ruby because it was my duty under the oath I had taken as a judge."

Brown next discusses his impressions of Jack Ruby, essentially summed up in these statements: "Jack Ruby, I think, is a man with a starved ego. . . . He is a religious man who spent hours with his rabbi but was capable of crude violence upon a drunk in his strip joint. . . . Such a man may seem a little pitiable, but there was nothing pitiable about what he did."

Brown flatly states that "Jack Ruby got a fair trial," although he admits the problem of achieving exact justice and says he did not think Ruby received "exact justice." Ruby "had the best lawyers that money could hire, and he got a fair trial. It is only in retrospect that I can say that I do not think his defense made the most of his case."

In a chapter entitled "The Flavor of Texas Murder" Judge Brown tries to lay a foundation of Texas law and environment in preparation for a discussion of the trial. On occasions, homicide may be called justified under the law, but there are questions arising out of the application of the law:

Obviously there are quirks in the way the law of murder is applied in Texas which have to be understood in judging whether Jack Ruby got a fair trial or whether he was adequately represented. Only against the background of the Texas experience can one understand how Jack Ruby was able to walk into the Dallas police station with a gun. These quirks do not imply that Texans are less law-abiding than their neighbors of other states. Often the opposite is true. Our people may accept some excuses for killing that other states do not, but the fact is that most Texas killers are arrested and punished. . . .

It should not be forgotten that Texas is still very close to the frontier. . . .

Some colorful incidents are introduced to show Texas casualness in regard to guns and at least some human lives. The judge argues that, true to frontier tradition, there is "in much of our state . . . an unsophisticated hostility to the killing of an unarmed man," as Ruby had done. Thus venue changes to other parts of the state might have done him no good. Brown is himself particularly upset by the laxity of Texas gun laws, although even in that area he insists that Texas mores require greater freedom in the use of arms than in other states.

He discusses the law of homicide. There is no crime of manslaughter in Texas, but rather murder is divided into

murder without malice and murder with malice aforethought. He differs with Belli on trial strategy, for, he insists, the thrust of the case should have been aimed at this
distinction.

This was the classic "sudden flash of anger" case. . . . I think all
the expert psychiatric testimony in this trial would have but-
tressed this plea and that the jury might actually have decided
that Ruby was out of his mind at the time of the killing. At the
worst it might have persuaded the jury that this was a murder
without malice.

The question of Belli's tactics arises again:

With no criticism intended of Mr. Belli personally or his un-
deniable talents as a lawyer or his intentions, I suggest that he
made a tactical error. The defense in the Ruby case, if it was to
fall back on a murder without malice case in the event of the
collapse of its insanity plea, had to keep out of the record certain statements that Jack Ruby made immediately after he
killed Oswald from which malice aforethought could be properly inferred. The defense actually assisted in getting these
statements in the record. I think that Melvin Belli, in his life-
long enchantment with medicine, pitched his whole case on an
esoteric defense that forced him to admit these damaging statements. I don't know that he did. I don't know anything about it.
I was merely the judge.

A chapter entitled "The Criminal and the Crime" deals
with Ruby's activities during the fatal weekend. It comments on Jack Ruby's being upset about the notorious
Weissman advertisement, and Judge Brown makes it clear
that he did not think much of the advertisement either.
Brown again tries to analyze the personality of Jack Ruby
and in the process appears to be trying to separate Ruby
from the city of Dallas:

Trying to trace the movements of this peculiar man through
the next 48 hours of his life in a city suddenly stilled by grief

and anxiety is as fascinating as reading a spy story, dimly lit, mysterious, fascinated as he seemed to be by every focal point connected with the Kennedy tragedy. Ruby himself was a character fit for Alfred Hitchcock. Here is the protagonist, a creature of strange angers and impulses, the product of a Chicago West Side gang, a food faddist, a health worrier. . . . This was the man who needed status. . . .

One mystifying aspect of Chapter 3 is the judge's comment that Ruby had entered the third-floor corridor of the City Hall on Friday, "bent over low, apparently scribbling on a piece of paper." Brown defends Wade's public revelations on television by citing the extraordinary public nature of the case. He sums up his analysis of Ruby's early week-end activities:

All this is the picture of a man not distraught, not emotionally upset, merely afflicted with the all too human need to tell everybody about it. A short time later, however, . . . he was again the upset and grieving man.

Brown deals with the possible recognition of Ruby by Oswald at the time of the shooting by stating (erroneously, in my opinion, if all the available evidence is considered):

In the movie film of the incident, there is a vague look of recognition in Oswald's eyes, but I put that down to sudden recognition of the gun. Some officer had just mentioned the possibility of someone trying to shoot him a few minutes before, and Oswald had sneered at the idea.

He comments on the admissibility of statements allegedly made by Ruby after the shooting of Oswald, saying that this was a matter of interpretation under Texas law of what *res gestae* means. His interpretation of *res gestae* was clearly a broad one.

What did the jury have to decide?

This was quite a week-end in the life of any man. Did Jack Ruby's mind or consciousness snap as he confronted Oswald there in the police basement? Did the strain of all this induce the "fugue state" of psychomotor epilepsy where he was then completely unconscious of what he was doing. Or did the peculiar mind of Jack Ruby, a quick and alert mind as many testified, overwhelmed perhaps by the unaccustomed glory and attention which he craved decide on even greater glory? This a jury, one of the best juries that has ever sat in a criminal trial to my knowledge had to decide.

The next chapter, "The Magic Word," begins with a discussion of the Ruby bond hearing. The judge states that nobody wanted Ruby to get out on bond, including the defense.

He probably couldn't have got six blocks from the courthouse alive, not because Dallas is more lawless or less civilized than other cities but because events like the Presidential and Oswald murders have a way of triggering others.

According to him, in Texas a man is entitled to post bond unless it is shown, as in Ruby's case, that he might be sentenced to death. He insists that Belli was unsuccessful in his efforts at the bond hearing to sound out the prosecution's case.

He describes the bond hearing as mainly an argument over the stability of Ruby's mind, and he says that the eventual agreement to procedures for psychiatric examination met Belli's main purpose in arguing for bond and allowed the defense to get out of the hearing "gracefully."

Brown expresses considerable skepticism about the psychomotor epilepsy defense, a skepticism that may have been enhanced when his "psychiatric consultant . . . told him later, when it made no difference in the trial . . . that in his opinion Ruby did not have psychomotor epilepsy and probably never would have." He speculates a good deal about the psychiatric testimony, and again takes Belli to task. He says it was not smart to forewarn the prosecution by bringing up psychomotor epilepsy at the bond hearing. He appears to approve the idea that Ruby should have been put on the stand and that the psychiatric testimony should have been used to mitigate a guilty plea.

The next chapter contains a discussion of the city of Dallas and is obviously protective of the judge's home town. Dallas is described as a friendly down-to-earth merchandising and financing city. The Citizens Council, that group of civic leaders of great influence, is described as a positive force of responsible leadership. It is defended against charges of extremism, and described as an organization of men who can on their own word commit great resources and power to a particular program. Brown says that no written records are kept of Citizens Council meetings. He insists that the Council in no way pressured him about the case.

He defends Dallas against charges of right-wing extremism:

These few people [right-wing extremists] the police feared when, Mr. Kennedy arrived for his visit. As it turned out, they did nothing but the concentration of law officers on the right wing problem in Dallas may have made Lee Harvey Oswald's work a little easier for him. . . . The fatal drive through the downtown was aided at the last minute because some liberal Democrats objected that the men of the Dallas power structure would be monopolizing the President on his visit. If he had followed the original plan, he might still be alive.

Brown admits a Dallas "proclivity for killing," citing the Negro population of Dallas as major offenders, but at the same time arguing that Negro murders of other Negroes are prosecuted with impartial zeal unlike other places and Dallas in the past. (Brown views "our Negro people" in nonbigoted, but patronizing manner.) He points to the low conviction rate for homicides, arguing, in *non sequitur* fashion, that this shows Dallas is not a "witch-hunting town."

The following chapter, "The Belli Poll," deals with the

venue problem. He appears to resent Belli's use of publicity in arguing that the people of Dallas needed "to make Ruby a sacrificial goat . . . in order to cleanse themselves." Belli promised to stop this and was "as good as his word." The judge thus avoided pressure to hold Belli in contempt.

This chapter deals, among other things, with the specifics of the hearing, problems with reporters, and the informality of his court. The decision at this point was to make an effort at getting a fair jury and to withhold any decision on a change of venue until the outcome of that effort.

"My Term in the Goldfish Bowl" is more specifically concerned with press problems. His conclusion is that he should have been more stringent on press coverage and allowed only a small reporter pool in the courtroom. He gives an explanation of the activities of advertising man Sam Bloom and his employees, contributed to him by the Citizens Council.

Chapter 8 appeared to be missing. (This may have accounted for some differences in numbering of pages.) Chapter 9, "The Case Against Jack Ruby," is a description of the trial proceedings. He quotes, disapprovingly, a statement by Belli as an example of his oral style at its worst. He gives his views of the theories and trial strategy of the defense and prosecution:

It quickly became apparent that the State meant to retrace Ruby's footprints over a period of two days, that it meant to show that Ruby had made up his mind to kill Oswald hours before the shooting. The defense, naturally, was going to block from the record anything indicating this if it could. It was also going to keep digging away at the State's witnesses to try to get some admission that Jack Ruby looked or acted abnormally—anything that might lend weight to its plea of insanity.

A significant chapter is called "The Police Station Murder Case." The description of the trial testimony is continued. It includes a discussion of *res gestae* problems in admitting Ruby's post-shooting statements and the matter of police connections being responsible for Ruby's presence at the scene of the shooting. He tells of the state's illiberal discovery rules, showing the difficulty in getting certain police records into evidence.

The ensuing chapter, "Portrait of a Character," deals with testimony concerning Ruby as an individual. It rehashes the story of his temper, his occasional acts of violence, his dogs, and a little of his unfortunate history.

The final chapter, "Sergeant Dean's Story," mentions the vagueness of the film clip, showing Ruby's homicidal act, and covers Dean's testimony, which the judge, of course, feels is very important.

Dean's testimony finally was this: Ruby had told him that he had first thought of killing Oswald when he had seen Oswald with a sneer on his face at the police lineup the night after Kennedy was killed.

This was the key to showing previous intent, or malice.

Brown draws the conclusion that "the State was consistently more adroit and abler than the Defense." From reading the book, we developed doubts about the adroitness and ability of the judge.

How would he face up to his manuscript as we subjected him to courtroom examination?

# 16

## THE HEARING BEFORE JUDGE HOLLAND

WE HAD PREPARED for the hearing on the writ of habeas corpus with care. Perhaps we were too sure of ourselves, because we felt that now, at last, we had Judge Brown where we wanted him—on the witness stand before a firm and fair-minded judge. What was about to be realized was true beyond our wildest hopes. Moreover, we felt (wrongly, as it turned out) that Henry Wade was silently on our side and that he wanted us to win as an easy way out of what had become an embarrassing situation.

At times I found myself taking a grudging liking to the district attorney. He seemed amiable, folksy, charming even. He assumed an air of ignorance, pretending that he left the law books for others and that he practiced instead by sound and smell. One erred, however, if one underrated him, as Belli learned. Wade seemed to let such vengeful spirits as Bill Alexander do his dirty work, but it was apparent to the perceptive that Wade really ran his office. He knew how to use those around him shrewdly and skillfully.

Now and then we conferred with Wade privately in hopes of settling the case by a short cut. He told us that he would be willing to forego the execution of the death sentence if we would settle for a life term, which he assured us would mean about seven years. He would not promise even that, and we desired a shorter term. Turning down Wade's proposal was a gamble we had to take, on the theory that once Wade had expressed a willingness to have the death sentence set aside, he could not later change his mind.

In the afternoon before the habeas corpus hearing, Wade met privately with us in Phil Burleson's office to review our discussion of a settlement. We had just finished our habeas corpus trial brief, and were pleased with it. We had not yet served copies of it on the district attorney or Judge Holland. After a few amenities I turned to our principal opponent and said, "Henry, if you read our brief, you would be persuaded that Judge Brown was disqualified." He chuckled and retorted at once. "Elmer, it would be harder to persuade me that Judge Brown was ever qualified."

Such a remark was characteristic of Henry Wade. Publicly as well as privately, he could be indiscreet if a point could be made. Then and later, I was shocked by the things he said. Accustomed to more timid souls in our courts, I could not get used to the droll candor of this unusual man.

The candor was a source of deception, a stratagem. For a while we thought Wade did not much care if we prevailed in the habeas corpus proceedings. His choice of the relatively mild Jim Williamson for the State lead, rather than the more resourceful and dynamic, not to say savage, Bill Alexander, helped to create this impression. We were to be disabused of this notion. Although Wade was not in the courtroom most of the time, we felt his presence even when he was not there.

When the hearing began, on September 9, 1965, the first witness we called was Mary Paul, Judge Brown's only sister. We were taking a chance in using Mrs. Paul, as we could be bound, as a matter of law, by what she said from the stand. We were relying upon the expectation that even if she tried to shield her brother, she would yet be compelled to speak the truth on the facts, and the truth could only help us. Sam Clinton, who had a special skill in the interrogation of women, examined this lady who, on the surface, was so different from her brother—self-contained, careful of speech, and altogether proper.

Mrs. Paul said she had been a book reviewer since about 1941 and was presumably the one referred to in her brother's letter to Mr. Stewart as being so enthusiastic about the manuscript. (This letter was constantly referred to throughout this proceeding as one of the principal proofs of our contention that Judge Brown was disqualified as having a pecuniary interest in the proceedings and that, therefore, the Ruby death sentence was a nullity. We wanted to connect Mrs. Paul with the letter or, at least, get the benefit of anything that she and her brother might have discussed.)

Mrs. Paul said that one needed a formal education to be a book reviewer, but no special education; she belonged to no professional groups of book reviewers and had never attended any conferences of authors and publishers. She had never published any reviews. She might have known "one or two writers, I don't know any publishers at all." Her reviewing consisted of speeches, "mostly to groups of women who are interested in good books." These were frequent, and she was paid for them. She was eager to leave the witness stand as soon as possible, because she had a review scheduled for early that morning.

She tried to pick out the very best books, she said. "That is left entirely up to me. I do it by reading the reviews and reading of the books themselves, and I make my selections in that manner." She bought all her books. "I have never received one from a publisher. . . . I would think by the very fact that I give a review of the book that it would be a recommendation before whom I speak. I am not on the selling end. . . . If I weren't convinced of the authenticity of the books, I wouldn't bother with them and take up my time and the time of other people to listen to them."

Having satisfied himself that Mrs. Paul was, indeed, a reviewer, Clinton proceeded to the matter of her opinion of her brother's manuscript.

Q. Now, your brother in that letter says that you have read the manuscript that had thus far been done, and I believe you told us that you had?

A. I didn't tell you that I had.

Q. You didn't?

A. No, you read it out of the letter just now. You didn't ask me that.

Q. May I ask you now?

A. You may.

Q. Did you read the manuscript that was thus far prepared at the time he is commenting you did?

A. He showed me some typewritten pages. I read them with a good deal of pleasure.

Q. According to Judge Brown, you reported that it was one of the most interesting things you had read in years, I think.

A. Yes.

She went on to volunteer, after an interruption by the ever-alert Bill Alexander: "I have not read the entire book. I have read only perhaps twenty or twenty-five pages of the typewritten material."

And on this limited basis, the judge had written so glowingly to his publisher! Had the publisher known the facts upon which Judge Brown based his report, the surprise might have equaled ours.

The judge had lived in her home *from about September 1, 1963, to about March or April, 1964.* The dates were of some consequence, as they helped fix the time when the judge first thought of writing a book and set about making arrangements for it. The earlier the latter date could be placed, the more likely it was that the proceedings were contaminated by the judge's disqualification. It was during the weeks immediately after the death verdict of March, 1964, that the first of the post-verdict motions were made by the defense and overruled by Judge Brown.

Mrs. Paul admitted that her brother had discussed with her that he was going to preside over the trial. This was in the period when there was a plethora of publicity about the case. She had attended court at the time of the Ruby proceedings: "Several times, probably, though it might be just one time, and that was in the selection of the Jury." She saw very little of her brother at the time because he was "pretty busy." She "imagined" that she discussed the proceedings with him as they went along. "I don't recall any discussions specifically regarding the trial." It never occurred to her then that her brother might be in a position to write a book on the case. She was aware of some of the events during the trial and not of others. "I don't know about the little strip tease. I know about the jail break; I remember that." It was very difficult to recall exactly what was discussed with her brother and what was not, since it was a long time ago.

It was some time in July, 1964, when the judge mentioned to her that he contemplated writing a book "and I was surprised and delighted." She had asked him, "Are you going to write a book?" and he had said, "Yes, I think it's about time that somebody told the truth about Dallas." He hadn't asked her for help, but if he had, she would have given it.

Had she ever heard of Holt, Rinehart and Winston? "Frankly, I had never heard of them until he told me the publisher."

She had not seen any more of the manuscript since her brother showed her the twenty-five or thirty pages.

"He didn't discuss anything with me regarding public relations. I don't really know what you mean by public relations."

She had never discussed Melvin Belli's book on the case with her brother.

And with this her examination was over. The State did not choose to cross-examine.

What had we gained by our calculated risk in putting Mrs. Paul on the stand? On balance, one could not be sure. Certainly, we had established the date when Judge Brown had lived with his sister. More was expected from the other witnesses, and infinitely more from the documentation, the many exhibits that we intended to introduce into evidence, including particularly the manuscript itself.

Paul Crume now took the stand. He was the well-known columnist of the Dallas *Morning News* who had been selected as Judge Brown's collaborator or, more accurately, ghost writer. "Big D," his column, has appeared on the front page of the paper for many years; he has been with the *Morning News* since 1936, except for the war years, and his only book was a collection of "Big D" pieces. He is a man of good reputation, and we felt that he was trying to tell the truth as he was questioned by Phil Burleson.

Crume had ghost-written "magazine articles, speeches and that sort of work," but never a book. He had really known Judge Brown only since July, 1964, "though I had met him before, knew who he was, and had possibly said 'hello.'" He had been approached to assist the judge in writing a book. "It was the 15th of July, but probably a day or so earlier, that is just a guess." Mr. Edwards, president of Holt, Rinehart and Winston, "telephoned me. . . . At the office. . . . I don't remember just exactly what the date of the conversation was. . . . Well, Mr. Edwards mentioned that Judge Brown wanted to write this book and he asked me whether I would be interested in helping him with the writing job. He asked me whether I would have time. . . . I thought sure that it was during that conversation he asked me what I would consider doing it for. . . . I told him I would be very interested in doing it, but that I would have to finish it before the first of October. . . . I had in mind there a three or fourth month period. . . . I think perhaps in mentioning he said something about they had —well, I don't know exactly, but there was some phrase in there, he said, 'we know what you can write,' and I think he said some other names had been mentioned, but I don't believe he mentioned who they were."

Crume later learned that his associate, Frank Tolbert,

another Dallas *Morning News* columnist, had also been approached about the book.

Burleson asked Crume about "the status of the book right now." Crume answered, "The status, I would suppose is—that would be hard to say, two-thirds at least 'rough drafted.' I would say it is pretty far along toward completion."

In the beginning he and Judge Brown talked a great deal. "It was done here in Dallas, and on a trip we made out to La Jolla, California." The trip was made in late August of 1964 for a week, he believed. The discussions in Dallas were "mostly at Judge Brown's apartment." He took very few notes. "Normally, I take notes on dates or names or something like that, but not on narrative material." He relied on his memory—"Subject to checking later, of course, yes." Judge Brown furnished him with a copy of the record of the trial, but no other notes or documents: "That is all except a box of letters that he had received which was full of newspaper clippings from over the country." He attended no part of the proceedings.

Crume knew the judge's sister, Mrs. Paul.

Q. Was she present during any of these discussions?

A. I don't believe so, during the actual—

Q. During the actual—

A. —actual talking itself. She may have been but it is except for the people involved, a rather dull thing to listen to.

What was the manner of approach at La Jolla? "We did talk some out on the terrace, but there was hardly anyone around. In other words, he was trying to get the details that a man might remember, the little things—and you can't do this by direct questions, but by an offhand comment that will start somebody to remembering, so there were people around at times and we might have been sitting at a table with somebody and I might have—"

"We did a great deal of talking just there in the room also." And they did some talking while driving down in the car. "The only person who was ever present was Mr. Stewart the editor that I mentioned. . . . I wrote perhaps three or four letters to Mr. Stewart, certainly no more than a half-dozen, and he wrote me about the same number."

Mr. Stewart had discussed the necessity of speed. "It was a matter of concern to everybody. . . . I was aware of the delivery date. Actually, I mentioned October, and as I said, I thought it would probably run over into November. . . . I suppose it was important to them because the sooner you get this out after the trial, the more public interest there was likely to be in it. . . . I am presently working on it as I can. . . . I am trying to patch together the newspaper clippings and what I can get from people who were at the trial and from what Judge Brown has told me and trying to shape up a Chapter on Selection of the Jury." The clippings did not come from Judge Brown. "I have a complete file of the Dallas Morning News."

He had heard Judge Brown say that there was a hearing to disqualify him, "and we haven't discussed it any further than that."

He and Mr. Edwards, the president of the publishing firm, discussed the matter of keeping his name out of the book. "I think this was on the first telephone call when he asked me whether I would mind not appearing as ghost writer. I said it made no difference to me one way or the other. . . . It was to be Judge Brown's own story of the trial and the events around it. . . . This was part of the point of all of the talking. I was trying to tell the story from the mind of another man. My personalities, as far as I could get them out, wouldn't be in it. The judgments wouldn't be mine. . . . I don't know what that he ever told me, I got the impression that he was angry and perhaps a little hurt by things that had been published about him and he wanted to tell his side of it." The judge had mentioned two articles in the *Saturday Evening Post* and *Life*. "He resented some of the comments." "Well, some of the time we used some of the material and discussed some of the material which had occurred during the trial, I think for instance, he told me of an incident between he and Mr. Lynn [sic], I don't know whether it was during the main trial or at one of the hearings before the main trial actually started, when he refused to cooperate with Mr. Lynn on this magazine article he had been commissioned to do. . . . He is not the kind of person who is particularly vengeful, and I think that 'angry' is perhaps too strong a word—irritated. . . . He just wanted to tell his side of the thing."

In the manuscript he would try to support Judge Brown's rulings. There were conversations between himself and Judge Brown about changes. After the judge saw the manuscript, "He would then make the deletions, corrections or changes or whatever he thought proper." He tried to make the manuscript reflect Judge Brown's judgments. "I am sure however, when he rewrites it, he will modify some of it. We haven't gotten to that yet." If the book had been completed "at the first part of November it would have been very profitable. . . . I wasn't particularly concerned with the success of the book, I had no interest in that, after I had turned it in." He was not sharing in the royalties.

"I attended one of the Ruby hearings in April, I believe." This was the hearing that involved the questions as to whether Joe Tonahill was to represent Ruby. "My purpose in being there actually, was to get a good look at Mr. Ruby. . . . I don't know whether I told him [Judge Brown] I was coming to sit in on the hearing or not. . . . One of the ladies in the office told me that I could sit there." He had written nothing as yet about this hearing. "Eventually, I will have to tie it all up to show how it all works out. It is quite possible that I will have a sentence or two on it."

He had had about three conversations with Mr. Williamson, District Attorney Wade's assistant, before coming to testify.

When Judge Brown wrote to the publisher in March,

1965, about 200 pages were completed. Now there were 235 pages. (In other words, Judge Brown had not turned over everything to us. The manuscript we had did not contain that number of pages. We never learned whether the omissions were intended or inadvertent, and if the former, the content of the missing manuscript pages.)

Crume had discussed "a detail or two" of the manuscript with Williamson, who corrected a phrase or so. "I believe he told me that he had looked at a copy that he had gotten from Judge Brown and looked it over."

At this point, we completed our examination of Crume, subject to what he might bring in to us in the way of further documentation, which we had asked him to look for.

Williamson now took over the questioning of the witness.

Crume said, at the outset, that the book was written for the layman. "This was to be a story of the trial within context, so to speak, it was to develop some material about the city itself, the scene—the locality—the circumstances." "It was to be biographical to the extent that it—that the biography had to do with the trial itself, and of course, it had to be a personal book." Judge Brown's views would be given. "And the Judge expressed his views as to the quality of the lawyers and of course, the homicide rate in Dallas County. . . ." He understood that the book was to end with the verdict, and not go on to the appeal. "I don't think he [Stewart] urged us at all. That was a casual talk about what we were going to try to do. He didn't say this has to be done or anything like that." Stewart had never threatened them in any way. "Well, I was concerned, because if you set a date, you want to meet it. . . ."

Williamson concluded his examination of Crume with two questions which he thought went to the heart of the matter, and he appeared satisfied with the witness's answers:

Q. Did Judge Brown ever express any opinion or concern as to whether or not the Ruby case being affirmed or reversed would affect the sales of the book?

A. No sir.

Q. Has the publisher ever expressed an opinion or concern as to whether or not the case being affirmed or reversed would have any effect on the ultimate sale of the book?

A. No sir.

In redirect, Burleson tried again to get Crume to admit that there had been discussions with Judge Brown of matters pertaining to the case which had occurred subsequent to the jury verdict, the motion for a new trial, for example. There had been discussions, but not with Judge Brown. "Well, here again, we are talking about something that I haven't written yet and if I do use it, I don't see now how it could be more than a sentence or two. In other words the people are interested in Mr. Ruby and you can't just leave him hanging—so you don't know what you are going to do." He was not sure about how the sanity trial, if it occurred, would be handled.

He had seen no one from the publisher's since the previous July. He had exchanged letters or had received copies of letters.

He thought that if Judge Brown had not been the judge in the case, he might still have written a book about it, a different sort of book. He evaded efforts to pin him down with more particularity, but admitted that there would then have been no explanations of the different rulings. He finally admitted that, as judge, Brown gave the book authenticity. "From a certain point of view, yes." "Well certainly the Judge's point of view would be different than if he were in the audience."

Pressed by Burleson, Crume began to make more admissions: "I don't know, I think that probably a person who had produced this from the outside, unless he was a very established author, would not have had the interest to a publisher that Judge Brown had, about the saleability of the book and so forth, now that is something else."

He conceded that the judge discussed other attorneys involved in the case and his reasons for rulings, and he was

aware that all of this occurred before the case was actually
heard on appeal.

In the manuscript he put Judge Brown's ideas into words,
as with the thought "that the Presidential assassination
was covered by the press as no others in history were" and
"that a man could live all of his life without the kind of
publicity he was going to get" in the Ruby trial. The judge
did not like some of the publicity. "He didn't like a great
deal of it, I know. . . ."

Then, suddenly, Burleson scored, establishing a point
that we were to make good use of in all the later proceedings and in our own public relations.

Q. Did he make the statement to you that he did not believe
that Jack Ruby received exact justice?

A. Yes sir.

Q. Those are his words and not your words?

A. Substantially his words.

This exchange was followed by yet another significant
statement: "I don't think he said that he might go with the
trial. I think he said that Mr. Belli, or one other of the
defense lawyers said that if the trial were sent to another
county, he hoped he would be able to go with it. I think
that is the statement." This was said, he thought, prior to
the determination of the change of venue hearing.

At this point the court recessed for lunch and to permit
Crume to pick up the documents that he had neglected to
bring with him that morning. When the hearing resumed,
Burleson tried to get Crume to admit that Judge Brown was
the source for various provocative passages in the manuscript. There was a crucial exchange:

Q. All right, what did you mean when you said in the book,
"I want to say flatly that none of them, referring to the Citizen's
Council, even so much as breathed a suggestion to me about
how I should conduct the trial"?

A. I think the Judge here was talking about certain reports

that pressure had been brought to bear on him by members of the Citizen's Council or the establishment or whatever you want to call it, on the actual conduct of the trial and not from the public relations angle.

*Mr. Alexander:* Do you mean the seating arrangements?

A. (By the witness) Yes.

The ever-alert Alexander had got the witness to convert "the public arrangements angle" to "the seating arrangements." For the moment Burleson did not attempt to restore Crume's original statement. He asked, instead, for verification, which was forthcoming, that Judge Brown had said that Clint Murchison, Sr., was the kind of man he would like to be himself. Then he went back to Sam Bloom and the matter of public relations.

Q. Now, in reference to this Sam Bloom, did [the] Judge tell you how he got into the case or—

A. Yes.

Q. Did he say anything to the effect that he had asked Mr. Bloom in?

A. No, he didn't say that. He said another man, I believe a Mr. Watson—

Q. Charlie Watson?

A. —had come around for—yes—come for advice and he sent Mr. Bloom around.

Q. Did Judge Brown tell you that he felt like Belli and Tonahill had a subtle campaign to put Dallas on trial before the country or words to that effect?

A. Yes, but I don't think he was so specific as to Mr. Tonahill.

Q. Mainly Belli?

A. Yes.

Q. Did he tell you, that is, did Judge Brown tell you his feelings about such things as that?

A. Yes sir.

Q. That he resented it or—

A. He resented it.

*Q.* Now, I think that Judge Brown also told you that he had delegated the press seating arrangements to Sam Bloom, is that correct?

*A.* Or the agency, yes.

*Q.* The agency—and I believe that Mrs. Helen Hankins actually—

*A.* I think she did most of that, yes.

*Q.* Now, in reference to the seating arrangements, did Judge Brown tell you something to the effect that he did not know whether it was a wise idea to have them in the courtroom in mass, and that it undoubtedly had an effect upon the jury and the jurors were bound by the sheer numbers of the press to be impressed of the importance of the trial, or words to that effect?

*A.* He—

*Mr. Alexander:* We object to that your Honor. He is going into something that is not contained in the manuscript.

*The Court:* Well, the record doesn't say where it was coming from. You may answer the question. I will overrule you.

*Q.* Did he tell you words to this effect?

*A.* Well, yes, he did, as a comment or an afterthought in the discussion of this thing somewhere.

*Q.* And in this discussion, what I stated in substance was generally what he told you?

*A.* Yes, I think what he was stating, he was sort of thinking it over as well as—

*Mr. Alexander:* If I understand you right, to keep from misrepresenting the record, Judge Brown said that as a question and not as a circumstance?

*A.* I wouldn't call it a question, Mr. Alexander, but it was just sort of a question about it in his own *mind* at the time and I think he was *thinking* it over in his own mind and it came out loud.

*Q.* At any rate he did discuss that with you?

*A.* He mentioned it, yes.

*Q.* Did he discuss with you the relationship between the press and the police and their relationship to Chief Curry and the fact that he had exposed Oswald to the public so to speak and to the press up there and later the press got on Chief Curry about this and it was very critical?

A. I don't think so, in that form, No sir. I think somewhere, I believe it's in there that he mentioned that this kind of thing in an effort to please the press could influence you to do things that perhaps you wouldn't want to do.

Q. Did he say words to the effect that the power of the press is subtle and when directed against you day after day, it can almost be overpowering and almost cause you to lose your values and make you seriously consider doing things that normally you would instantly reject, or words to that effect?

A. I wrote those words in a tentative chapter, but that was his idea that he talked about.

Q. This was an idea that you got from talking to Judge Brown?

A. Yes sir.

Q. Did he discuss with you about why he finally let the television in for the televising of the jury verdict?

A. Yes.

Q. Would you tell us what the general nature of that was?

A. Well, he said as I remember it, that he had been under pressure from the television people since the beginning as early as December, I believe, and that he had consistently turned them down and that when the proposal to televise the verdict came up he could see no harm in it—that the trial would be over and that it wouldn't influence the verdict in any way, so he allowed it.

Q. Did he also state in essence that he eternally regretted that decision?

A. I think he said that this—he regretted it.

Q. I will ask you if during your conversations with Judge Brown, he at any time made a statement to the effect that from the beginning I have realized this case might backfire and ruin me politically?

A. Yes sir, he has said that.

We had been able to prove far more than the morning's

session might have indicated, because we were dealing with an essentially honorable man. In the same vein, Crume admitted that he and the judge had discussed Sergeant Patrick Dean's crucial testimony—the testimony which, in our judgment, had been more responsible than anything else for the jury's death verdict. This testimony had caused Judge Brown his one uneasy or uncomfortable moment during the trial. The judge had thought that if the alleged conversation between Sergeant Dean and Ruby had occurred within ten minutes of the shooting of Oswald it might be admissible as part of the *res gestae,* but not if the interval was forty minutes. "I remember Judge Brown saying something to the effect that he could sense a possible mis-trial—possible reversal, or the danger of one." This was followed by an equally important question and answer:

Q. And did he say words to the effect that if Belli had stopped right there he might have left him in a pickle?
A. Yes, he did.

By now the astute Alexander was quite alarmed, as well he might be. He feared that we were going through the manuscript, paragraph by paragraph, to drive home certain damaging conclusions; but we did not want to take undue chances, and the interrogation was terminated when we learned that Crume had been unable to find the most recent letter that he had received from the publishers.

Williamson's cross-examination was brief, and we were not displeased with it. He brought out what Crume meant by an authentic book: "Authentic to me means in this sense it would be the truth to the best of a man's knowledge." He did not mean "any judicial effect. . . . They are two distinct words to me. . . ." Judge Brown had never told him that the book was to be made a part of the record, so that it might have "some authoritative effect" on the Court of Criminal Appeals. "Offhand I don't know of anything that wasn't his own personal opinion," not his opinions rendered as a judge. Crume was hired, he said, "to write, as it developed, a story of the trial of Jack Ruby within the context of dealing with the local characters and so on that were a party to it." This did not include events after the verdict, but he was not sure of the extent that such events might be dealt with.

Little, if anything, was added to Crume's testimony in the redirect.

The next witness was L. B. Bailey, Jr., the official reporter in Judge Brown's courtroom. We had always had trouble with Bailey, because of his slowness in preparing transcripts of proceedings and because of his errors, which we could not always believe to be inadvertent. We did not know whether the trouble was due to Jack Ruby's status as a poor person, which required that the services be performed without cost. Sometimes we thought there were other explanations, such as editing by the judge or prosecutors. Bailey sometimes appeared a bit furtive, certainly less than forthright.

He had been employed as official reporter for Judge Brown for two years. This was a full-time job, for which he was paid by the county.

"Have you had occasion to do any work for Judge Brown in reference to the proposed book . . . ?" he was asked.

"Yes, sir," he replied. "I did some typing for the judge . . . portions of the manuscript. . . ."

He identified such portions when they were exhibited to him. Apparently, he had copied material which sometimes bore corrections or deletions in the handwriting of the judge. Often the pages had been untouched. Then he had turned all of it over to the judge. He had last done any typing on the book "within the last five months I am sure that would cover it."

"Now, were you paid extra for doing this typing?"

"I was offered payment, but I refused payment."

The pages copied by Bailey were offered in evidence. Williamson had no objection except with respect to what

he called "the privacy of the author." "We are talking about
an unpublished manuscript here," he said, "and we would
like to have it restricted to keep it from the general public."
It should be handled, he said, so as to protect the author,
Judge Brown, "and still go up as a part of the record."

Burleson suggested that it be placed in an envelope and
sealed, and Williamson thought "that will be fine." (But
this was never done, in fact. There was no practical or
judicially sanctioned method of observing the understanding.)

Bailey, still on the stand, was then shown a copy of the
amazing letter that Judge Brown had sent to Stewart, the
letter in which he had proclaimed, among other things,
his intention to deceive those who might inquire about his
book. Bailey was asked if he had typed the letter. "I believe
I did," he answered.

". . . at the request of Judge Brown?"

"Yes, sir."

He was quite sure that the letter was dictated to him by
Judge Brown, rather than transcribed from any long-hand
text.

Was his work to be kept secret?

"I assumed it was not to be discussed with the general
public, but he didn't say anything to me about it being a
big secret."

Williamson then took over the cross-examination. He
brought out that Bailey was not expected to work twenty-
four hours in the day for the county. He could "work for
other attorneys" so long as it did not interfere with court
proceedings. Judge Brown, it was brought out under Williamson's prompting, did not consider what Bailey did for
him as part of the official duties of either person; Bailey
did this special work for Judge Brown "as an individual."
He also understood that Judge Brown had a right to look
over the material typed by him and to change it if he
thought it necessary!

By agreement, the State was permitted to interrupt our presentation by calling in its behalf William J. Tribe, of New York, vice-president and corporate secretary of Holt, Rinehart and Winston. Tribe testified that he had "very little to do" with evaluating the sales potential of books, but he attempted to do just that in response to Williamson's inquiries and the cross-examination. He seemed to flip-flop in his views, not because of any too-patent desire to deceive, but because the prediction of sales in publishing is highly speculative, even for so-called experts. The book by Judge Brown that his company contemplated, he said, was "a story of the trial up to the point of the verdict . . . and the setting in Dallas, and Texas law." It was to deal with "his experiences as Judge in this trial; not as a definitive statement of the law, but written for the public." Judge Brown was to be paid royalties; the advance was to be at the publishers' risk. In his "opinion as an expert," he did not think it would make any difference in the sale of the book whether Judge Brown were reversed or affirmed on appeal.

The ponderous Williamson propounded a long question: "Now, this is in the nature of a hypothetical question. Now, the contract was made in July, and the trial had already taken place prior to that time and the case was on appeal when the contract was made, but from the salability of the book, if Judge Brown had approached you to sell his experiences, and provided Jack Ruby had been acquitted on the main trial, would the fact that he had been acquitted had any effect on the potential sale of the book by Judge Brown as compared to the fact that Jack Ruby was convicted?"

Tribe took the question in stride, with less verbosity than his interrogator:

A. I would say that the fact situation in that hypothetical case, would have made the potential profits out of the book more valuable.

Q. More what?

A. More valuable.

Q. And by that do you mean by the number of books that you see sold?

A. That is the only value we have.

The deadline for the book, Tribe said, was November 21, 1964. It was not met. The publisher had the right, seldom exercised, to the refund of the advance. The publisher had sought, vigorously but unsuccessfully, to get Judge Brown to complete his task.

The questioning went on:

Q. In evaluating a book, especially one like this one, about a trial, do you believe that the closer to the trial that the book could be published the more interest the public might have, and the more it would sell?

A. That's right.

Q. And your company has tried to expedite—

A. Yes, right.

An effort was made to find out what the sale of this, or any, book might be:

Q. And when your company publishes a book, are you catering to a sort of captive audience?

A. No.

Q. And you don't order them to buy the books from you?

A. We do not.

Q. So the number of books you ultimately sell, depends solely upon whether the public wants to buy them or not?

A. That is the only consideration.

Q. And it is purely speculative as to how many they will buy?

A. That's right.

Q. And you simply try to evaluate and guess what the public will buy.

A. That is exactly it.

And on this dubious note the direct examination ended.

It was difficult to ascertain what Williamson, or the State, had in mind in calling Mr. Tribe from New York to testify. The cross-examination proceeded. We had more definite designs upon the witness. Very quickly Sam Clinton, who took over at this point, began to draw him out.

Q. What connection, if any, do the Murchison brothers have with Holt, Rinehart and Winston, Inc.?
A. John Murchison is a member on the board of Directors.
Q. And is he of Dallas?
A. Yes sir.
Q. And he is one of the Murchison brothers?
A. He is one of the Murchison brothers.

Tribe was shown some bills from the Hotel Del Charro in La Jolla, where Judge Brown and his collaborator Paul Crume had sojourned shortly after Judge Brown had entered into a contract to write the book.

Q. What was the reason why, if you know, why the bill for Judge Brown and Mr. Crume out in California was sent to Murchison brothers in Dallas instead of your Company in New York?
A. I don't know why.
Q. You do not know why.
A. I do not know why.

Then he was shown a remittance from the publisher to Murchison Brothers, and asked: "... do you know how that happened?"
"No, I don't."
Clinton then took Tribe over the ground of Williamson's direct examination and there was less assurance on Tribe's part than earlier:

Q. Would you agree then, that Mr. Stewart [to whom Judge Brown had sent his remarkable confession of deception] is really the expert about sale appeal, authenticity and so on?

A. He would be one of the experts.

Q. At least is one of the experts—or expert enough for you to rely on his advice before you act?

A. That's right.

Q. Then when you answered counsel's questions about your opinion as to the effect of a reversal of the case, do you have an opinion as to the effect upon the book if it were reversed due to actions and rulings made by Judge Brown?

A. I would have no opinion on that.

Q. You would have an opinion?

A. No sir.

Q. Isn't it generally true in a book of this kind . . . that a significant factor in its success is public appeal and that the public appeal is greater the closer it is published to the event that is described?

A. Yes, I think that would be so.

He thought that fifteen thousand copies of the hardbound book would have to be sold to cover the $10,000 advance to Judge Brown. Was such an advance "generally considered unusually high?"

A. No, that is not unusually large at all.

Q. I take it then by that answer that is larger than normal. That is,—

A. Well—

Q. —for a trade book.

A. Yes, it is larger than normal.

He had consulted with Stewart before the latter had written to Judge Brown "the further we get from the trial, the harder it is going to be" to make sales. He did not disagree with the statement. Nor did he disagree with Stewart's admonition to Judge Brown that "the whole Ruby business is getting further and further away. . . ."

Williamson tried to rescue the situation in which Tribe's cross-examination seemed to place him:

Q. (By Mr. Williamson) All right, I will ask you if you have had any conversations there in your office with what you would call assistant experts on the question of the effect of the sale potential of this book based on a reversal or an affirmance?

A. Yes, I did.

Q. And what seemed to be the opinion?

A. That is to the effect that it would have made or will make no difference.

Q. You are not saying that the publicity given to some action by the Appellate Court will not re-create a certain interest which might effect sales?

A. No.

Q. Are you saying that?

A. No, not at all.

*Mr. Williamson:* Pass the witness.

Sam Clinton made an attempt at recross examination, and then Phil Burleson took over the examination of the so-called relator's witness, the obviously disconcerted Judge Joe B. Brown, through whom we hoped to establish the validity of the writ of habeas corpus we had filed in behalf of Jack Ruby.

Jack sat between Sol Dann and myself, deeply interested, if not always comprehending. He whispered first to one of us, then to the other. He passed notes. He still tried to make himself the center of attention, rather than the bumbling figure on the witness stand. He continued to resent our efforts to keep him in line, more silent than was his wont. Our task was not an enviable one, but it was easier than Judge Brown's. He had to explain what was largely unexplainable. The tone was quickly set.

Q. And I believe you are the elected, qualified and acting Judge of Criminal District Court No. 3 of Dallas County, Texas?

A. I am not acting today.

He had been judge of the court of which he was "not acting today" since January 1, 1957. He had been a judge for twelve or fourteen years, he thought; a justice of the peace "for a number of years before that"; in all, serving on the bench in the neighborhood of thirty years—long enough to learn wisdom, it might have been said, or simply to become confirmed in one's foibles.

Although belonging to the State Bar of Texas, and a member of its judicial section, he was not a member of the American Bar Association, the pre-eminent organization of the profession.

He confirmed that he had presided over all phases of the Jack Ruby case until recently:

Q. As a matter of fact, you were the Judge that was on the case up until a few months ago I believe when you wrote a letter asking to be excused from further duty in connection with that case?

A. Yes sir.

He confirmed the execution of a contract with Holt, Rinehart and Winston on July 21, 1964, in New York, for the writing of a book on the Ruby case under which he was to receive $10,000 in advance against royalties, modified by a subsequent agreement which involved the paying of half of the advance to Paul Crume. Returning to Dallas, Judge Brown contacted Mr. Crume and subsequently had conversations with him in his apartment and at La Jolla, at a hotel owned by the Murchisons, who also had an interest in the publishing company. The judge had known the Murchisons for some time, Clint, Sr., and his son John casually, and Clint, Jr., more closely. He had talked with the younger Clint about the purpose of his trip with Crume, and the Murchison secretary had made the reservations. What was the exact purpose of the trip with Crume? "Oh, to be with each other as much as possible so that he could get an idea of my style of speech, my phraseology and my way of thinking—"

No notes were taken, nothing was furnished by him except a portion of the record of the Ruby trial. He took it with him to La Jolla and back and they examined portions of it "very casually."

*Q.* Did you at any other time after that, furnish Mr. Crume with notes, documents or other Statements of Fact?

*A.* No sir.

*Q.* Have you read any of the work that Mr. Crume has done?

*A.* I have read a portion of it, yes.

*Q.* Has any of the work been sent into the publisher?

*A.* Yes, there was a portion of it sent.

*Q.* Has that portion that has been sent in been approved as to form and substance?

*A.* No sir, it is in its roughest notes—the first drafting.

*Q.* The first drafting?

*A.* Yes sir.

*Q.* Speaking of the way Mr. Crume gave it to you or the way it was after you had it typed?

*A.* The way it was after I had it typed.

*Q.* Approximately how many pages has already been sent to the publishers?

*A.* Mr. Burleson, I couldn't tell you. I imagine around 80 or 90, or maybe 95 pages. I just don't know.

No, he had not read Melvin Belli's book, *Dallas Justice*, nor any part of it, only a brief review of it in the Dallas *Times Herald*. His attention called to the manuscript of his book, produced by court order, he was asked if he had read everything in it. "Very lightly, yes," he replied. "Very lightly?" Burleson pursued. "Yes, sir," he agreed.

*Q.* Now, just exactly what were you going to do in connection with the writing of this book or the fulfillment of the contract that you entered into with Holt, Rinehart and Winston? What were your duties?

*A.* Well, I don't know what duties I had, Mr. Burleson.

*Q.* Well, I assume you read the contract before you signed it?

*A.* Yes sir.

*Mr. Alexander:* That contract is in evidence and it speaks for itself. He can't alter or vary the terms of a written contract. It is therefore the best evidence and speaks for itself. We object on that ground.

*The Court:* Overruled.

*Q.* Were you going to write a book?

*A.* Paul Crume was going to write it. I was going to edit and rewrite portions and revise what I thought needed revision and submit it to the publisher.

Mr. Edwards, the president of the Holt firm, had contacted him in the first instance. Before that, Judge Brown had talked with Clint Murchison, Jr. "Well if I remember correctly, I called Clint, Jr., and told him that I had been reading some stuff that had been read—or printed about the Ruby case that was so grossly exaggerated that—and out of context that I thought that somebody ought to write a book and tell the truth about the Ruby case. . . . And I said 'Do you know of a publishing company?' He said, 'Yeah, Joe, I think I own one, but I can't tell you the name of it right now.' He said, 'I'll have my secretary look it up and call you right back.' A few minutes the secretary called me and said 'Holt, Rinehart and Winston, Inc., 383 Madison Avenue, New York.' Clint said are you pretty serious about writing the book and I said yes and he said that he would contact him and see if he could help and I said that I would appreciate it and I had heard that they were very good publishers and he said, 'I will let you hear from me.' And I think the next thing that happened was a day or two later his secretary contacted me and told me that he had talked to Mr. Edwards and they would like an appointment with me within the next week and I believe if I am not mistaken I was on vacation at that time and was at home and Mr. Edwards came to see me in my office some Tuesday morning, I don't remember the date. So I came down to my office and Mr. Edwards came down and we discussed it. . . ." Yes, the Judge repeated, he had been thinking about writing a book.

"Yes sir, actually, I received about five bushels of mail Mr. Burleson, preceding, during, and after the trial.

"I see—"

"None of which I opened."

Burleson asked about a couple of articles that had appeared in *Life* and the *Saturday Evening Post* at the time of the trial; they had been referred to in the manuscript. "I probably mentioned them to Paul, then." Pressed by Burleson, he said: "I don't know if they had any direct or positive bearing on me writing a book."

*Q.* Was it an accumulation of many things?

*A.* Yes.

*Q.* And something you had thought about and given serious thought to?

*A.* Yes sir, I gave serious thought to it.

*Q.* And then it wasn't something you just on the spur of the moment decided to do?

*A.* I decided to write a book on the spur of the moment.

He did not explain how the matter could have been one of "serious thought" and yet undertaken "on the spur of the moment."

He had first talked with Murchison while he was still living with his sister. (She had testified that this was from about September 1, 1963 to about March or April of 1964.) He had not talked to her ("No, sir, I don't believe I mentioned it to her at all") or to anyone else about the book, despite Mrs. Paul's being a good book reviewer. He repeated that it was a sudden decision on his part; the thought of writing a book about the case had not entered his mind earlier than the few days before he had talked with Murchison. Burleson tried to drive the point home, to the discomfiture of opposing counsel.

*Mr. Williamson:* It sounds like we are on a broken record here, and—

*The Court:* Overruled.

*Mr. Alexander:* Let's move along.

When Judge Brown had talked with Mr. Edwards about the book, "They told me to write a list of five authors that I would like to have, and I gave them a list and Mr.

Crume's name was on it." Crume's name was second on the list, but the judge had not talked with him or with the others. His first choice had been Jim Bishop, who had written *A Day with Kennedy* and *The Last Days of Lincoln;* but Bishop was not available.

Q. Would you tell the Court and myself why it was that you felt like you wanted to write a book?

*Mr. Alexander:* To which we object.

*The Court:* Sustained.

Q. Judge, you feel like you had been hurt politically by the written words in the magazine articles or the books or comments or anything of that nature after the end of the Ruby case?

A. No sir; not politically, no sir.

The judge tried to evade questions about whether he had discussed this with Crume. Burleson turned to another line of inquiry.

Q. Let's get into the mechanics of the writing of the book then. How is the book being written?

A. What do you mean?

Q. Are you writing anything yourself?

A. I am waiting for Paul to get through. We are going to put it all together and then go back and rewrite the whole thing again. I am going to go through and edit and revise the book in places that I think ought to be revised and make whatever changes I deem necessary or think advisable in the book.

Q. You are not doing any original writing yourself?

A. I haven't so far, no sir.

He would do more writing later, he thought. As Crume gave pages of the manuscript to him, he would turn them over to Bailey, his official court reporter, to be typed after he had corrected a few "obvious errors." "It is nowhere near completion, Mr. Burleson. . . . I have read it over. I haven't read all of it over."

Listening to the judge as he made these contradictory statements, I felt a little sorry for him despite the harm he had done to our client. When, later, I expressed this thought to another judge, he said to me, "Don't feel sorry for Judge Brown; he has done a terrible thing."

Judge Brown was shown copies of the letters from his publishers in which he was implored to speed up the completion of the book, lest the sales suffer. Yet he persisted in testifying that he and Stewart had never talked about getting the book published in a hurry or about time being of the essence.

Before he wrote the famous letter of March 12, 1965, the Court of Criminal Appeals had remanded the Ruby case to him for a hearing on Jack's sanity, and he had turned down peremptorily, on March 8, the several motions we had filed with him, including one to disqualify him on the ground that he had a pecuniary interest in the case. Now the judge said, "I was not conscious of it at the time I overruled your Motions."

Burleson pretended he had not heard the judge: "I'm sorry, I don't quite follow you."

Judge Brown repeated: "I wasn't conscious that the Motion had been overruled when I wrote that letter."

Now the judge was tormented with questions about what he had said in that greatly to be regretted letter:

Q. And had you begun to write a book at that time.

A. I expect Paul had.

Q. The question sir, is had you started writing a book at that time?

A. No sir.

Q. You had not?

A. No. I haven't begun yet to write a book.

Q. I am directing your attention now to the very first sentence. You state "we are coming along nicely." Whom did you mean by that?

A. Paul and I.

Q. What were you coming along nicely on?

A. Writing a book, but Mr. Crume is doing the writing, I am not.

Q. And the next sentence—

*A.* —in other words, I can say we're coming along nicely, however I had not written any book or written any part of a book at that time.

*Q.* "—we have about 190 pages of it complete." Are you talking about you and Paul Crume again?

*A.* No, Mr. Crume did it. Paul and I hadn't even seen it at that time.

*Q.* You hadn't even seen it at that time?

*A.* I don't think I had.

Judge Brown wove in and out as he met question after question. He was not the only one who was becoming dizzy. We tried again to drive our point home:

*Q.* Now, Judge, did you consider yourself to be the author under this contract and agreement?

*Mr. Alexander:* To which we object, the contract speaks for itself.

*The Court:* Overruled.

*A.* In the sense, Mr. Burleson, that someone has what is known as a ghost writer.

*Q.* And Mr. Crume was going to be your ghost writer?

*A.* Yes sir.

Here the court adjourned to the next morning. Again, as ever, Jack Ruby was eager to become the star of the show. The press was willing to oblige him, for he always had something whimsical or dramatic or otherwise publishable to say. When we asked Judge Holland to restrain the representatives of the communications media from taking over to the prejudice of our client, he assured us that Ruby, in his obviously sick manner, was helping himself and that the press would depict him in a light that was bound to help rather than harm him. Sol Dann and I politely dissented, and the judge reluctantly told the press that they could not talk with Ruby without our approval. Jack was taken back to his cell. Elated by what had happened, we planned for the next day's session.

When the hearing resumed, Judge Brown was asked what he had done to fulfill his contract.

A. I expect that I have done practically nothing, Mr. Burleson.

Q. When you say "practically nothing," have you done anything?

A. Oh, I have scanned the manuscript and made a few corrections.

Q. Have you done anything else?

A. No sir, not that I know of or can think of at this time.

The trip to La Jolla had nothing to do with the contract, he said; then he corrected himself: "I suppose you could say yes, in a sense, it did."

He and Crume got together "rather infrequently," "from probably the first of July or so, up until about three weeks ago." The sessions would last about "15 or 20 minutes . . . maybe 30 minutes." "There was a long period of time in there that I didn't see Paul. We would talk on the telephone briefly. I would ask him how he was getting along and so on." Then the meetings began to stretch to about two hours; "maybe we would go a month or six weeks and not even contact each other."

Burleson wanted to know what Judge Brown did when he "scanned over" Crume's work. "You know what scanning over means, Mr. Burleson, you are an attorney," said our "author," rather sharply. "Well, Judge, I know what it means to me," Burleson responded. "Well, it means the same thing to me," Judge Brown insisted.

No, he had not given Crume "some notes and clippings in a box," only some borrowed parts of the record of the case. He thought he had borrowed parts of the record from Bill Alexander and even from the unwitting Burleson. He was asked about the court reporters' copyrighting of the record of the trial. "When they did it, it was unbeknownst to me. I was very displeased when I was informed of it."

*Q.* Now, have you had any recent correspondence from anybody that has anything to do at all with the writing of the book or with your position as author of the book?

*A.* None other than I got a letter from Mr. Belli yesterday morning.

*Q.* Did that have to do with anything about the book?

*A.* He made a comment about it.

*Q.* He made a comment about it?

*Mr. Alexander:* Was he ugly, Judge?

*Mr. Burleson:* We object to him continually commenting and coming in and asking questions.

*Mr. Alexander:* I am very sorry.

*Mr. Burleson:* He did it yesterday several times.

*Mr. Alexander:* Please forgive me, will you?

It was Bill Alexander's tendency to take over when he felt his colleagues were faltering, and Williamson often seemed to be less hard-hitting than his tougher associate. Generally, we at the counsel table were publicly philosophical about Alexander's savage forays, but we privately resented him as the prime cause of the death sentence. Judge Brown was not looked upon with the same anger, although he had presided in a way that was dubious at best, and his pecuniary interest in the case had brought about the present proceeding. It was necessary now to be even less delicate in our handling of him.

*Q.* Now, at any time after the signing of this contract back in July of 1964, did you deny that you were writing a book?

*A.* I probably did, yes.

*Q.* As a matter of fact, did you deny to me that you were writing a book?

*A.* I probably did Mr. Burleson, I was denying it to most everybody.

*Q.* Why?

*A.* There were a lot of stories going around. I heard that Henry Wade was writing a book and that you were writing a book and—

*Q.* What, you heard what?

*A.* I heard Mr. Wade was writing a book and you were writing a book and Mr. Belli was writing a book.

Burleson went on, heedless that he might thereafter have to try cases in Judge Brown's courtroom.

*Q.* Why were you keeping it quiet or trying to keep it quiet?

*A.* So that I wouldn't have to discuss it.

*Q.* Discuss it with whom?

*A.* Anybody who asked.

*Q.* Did you discuss with Mr. Crume that you should keep it a secret?

*A.* Yes sir.

Judge Brown protested, again, that he was shunning publicity and had always done so in connection with the Ruby case.

*Q.* Well, do you think by authoring a book that talked about Ruby and showed you as being the presiding Judge that you were escaping and shunning publicity?

*Mr. Alexander:* This is argumentative.

*The Court:* Overruled.

He was asked about participating in a book while the case was still pending in his court and on appeal and might be going to the United States Supreme Court. Judge Brown struck back, charging that Burleson had been seen on television signing the statement of facts. Burleson questioned this, and Bill Alexander intruded again. "It was a great ceremony wasn't it Judge?" Burleson responded sharply: "I object to Mr. Alexander sitting over here testifying." The exchange continued to enliven the courtroom:

*Mr. Alexander:* I was only refreshing his memory.

*Mr. Burleson:* I would ask the Court to instruct Mr. Alexander not to refresh his memory.

*Mr. Alexander:* No, not his memory, your memory. I remember you being on T.V., Phil.

*Mr. Burleson:* Would the Court instruct Mr. Alexander not to make any side-bar remarks?

*The Court:* You gentlemen, all of you, are instructed not to make any side-bar remarks.

It was difficult to pin the judge down to the implications of various passages in the manuscript that were pointed out to him. On the one hand, he persisted that he had read it only briefly, that it was "the very roughest of drafts"; on the other hand, he insisted that he was "not ashamed of anything I did," or of anything in the book.

A. I wouldn't deny anything in the book, Mr. Burleson.

Q. How about Mr. Crume, will you accept the responsibility for him?

A. I will accept the responsibility for everything written.

Q. Is it then safe to say you agree with all of it?

A. That which I don't think is correct will be taken out and that which I do think is correct will be added.

Q. All right sir, we will have to go through it page by page then.

A. I don't mind at all.

By now the State was as much concerned with his discomfiture as was Judge Brown himself. Williamson again explained his viewpoint:

Your Honor, I will take it upon myself to again state the State's position in this matter, and that is: We see the disqualification of the Judge on pecuniary interests depends on whether he had a financial interest in some way in deciding some issue before him to the Judge's financial interest. We think these things do not show any financial interest in the sense of the Judge ruling. What he may say after the trial—we just wish the record to show that the State is not contesting a full hearing, but still, I believe these matters are wholly immaterial to the interest of the pecuniary interest.

*Mr. Burleson:* It ties in with other statements in the book in support of our position that this may have been in the Judge's mind either consciously or unconsciously back to or during part of the trial.

*The Court:* I will overrule the objection.

Judge Brown resumed his explanation: "Mr. Burleson, please remember that I didn't write any of this. These are all Mr. Crume's conclusions that are written."

Questioned further, he went on: "I think I can simplify it, Mr. Burleson, I will accept the responsibility for the things that are written in there, even though I didn't write them. They are not my conclusions, they are Mr. Crume's, but since it is my book, and as the book stands right now, far from being finished, I don't know whether that will be in there or not."

And having manfully accepted the responsibility, he quickly dropped it. Clearly, an author and his ghost do not always observe things in the same spirit.

While the Brown manuscript had been received in evidence and could be read by the court, we felt that it was important to underscore what was in it, lest the court and the press miss it. Judge Holland seemed to agree with us. Over the continuing protest of the State, he permitted us to attempt to wring from his predecessor the implications of what was said in his name in the manuscript. These passages showed, at the very least, that Judge Brown might have been affected or even prejudiced in his rulings and toward the defense during the course of the trial and its aftermath. It was legitimate to inquire if the thought of writing a book, the actual writing of it, the passages we pointed out, proved that there was a disqualifying pecuniary interest on his part. It was not simply an interest in who would win or lose in the ultimate sense. Judge Holland was more sophisticated about the matter than the representatives of the State professed to be. This was illustrated in an exchange between the witness and counsel:

Q. Did you tell Mr. Crume of words to the effect, that a lot of abuse was directed toward you?

A. Yes sir, I probably did.

*Mr. Williamson:* We can't see how anything of this nature can go to the pecuniary interest of the Judge Brown—what his feelings were, his general attitude—what does this tie in with.

*Mr. Burleson:* If you will just wait, Judge Williamson, I will try to get there. But I have to ask some questions before I can do that.

*The Court:* I will overrule your objection.

Judge Brown declared that he read and saw nothing during the course of the Ruby trial: "I didn't even look at your and Mr. Belli's television interview." This led to a revealing exchange between Burleson and Judge Brown, terminated by Judge Holland:

Q. Judge, are you bitter at me for bringing this action?

A. No, I'm disappointed, Mr. Burleson, not bitter.

Q. Do you feel like it is frivolous—that this Motion to disqualify is frivolous?

A. No sir, I don't think frivolous is the word.

Q. Do you think it may have some merit?

A. No sir, I don't think it has any merit at all.

Q. This is highly argumentative but I don't appreciate you making digs at me.

A. You were making digs at me, too.

*The Court:* Gentlemen, this is not the place to show your personal feelings toward each other. I am here to conduct a Hearing, and that's what I am going to do.

Burleson again tried to get Judge Brown to admit that he was motivated by his disapproval of various magazine articles that appeared at the time of the trial, but the latter still declared that he read, saw and listened to nothing while the trial was going on—notwithstanding that huge quantities of such material had been received in evidence during the hearing on the Ruby motion for a change of venue. The defense had wanted to show thereby the prejudiced atmosphere in the community. This, apparently, was far from Judge Brown's mind as he now faced his interrogator. Finally, Burleson wrung some admissions from the unwilling witness:

Q. Did you tell Mr. Crume and discuss with him to the effect that Mr. Belli attempted to put Dallas on trial before the nation's press and before the nation's people, or words to that effect?
A. I don't know whether I did or not.
Q. Could you have?
A. I could have maybe, I don't know.
Q. Did you feel that way?
A. More or less, yes.

After many sallies in this direction and that, Burleson tried to pin Judge Brown down as to the arrangements that had been made for him by Sam Bloom of the Dallas Citizens' Council. Williamson objected that this was already before the Texas Court of Criminal Appeals. Judge Holland overruled the objection, saying that he had no way of knowing what was before any reviewing court. Alexander again tried to get Williamson out of the morass:

*Mr. Alexander:* We are willing to stipulate that Mr. Bloom handled the seating arrangements.
*Burleson:* We are not willing to take that stipulation.
Q. What did Mr. Bloom do?
A. Mr. Bloom himself did nothing.
Q. What did Mr. Bloom's employees do?
A. They handled the seating arrangements and the press.
Q. Just what Mr. Alexander said?
A. Yes, exactly.
Q. Nothing else?
A. That's all.

Judge Brown apparently missed the irony of Burleson's summing up of what Bill Alexander had said. By now, he was very eager to disown almost everything written in his name by Paul Crume, although he had not altered the passages in the manuscript, nor had he advised his publishers that he objected to anything in the very manuscript that had been sent by him to them. Apparently, he was learning, for the first time, that authorship, even with the assistance of an experienced ghost writer, could be very difficult, with consequences beyond one's imagining, especially when questioned by a relentless defense counsel who aspired to set aside what he regarded as an unjust result. Authorship was more than the receiving of advance payments on account of royalty, more than sojourning at a Murchison resort in La Jolla.

When Burleson turned again to the letter of March 12, 1965, Judge Brown could not rely upon disclaimers or pass the responsibility to Paul Crume.

Q. And did you express an opinion in that letter as to the sanity or insanity of Jack Ruby?

A. Yes sir, it was an erroneous opinion, but it is in there nevertheless.

Q. What did you mean by erroneous opinion?

A. I mean that I had no opinion up until the time I wrote the letter.

He was asked: "What did you mean when you said that you were going to have to have a sanity hearing, what was going to keep the case far from being over?"

"Well, I don't know what I meant by the thing, Mr. Burleson."

He was reminded once more that he had overruled our motions on March 8, 1965, without a hearing.

His bias was brought home to the court, if not to Judge Brown, by some blunt questioning:

Q. Prior to this hearing had you let the District Attorney or any of the assistants see a copy of your book?

A. Yes sir.

Q. And prior to the time that I filed this Order to produce the book, had I requested the same opportunity?

A. Yes sir, I believe you did.

*Q.* And did you allow me to do that on behalf of the petitioner?

*A.* No sir.

Burleson asked: "When is the last time that you did any work on the book?" To which Judge Brown answered: "I believe I went through it last week or ten days and numbered the pages, Mr. Burleson. . . ." No inquiry was made as to how exhausting this task of numbering pages might have been; but it appeared that either something was wrong with the numbering or more was done than was produced in court.

He was asked if he had ever said that the book was completed, and he denied this vehemently. He was asked if he had made the remark when interviewed by a radio interviewer, just a month previously, when our motions to disqualify him were being heard by Judge Holland. Again he denied it. He was confronted after a recess with the name of the radio interviewer and the exact quotation: "We are coming along fine, I am just about finished." He now admitted that he "probably did" make the statement.

*Q.* Was it a true statement at that time?

*A.* No.

*Q.* It is not?

*A.* It is a flat-out lie, Mr. Burleson, if that is the way you want to construe it.

He, seconded by Alexander, insisted upon the return of this manuscript, but was assured that the original would be returned to him after it was copied and the copy sealed for the record. He said he would not have produced the manuscript if he had known this—"not that I want to hide anything. . . ."

The next question stung him: "Now, have you ever written anything previously for publication?"

*A.* I refuse to answer that question.

*Q.* On what grounds?

A. It is immaterial whether I have written anything for publication or not.

Q. Your Honor, am I entitled to an answer?

*The Court:* Judge, I don't think it is up to you to pass upon the immateriality or materiality of the question, you may answer the question.

A. No sir.

Q. Has anything you have ever written [been] published?

*The Court:* You may answer.

A. I know I may, but do I have to? No sir. Am I not allowed some protection from the Court?

*The Court:* You will get protection, Judge, you answer the question.

No, he had written nothing.

Judge Brown must have felt that his ordeal was over as Williamson took over the questioning in behalf of the State. Although labeled as cross-examination, what followed was essentially an effort to rehabilitate Judge Brown in order to preserve the death verdict against Ruby. If we prevailed in this proceeding, it should be remembered, that verdict would necessarily be set aside and a new trial of the murder charge would have to take place. Williamson began his examination rather ponderously, as if he were trying to decide what to do:

Q. Judge Brown, I wish to direct your attention to the development of facts that I intend to prove or which are material or which forms the basis of a decision of the question as to whether in the main case of the State of Texas vs. Jack Ruby, at the time you performed any official act therein, if you had pecuniary interest in reaching a conclusion against Jack Ruby—

*Mr. Clinton:* Excuse me Judge, I submit that this is a legal question, asking the witness—

*Mr. Williamson:* I am directing his attention to these facts. That isn't a question.

Q. Previously now, in connection with this, so we would understand each other and the record will show the term used, I am asking and referring to pecuniary interests as a monetary interest not necessarily in money itself—in some property which can be estimated for value in money as a pecuniary interest. Do you understand that?

A. Yes sir.

Williamson then went on to explain that he was trying to show that Judge Brown had not formed the intent to write the book at any time prior to the verdict and that thereafter he did not have a financial stake in the outcome and that, in any event, nothing of great seriousness occurred in the post-verdict proceedings. The interpretation of what constituted disqualifying "pecuniary interest" offered by the State was a very primitive one, it should be repeated; there was no pecuniary interest, according to the State, unless Judge Brown would make money in accordance with the result of the case. Some such concept might have been acceptable in a civil case, we thought, but not in a criminal case, one in which a human life hung in the balance. Williamson took up each item listed on the docket of the case and had Judge Brown aver that what he did was not the result of any contract for the writing of his book. This was best illustrated by one phase of the examination, characteristic of the rest:

Q. Now, your contract with the publisher speaks for itself as to the terms and the compensation, as to whether they were to be contingent or not or direct. Now, was that contract supplemented to make your compensation directly contingent on your performing a judicial act so that your conclusions of how you acted would be detrimental to Jack Ruby?

A. I don't think so.

Q. Do you think so, or do you know so, this is very important. Did the publisher ever pay you anything—

A. No sir.

Q. —if you would do—

A. No sir.

Q. And did the contract depend on any act one way or the other in this matter?

A. No sir.

Sometimes Williamson's questions miscarried, as when it was evident that in considering the bills of exceptions, filed by the defense, after he and the publisher had entered into their arrangement, Judge Brown took a good deal of time in considering the matter, giving thought to the pros and cons, before denying the bills. Williamson then tried to lessen the harm that had been done:

Q. Now, did the time you spent with Paul Crume have any effect on your considering the Bills of Exception?

A. No sir.

Q. Did you feel that you had to get something done to the book in a hurry?

A. I had no haste at all.

Q. You didn't meet your deadline, at least you weren't in that much of a hurry.

A. I still haven't met it.

The matter would not be straightened out, because it could not be. Judge Brown confounded Williamson by declaring, despite Williamson's guidance: "Probably the quicker the book could have been published the more sales could have occurred." So that the necessity for speed must have been in his mind, no matter how he tried to forget it and even assuming he tried to act with complete judicial decorum and in good faith. Thus Judge Brown and Williamson tried to explain away the hasty overruling, without a hearing, of our now celebrated motions on March 8, 1965:

Q. Now, on that morning there were certain Motions, among them the motion to disqualify you?

A. Yes.

Q. Now, what did you do when those Motions were filed, you said you wanted to go ahead first and determine whether the defendant wanted an insanity hearing or not in substance?

A. They requested their Motions be acted on.

Q. They requested their Motions be acted on first, is that correct?

A. Yes.

Q. Did you overrule them?

A. Yes, I overruled them.

Q. Based on what, without a hearing?

A. Well, they were filed at an improper time.

Q. All right, and you felt that the time for acting on them wasn't at that time?

A. Yes.

Q. Did you have in your mind any prejudice about them reurging them at a proper time?

A. They could have been reurged at any time.

Q. Now, did your writing of this book effect in any way your overruling these Motions?

A. No, none whatsoever.

The State now tried to show, through the questioning of Judge Brown, that the writing of the book "was not a judicial act," but was "an act of an individual relating some certain experiences when you had sat as a Judge." This was perilously close to the proverbial distinction without a difference, and it became more so as the judge answered the questions put to him:

Q. Now, was the compensation in your mind to be paid to you by the publisher to be paid to you solely because you were the Judge who had sat in the Ruby trial?

A. No.

Q. Was it because you were going to write a book?

A. Yes.

Judge Brown said that he was not going to make the book a part of the record in the appeal pending on the death sentence. He opined that the book could not affect or influence the Court of Criminal Appeals in making their decision on the appeal, and it was not calculated to do that. The book was being written primarily for laymen. Having said this, Judge Brown became impatient of Williamson's efforts to get him to expound further:

*Q.* In the writing of your book, did you have in mind something like this: to kind of indicate your reasons for certain of your actions in the Ruby case and to show that you did not disregard—had not disregarded or overlooked serious arguments of counsel—

*A.* Counsel, the book is for laymen.

*Q.* Let me get it all out first, Judge.

*A.* Well, you make them so lengthy that I forget them.

*Q.* Let me get it all out first— Was it to show your full understanding of the case and to avoid the suspicion of arbitrary conclusions? To promote confidence in your intellectual integrity and maybe to contribute useful precedents to the growth of the law? Is that kind of what you had in mind?

*A.* Not particularly, no sir.

*Q.* I was basing it on the American Bar Association. They say it is all right if you want to do it.

*Mr. Burleson:* Are you testifying?

*Mr. Williamson:* No, I am just state— I only state that for the record.

*Q.* After you denied those Bills of Exception, do you know of anybody that was legally liable to pay you more money if you had approved them?

*A.* No sir.

*Q.* And do you know of anybody that would pay you or were you entitled to any more money from anyone if the case is reversed or affirmed.

*A.* No sir.

*Q.* Is there any Order of any kind that you have entered in the Jack Ruby main case or any other part of the thing commanding anyone to buy your book?

*A.* No sir.


And on this note Williamson's examination ended; but Judge Brown was not through. We availed ourselves of our right to redirect examination, again through Burleson. We thought we had only "one or two short questions," but Judge Brown's responses invited fuller questioning. It will be remembered that Judge Brown had considered certain bills of exception following the signing of his contract with the publisher. This was promising from our viewpoint, and Burleson pursued the matter skillfully:

Q. Now, in this seven and a half or eight hours that you spent qualifying and refusing the 15 formal Bills of Exception, did you exercise your judicial discretion in making those ultimate decisions on those 15 Bills?

A. I did.

Q. And that was of a judicial nature?

A. Yes.

Q. And that was after you had already entered the contract and to receive the money and actually had received $5,000 cash?

A. I believe so, Mr. Burleson, yes.

Burleson then brought out other judicial acts performed by Judge Brown while he was, in our opinion, disqualified by reason of a pecuniary interest:

Q. Also, after obtaining some of the money and signing of the contract, did you not approve the minutes of your Court?

A. Yes, at the end of the term, I probably did, Mr. Burleson.

Q. And is that a judicial act, when you do that?

A. I think it is an administrative act, Mr. Burleson.

Q. At sometime after you got the idea to write the book, in the latter part of June you would have approved them then, would you not have?

A. Yes.

Q. Now, the Judgement entered in the Ruby case and the overruling of the amended Motion for New Trial were approved after you got the idea to write the book?

A. Well, it could and it could not. I know I signed the minutes on the last day of the term.

Judge Brown was finally through. His public exposure was at an end. At the moment, I was again torn between a sense of pity and a feeling of disgust; the latter strengthened when we introduced into evidence, without objection, the Judicial Canons of Ethics of the American Bar Association and the Texas Bar as well.

Other than the testimony of William J. Tribe, an officer of the Holt firm, with which it had interrupted the giving of our testimony, the State presented only a stipulation, to which we readily agreed, that if Judge W. A. Morrison, of the Texas Court of Criminal Appeals, were called as a witness (which was altogether unlikely), he would testify that he and George P. Blackburn wrote *Wilson's Texas Criminal Forms Annotated*, 6th Edition, commissioned by Vernon Law Book Company, and that he received a royalty of 6½ per cent on the sales of the $25 volume, that no law library in Texas is complete without it, and that criminal lawyers purchase it. At first, in offering the stipulation, Bill Alexander described the book as "this literary work," but he dropped the inapplicable phrase when we objected.

The State's purpose, obviously, was to persuade either Judge Holland or the Texas Court of Criminal Appeals that since one of its members was the "author" of a law book in collaboration, Judge Brown should not be criticized for writing his kind of book—a book totally different in contents and context. We hardly thought either Judge Holland or the reviewing court would be impressed by the analogy.

Judge Holland was in a mood to move along. No sooner was the hearing of the evidence concluded than the arguments of counsel began. Phil Burleson led off for our side, effectively. We had discussed the argument thoroughly, and had agreed upon those matters of evidence and law that ought to be stressed. We felt that our briefs, already filed, covered the law completely; it was the significant points of the evidence that had to be made clear to the court, if it had not already grasped them. We felt certain that little, if anything, escaped Judge Holland, ever attentive, intelligent, and self-assured.

There were matters, Burleson said, that we had not covered in our briefs because we had not known of them until the hearings. He stressed Judge Brown's letter to Administrative Judge Blankenship in which he had "recused" himself. Recuse meant, Burleson pointed out, "to reject, as disqualified to act." Judge Brown finally recognized this. Where he had found the word we did not know; but it was apt, it carried the right meaning.

Burleson then went on to the contract of July 21, 1964, between Judge Brown and Holt, Rinehart and Winston, as a result of which he had received $5000 on account. This gave him a pecuniary, or monetary, interest in the case, we contended. He utilized his position as judge for the purposes of the book; this was reflected in the proposed dust jacket, the manuscript, the testimony of Paul Crume. Above all, the letter Judge Brown had sent to managing editor Stewart reflected how he was using his judicial position for the purposes of the book: in it he had declared emphatically that he was not going to disqualify himself, and he was going to produce a "much, much better book" because of the sanity hearing and other pending matters. He had had the writing of the book in mind for a long while before the signing of the contract, Burleson argued; the negotiations occurred as far back as "the spring of 1964." What is the definition of spring? In North America it comprises March, April, and May—the very time of the trial and first post-trial proceedings. (This I had stressed in the discussions among counsel, and Burleson made the most of it in court.) He showed, once again, how Judge Brown's pecuniary interest was reflected in his shooing us hurriedly out of court, like village bums, when we presented our four motions—to disqualify him, for a change of venue, for the selection of counsel of Ruby's choice, and for a reasonable continuance of the pretrial conference and sanity hearing. He demonstrated that Judge Brown's "explanation," by affidavit and otherwise, of why he ruled as he did simply did not convince. He was in an excessive hurry because of the book. That was why he had refused every one of the fifteen formal bills of exception in connection with the appeal of the death sentence.

Burleson referred to the Canons of Judicial Ethics of

both the Texas State Bar and the American Bar Associations. If Judge Brown was disqualified, he said, then all his
judicial acts were void and not simply voidable. "Judge
Brown did not recognize that he was disqualified or that he
had any malice. I don't think he is that type of person. . . ."
But a judge may be disqualified whether or not he recog-
nizes that he is, and Judge Brown's disqualification rendered the entire judgment of conviction void.

Williamson responded for the State. His argument was
simply expressed:

If the Court please, I will argue the easy points and leave the
hard ones up to the Court.

The first easy point I would like to take up is that when Judge
Brown recused himself he didn't disqualify himself.

A Judge is disqualified, depending on the circumstances and
the law as to whether the Judge is disqualified or whether he
thinks he is disqualified. We have cases where a Judge has been
made to sit, and it is his duty to sit, unless he is in fact,
disqualified.

Now, the only person that I could see that had any pecuniary
interest in the outcome of this is Paul Crume, who testified here
before the Court. Now, there has been testimony concerning
the fact that regardless of what Judge Brown did or didn't do
wouldn't affect the amount of money he would get in writing
about a trial that had already happened and it wasn't contingent on what had or had not happened.

There was testimony to the effect that regardless of any
judicial acts of his, it wouldn't have any effect on the sale or
the amount of money involved as an advance. It was not contingent on this at all.

To us it was appalling that Williamson really believed
these things. They would reduce the matter of due process
and fair trial to an empty formula: Were you paid for the
ultimate result? This would mean that one might be saturated with prejudice and yet be qualified in a legal sense.
As Williamson phrased it:

A book about a case where a man shot another man in view of five million people, the public would take it as routine that he was very quickly convicted of doing an act of that kind. That is the testimony. That is obvious in Judge Brown's testimony.

We had expected Judge Holland to take his ruling under advisement (that is, to consider it for a time), as lawyers say; he would have been justified in this course by the importance of the issues and the far-reaching effect of his decision. But he was eager to dispose of the case. Without hesitation, he announced the result at the conclusion of the arguments.

Under the law and the evidence in this case, it is my opinion that it would be fair and just to both the defendant [and] to the State, for this Court to Certify this record to the Court of Criminal Appeals to be for their review and for their consideration. And, in connection with it—the other record in the case which they have before them. [This was a reference to the appeal from the death sentence.]

It is my opinion that in fairness, this court can do no more, and should do no less. This action is taken so as to not disturb the present status of the defendant in this case, and this action is taken—is not to be taken as condemning and certainly not condoning the acts or conduct on the part of Judge Brown in writing this book.

This matter is squarely now before the Court of Criminal Appeals to be considered by it, in connection with the other record in this case.

This is my judgment, gentlemen: you may prepare your Order accordingly.

All the way back to Chicago, Dann and I discussed the hearing. We were pleased as never before. The more I thought about the result, the more pleased I was.

Strange to say, we were in some respects better off with the order contemplated by Judge Holland than with a complete victory. In the latter event, the case would have gone back to the Dallas court for retrial, presumably before Judge Holland. Of course, we were enthusiastic about Judge Holland, but we still could not be sure of Dallas. The same prejudice might exist. Then if we asked for a change of venue from Dallas County, we might lose Judge Holland and get an inferior presiding officer, another sort of Judge Brown. There was a dilemma.

Nevertheless, had we won completely, we would have rejoiced and forgotten, for the moment, the ensuing risks. And in due course, we would appeal Judge Holland's order. For one thing was clear: an ultimate victory on the habeas corpus proceeding would throw out the death verdict and, at worst, we would begin the defense of Ruby without some of the handicaps that confronted Belli and his associates.

Here, as always, in every legal maneuver, there were plus and minus factors. One can seldom be absolutely certain that a particular result is good in all respects.

Now before us were a series of actions to which some thought had to be given. In addition to the appeal of the habeas corpus order, there remained the sanity hearing and, obviously, continuing discussions with Henry Wade on a settlement. It seemed that the sanity hearing should not proceed, but should not be dropped. In either case, the Court of Criminal Appeals might give us little choice in the matter and insist that we go ahead with it before hearing either the original appeal or the habeas corpus appeal.

As we were deliberating our course of action, Judge Holland, on September 21, 1965, formally entered his order. It was shrewdly calculated to give us the elation of victory though cast in the form of a denial of our petition. Judge Brown could have found little comfort in it, and the district attorney's office must have felt the singeing tongues of an ultimately consuming fire.

On the 9th day of September, 1965, came on to be heard the Application for the Writ of Habeas Corpus on behalf of Jack

Ruby, Petitioner, against J. E. (Bill) Decker, Sheriff of Dallas County, and . . . the Court proceeded to hear the application and the evidence in support of same.

The Court . . . finds that under the law and evidence in this case, that it is the Court's opinion that it would be fair and just to both the Petitioner and to the State, for this Court to certify this record to the Court of Criminal Appeals for its review and judicial determination and that this action is taken so as not to disturb the present status of the Petitioner in this case and said action is not to be taken as condemning or condoning [From the bench of Judge Holland had said, "certainly not condoning."] any act or conduct on the part of Judge Brown in writing this book and that for the sake of Petitioner seeking appellate review, the Court denies the relief prayed for in the Application for Habeas Corpus and Jack Ruby is to be remanded to the custody of the Respondent Sheriff.

In effect, Judge Holland was passing the matter on to the higher court for its consideration. He knew that if he followed what was undoubtedly his impulse and sustained our petition, the death sentence would be set aside peremptorily, and on him would fall the onus of this result. Such action, he evidently reasoned, was a responsibility of his judicial superiors. After all, he and Judge Brown were peers in the judicial hierarchy, both responsible to the Court of Criminal Appeals. It was up to that court to brand Judge Brown's conduct, not him. Judging another judge is always difficult, and seldom is a lower-court judge strong enough or compulsive enough to do so.

In due course, we gave notice of appeal in the precise manner required by the Texas Code. We were now supposed to turn our attention to the preparation, certification, and filing of the statement of facts in the case. As Burleson proceeded with this chore, Dann and I in particular turned our attention to another matter that could prove significant in determining Jack Ruby's fate.

# 17

## THE A.B.A. REFUSES TO INTERVENE

GENERALLY, it is well that litigation be confined to the actual parties, so that it is not confused by meddlers. Now and then an unusual situation arises when there are public interests and potentialities beyond those of the participants in a case. This is true of those cases that capture the headlines because they are historic or sensational or that involve great constitutional issues, the public welfare, the security of the state, the meaning of the resounding phrases of the Founding Fathers.

The Ruby case was filled with such paramount matters as the effect of rampant publicity and a possibly prejudiced community upon the judicial process; whether or not those who had viewed a killing on television, like eye witnesses, ought to be ineligible to serve upon a jury deciding the fate of a killer; the test of what constitutes malice or premeditation; such newfangled concepts as psychomotor epilepsy and insanity generally; whether or not a judge under contract to write a book about the case had such pecuniary, or prejudicial, interest as to be disqualified from passing upon proceedings arising either before or after the verdict; the admissibility of statements allegedly made by the defendant, without benefit of counsel or proper warning, after he was under arrest. Seldom had a case been more filled with momentous issues, rulings, and results.

We felt that the American Civil Liberties Union, that great guardian of individual rights, ought to be in our corner, and it was. Sam Houston Clinton, Jr., was the counsel for the Texas Civil Liberties Union, and his participation in the case was by assignment of that state branch of the A.C.L.U. Kunstler was on the national board of the A.C. L.U. and active in other civil rights organizations.

We felt that we needed other participation, as well, to indicate that more than one deserving, or undeserving, individual was involved. We thought that the American Bar Association, the organization to which most reputable lawyers and judges belong, ought to be in our corner. The Association has great influence in molding judicial opinion, and had only recently intervened successfully in the *Estes* case on the issue of television in the courtroom. I despaired of persuading it, and I was not eager to extend myself on peripheral matters. But Sol Dann desired the involvement of the A.B.A. from the beginning, even before the rest of us had fully considered the matter. There is no doubt that he was always eager to have some of our work done for us.

On March 16, 1965, Dann wrote to Joseph D. Stecher, counsel of the American Bar Association, that at the suggestion of Glenn Coulter, long prominent in the Association, he desired to visit with him to obtain his assistance and that of the Asociation in the pending Ruby case. Mr. Stecher replied bluntly: "I see no point in our discussing this matter, because neither I nor the American Bar Association will become involved in any way in this case."

Earlier, on March 11, Dann had written to Judge Walter E. Craig, who had been the president of the Association. Judge Craig replied, on March 24, with more courtesy and encouragement than had the Association counsel.

Please accept my apologies for not replying sooner. I note from the press reports that Judge Brown has been relieved of further responsibility in the sanity hearing, which indicates at least some degree of progress in your efforts in the case.

In my present position I am not currently able to take any

affirmative action in the matter. I am, however, taking the
liberty of forwarding your letter ... to Mr. Lewis F. Powell, Jr.,
current President of the American Bar Association. ...

A few days later, on March 29, Mr. Powell wrote to
Dann.

Our counsel, Mr. Stecher, has already written you on this
subject.

For reasons which I am sure you will understand [the reluctance to interfere with private litigants who might resent such
intrusion], the Association rarely intervenes in litigation, and
then only pursuant to express prior authority by Board of
Governors. Such authority is normally given only in situation
involving principles of the broadest application. An example
of this is the decision to intervene in support of Canon 35, which
is directly in issue in the *Sol Estes* case. [Dann and all of us felt
that the Ruby case *was* as important as the Estes case.]

The Board of Governors does not meet again until late in
May. I would not expect it to act favorably on a request of
this kind.

Why were Messrs. Stecher and Powell so sure of the Association's inaction? Dann would not let the matter drop
so easily. He immediately wrote to Powell again, urging
the calling of a special meeting of the Board to consider
the situation. He explained the nature of the proceedings
then pending before the United States Court of Appeals
and complained of the violations of the constitutional
rights of Ruby by Judge Brown and the Dallas District
Attorney's office. He stressed that federal Judge Davidson
had also been overly hasty in forcing a hearing in the absence of Ruby's counsel, with the result that Ruby's rights
had been brushed aside. Our motion was to be argued
before the Court of Appeals in Jacksonville, Florida, on
April 20, 1965. With more urgency than tact, Dann concluded his letter with a strong appeal to the Association to
intervene. Seizing upon the precedent mentioned by Powell

in his letter, Dann drew a direct comparison between the Billy Sol Estes case, in which the A.B.A. had intervened, and the Ruby case. To Dann, the legal and ethical violations in the latter surpassed those in Estes, and could have a bad effect on public respect for bench and bar. Therefore it was certainly a matter requiring the intervention of the foremost legal association in the United States.

Dann also persuaded Chicago attorney Michael Levin, the old Ruby family friend through whom I had been brought into the case, to write to the President and Board of Governors of the ABA, on April 7:

I am greatly concerned about the conduct of the lawyers and judges involved in the case of Jack Ruby. It appears, from the information which I have at hand, that the canon of ethics of the American Bar Association have been violated and the constitutional rights of Jack Ruby have been ignored and denied.

If ever a case demanded the intervention of the Association and the filing of briefs amicus curiae this case cries out for such action. The matter is now pending in the U.S. Circuit Court of Appeals, and is set for hearing in Jacksonville, Florida on April 20, 1965. I would appreciate knowing what action, if any, you have taken in this matter, and if you have not looked into it, will you kindly do so immediately.

Levin received a courteous but ineffective response from Mr. James M. Spiro, Director of Professional Activities of the Association, on April 14:

On behalf of President Lewis F. Powell, Jr., I thank you for your letter suggesting that the Association consider intervening as amicus curiae in the Ruby case pending in the U.S. Circuit Court of Appeals.

For reasons which we are sure you will understand, the Association rarely intervenes in litigation and then only pursuant to prior authority by the Board of Governors. Such authority is normally given only in situations involving principles of

the broadest application. An example is the decision to intervene
in support of Canon 35 which is directly an issue in the *Sol
Estes* case.

The Board of Governors has been fully informed about the
proceedings in the Oswald and Ruby cases and would not be
expected to act favorably on a request of this kind. This is
particularly so since the Board of Governors does not meet again
until late in May.

I do not know if the results would have been any different if any other Ruby counsel had been involved in the
venture. Certainly, the situation then hardened, as we
were to learn later, when I was more directly involved.

Dann had not been content to carry the case to the
American Bar Association. Again without conferring with
co-counsel, he wrote, on March 18, 1965, to Mr. Arnold
Forster, General Counsel of the Anti-Defamation League
of B'nai B'rith, one of the leading Jewish organizations. He
had earlier written to Mr. Dore Schary, Chairman of the
National Commission of the A.D.L. This time Dann had
argued the Jewish implications of the case. Mr. Forster and
the others did not dismiss him without careful consideration. There were consultations, apparently, between various leaders—the national president of B'nai B'rith, the
national director, the general counsel, and the chairman of
A.D.L., and others. On March 31, Mr. Forster replied to
Dann:

Impressed as we are by your arguments in respect to the
manner in which the Ruby case has been handled, we are nevertheless, unable to find a basis for intervention by B'nai B'rith or
the ADL. Such a basis would exist if the evidence satisfied us
that the fact that Ruby is Jewish had any relationship to his
conviction. In our opinion, such evidence has not yet been put
forth. In addition, we are mindful that the issue of Ruby's
sanity has not been resolved. Should he be adjudged insane
and committed, as you believe he should be, your own position

is that justice will have been done. Should he be adjudged sane, there will then be opportunity for his attorneys to argue an appeal before the highest Texas court, and presumably, the Supreme Court of the United States. In these circumstances, it is our belief that we ought not to intervene at this time.

Obviously, if at some future date evidence is adduced to show that Ruby has been denied equitable treatment because he is Jewish, we would want to see that evidence and reopen our consideration.

Despite these rebuffs, Dann never abandoned his hopes for magical solutions, and he never retreated from the view that we had to seek aid outside our own forces. But as the defense team became more closely knit, there was less tendency on his part to go it alone, as he had in this instance, without consultation with co-counsel.

After the habeas corpus hearing before Judge Holland, it seemed that another effort to obtain assistance might be fruitful. I had learned that Sol had been turned down in the earlier attempt, and there was no obvious reason to expect success now. On the other hand, the proceedings had moved along, and the situation was much different from what it had been. In this spirit, on October 27, 1965, I wrote to my colleagues:

I feel that it might be well to have the American Bar Association intervene in our habeas corpus matter, but I am afraid that if we concentrate too much on such intervention we may leave insufficient time for the actual appeal. Perhaps, the way to handle the matter is to write to both the American Bar Association and the Texas Bar Association after the appeal is perfected and to state our conviction that their intervention is in order. We can offer in the same letter to supply copies of the pleadings, the briefs and the transcript of the proceedings. We can also suggest a conference on the matter. I do not think that we should make a career of it, however. As to requesting the American Bar Association to furnish us all the material about the judicial codes of the various states, I see no harm in that. I just want to make certain that we are in the state of mind in which we rely upon ourselves rather than Santa Claus.

Thereafter, Burleson wrote to Joseph D. Stecher, counsel for the American Bar Association, telling him, succinctly, about the habeas corpus proceeding and asking him for "court decisions, administrative opinions, ethical opinions, published reports and papers or speeches" relating to violations of the canons of judicial ethics. Burleson carefully refrained, at this time, from asking for intervention in the case. Perhaps, Mr. Stecher would suggest that himself. His reply a few days later had hopeful undertones:

The only thing we have here in addition to Henry Drinker's excellent book on legal ethics are the opinions and decisions of our Committee on Professional Ethics. I have checked them carefully, and there appears to be only one opinion which is germane to the question you are presenting. That is Opinion No. 52, issued December 14, 1931. I enclose a photocopy of that Opinion. I am sure you will agree that the conduct there held to be improper is much less objectionable than the conduct you alleged in your proceedings. I hope this will be of some value to you.

Mr. Stecher's response encouraged us to pursue the matter. I prepared a rough draft of a letter to be sent to the Association, and my associates made suggestions for its improvement. On November 16, 1965, with the blessing of my associates, the letter was sent off to Mr. Stecher of the American Bar Association, Mr. Clint C. Small of the Texas Bar Association, and Mr. W. St. John Garwood of the Texas Civil Judicial Counsel. The letter to Mr. Stecher carefully eschewed rhetoric. We thought it was a brief but persuasive argument for intervention by the great national professional association to which we all belonged:

This letter is being sent to you in behalf of Messrs. Phil Burleson, Sam Houston Clinton, Jr., Sol A. Dann and William

M. Kunstler and myself as attorneys for Jack Ruby. It supplements Mr. Burleson's letter to you of October 28, 1965, and your reply of November 4, 1965. Because I practice in Chicago, in the headquarters city of the ABA, I was delegated by my colleagues to pursue with you the matter of your intervention in the pending habeas corpus proceedings. We feel that the American Bar Association should intervene as *amicus curiae* and file a brief in connection with the appeal of the matter in the Texas Court of Criminal Appeals, since the canons of judicial ethics are involved.

The habeas corpus proceeding seeks an adjudication that the judgment of conviction and the imposition of the death penalty are void by reason of the disqualification of the presiding judge, the Honorable Joe B. Brown. The gist of the action is that Judge Brown had a pecuniary interest in the case during the pendency of the trial proceedings and, certainly, while he had under consideration matters requiring his judicial discretion, without which the case could not be reviewed properly in the Texas Court of Criminal Appeals. During this time, as we showed in the hearing on our petition, he was under contract to write a book about the case and received $5,000 as advance royalties. He was able to obtain this contract and money through persons he had known in Dallas for some years, who were associated with a large New York publishing firm.

Mr. Burleson sent to you some of the relevant material with his letter of October 28, 1965. We will be glad to deliver to you a complete transcript of the proceedings, and we will be happy to confer with you or your representatives at any time.

We believe that your intervention is a necessity in this case because the issues involve the honor of the legal profession and the judiciary and far transcend anything personal to Mr. Ruby or us. We believe that, as in the Estes case and other matters in which the American Bar Association has intervened, the reputation of the judicial system is at stake, matters going to the very essence of what constitutes a fair trial and due process.

At this time we want to call your special attention to the letter which Judge Brown sent to his publisher, Holt, Rinehart

& Winston, Inc., on March 12, 1965, in which he declared his intention to conceal or misstate the facts with respect to his pecuniary interest and gave every indication of pre-judging the remaining issues, such as the sanity hearing. . . . Of course, this is only part of the relevant evidence set forth in the transcript of the proceedings or, as it is known in Texas, the statement of facts.

We have sent copies of this letter to Mr. Clint C. Small, Jr., president of the Texas Bar Association, and Mr. W. St. John Garwood, chairman of the Texas Civil Judicial Council.

As it is likely that the hearing of this matter will be advanced by the Texas Court of Criminal Appeals, so that it will be heard within weeks, we want to stress that time is of the essence.

The very next day, Mr. Stecher replied, referring to the previous appeal by Dann. The letter was not encouraging:

You may not know that earlier this year Sol A. Dann, of Detroit, appealed to the Association to file a brief as amicus curiae in the Jack Ruby litigation. His request was considered by the full Board of Governors of the Association which, at its meeting in May, 1965, determined that it would not be appropriate for the Association to intervene in this matter, and the request was denied. In view of the record, I am therefore unable to give you any assurance whatever that the Board would agree to intervene in response to this latest request. Furthermore, the Board will not meet again until February 17, 1966.

A far more encouraging and, we thought, more understanding letter from Mr. W. St. John Garwood, President of the Texas Civil Judicial Council, arrived the next day:

The situation reflected by Judge Brown's letter of March 12, 1965, to Editor Sam Stewart does, indeed, approach the fantastic, and I accordingly infer a suggestion on your part that the Texas Civil Judicial Council might take some active part in the matter, such as intervening along with the A.B.A., in Ruby's behalf. However, I do not consider myself empowered to speak for the Council without authority from the membership, and, in any case, my present view of our statutory powers (Art. 2328a, Tex. Civ. Stats.) is that they do not include action of the kind in question, considering primarily that we are restricted to the non-criminal field of justice and secondarily, that our functions are largely advisory to the State government through the Governor, Supreme Court and Legislature. Nevertheless, I am sending the Council membership a copy of Judge Brown's mentioned letter with request for immediate advice as to any action it may think I should take.

True, Mr. Garwood pointed out the legal disabilities under which the Council labored; but he readily grasped the importance of what we were attempting. So I wrote again to Mr. Stecher, on November 22, 1965:

I hasten to advise you that the earlier request by my associate, Mr. Sol A. Dann, that the ABA file a brief as amicus curiae in the Jack Ruby litigation, pertained only to the pending appeal from the judgment of conviction, and not to the habeas corpus proceeding. The latter proceeding was not filed at the time Mr. Dann wrote to you; indeed, we had not known with any degree of certainty at that time of Judge Brown's pecuniary interest in the case. This knowledge came to us with some particularity when we took the deposition of his publisher in New York, after we had learned in general terms of the possibility of the judge's disqualification. The copy of Judge Brown's letter that I sent to you was one of the documents that we adduced at the deposition.

At the hearing in Dallas on our petition for a writ of habeas corpus, Judge Brown admitted that he had publicly denied receipts of any money from his publisher and had denied that he was writing a book, because he wanted it to be kept secret. But, as he said, "it leaked out." He then admitted that he had "recused" himself after the deposition was taken of the publisher that disclosed that negotiations had begun in the spring of 1964, when important aspects of the trial proceedings were still pending.

We feel very strongly that ABA intervention should be forth-coming in the habeas corpus proceeding, even if it means a special meeting of the Board. That our feelings are not personal or the result of mere advocacy is shown, I believe, from the reaction of the Honorable W. St. John Garwood . . . to whom, as you know, we sent a copy of our letter to you of November 16.

After quoting from Mr. Garwood's response, I concluded with an offer to sit down with Mr. Stecher to discuss the matter.

On the same day, Mr. C. C. Small, Jr., the President of the State Bar of Texas wrote to me in what I construed to be encouragement:

I have submitted the letter of November 16, 1965, and the attached material in the Jack Ruby matter to the members of the Board of Directors of the State Bar. Any action such as you request requires concurrence of a majority of the Board of directors.

Regardless of whether or not the State Bar would file an *amicus curiae* brief in the habeas corpus proceedings, it is obvious that Judge Brown's conduct as shown by his own letter of March 12, 1965, deserves attention from the disciplinary machinery of the State Bar.

I will advise you as soon as possible of the attitude of the Board of Directors of the State Bar in regard to your request of an *amicus curiae* brief.

Mr. Small, like Mr. Garwood, sent a copy of his letter to Mr. Stecher, Counsel of the A.B.A. Abruptly, on November 23, 1965, Stecher wrote to me:

I am well aware of the fact that the earlier request by Sol A. Dann that the American Bar Association file a brief as amicus curiae pertained only to the pending appeal from the judgment of conviction and not to the habeas corpus proceeding. In any event, however, I am entirely without authority to do anything in this situation. There is nothing I can add to what I had in my letter of November 17.

A few days later, Sam Clinton wrote of his further efforts to win the assistance of the leadership of our profession:

After I received St. John Garwood's reply to Elmer's letter I called him and personally discussed the matter with him. He expressed more distaste for the actions of Judge Brown than indicated in his response but, at the same time, indicated that he had strong reservations about the power and authority of the Texas Civil Judicial Council to intervene. Whereupon I told him that while we would like for the Council to take an active interest in the matter, we recognized its limitations and that he and the Council could be of great assistance and help by letting the Board of Directors of the Texas Bar Association know of his and its reaction, and, if it could be done, to urge the Board of Directors of TBA to intervene or to assist ABA in such intervention. Judge Garwood thanked me for my clarification and again indicated that he thought something ought to be done but that he was pretty sure the Texas Civil Judicial Council was not the vehicle to undertake it and would keep the matter in mind if and when the Board of TBA was requested to take any action.

It seems to me that the judicial section of the State Bar of Texas would be in much the same position. That is, it will lack the power and authority to intervene in its own name but could present its views to the Board of Directors of the TBA and request the Bar to intervene or to urge and assist ABA to intervene.

As anticipated by Clinton, Mr. Small, President of the State Bar of Texas, indicated on December 7, 1965, why his organization could not intervene in our case:

I have now received replies from a majority of the Board of Directors of the State Bar in respect to the request made by you in your letter of November 16, 1965, for an *amicus curiae* brief from the State Bar in the habeas corpus proceedings now pending in the Jack Ruby matter.

The unanimous opinion of those replying was that the State

Bar should not participate in any manner in the habeas corpus proceedings. The effect, if any, of Judge Brown's conduct on the rights of Ruby can and will be, of course, decided by the courts in the course of the present pending proceeding.

This does not mean that the Board of Directors is not interested in exploring the matter of Judge Brown's conduct as a judicial officer, but any action in this respect will undoubtedly be taken outside the framework of the Ruby case in all its ramifications before the courts.

We appreciate your calling this to the attention of the State Bar, since many of the officers and directors were not aware of this facet of Judge Brown's conduct in the trial of the Ruby case.

At least the State Bar of Texas was not going to ignore the situation. This would not help us or Ruby in our immediate problems, but we felt that we had performed a necessary professional duty; it was up to others to pursue the matter. We would continue alone on the habeas corpus appeal—if we could ever get the official court reporter to complete the so-called statement of facts, the transcript of the trial proceedings.

We were learning, at first hand, about whom God helps.

# 18

## TO STRIKE A DEAL

OFF AND ON during the spring and summer of 1965 we had been holding secret discussions with District Attorney Wade, with Judge Brown, and with others. Our hope was that we might work out a just deal that would end Jack Ruby's legal nightmare. We were pledged to tell no one of these meetings. Suddenly, the secrecy was ended, not by us, but by the man who had so insisted upon silence, District Attorney Henry Wade.

In its November 4 issue, the Dallas *Times Herald* spread a headline across the front page: WADE AGREEABLE TO LIFE FOR RUBY. Above this banner were the explanatory words: —WOULD RECOMMEND COMMUTATION— Jim Featherstone, a staff writer who had often obtained beats in covering the case, had dug up the story, and his account was repeated in newspapers all over the country. Wade, according to Featherstone, had said he had offered to Ruby's attorneys to reduce the death sentence to life imprisonment "on at least two occasions" but that we had not accepted. "One of their attorneys—Mr. Sol Dann of Detroit—wants to hold out for a five-year sentence." (Not only had Dann wanted a short sentence; Burleson and I, too, had told Wade that.) "We do not feel this would be a proper punishment. The punishment should be at least life imprisonment."

Wade had outlined for the reporter the procedure: we would have to apply for a commutation of the death sentence to the Texas State Board of Pardons and Paroles; then, on the recommendation of Governor Connally, the sentence could be reduced. "If they [Ruby's attorneys] apply for a life sentence, we would join with them in recommending a life sentence." To justify his position, Wade added, "There is an advantage to keeping Ruby alive for interviews and historical purposes. There are still a lot of unanswered questions."

Dann, for once, would not comment on Wade's remarks when asked to do so by the reporter, although he did say that it was only a case of murder without malice. Burleson, too, was reticent, but he repeated what Dann had said: "Why should we accept the offer when there are reversible errors in the case?"

Featherstone said that Judge Brown, now out of the case, had told him "several months ago that he did not feel Ruby would ever die in the electric chair." The judge had said: "After all, we are talking about the man who killed the man who killed President Kennedy."

The next day, November 5, the Dallas *Morning News* developed the story. At a hastily called press conference, Wade said that his offer had nothing to do with his failure to obtain a federal judgeship. (It had been widely assumed in Dallas that Wade was assured a place on the federal bench, but the appointment had, in fact, gone to Irving Goldberg.) The mounting expense of the case was one reason for the offer; the crowded docket of the courts was another. He and his staff, Wade declared, had plenty of work to do. He was concerned that "some people are still asking questions about the assassination—it is just as well to have [Ruby] available."

He did have a definite opinion about Ruby's mental condition: "Although he is sane, there is no question he has some neurotic tendencies that could be treated in the penitentiary."

Gratuitously, he added that Ruby's sentence would have been less severe if Belli and his associates had asked for leniency at the trial. And he took pains to stress that there was "nothing new" in the offer of commutation.

Later in the day Burleson commented on the story: "We are still processing our appeals—one from the trial itself and the other on the habeas corpus hearing based on [the allegation of] Judge Brown's disqualification. My position in the trial was that Ruby was guilty of murder without malice, if he was sane at the time. If we had accepted any compromise, we wouldn't have been proceeding with our appeal, would we?"

The State Board of Pardons and Paroles indicated that same day, through A. C. Turner, one of the three members, that it was premature to consider action by the Board. "As long as Ruby's case is on appeal, we would not have jurisdiction," Turner said. "We could not consider it until there was a final conviction and he had been delivered to the custody of the Department of Corrections at Huntsville." The Board, Turner added, gave "considerable weight" to the opinions of the trial judge and the prosecutor, but it considered other factors as well. In any event, the Board could not make a final decision; only the Governor could. Nor could the Governor commute a death sentence without a Board recommendation.

Wade apparently thought the Governor would agree with him, although Connally was reported as saying some months before that he would not recommend commutation. Apparently, either the report was erroneous or the Governor had changed his mind, for his press secretary, George Christian, declared that the Governor never commented on a case until it actually came before him: "I do not know what he would do in Jack Ruby's case," Christian said. "I have never heard him mention how he feels about it."

A life sentence, it was pointed out, would require Ruby to spend at least seven years in prison: all life sentences were reviewed after fifteen years, and with credit for good behavior the sentence would become only seven years.

Now Judge Brown wanted to correct the account of Featherstone. He had been misquoted: "What I did say was that I thought the death penalty would be abolished before he would ever die in the chair."

Of course, Marguerite Oswald, the mother of the President's assassin, could not resist commenting on the district attorney's offer. She was concerned that a life sentence would not be exactly that. "There is no law now that says Ruby would remain in prison for life if the sentence is reduced to life imprisonment," she said. "The lawmakers will have to hold a special session and pass a law that he will not be eligible for parole." Characteristically, it did not occur to her that such a special law might be unconstitutional. She still believed in her son's innocence and clung to the hope that, if alive and interviewed, Ruby might somehow prove this; but she would not, in an excess of charity, free the man who had shot her son.

When asked whether the offer to commute the death sentence would be withdrawn if the Ruby appeal went on, Wade refused to speculate. But many thought that he would be compelled to stand behind his offer in the future. As one acute observer phrased it: "If he offered to intervene and upset a jury sentence—and then refused to do it later—it would be like he pulled the switch [on the electric chair] himself." The defense, it was agreed, had nothing to lose by continuing the course it had chosen.

We could try to get something better and, if necessary, accept Wade's offer in the end.

# 19

## APPEALING JUDGE HOLLAND'S ORDER

As MORE AND MORE TIME went by without our filing the so-
called statement of facts (the transcript of the evidence
and proceedings) in connection with the habeas corpus
appeal, the district attorney's office became increasingly
impatient. They could not know that I shared their impatience. After the hearing we had assumed that Burleson,
who had the on-the-scene familiarity and responsibility,
would immediately get the court reporter's transcript and
distribute copies to all of us. We would then agree upon
the necessary corrections. As time passed, without any
transcript, I in particular fretted about the matter. Burleson tried to calm my fears, but they persisted, despite his
assurances that we could not be penalized because of the
delay.

At last, on March 16, 1966, the State filed a motion requesting a hearing to determine whether there was good
cause for the long delay. Judge Holland had denied our
petition to set aside the death verdict on September 9,
1965, the motion recited; we had given notice of our intention to appeal, and fifty-six days later, on November 5,
we had asked that Ruby, as a pauper, be furnished a statement of facts without charge. Before that, the State set
forth, we had asked the court to continue, until the habeas
corpus appeal was disposed of, the post-conviction sanity
hearing that had been set for October 18; the court had
complied with our request, cautioning us to be diligent.

On November 18, the motion went on, the court reporter prepared, certified, and delivered the statement of

facts and the judge approved it. We, however, had never submitted the document to the State for approval and did not file it within ninety days, as required by law. The State's motion contended that we had not taken the proper steps to secure the correction of the document if we deemed it inadequate or inaccurate and to extend the time for filing it with the record of the case. There was no excuse for our neglect and delay, it said. Fearing that Judge Holland might be unduly kind to us, the State asked the court not to determine arbitrarily that good cause was shown for our inaction, but to force us to prove it.

The court, unusually charitable to us in the circumstances, found that good cause was shown for the delay. For the moment I breathed more easily.

Then came proof that the gods are sometimes kind to the undeserving. Because of our not completely justified delay, we were able to place into the record for the appeal material that, without the delay, would have been left out.

Into our so-called Formal Bill of Exception No. 1 we incorporated the text of Judge Brown's guest appearance on "The Mort Sahl Show," in New York, on November 27, 1965. Preliminarily, we explained that the television interview contradicted what Judge Brown had said at the habeas corpus hearing; since it was too late to make a motion for a new trial in either the original case or the habeas corpus proceeding, we were taking this means of bringing the material to the Court of Criminal Appeals in connection with our appeal.

Mort Sahl, a nightclub intellectual dearly beloved by the Beat Generation, was trying to make a new career on television with his program. So far as we were concerned, he was serving a great purpose as he drew from Judge Brown the truth about matters on which he had earlier dissembled.

"This is the first appearance I had made since the trial," the judge said, after a few words of polite palaver. Sahl suggested that the press had urged him on. "Well, you would be amazed at the power of the press," Judge Brown continued. ". . . You know you've always heard that if your foresight could be as good as your hindsight, you would act different probably from what you really did. But this case has received more publicity than probably any case ever tried in the history of our United States jurisprudence." Sahl asked: "You mean it would surpass the Sacco-Vanzetti case?" "Yes, and, well, of course, we have more news media now than we had then. We have more news media now than at the Lindbergh trial. And you can't stop the power of the press. It is too formidable."

The judge was obviously warming up: "Well, there's nothing wrong with getting the truth to the people, but I think as a result of the Ruby trial, the newspapers have distorted the facts and made innuendos and have taken things out of context until actually nobody knows the real truth of the Ruby trial. I have read many accounts written by people who were not present at the trial, and couldn't possibly know what actually went on, without having taken someone else's word for it—it's all hearsay."

He disparaged the Kaplan-Waltz book: "I think that Mr. Kaplan has taken gossip really and documented it as fact. I don't mean to criticize his book—I hope he makes money—I think that's the reason he wrote it."

Sahl referred to Belli's book on the case. This, he said, led to the "forthcoming book" by the judge.

Brown, at Sahl's invitation, "took off" on his own book. He said he had re-read all the testimony, almost a million words, in order to correct the "many misconceptions."

"I don't know who employed Mr. Belli in the case; I presume that the Ruby family did because they have employed some 20 to 25 lawyers since, and there is only one lawyer left in the case who actually was present during the trial and he wasn't present in the courtroom a great deal because Belli had him out doing a lot of investigative work." The reference to the number of lawyers was hyperbole rather than fact. Like the proverbial Arab, the judge could not always confine himself to the literal truth.

Judge Brown discussed the withdrawal of Tom Howard

from the defense, the law of insanity in Texas, the charge that he had been reading a comic book during the trial, and, prodded by Sahl, anti-Semitism. "There is no anti-Semitism in Dallas," he said. When the studio audience laughed, he amplified on his belief as to the absence of anti-Semitism.

He charged that Belli and Tonahill really did not want a change of venue. Why did they make such motion? "Mr. Belli said he wanted to look good."

He dwelt upon the issue of Ruby's sanity and the status of the case. At the very least he seemed somewhat confused. He was vague, too, about Henry Wade's willingness to accept a term of years in the case, rather than the death penalty (this had just been revealed publicly). The Warren Report was brought up, and he opined: "I doubt if it has been very widely read. It's a very lengthy thing . . . after the first 150 or 200 pages. Then it starts with graphs and special reports." He thought there was no evidence of any link between Oswald and Ruby. And again the matter of television and the press came up. It was clear that the judge was oppressed by the power of the communications media. He admitted that the jury had not deliberated "very long." He offered an explanation:

I have talked with the jury since and they said that Belli offered them no alternative but either an acquittal or an extreme penalty. There was nothing in between and you know under the Texas law, there is murder with malice and murder without malice, and perhaps I should try to explain a little bit—murder with malice is a murder done in an instant—actually malice is a wrongful act done intentionally without just cause or excuse and malice aforethought is a condition of the mind in which— during which a person commits an act with a heart regardless of social duty and fatally bent on mischief. Now had he qualified the jury on murder without malice which carries a five year maximum penalty, murder without malice are those murders or homicides committed while under extreme passion created by passion or horror, or resentment or terror, that renders a mind incapable of cool reflection. Now the maximum penalty for that is five years.

*Sahl:* That's all?

*Brown:* Uh huh. But they never qualified the jury on murder without malice.

*Sahl:* What you are saying is that they didn't give them any way out?

*Brown:* That's right. The jury had no alternative—either they had to render an acquittal or the extreme penalty and they could not acquit. Twenty million people saw Jack Ruby shoot Oswald on television.

Belli, he said, had approved the jury in the first instance. (The judge was conveniently ignoring Belli's strenuous efforts to get a panel that had not seen the shooting on television. When these efforts failed, Belli could only make the most of it, by appearing to like the jury. He would not prejudice them further by insult—until the verdict was in.)

Sahl turned the judge over to the audience for questioning, and there were some revealing exchanges:

*Audience Participant:* Judge Brown, you mentioned the excessive press coverage that this trial received. I was wondering if you felt any undue pressure or inability to perform your functions as presiding judge in this trial because of that extensive coverage and also whether you believe any of the other participants in the trial, namely Wade or Belli, might have acted differently than they otherwise would have had this trial not received the publicity that it did?

*Brown:* Yes sir, I think you're—that is correct. From—I was under great pressure because of the press. They wouldn't leave me alone. Every recess we would have, I'd go back to my chambers—there would be four or five reporters or photographers. See I have no jurisdiction out of the courtroom whatsoever. I could not banish them like the Federal Courts do from the corridors outside the courtroom. Would that I could, but I

couldn't, so they consequently congregated out in the corridors.
And every time anybody would come in and go out and me in
particular—every time I went in or out they shot my picture.
I asked them not to; they did it anyway. And I think in the
courtroom the very fact that there were over 370 accredited
news people in the courtroom had some bearing on the
participants.

*Audience Participant:* If I may continue, do you think Jack
Ruby and the State of Texas each got as fair a shake as they
might of had the coverage not been so extensive?

*Brown:* Yes, I think he did.

*Audience Participant:* You don't feel that tactics were altered
to accommodate the press in any way?

*Brown:* No sir, I don't think so. We tried awfully hard not to,
and if it was done, it was done subconsciously, because I paid
no attention to them and the press in the courtroom were models
of decorum. They were very nice, but outside the courtroom
they hounded us to death.

Judge Brown gave a colorful account of what happened
after the verdict, with special reference to Belli's outcry.
". . . if I'd been in the courtroom, he would have still been
in jail for contempt." The judge was told, "They're raising
hell in the courtroom," so he returned. "The photographers
were standing on the furniture; standing on the rail; and
as a matter of fact, it cost $3,000 to repair the damage that
they did—it cost the taxpayers." This led Sahl to inquire:
"Well, in other words, Judge, what you are saying is when
the press is present you are afraid the principals will play
to them as an audience instead of their being eavesdrop-
pers on the judicial action? That's always the problem?"
"Yes, that's one of them," Brown replied. He then eluci-
dated: "I think to a great extent the case was tried on television outside the courtroom. Things which happened that
I had no control over— The Bar Association complained to
me that Belli was making statements up and down the
street—they followed him into a night club, to his suite
in the hotel; he was telling what he was going to put on in

the way of testimony. The Bar Association complained to me and asked me to hold him in contempt and I couldn't, because he was talking on his own time, but I did call him in and ask him to quit and he agreed to and did quit."

Sahl turned again to the findings of the Warren Commission, and drew from the judge an unexpected response: "I am not satisfied as to the reasons Oswald killed the President. I have my own theory as to why Oswald shot the President. I have not expressed it; don't intend to, but I have read a great deal about Oswald and I don't think really that he was shooting at the President."

Having declared his unwillingness to express his theory, Judge Brown did just that: "I really think that Oswald was shooting for Connally. . . . Yes, and the President got in his line of fire. You know he squeezed three shots off in five seconds—the first shot missed the car altogether and hit the curb and richocheted over to the street where some deputy sheriffs found it. He had cause to hate Connally, but he really had no cause to—"

The audience and the judge and Sahl could not get away from the implications of the conduct of the press. They returned to it again and again. Judge Brown declared, "I am not talking about the fairness of the trial itself. I think that Ruby got a fair trial. He thinks he got one too. He told me two weeks ago." (We would have welcomed the opportunity to cross-examine him on this often repeated, but untrue, statement.)

One informed audience participant asked: "Now, if the Supreme Court reverses or upholds that lower court decision in Sam Sheppard's case will that have an effect on a possible appeal—new avenue of appeal for Ruby? Do you think?" And Brown replied: "Yes, I think it will, uh huh."

Then the show took on a new excitement for us. Almost everything that was said had relevance to our efforts to vacate the judgment of death:

*Audience Participant:* Judge Brown, you indicated that the defense did not give the jury an alternative between acquittal and a conviction. What right did you have under Texas law and procedure to instruct the jury about the various levels of balance?

*Brown:* I had no authority to instruct them other than give them the law pertaining to murder. They in turn put the facts to the law, and reached a conclusion based upon the law as I gave it to them and the facts as they heard it from the witness stand.

*Sahl:* Does that answer your question adequately? You look like you have an afterthought.

*Audience Participant:* I am not sure that I understand.

*Sahl:* That's all right, that's why we are here.

*Brown:* Well, what I am trying to say is that the jury hears the facts; the only charge I can give—instructions I can give to the jury is the law on murder. He was indicted of course for murder with malice in that he did with a gun voluntarily shoot and kill Lee Harvey Oswald. I am bound to instruct the jury on the law of murder with malice. Now the jury in turn takes the facts as they hear them from the witness stand and applies them to the law as given to them by the Court and arrive at a verdict that way. They took the facts as given to them by the witness stand—as they came from the witness stand—and applied it to the law of murder with malice and arrived at that verdict.

*Audience Participant:* So then with some change in the—

*Brown:* Now, I did instruct them on murder without malice, but the facts did not fit murder without malice as they were presented to the jury. In other words, what I am trying to say is this, that had they offered some alternative, had put in some testimony that would allow the jury to find anything other than the death penalty, I think the jury would have.

*Audience Participant:* Then the question comes up, why did they fail to do this?

*Brown:* Well because—well you ask Mr. Belli.

Laughter.

*Brown:* He was the man in charge. And I could not under any circumstances suggest to him how to conduct his case no more than I could suggest to the State how to conduct their case because then I would be involving myself in the case and my job is to sit and see that the defendant has a fair trial, gets a fair trial.

*Sahl:* Thank you very much.

*Brown:* And all of the publicity that has come out of the Ruby case, yet nobody has ever said that he didn't get a fair trial.

*Sahl:* With the exception of Melvin Belli. Has he maintained that Judge?

*Brown:* Well I can understand Mel's attitude.

Laughter.

*Sahl:* Judge, when are we going to see, "Dallas, Ruby and the Justice"?

*Brown:* I hope we get to it—or get it out by late spring anyway. I've got three more chapters to write on it and I'll have the preface to write, and I sent most of it to the publisher.

*Sahl:* So, it's almost down the chute huh?

*Brown:* Yeah, but you know how long it takes to get a book—it's the first time I ever tried to write anything, and it's difficult, let me tell you.

*Sahl:* It's a lonely occupation.

*Brown:* You read and read and read, Mort, and then you write one paragraph.

Thus did Judge Brown repudiate all he had said at the habeas corpus hearing with respect to his nonparticipation in the writing of the book. Now that the book was virtually complete he was taking all the credit.

We could now prepare our brief for the habeas corpus appeal with a good deal of enthusiasm and confidence. This brief was the only one in all the Ruby proceedings that we had printed. All our other briefs, in all proceedings and all courts, were either mimeographed, photostated, or simply typed, for the family never had funds for printing even the more important documents. On this one occasion, with so much at stake, we wanted to present our argument in the best possible form.

With hindsight, I now think our brief was too diffuse. There was extremely good material in it, but it would have been much better if we had reduced it in size and concentrated on the highlights of law and fact. Our argument was simple enough. Judge Brown, having a pecuniary interest, was disqualified within the meaning of the Texas constitution. Ruby was denied due process of law guaranteed by the Texas constitution and the Fourteenth Amendment to the Constitution of the United States because Brown was writing a commentary account of the trial proceedings while matters involving his discretion were still being considered by him. This rendered the judgment of conviction void and the subsequent proceedings invalid. All that we said in the fifty-eight printed pages was an elaboration and extension of these few simple self-evident propositions.

The State's brief acknowledged that, after the Court of Criminal Appeals had sent the original case back to Judge Brown for a sanity hearing, he had "made certain interlocutory orders and rulings on pending motions," but, it pointed out, these "were vacated and each and all of them have been or will be reheard, considered, and ruled on independently by Judge Holland." *Ergo*, there was nothing wrong with the situation. (Of course, we had drawn exactly the opposite conclusion from these facts. We did not believe that such errors could be corrected in the manner suggested by the State.)

Further, the State argued, if facts were belatedly discovered showing that Judge Brown "was legally disqualified at the time he performed discretionary duties in connection with the trial as to the accused's guilt or innocence" and we could not have discovered these facts earlier, then we might file some sort of pleading in connection with the appeal from the conviction, but not through a habeas corpus proceeding. (This was a highly technical point, as were others raised by the State in its brief, but Wade's staff pressed them with some ingenuity.) At the same time, they chided us for the delays and stratagems that had prevented an earlier ruling on the merits and with respect to Ruby's sanity. The State made much of our "dilatory tactics and collateral flanking proceedings." It also contended, contradicting itself in the process, that we had rushed Judge Brown into premature and precipitous consideration of our motions. (The brief consisted largely of an annotated chronology of our many adventures and misadventures in various courts, shrewdly calculated to persuade the high court that we were not acting in good faith, regardless of what Judge Brown had done.)

We were criticized again, and with considerable particularity, for the great delay in presenting our statement of facts. It was suggested by the State, but not insisted upon, that perhaps we ought to be denied a review because of the inexcusable delay.

Finally, the State argued that the disqualification of Judge Brown, if it existed at all, related to matters occurring after the completed trial. What Judge Brown had done, it was maintained, did not necessarily affect his personal or pecuniary gain or loss, and it should not be assumed that we were adversely affected. (This argument would have required us to prove the largely unprovable, that even the most reprehensible conduct directly affects the result of a case. We could not believe that the State was serious in its excessively narrow interpretation of what constituted judicial disqualification.) True, it said, Judge Brown was not perfect when measured by "the Canons of Judicial Ethics or by generalizations in certain cases decided by the United States Supreme Court." Other judges sold books, it said, and were not criticized. Why, then, pick on Joe Brown?

My colleagues and I arrived in the courtroom at Austin early, after cordial exchanges with some of the personnel

around the building. We were inordinately pleased and
confident about the situation. The luxury of a printed brief
betokened this new state of mind. As we quietly talked
over the discoveries that we had made with respect to
Judge Brown and the impression they had made in Judge
Holland's courtroom and upon the public, we expressed
the hope that the habeas corpus proceeding would afford
the Court of Criminal Appeals a short-cut to achieving a
just result. It still seemed to us that even Wade's office
would welcome such result.

Suddenly Judge Morrison, a tall Texan, walked into the
room. Greeting each of us in the friendliest manner, he
made a point of learning our names and letting us know we
were completely welcome. Whether or not this is usual in
the judge's part of the country, I do not know, but I had
never experienced such a ceremonial at home.

Whatever the cause, our own confidence or the judge's
welcome, we were in exactly the right mood for effective
oral argument when the public session opened. I thought
full justice was done to the case in the argument. All the
judges seemed to be much interested, but they said nothing. I thought the State's response was not especially effective. Hopefully, we all looked forward to the court's
ruling.

On May 18, 1966, the Texas Court of Criminal Appeals
decided the habeas corpus appeal. To say that the *per
curiam* (unsigned) opinion was curt is to understate the
matter. Considering the effort put into the trial and into
the appeal, it was almost insulting. Where Judge Holland
had seen much merit in our contentions and had denied our
petition only to permit an appeal, the reviewing court
acted almost vengefully:

This is a habeas corpus proceeding. The petition was pre-
sented to the Honorable Louis T. Holland, Judge of the 97th
Judicial District of Texas, who was sitting for the Judge of the
Criminal District Court No. 3 of Dallas County.

Judge Holland granted the writ and after hearing denied the relief prayed for and remanded the Petitioner to the custody of the Sheriff of Dallas County "for the sake of allowing Petitioner appellate review." This is an appeal from such order. Jack Ruby is in the custody of the Sheriff of Dallas County as the law requires him to be for this Court to have jurisdiction of his appeal from his conviction, with punishment assessed at death, which is pending before this Court in our Cause No. 37,900, styled Jack Rubenstein, alias Jack Ruby vs. The State of Texas.

This Court is and has been since February 24, 1965 ready, able and willing to hear, consider and decide the questions raised in the said appeal in Cause No. 37,900, including the question of the claim of denial of due process and the validity of the judgment of conviction.

Controversy continues as to whether Honorable Joe Tonahill, one of Appellant's trial counsel, should be permitted to represent him on appeal from his conviction for murder.

Judge Holland has indicated his readiness to empanel a jury and determine the question of Appellant's present sanity or insanity. He is directed to do so without further delay and to certify to this Court the result of such hearing.

At such hearing, Appellant's trial attorney, the Honorable Joe Tonahill, as well as counsel representing Appellant in this habeas corpus proceeding should be given the opportunity to present any competent evidence relative to Appellant's present sanity.

The writ of habeas corpus is not available to secure a judicial determination of any question which, even if determined in the prisoner's favor, could not result in his immediate discharge. The judgment remanding Appellant to the custody of the Sheriff of Dallas County is affirmed.

No motion for re-hearing will be entertained.

The last sentence was a gratuitous slur, since the rules of the court provided for such motions as a matter of course. We decided to ignore the injunction and asked leave to file a motion for rehearing. We called the court's attention to the voluminous record, recently augmented, in the appeal from the death sentence and its relevance to the habeas corpus proceeding. We referred, as an example, to the order entered by Judge Holland removing Joe Tonahill as attorney for Jack Ruby and relieving him of all duties. We referred the court to the supporting documents for such removal, including Ruby's own request. For this reason, we said, the court should reconsider that portion of its opinion which permitted Tonahill to participate in the sanity hearing and the appeal. We called the court's attention to the authorities sanctioning the writ of habeas corpus even if it does not result in the immediate discharge of the applicant and he is held for trial. We urged that the validity of the judgment of conviction must be decided before the determination of the other issues, such as change of venue, selection of jury, res gestae, etc. It did no good. The court denied our motion.

We had to ask ourselves what this denoted. Was it prejudgment of our case, impatience with the failure to hold a sanity hearing, annoyance that "foreign" attorneys were involved, irritation by the effort expended in behalf of an indigent person, or other undisclosed circumstances?

Clearly, we had to petition the United States Supreme Court for a writ of certiorari and, if possible, obtain a delay in the sanity hearing and other proceedings. We would ask Judge Holland, then the Texas Court of Criminal Appeals, then a Justice of the United States Supreme Court for this delay. If we could not obtain a stay, then we had to decide what to do about the sanity hearing and, in any event, be prepared to proceed on the appeal from the death sentence, while pursuing our application for a writ in the highest court of the land.

# 20

## JACK RUBY IS HELD TO BE SANE

THE MATTER of a sanity hearing for Jack Ruby was long under consideration. One of the last actions taken by Melvin Belli before the trial was the filing of a motion for a pretrial sanity hearing. Judge Brown immediately denied the motion, without consideration, as having been offered too late.

After the trial, as has been related, the Ruby family offered affidavits attesting to their belief that Jack was insane. Nothing came of this at the time, as the hearing was continued again and again. Then, when Kunstler tried to enter our appearances as counsel for Jack, the Texas Court of Criminal Appeals had seized upon the affidavits as a means of determining who should represent Jack in the courts. That court directed Judge Brown to proceed with the sanity hearing.

It was then, in March, 1965, that we entered the four motions that had taken us into so many different courts. As we had sought, we did achieve most of our goals, indirectly and in time. Tonahill was removed; Judge Brown had "recused" himself; the sanity hearing had been effectively stayed.

The attitude of counsel toward a sanity hearing had never been precisely determined. There was a risk, since if Jack were found to be insane, then he might be confined to a mental institution for life, an institution, moreover, where he would not be likely to get the psychiatric attention he needed. Then, too, a decision would have to be made about prosecuting the appeal after his incarceration.

(Texas law permits counsel some discretion in the matter.) And, of course, if he were found to be sane, the appeal would proceed, and then the sentence might be affirmed and Jack executed—or there might be another result, depending on our skill and good fortune.

Sol Dann, early in 1964, had begun to search for evidence that could be used in a sanity hearing. The tactic then was to show that Jack was mentally incompetent at the time of the shooting of Oswald. There was, in fact, much evidence of Jack's unstable temperament, but it had not been used at the original trial. After I entered the case, I turned to amassing additional material for possible use in the sanity hearing.

With the order of the Texas Court of Criminal Appeals, on May 18, 1966, we were confronted, whether we wished it or not, with the likelihood of an immediate sanity hearing. To compound the difficulty, the court had expressly granted to Joe Tonahill the right to participate in that trial, even though he had been removed by Judge Holland after a hearing. Yet when we asked the court to reconsider the order, it refused.

On Friday, May 20, 1966, Clinton filed a motion in the Court of Criminal Appeals for a stay of the sanity hearing. Like our previous motion, it was promptly overruled by Judges Morrison and Woodley. The judges' attitude, Clinton informed us, seemed to be that they wanted the sanity hearing to proceed without delay. Privately, Judge Morrison told Clinton that he and the members of the court had been criticized for the long delay in the case; they wanted nothing to stand in the way of an immediate sanity hearing.

We were no more successful with Judge Holland. On May 24, he, too, refused to delay the hearing. When he set the Ruby sanity hearing for June 13, 1966, to be preceded by a pretrial conference on June 10, we had no choice but to apply to a justice of the United States Supreme Court for a stay, pending the filing of our petition for a writ of certiorari. Justice Hugo L. Black was the one before whom this petition would come up, as he was the justice assigned to all Fifth Circuit matters. Normally, we would have regarded this as fortunate, for Justice Black has a profound respect for constitutional rights and is a very compassionate and perceptive human being. But he also dislikes anything that is presented to him in a blaze of publicity, and we were afraid that others might be the incendiaries in this respect—Joe Tonahill, for one. Justice Black, despite his reputation in some quarters to the contrary, has a great regard for the rights of lesser tribunals, be they state or federal. We feared that he might not be receptive to interfering with the lower courts until they had had the chance to deliver their rulings. Then would be the right time to petition the Supreme Court for a writ of certiorari. He could not be as oppressed as we were by the hands on a clock: if we waited too long, the statutory ninety days for appealing to the highest court of the land would go by.

As always, the five of us went over Kunstler's proposed text of the application for a stay with infinite care, suggesting many changes that, in the end, produced a cogent document. If we could not persuade Justice Black, we would certainly convince ourselves.

After giving a condensed history of the proceedings through the various courts in which we had traveled—the reader knows this story by now—we summed up the reasons, as we saw them, for a stay.

Concededly, the question was limited to whether the pretrial and the sanity hearings, scheduled for June 10 and June 13, 1966, respectively, should be stayed pending further proceedings in the United States Supreme Court. But in deciding this application we felt that some knowledge of the totality of the circumstances was indispensable. The past saga of this celebrated and historic case, with its many examples of the patently flagrant disregard of Ruby's fundamental constitutional rights as well as the novel nature of the federal questions raised in the habeas corpus proceeding, suggested at the very least a reasonable possibility that the Supreme Court would grant the petition for certiorari and eventually reverse the inexplicable decision of the Court of Criminal Appeals in the habeas corpus matter.

The request for a stay of the state court proceedings was based upon two basic and fundamental constitutional questions:

(1) Was petitioner Ruby being denied his right to counsel of his own choosing when a state appellate court forced a lawyer upon him after the trial court, following a full hearing, had ordered his removal and there was no appeal therefrom?

(2) Did the interest of the original trial judge, based upon his well-rewarded undertaking to write a book about the trial, deny petitioner due process of law so as to cause that trial and all subsequent proceedings to be constitutionally defective and therefore null and void?

We dealt in detail with the denial of counsel of Ruby's choice. It still comes easily to my tongue when I reread the outline of the argument against Tonahill:

(1) Petitioner has stated in open court that he does not want Tonahill to represent him.

(2) Petitioner has told Judge Brown he does not want Tonahill to represent him.

(3) Petitioner has told Chief Justice Earl Warren [when he was examined by the Warren Commission] that Tonahill is not his lawyer.

(4) Petitioner's immediate family, including his attorney-in-fact, does not want Tonahill to represent him.

(5) Tonahill has been discharged by petitioner and his family.

(6) Judge Holland has ordered Tonahill removed as an attorney of record.

(7) Tonahill has not participated in petitioner's representation for over a year.

(8) Tonahill has publicly attacked the integrity, wisdom, and competency of the attorneys of petitioner's own choosing.

(9) Tonahill and the present attorneys of petitioner's own choosing have differed and do differ on the manner in which to proceed for petitioner's best interest, and for another and antagonistic lawyer to be forced upon petitioner and his present attorneys to conduct a jury trial involving petitioner's sanity would create, *inter alia,* the following problems detrimental to petitioner:

(a) Which witnesses to be called on behalf of petitioner?

(b) The nature and extent of their direct examination?

(c) Whether Tonahill will bring additional attorneys into the case?

(d) Who will voir-dire [interrogate] the jury?

(e) What pretrial motions will be filed?

(f) What pretrial stipulations, if any, will be made?

(g) What questions will be asked of the State's witnesses?

(h) Who will be allowed to waive certain rights of petitioner?

(i) What objections will be made?

(j) Who will have authority to make objections?

(k) Who will argue to the jury, and

(l) What will be the nature of such jury argument?

There was more. To us it passed belief that any court viewing all the circumstances could foist Tonahill upon Ruby.

We summed up the consequences flowing from the disqualification of Judge Brown. In essence, if we were right in our contention that the proceedings were a nullity, there could not validly be a sanity hearing as part of the same void case. So we argued that the sanity proceeding and all other state court action should be stayed until the Supreme Court could act upon our petition for a writ of certiorari.

In token of our good faith, we offered to file our petition within such shorter period than ninety days as the court might suggest.

On June 3, we were informed by the clerk of the Supreme Court of the United States that Justice Black had denied our application for a stay of the proceedings in Texas and had attached a memorandum to his order. Just as we had feared, Justice Black, after summarizing the situation, delivered the telling philosophical judgment:

I do not feel justified in granting a stay which will interfere with the orderly and customary processes of the Courts of Texas in attempts to give Ruby a fair and prompt determination of his rights.

Although unhappy at the setback, a temporary one in fact, we had at least had the satisfaction of consideration by a justice whom we all admired. Our petition for a writ of certiorari was still before the Supreme Court, and this was insurance against any miscarriage in the Texas courts. Now, however, we were confronted with the problem of what to do about the sanity hearing. Should we participate, and so in effect recognize its validity? Should we decide that, since it was a void proceeding—according to our theory—we would have nothing to do with it? If the latter, then there would have to be a finding that Ruby was sane. How would that affect us? First of all, it would mean that Tonahill, at last, would be completely out of the case: a sane man can hire or fire his attorneys at will. There were other consequences to consider. Might not a finding of sanity, even in a void proceeding, indicate that we had not been in good faith in our contention, over a long period of time, that Ruby was insane? Might not the reviewing court seek to punish us by giving only cursory attention to our other arguments? In any event, there would be less sympathy for a sane Ruby than for an insane one.

As the sanity hearing neared, the attorneys on various

sides of the case made their views known publicly. Tonahill, for the first time, admitted that a sanity hearing might
not be good for Jack. The filing of our motion indicated to
him "a lack of enthusiasm for an adequate sanity trial. It
indicates the sanity trial would be a pretty futile thing,
because they don't want it."

"I would work with them and bend over backwards to
cooperate," Tonahill said, "but if those people don't want
him to have a sanity trial it may be difficult to get full-
fledged cooperation."

Henry Wade, shrugging his shoulders in characteristic
fashion, responded: "We're ready for the sanity trial and
have been for a long time, but it's not up to us to ask for a
sanity trial." He said that it was a matter of indifference to
him who represented Ruby. "That's a question between the
lawyers and the courts." Then, shifting his ground when
asked about the Ruby motion for the quashing of the
sanity hearing, he said: "From our standpoint, the district
attorney's office takes the attitude that the trial court will
overrule the motion and follow the mandate of the Court
of Criminal Appeals."

Tonahill agreed with his old adversary.

On June 8, 1966, we had another in our long series of
conference calls. Everything seemed to be going exceed-
ingly well. For the first time, the proceedings seemed
almost completely free of the complications that had
dogged us for so long. We agreed upon a series of steps,
some of which, it turned out, were based upon misconceptions.

We agreed that we would file a motion in Eva's name,
or some other document, with Judge Holland in behalf of
the members of the Ruby family and Jack, setting forth
that, to hasten a final disposition of the case, and without
prejudice to the right to ask for a sanity hearing later, Eva
was withdrawing the request for a sanity hearing at this
time. This motion, we were told, would be taken up before
Judge Holland at the imminent pretrial conference. We

were told, erroneously, that it would not be opposed by Wade or Tonahill.

Burleson and Clinton would immediately file a motion with the Texas Court of Criminal Appeals, asking that the record in the habeas corpus proceeding be incorporated with the record in the appeal in the main case, so that all aspects of the situation, including due process, might be considered by the court in reaching a fair and expeditious decision. This, too, we were told, would not be opposed by Tonahill, but we were not sure what Wade's attitude would be.

Kunstler would prepare a draft of the certiorari petition for the U.S. Supreme Court in the habeas corpus matter, so that I might revise it before I left on a long-scheduled trip to Europe on June 28. If, meanwhile, the Texas Court of Criminal Appeals allowed our motion with respect to the consolidation of the record, the material prepared by Kunstler would be used in connection with the brief for the Court of Criminal Appeals.

Burleson and Clinton would work immediately on a draft of the brief for the Texas Court of Criminal Appeals and submit a copy of it to me before I left on my trip, so that I might make suggestions and revisions in it. (While I was away, my young associate, Wayne B. Giampietro, would substitute for me, as, indeed, he did.) Our aim would be to file a brief, in some form or other, without delay. We could supplement it later, as was the custom in this sometimes informal court.

Our intent was to secure oral argument on the main appeal early in the October term of the Texas Court of Criminal Appeals, so that soon thereafter there might be a decision by that court (assuming that we had not meanwhile gone up on certiorari in the habeas corpus matter).

With respect to the gadflies Tonahill and his then associate, Colvin, we would reach a tacit understanding in which they recognized that we did not have the right to agree to their being in the case in any way because of the opposition of Ruby and his family, but that in order to avoid any further acrimony or anything that might be disadvantageous to Jack we would not object, nor would they object, to working along parallel lines. That is, we would file our own brief with the Texas Court of Criminal Appeals and not object, except possibly *pro forma*, to their filing a separate brief or briefs. In the same way, we would argue the case before the court and would not object, except in a formal way, perhaps, to their arguing the case. We would reserve the right to open and close the oral argument, and we would try to agree upon some division of the oral argument along logical lines, so that there would be no undue repetition of any point. Thus Burleson would take one point or perhaps the statement of facts, Clinton another, Kunstler a portion, myself a part. Because of the importance of the issue, we would make every effort to secure additional time for oral argument from the court.

In view of the *Sheppard* decision by the United States Supreme Court, we would get copies of the various briefs of Sheppard's attorneys and the American Civil Liberties Union, which had intervened in his case, and make the same sort of argument in compressed form. We would do this both with respect to the petition for certiorari and with respect to the appeal in the Texas Court of Criminal Appeals.

I would do no further work, for the moment at least, on the certification of the records for use in the sanity hearing, until and unless the pretrial conference indicated the necessity of our pushing ahead.

After we had concluded that we ought not to participate in any way in the sanity proceedings, we drafted a protective motion with the utmost care, and promptly presented it to Judge Holland, risking his displeasure but doing what our best professional judgment dictated. Despite the technical language, the motion is an interesting one.

Now comes Jack Ruby, Defendant, by and through his undersigned attorneys and represents unto the Court that [the]

Affidavit of Eva Grant, his sister, filed here on April 27, 1964 requesting a hearing under Article 932b V.A.C.C.P., having been withdrawn, vacated and annuled by verified instrument filed by said Eva Grant on June 9, 1966, he does not now desire and, with counsel, protests holding any such sanity hearing at this time in deprivation of his rights guaranteed by the Constitution of the United States, particularly the Fifth and Sixth Amendments thereto, and by the Constitution of Texas, particularly Article I, Section 10 thereof, and to the prejudice of his other rights in that such proceedings arise out of a judgment of conviction which is void and in that a finding of sanity or insanity may be used against him in future proceedings; and, accordingly, if such hearing is nevertheless held over this protest, so that Defendant's rights will be in no way waived, further represents that Defendant's counsel, with deference to this Court, will be present in the courtroom but will not actively participate in examining members of the jury panel, presenting and interrogating witnesses, cross-examining witnesses, making oral argument or engaging in any other aspects of such hearing, save and except the making of objections and taking exceptions to proceedings and occurrences during the court of said hearing in a further effort to protect Defendant's rights.

WHEREFORE, premises considered, Defendant respectively moves that the sanity hearing presently set for June 13, 1966, be dismissed and the supplemental record made herein pursuant to May 18, 1966 Opinion of the Court of Criminal Appeals of Texas be certified to that Court in order that Defendant's appeal in this cause may be reviewed at the next term of said Court, or continued pending said certification and ruling by Court of Criminal Appeals on the issue thus presented.

Judge Holland promptly denied the motion at the pretrial conference on June 10. We immediately filed a motion with the Court of Criminal Appeals, asking it to vacate its orders of February 24, 1965, and May 18, 1966, setting the case down for a sanity hearing, and asking the high tribunal to proceed, instead, with the appeal on its merits. Tonahill and Colvin filed a similar motion. For once our antagonists saw eye to eye with us. When these motions were categorically denied by the Court of Criminal Appeals, it became clear that the court was determined to allow nothing to stand any longer in the way of our following its several times expressed wish. Notwithstanding this judicial disapproval, we still felt that we could not participate actively in the sanity hearing. We would be there physically, but we would stand mute. Lest our silence and our motion be misconstrued by either the court or the public, we filed, posthaste, certain suggestions for the consideration of Judge Holland:

Now COMES Jack Ruby, Defendant herein, by and through his undersigned attorneys, and without waiving, and especially reserving all his rights, privileges, and immunities in the premises, and as officers of this Court and under the Court's direction, would show as follows:

### I

IT IS RESPECTFULLY SUGGESTED . . . that to avoid any waiver or misunderstanding, the presence of the . . . attorneys at the sanity hearing set by the Court, who are counsel of Jack Ruby's own choosing, are present under the Court's directive and over the expressed protest and objection of said . . . attorneys in seeking to render effective aid . . . to said Defendant and such presence . . . at the sanity hearing is not a waiver of any of the Defendant's Constitutional and statutory rights.

### II

. . . that said Jack Ruby should not be present during the course of the sanity hearing for the reason that his presence is not necessary and to subject [him] to a sanity hearing raised by evidence offered by the State . . . at the pretrial hearing . . . would be harmful to [his] person and to his . . . rights.

### III

. . . that in the event Jack Ruby is present in Court . . . the Court prohibit any interviews with news reporters or with anyone and that the Court not allow Jack Ruby to make any statements to

or be interrogated by the Court, the attorneys or the news
media to the end that his rights against self incrimination and
due process and otherwise under the Constitution[s] of the
United States and . . . Texas will be fully protected and in no
way be infringed or denied.

## IV

. . . that the Court not allow into evidence any alleged statements or conversations . . . after Jack Ruby's arrest . . . and . . .
to the present time. . . .

## V

. . . that all news media be excluded from the courtroom, the
corridors outside the courtroom . . . wherein the hearing will be
held and all places where the Defendant, members of the jury
panel, witnesses and all counsel are likely to be or may be, all
as provided under the rules and procedure set forth by the . . .
Supreme Court in the recent decision of Sheppard v. Maxwell
. . . and the cases therein cited.

## VI

. . . that a fair and impartial sanity hearing cannot be held on
June 13, 1966, for the reason that the news media accounts and
stories circulated to the prospective jurors and to the public
generally in and around Dallas County were [of] such a nature
as to come within the principles and doctrine of Sheppard v.
Maxwell. . . .

## VII

. . . that the Court lacks the jurisdiction to proceed with the
sanity hearing in that there is no valid pleadings on file raising
the issue and nothing is in controversy for the Court or jury to
decide.

## VIII

. . . that in the event the sanity hearing proceeds . . . the Court
insure Jack Ruby a fair and impartial trial following the rules of
procedure and evidence during all stages of the hearing and
this should be done regardless of objections and especially in
light of the . . . attorneys' position that they will not present
objections or actively participate in the trial.

## IX

. . . that no person or attorney be allowed to represent the rights of Jack Ruby to the end that any such rights be waived or infringed upon in any manner by motion, verbal representations or otherwise to the end that all of the rights of Jack Ruby will be fully protected.

X

. . . that a continuing objection to each phase of the sanity hearing and to each witness and to each question of each witness and to each piece of evidence be noted on behalf of the . . . attorneys and that it not be necessary to re-urge said objections during the course of the sanity hearing and that it be fully understood that the aforementioned objections shall continue through the entire proceedings. . . .

The sanity hearing, such as it was, took place on June 13, 1966. Jack Ruby and some of his attorneys were physically present in court, but it was clearly understood that they would not participate in the proceeding. Judge Holland understood their position and protected it.

The hearing had been preceded, after all, by private conferences between defense counsel and Tonahill and Colvin. At the meetings, Colvin acted as a sort of referee in what would otherwise have been a tense struggle between Tonahill and Dann. Although Tonahill threatened, at one point, to participate actively in the hearing and even to offer evidence to prove that Ruby was insane, all counsel agreed finally that the district attorney should be permitted to have the hearing to himself.

With his opponents maintaining a self-imposed silence, Bill Alexander had the stage. Strutting about as if he were confronting mighty opposition, he presented himself as the great defender of Ruby against his would-be attorneys. They, rather than Ruby, were to blame for this sham battle over sanity. No psychiatric testimony was offered, and the only evidence at all was provided by the jailors and the prison doctor.

A jail guard described Ruby as a "pretty good gin rummy player." Deputy K. H. Croy said Ruby cheated "occasionally" at cards but was caught in the act. "He didn't like it

too much," Croy opined with a smile. Four deputies said
that Ruby knew where he was, what he was in jail for,
and what penalty had been assessed against him—a legal
test of his sanity.

Deputy W. S. Elliott said that during his time guarding
Ruby he noticed that he "loved to read" and "knew quite a
bit about current events."

"He has a very fine mind," Elliott said, unsmiling.

Deputy Don Standridge said Ruby preferred to read
legal material and had an "exceptionally good memory."
Ruby was concerned with personal appearance and always
followed orders, although "he didn't like to."

Deputy Archie F. Watson said he played dominoes and
cards with Ruby. He said that he never noticed any hallu-
cinations or delusions in Ruby's actions.

The jail doctor, John W. Callahan, said he had seen
Ruby twice a week. Ruby, he said, worked crossword puz-
zles and his attitude was "very good."

He was in good physical condition "in keeping with his
age and sex," Dr. Callahan insisted. His last blood pressure
count was 130 over 80 and he had a 72-beat-per-minute
pulse.

Asked if Ruby appeared suicidal, Callahan answered
"definitely not." (Later, after Ruby's death, Dr. Callahan
said in a published article that Ruby was suicidal.)

Alexander tried to create the impression, within the
limited scope of the hearing, that only a cabal of lawyers
and pseudopsychiatrists pretended that Ruby was insane.
In this the irresistible Ruby agreed. He was determined to
make the jury and the wider public believe that he was a
rational man who had acted in a moment of uncontrollable
passion.

When Ruby unexpectedly rose from his seat to address
the court, his sister shouted a warning to Burleson; but her
brother would not be stopped.

"I try to answer every question intelligently," he said. "I
never tried to camouflage my true mental capacity."

"Never at any time since I was convicted have I done anything to make anybody believe I was of unsound mind," Ruby said, facing the jury. "I don't know who conspired to do that [spread the story he was insane]."

His attitude implied that it was his attorneys, particularly Tonahill, and the prosecution.

Alexander made a pretense of explaining to the jury that Ruby's attorneys were silent for constitutional reasons. "Sometimes I think we're supposed to get the nose bleed when they mention constitutional rights," he said. "They started this proceeding and now they want to hold back claiming this constitutional rights business."

He accused us of "piddling around." "I almost feel sorry for Jack," he said. "Jack Ruby is in a better position than his lawyers because he takes a realistic view of things."

After the jury returned its verdict of "sane," Judge Holland drawled, characteristically: "This sure has been an odd case for you. You've done your job and I've done mine. Maybe this looks like much ado about nothing. I hope that history records that I haven't done any violence to our profession."

The attorneys then masked their antipathies in praise of Judge Holland, and he in turn complimented them. Everyone, including the audience, had a good time, and there was frequent laughter. In the audience was Marguerite Oswald, the mother of the one charged with slaying Kennedy. She explained that she was still investigating the case to prove that her son was only a "patsy."

The judge commented to all and sundry: "I hope you don't think this turned out to be a testimonial."

"Are you going to appeal the verdict that Ruby was sane?" Dann was asked by a reporter.

"We are going to appeal everything," he said, without consulting anyone.

(In fact, there was no appeal of the "adverse" ruling; under Texas law there can be no appeal in a sanity hearing. Our contention would have to be that the proceeding was absolutely void. If there was a second trial and the State attempted to introduce the finding of the jury, we could object to it and have a bill of exceptions if the finding was admitted into evidence. In addition, there was always the opportunity to raise the matter in a habeas corpus proceeding.)

Before the Court of Criminal Appeals could have received notification of the jury's verdict in the normal manner and while our motion for certiorari was pending in the United States Supreme Court, the court entered an order on June 15, 1966, setting the appeal from the death sentence for the filing of briefs and oral argument on Friday, June 24, 1966, at 9:30 A.M.

The court directed Ruby to designate in writing the attorneys authorized to represent him in that court and to argue the matter. To even the score, the State was directed to file a list of counsel to argue for it.

Then, as if reading our minds, the court, on its own motion, allowed us one hour and thirty minutes for opening and thirty minutes rejoinder, far more than called for by the rules. In addition, all who had been appellant's counsel of record after the filing of notice of appeal were given thirty minutes to argue as friends of the court. After all our struggles, Joe Tonahill would be permitted to supplement our argument. By this time we did not much care.

The State was given a similar allocation of time.

And the parties were given until August 1 to file additional briefs, the State being allowed twenty days to reply to the last of our briefs. (Significantly, Judge Woodley dissented from that part of the order giving Tonahill time to argue the case.)

Now, at last, we could say that we had ample time to present our argument against the judgment of death. We still might ask ourselves if this were only a modification of the old saw about being given a fair trial and then hanged. Perhaps Ruby was indeed going to be given that to which every American is entitled—if not a fair trial in the first instance, then a fair review, and thereafter a fair trial. If such turned out not to be the case, then our petition for certiorari in connection with the habeas corpus proceeding was still before the Supreme Court, and another petition for certiorari might be filed in connection with the present appeal, with the two matters possibly consolidated in the United States Supreme Court. There were other steps that resourceful and dedicated lawyers could take, and we hoped that we were both resourceful and dedicated.

# THE ARGUMENT OF THE APPEAL

# 21

## THE ESTES CASE

ANGLO-SAXON JURISPRUDENCE has as one of its basic tenets the deceptive principle that litigants have the right to rely upon the precedents. As the courts have ruled in the past, so are they supposed to rule in the present and future. In fact, the precedents, particularly where great constitutional issues are involved, change frequently. The highest court of the land may conclude that the precedents in a particular situation are wrong or outmoded and should be refined, restated, or overruled. So in every case a lawyer has at least one eye cocked upon the cases pending in the Supreme Court, in the hope that the uttering there of some magical words will vindicate his position.

At least three cases of overwhelming importance and pertinence were pending in the Supreme Court as we struggled to set aside the death verdict pronounced upon Ruby. We were hopeful that in the *Estes* or *Sheppard* or *Miranda* cases, or in all of them, or in some other ruling, it would be found that we were right and the Dallas court tragically wrong. We scanned the newspapers and what lawyers call "the advance sheets" of judicial opinions to learn what portended. In each instance, the opinion of the Supreme Court turned out to be of landmark proportions. To understand the Ruby case one must understand what the Court said in each of these cases.

The case of Billie Sol Estes was originally called for trial on September 24, 1962, in Smith County, Texas, after a change of venue from Reeves County, more than five hundred miles west of Smith County. (The tremendous size of the state of Texas permits such far-reaching changes of scene for trials, comparable elsewhere to the skipping of a couple of states.) At that time Jack Ruby was operating a small-scale night club in Dallas, relatively little known despite a lot of noise. Billie Sol Estes was a genuinely big man—in a fraudulent way. He had taken in bankers, farmers, his fellow churchgoers, and many others by a crooked scheme to induce them to purchase fertilizer tanks and equipment which had existed only in his own fertile mind. Carrying the fiction further, he had caused the purchasers to give him chattel mortgages on the nonexistent property. Ultimately, the scheme collapsed, and Billie Sol Estes, protesting self-righteously, was indicted. A national sensation was created; the pretrial press clippings alone filled eleven volumes. Naturally, there was a great demand for seats at the trial. Every seat was filled by eager spectators, and many persons stood in the aisles of the courtroom. Any legitimate theatre, in the heyday of Broadway, would have been proud of such attendance.

At the time, there were two conflicting codes of propriety for the conduct of trials. The American Bar Association Canon 35, born of the Lindbergh kidnapping-murder case debacle in New Jersey, for which Bruno Richard Hauptmann paid with his life in the electric chair, provided that judicial proceedings should not be broadcast, televised, or photographed, lest fair trials be impeded. This canon, which had no binding legal effect, resulted from the growing awareness of the responsibilities for "due process" created by the Fourteenth Amendment to the Constitution of the United States. Only Texas differed from the American Bar Association on this subject. Just as Texas had a separate court for criminal appeals, it had a different canon for judicial proceedings. Canon 28 of the State Bar of Texas leaves the telecasting and photographing of court proceedings to the supposedly sound discretion of the trial judge. Since the trial judge may be almost any kind of human being imaginable, including Judge Joe B. Brown,

all sorts of troubled results are foreseeable and unforesee-
able.

When Billie Sol Estes was called to trial on September
24, 1962, his attorneys moved to ban telecasting, radio
broadcasting, and news photography; at the same time,
they moved for a continuance. A two-day hearing was held
on these motions. This hearing was carried live—very
much alive—with all the communications media in full
operation. Later, when Justice Tom Clark of Texas delivered the opinion for the Supreme Court, he observed that
"the picture presented was not one of that judicial serenity
and calm" to which each accused person is entitled under
the American system.

The continuance was granted, but the judge refused to
ban radio, television, and cameras from the courtroom. A
bit less than a month after the original hearing, the case
came on again for trial, on October 22, 1962. The atmosphere in the courtroom was changed somewhat; that is,
the communications media were present, but less blatantly.
At the earlier hearing "cables and wires were snaked across
the courtroom floor, three microphones were on the judge's
bench and others were beamed at the jury box and the
counsel table," and there was "considerable disruption of
the hearings." This time the telecasters, broadcasters, and
photographers were less obtrusive. They were confined to
a booth at the back of the courtroom. The defense counsel
continued to object to the coverage, and the judge, apparently less sure of himself than his rulings indicated, restricted the media from time to time. Parts of the proceedings were covered live and parts not covered at all, and
there were variations in between. In any event, news
commentators made much of the case, using film clips "as
a backdrop for their reports." And on one occasion videotapes of the September hearing were rebroadcast in
place of the "late movie," and must have been equally
entertaining.

Whether or not the coverage of the case had any effect

on the proceedings in fact, Billie Sol Estes was convicted, and an appeal was taken by him to the Texas Court of Criminal Appeals. The Court, affirming the conviction, held there was no impropriety or impairment to a fair trial because of the limited telecasting and the like.

This ruling in the Estes case by the highest court of criminal review in Texas was in effect when Jack Ruby was tried. One can be certain that it was a temptation to Judge Brown and other judicial Thespians. Judge Brown did resist, after a fashion, the full coverage of the case by radio and television; but "to his eternal regret," as he phrased it, he consented to the televising of the jury's verdict. Objections to the circus atmosphere and the poisoned community atmosphere had been taken by counsel for the defense, even if many believed that Belli and Tonahill had themselves shared in the responsibility for the excesses of the press.

Meanwhile, the Billie Sol Estes case proceeded by certiorari to the United States Supreme Court. There a native Texan, from Dallas, was to write the majority opinion for a badly split court.

The case was argued before the Supreme Court on April 1, 1965, shortly after we had attempted to disqualify Judge Brown in our version of the Estes case. It was decided on June 7, 1965, as the highest court neared its summer recess. A rehearing was denied on October 11, 1965, after the court had returned to its judicial duties.

The Supreme Court, through Justice Clark, held that Estes was deprived of his right under the Fourteenth Amendment of the Constitution to due process "by the televising of his notorious, heavily publicized and highly sensational criminal trial." Four justices dissented. As so often happens in a landmark case, all the justices felt constrained to explain why they were for or against the majority opinion.

Justice Clark reminded his colleagues that two years earlier, in the Rideau case, arising in Louisiana, they had "constructed a rule that the televising of a defendant in the act of confessing to a crime was inherently invalid under the Due Process Clause of the Fourteenth Amendment even without a showing of prejudice or a demonstration of the nexus between this televised confession and the trial." The justice then gave an account of what had happened in a manner that was a model of succinctness and judicial eloquence.

Here, although there was nothing so dramatic as a home-viewed confession, there had been a bombardment of the community with the sights and sounds of a two-day hearing during which the original jury panel, the petitioner [Estes], the lawyers and the judge were highly publicized. The petitioner was subjected to characterization and minute electronic scrutiny to such an extent that at one point the photographers were found attempting to picture the page of the paper from which he was reading while sitting at the counsel table. The two-day hearing and the order permitting television at the actual trial were widely known throughout the community. This emphasized the notorious character that the trial would take and, therefore, set it apart in the public mind as an extraordinary case or, as Shaw would say, something 'not conventionally unconventional.' When the new jury was empaneled at the trial four of the jurors selected had seen and heard all or part of the broadcasts of the earlier proceedings.

Justice Clark was concerned about the possibility that the court might be discriminating between the newspapers and television; for newspaper reporters have a recognized right of access to the courtroom to assure the defendant a "public trial." He resolved the dilemma by observing that reporters are not permitted to bring typewriters or printing presses into the courtroom. When television reporting could be freed from "their present hazards to a fair trial," he said, "we will have another case."

There followed a long and learned discussion of what constitutes due process, a fair trial, the right of the public to know what is going on. He considered whether or not the defendant Estes had actually been prejudiced by the television of any part of the proceedings. He concluded that the risks were so great as not to require a showing of actual prejudice. He cited earlier cases in which the Supreme Court had dispensed with the need for proof of prejudice and analogized the Estes situation to these precedents. He phrased the matter in concrete terms:

Forty-eight of our States and the Federal Rules have deemed the use of television improper in the courtroom. This fact is most telling in buttressing our conclusion that any change in procedure which would permit its use would be inconsistent with our concepts of due process in this field.

The chief function of the judicial machinery, he said, is to ascertain the truth. Television does not contribute materially to this, he said. It injects "an irrelevant factor into court proceedings." It causes unfairness. He discussed the potential impact of television on the jurors, the quality of the testimony in criminal trials, the additional responsibilities on the trial judge, the impact on the defendant. Significantly, from our viewpoint, he cited at this point a document relating directly to the Ruby case, "Pye, *The Lessons of Dallas—Threats to Fair Trial and Free Press,* National Civil Liberties Clearing House, 16th Annual Conference." He went on:

The television camera is a powerful weapon. Intentionally or inadvertently it can destroy an accused and his case in the eyes of the public. While our telecasters are honorable men, they too are human. The necessity for sponsorship weighs heavily in favor of the televising of only notorious cases, such as this one, and invariably focuses the lens upon the unpopular or infamous accused. . . .

The State would dispose of all these observations with the simple statement that they are for psychologists because they are purely hypothetical. But we cannot afford the luxury of saying that, because these factors are difficult of ascertainment in particular cases, they must be ignored.

The justice's words had a fervor at times that many people, mistakenly, were not accustomed to expect from him. The final words before the formal order of reversal were especially stirring:

It is said that the ever-advancing techniques of public communication and the adjustment of the public to its presence may bring about a change in the effect of telecasting upon the fairness of criminal trials. But we are not dealing here with future developments in the field of electronics. Our judgment cannot be rested on the hypothesis of tomorrow but must take the facts as they are presented today.

Chief Justice Warren, his famous report on the debacle in Dallas being fixed, no doubt, in his own mind and in the consciousness of his countrymen as well, was not content to agree with Justice Clark's opinion for the court on generalities and abstract fears alone. Joined by Justices Douglas and Goldberg, he presented a long and persuasive recital of the facts with respect to the baneful consequences of the use of television in the courtroom during the Estes proceedings. He drew compelling conclusions from these facts, buttressing each with direct proof of what had actually occurred:

The televising of trials would cause the public to equate the trial process with the forms of entertainment regularly seen on television and with the commercial objectives of the television industry. . . .

The television industry might also decide that the bareboned trial itself does not contain sufficient drama to sustain an audience. It might provide expert commentary on the proceedings and hire persons with legal backgrounds to anticipate possible trial strategy, as the football expert anticipates plays for his audience. The trial judge himself stated at the September hear-

ing that if he wanted to see a ball game he would turn on his
television set, so why not the same for a trial.

Moreover, should television become an accepted part of the
courtroom, greater sacrifices would be made for the benefit of
broadcasters. . . .

There would be a real threat to the integrity of the trial
process if the television industry and trial judges were allowed
to become in the staging of criminal proceedings. . . .

Can we be sure that the public would not inherently distrust
our system of justice because of its intimate association with a
commercial enterprise? . . .

Broadcasting in the courtroom would give the television
industry an awesome power to condition the public mind either
for or against an accused. . . .

The sense of fairness, dignity and integrity that all associate
with the courtroom would become lost with its commercializa-
tion. Thus, the televising of trials would not only have an effect
on those participating in the trials that are being televised, but
also on those who observe the trials and later become trial
participants. . . .

Finally, if the televising of the criminal proceedings were
approved, trials would be selected for television coverage for
reasons having nothing to do with the purpose of trial. A trial
might be televised because a particular judge has gained the
fancy of the public by his unorthodox approach; or because the
district attorney has decided to run for another office and it is
believed his appearance would attract a large audience; or
simply because a particular courtroom has a layout that best
accommodates television coverage.

Here was the Chief Justice at his very best, combining
great skill in both the abstract and the concrete. We cher-
ished each word and made note, unnecessary in any event,
to quote him in the Texas Court of Criminal Appeals and
elsewhere when the Ruby case reached that point of ripe-
ness. The Chief Justice, familiar with what had gone on in

Dallas, would be a good audience for us; but, alas, we felt
that he would find it necessary to disqualify himself. (This
danger is always present when a justice of the Supreme
Court is selected for activity in any forum outside of his
own courtroom.)

Justice Stewart, with whom three other members of the
court joined, indicated that we had to bear in mind the
possibility that there might be different readings of the
facts in each case. He said, at the outset of his dissent:

I cannot agree with the Court's decision that the circumstances of this trial led to a denial of the petitioner's Fourteenth
Amendment rights. I think that the introduction of television
into a courtroom is, at least in the present state of the art, an
extremely unwise policy. It invites many constitutional risks,
and it detracts from the inherent dignity of a courtroom. But I
am unable to escalate this personal view into a *per se* constitutional rule. And I am unable to find, on the specific record of
this case, that the circumstances attending the limited televising
of the petitioner's trial resulted in the denial of any right guaranteed to him by the United States Constitution.

He then spelled out why he felt that Estes had not been
deprived of a fair trial. But even in dissent Justice Stewart
and those who agreed with him knew that there were
inherent dangers:

It is obvious that the introduction of television and news
cameras into a criminal trial invites many serious constitutional
hazards. The very presence of photographers and television
cameramen plying their trade in a courtroom might be so
completely and thoroughly disruptive and distracting as to
make a fair trial impossible. Thus, if the scene at the September
hearing had been repeated in the courtroom during the jury
trial, it is difficult to conceive how a fair trial in the constitutional sense could have been afforded the defendant. And even
if, as was true here, the television cameras are so controlled
and concealed as to be hardly perceptible in the courtroom

itself, there are risks of constitutional dimensions that lurk in the very process of televising court proceedings at all.

His conclusion, although it led to a different result, was as eloquent as that of the Chief Justice or of Justice Clark:

I do not think that the Constitution denies to the State or to individual trial judges all discretion to conduct criminal trials with television cameras present, no matter how unobtrusive the cameras may be. I cannot say at this time that it is impossible to have a constitutional trial whenever any part of the proceedings is televised or recorded on television film. I cannot now hold that the Constitution absolutely bars television cameras from every criminal courtroom, even if they have no impact upon the jury, no effect upon any witness, and no influence upon the conduct of the judge.

Justice Brennan underscored what was implicit in the many words written by his colleagues:

I write merely to emphasize that only four of the five Justices voting to reverse rest on the proposition that televised criminal trials are constitutionally infirm, whatever the circumstances.

In Dallas the press was well aware of the implications of the Estes case. The *Morning News,* which, we thought, had had so prejudicial an effect during the Ruby trial, reported on June 17, 1965, that the Dallas attorney for Jack Ruby "is underlining passages" in the Supreme Court's ruling:

Attorney Phil Burleson revealed he is "about half way through" with the federal judges' opinions on high-powered publicity and its effects on Estes' Tyler trial.
Dist. Atty. Henry Wade said he expected Ruby's lawyers to use the Estes ruling in the case of Lee Harvey Oswald's slayer but, "I don't think it will make any difference."
He pointed out that Estes' case was televised from pretrial hearings through much of the actual trial, but cameras were allowed in the Ruby courtroom only after the jury reached a verdict.

Other attorneys, who asked not to be identified, said that although most of the opinions concerned the use of television in the courtroom, there was also discussion of the "atmosphere" of publicity and the "national notoriety" of the case.

In due course, all the Ruby defense counsel read and re-read the Estes opinion.

# 22

## THE SHEPPARD CASE

A YEAR LATER, almost to a day, after the Estes decision, on June 6, 1966, the Supreme Court of the United States handed down an opinion in the habeas corpus case of *Samuel A. Sheppard* v. *E. L. Maxwell, Warden* that was even more far-reaching than the *Estes* opinion. This time only Justice Black dissented, and he did not offer an opinion. Again Justice Clark of Dallas delivered the majority opinion. Because we were about to file our brief with the Texas Court of Criminal Appeals and to argue the Ruby death sentence before that body, his words were of tremendous importance to us. Why did the *Sheppard* case mean so much?

Sheppard had been convicted of the second-degree murder of his wife in 1954 in the Court of Common Pleas of Cuyahoga County in Ohio. Samuel H. Silbert had been the Chief Justice of that court for many years, but one of his colleagues, facing re-election, had asked for the well-publicized privilege of presiding, and the Chief Justice had obliged him. Sheppard's conviction was affirmed by the Court of Appeals for Cuyahoga County in 1955 and by the Ohio Supreme Court in 1956. That same year the United States Supreme Court denied certiorari on the original appeal, and Sheppard seemed destined to serve his sentence in disgrace. After several years, Sheppard came up for parole, but the Ohio parole board refused him freedom. Then, in 1964, a brilliant new legal luminary, F. Lee Bailey of Boston, came upon the scene. In his application for federal writ of habeas corpus, Bailey contended

that Sheppard was deprived of a fair trial by the State
because of the trial judge's failure to protect him sufficiently "from the massive, pervasive and prejudicial publicity that attended his prosecution." The federal district
court agreed with Bailey, and, as the legal phrase goes,
"granted the writ subject to the state's right to put Sheppard to trial again." The United States Court of Appeals
for the Sixth Circuit reversed the district court by a split
vote, and the Supreme Court granted certiorari. Thus, as
has happened in other important cases, the Supreme Court,
despite its earlier decision to turn down the original appeal,
agreed to review the case in a different context. The Supreme Court concluded that Sheppard had not received a
fair trial, after all, and reversed the judgment. (Subsequently, the State chose to try Sheppard again, and under
Bailey's shrewd defense, aided by the passing of a decade,
the defendant was acquitted.)

The opinion of Justice Clark in the Sheppard case was
very much in our minds. There was in it a long review of
the circumstances surrounding the murder of Marilyn
Sheppard and the focusing of suspicion on her husband:

After a search of the house and premises on the morning of
the tragedy, Dr. Gerber, the Coroner, is reported—and it is un-
denied—to have told his men, "Well, it is evident the doctor did
this, so let's go get the confession out of him." He proceeded to
interrogate and examine Sheppard while the latter was under
sedation in his hospital room.

Justice Clark recited the facts with respect to newspaper
coverage:

On July 7, the day of Marilyn Sheppard's funeral, a newspaper story appeared in which Assistant County Attorney
Mahon—later the chief prosecutor of Sheppard—sharply criticized the refusal of the Sheppard family to permit his immediate questioning. From there on headline stories repeatedly
stressed Sheppard's lack of cooperation with the police and

other officials. . . . When Sheppard insisted that his lawyer be present, the Coroner wrote out a subpoena and served it on him. Sheppard then agreed to submit to questioning without counsel and the subpoena was torn up. The officers questioned him for several hours. . . . Sheppard's performance was reported in detail by the news media along with photographs. The newspapers also played up Sheppard's refusal to take a lie detector test and "the protective ring" thrown up by his family. . . . More stories appeared when Sheppard would not allow authorities to inject him with "truth serum."

The Coroner called an inquest:

The hearing was broadcast with live microphones placed at the Coroner's seat and the witness stand. A swarm of reporters and photographers attended. Sheppard was brought into the room by police who searched him in full view of several hundred spectators. Sheppard's counsel were present during the three-day inquest but were not permitted to participate. When Sheppard's chief counsel attempted to place some documents in the record, he was forcibly ejected from the room by the Coroner, who received cheers, hugs, and kisses from the ladies in the audience. Sheppard was questioned for five and one-half hours about his actions on the night of the murder, his married life, and a love affair with Susan Hayes. . . .

Throughout this period the newspapers emphasized evidence that tended to incriminate Sheppard and pointed out discrepancies in his statements to authorities. At the same time, Sheppard made many public statements to the press and wrote feature articles asserting his innocence. . . .

These brief excerpts from Justice Clark's summary of the background of the case scarcely convey more than the general flavor of what was occurring that summer of 1954. There were all sorts of sensational articles tending to prejudice Sheppard before a trial had taken place. These things, we felt, were similar to what had occurred with respect to Jack Ruby, except that in our case there was

more of this prejudicial material, because the presidential
assassination and its aftermath were naturally of greater
interest to the public than even the most sensational sex
murder.

Justice Clark quoted from front-page editorials demanding that Sheppard be jailed. He referred to the five volumes
filled with clippings from each of the three Cleveland newspapers. He assumed that the radio and television coverage
was equally large, because all communications media had
been in the courtroom in full force. He gave a graphic
account of what had happened in the courtroom, presided
over by Judge Blythin, "a candidate to succeed himself."
(Judge Brown was also a candidate to succeed himself and,
at the ensuing election, which followed the Ruby trial, he
garnered more votes than any other candidate for office in
his district, save President Johnson.)

Justice Clark's account of the trial very much resembled,
in many particulars but not in all, the arrangements for
the Ruby trial, but on a somewhat smaller scale. So far as
we know, Judge Blythin, unlike Judge Brown, was not
assisted by any public relations counsellor such as the
famous Mr. Bloom of the Citizens Council of Dallas. With
undertones of shock, Justice Clark reported: "Indeed, one
television broadcast carried a staged interview of the judge
as he entered the courthouse." How many more such
"staged" interviews did Judge Brown permit of himself,
contending counsel, and even defendant Ruby himself!
"In the corridors outside the courtroom there was a host of
photographers and television personnel with flash cameras,
portable lights and motion picture cameras." This was
the essence of what occurred during the Ruby proceedings.
"A rule of court prohibited picture-taking in the courtroom
during the actual sessions of the court, but no restraints
were put on photographers during recesses, which were
taken once each morning and afternoon, with a longer
period for lunch." So detail was piled upon detail by Justice
Clark, all having a reminiscent ring to the Ruby counsel:

All of these arrangements with the news media and their massive coverage of the trial continued during the entire nine weeks of the trial. The courtroom remained crowded to capacity with representatives of news media. Their movement in and out of the courtroom often caused so much confusion that, despite the loud speaker system installed in the courtroom, it was difficult for the witnesses and counsel to be heard. Furthermore, the reporters, clustered within the bar of the small courtroom, made confidential talk among Sheppard and his counsel almost impossible during the proceedings. They frequently had to leave the courtroom to obtain privacy. And many times when counsel wished to raise a point with the judge out of the hearing of the jury it was necessary to move to the judge's chambers. Even then, news media representatives so packed the judge's anteroom that counsel could hardly return from the chambers to the courtroom. The reporters vied with each other to find out what counsel and the judge had discussed, and often these matters later appeared in newspapers accessible to the jury.

If there were differences between the two trials, we felt that they were slight, differences without true distinctions. As in the Ruby case, so in the Sheppard case: "Every juror, except one, testified at *voir dire* to reading about the case in the Cleveland papers or to having heard broadcasts about it." Justice Clark concentrated now on nine of the more flagrant episodes of overreaching by the press and others during the course of the trial itself. Extensive as have been our quotations from the famous Sheppard opinion, we have only skimmed over the countless picturesque details.

Justice Clark went from the specific facts of the pervasive publicity surrounding the Sheppard proceedings to the law developed over the years and culminating in the Estes opinion the previous term of the Supreme Court. He posed the contrasting problems in the contest between a free press and a fair trial: ". . . we have consistently required that the press have a free hand, even though we

sometimes deplored its sensationalism." He quoted from
an earlier opinion of the court: "Freedom of discussion
should be given the widest range compatible with the
essential requirements of the fair and orderly administration of justice." He cited from that embodiment of judicial
liberalism, Justice Holmes, in a case more than a half
century old:

The theory of our system is that the conclusions to be reached
in a case will be induced only by evidence and argument in
open court, and not by any outside influence, whether of private
talk or public print.

He quoted, too, from Justice Black, the only colleague
who was dissenting from the majority decision in the
Sheppard case: "our system of law has always endeavored
to prevent even the probability of unfairness." He concluded that "the totality of circumstances"—a phrase dear
to the Supreme Court in many Bill of Rights situations—
makes the Sheppard trial and its result a miscarriage of
justice, a deprival of due process in the constitutional, as
well as the practical, sense. He analyzed what had occurred
in both the Estes and Sheppard proceedings and decided
that the constitutional abuses were greater in the Ohio case
than in the Texas case.

This analysis reminded us that there would be similar
weighing of the Ruby, Sheppard and Estes cases in the
Texas Court of Criminal Appeals and then in the Supreme
Court of the United States, when and if our case reached
that highest of tribunals. Glittering generalities were supposed to guide us, but not to blind us. It was "the totality of
circumstances," that magical phrase, that was to concern
the court and us. We were encouraged by much in Justice
Clark's opinion and by the footnotes as well. In a case in
which a client's life may depend upon one's attention to
details, it is necessary to seek out the meaning of each
word and phrase, and not alone the opinion as a whole or
long passages in it. A qualifying clause may destroy the

entire effect of an opinion, and a parenthetical phrase, or
a footnote, may be the clue to unexpected consequences.

As we saw it, Judge Brown in the Ruby case was guilty
of the same lack of understanding of fundamentals as was
Judge Blythin in the Sheppard case. As Justice Clark
expressed it:

The court's fundamental error is compounded by the holding
that it lacked power to control the publicity about the trial.
From the very inception of the proceedings the judge announced that neither he nor anyone else could restrict prejudicial news accounts. And he reiterated this view on numerous
occasions. Since he viewed the news media as his target, the
judge never considered other means that are often utilized to
reduce the appearance of prejudicial material and to protect
the jury from outside influence. We conclude that these procedures would have been sufficient to guarantee Sheppard a fair
trial and so do not consider what sanctions might be available
against a recalcitrant press nor the charges of bias now made
against the state trial judge.

The carnival atmosphere at trial could easily have been
avoided since the courtroom and courthouse premises are subject to the control of the court. As we stressed in *Estes*, the
presence of the press at judicial proceedings must be limited
when it is apparent that the accused might otherwise be prejudiced or disadvantaged.

And "the court should have insulated the witnesses,"
Justice Clark continued:

[T]he court should have made some effort to control the release
of leads, information, and gossip to the press by police officers,
witnesses, and the counsel for both sides. Much of the information thus disclosed was inaccurate, leading to groundless rumors
and confusion.

More specifically, the trial court might well have proscribed
extra-judicial statements by any lawyer, party, witness, or court
official which divulged prejudicial matters, such as the refusal

of Sheppard to submit to interrogation or take any lie detector tests; any statement made by Sheppard to officials; the identity of prospective witnesses or their probable testimony; any belief in guilt or innocence; or like statements concerning the merits of the case.

From the specific recital of what had gone on in the Sheppard proceedings, Justice Clark drew the guideline conclusions for our use and for the use of all courts everywhere, seeking a reconciliation of the twin requirements of fair trial and free press:

From the cases coming here we note that unfair and prejudicial news comment on pending trials has become increasingly prevalent. Due process requires that the accused receive a trial by an impartial jury free from outside influences. Given the pervasiveness of modern communications and the difficulty of effacing prejudicial publicity from the minds of the jurors, the trial courts must take strong measures to ensure that the balance is never weighed against the accused. And appellate tribunals have the duty to make an independent evaluation of the circumstances. Of course, there is nothing that proscribes the press from reporting events that transpire in the courtroom. But where there is a reasonable likelihood that prejudicial news prior to trial will prevent a fair trial, the judge should continue the case until the threat abates, or transfer it to another county not so permeated with publicity. In addition, sequestration of the jury was something the judge should have raised *sua sponte* with counsel. If publicity during the proceedings threatens the fairness of the trial, a new trial should be ordered. But we must remember that reversals are but palliatives; the cure lies in those remedial measures that will prevent the prejudice at its inception. The courts must take such steps by rule and regulation that will protect their processes from prejudicial outside interferences. Neither prosecutors, counsel for defense, the accused, witnesses, court staff nor enforcement officers coming under the jurisdiction of the court should be permitted to frustrate its function. Collaboration between counsel and the press as to information affecting the fairness of a criminal trial is not only subject to regulation, but is highly censurable and worthy of disciplinary measures.

So, because of the failure of the trial judge to "fulfill his duty to protect Sheppard from the inherently prejudicial publicity which saturated this community and to control disruptive influences in the courtroom," the case was reversed and remanded.

Thus, as the climactic moments in the Ruby case approached, we were encouraged, beyond our wildest hopes, by a landmark decision handed down by a man from Dallas.

We scanned the law reviews for the first commentaries on the Sheppard decision. Laymen do not always realize how important are these articles that appear in the publications of the various law schools throughout the country. The articles are often written by brilliant young students, leaders in their classes, who are trained by their faculty advisers to assimilate and analyze the best legal knowledge of their day. The average note in the better law journals is the result of the reading of every analogous authority in the English-speaking world. One such note about the Sheppard case opined, as did we: "The major elements of the 'totality' which the Court found violative of petitioner's rights were the trial judge's failure to protect petitioner from massive prejudicial publicity, and his refusal to exercise control over the activities of news media personnel in the trial chamber." The prejudicial items could be divided into four categories, the writer said: "1) articles containing information released by officials involved in the investigation into the murder of petitioner's wife which suggested petitioner's guilt and emphasized alleged inconsistencies in his account of events on the night of the murder; 2) articles and headlines demanding that petitioner be arrested for the murder; 3) publication of highly prejudicial 'facts' which were never offered in evidence at the trial and thus never subject to refutation; and 4) deliberate attempts by various news media to discredit petitioner's personal character." Other facts to be considered in this "totality of circumstances" were: "the fact that the trial was conducted in the midst of a heated election campaign in which both the trial judge and the chief prosecutor were candidates for judicial office; the fact that petitioner was interrogated for five hours without the benefit of counsel at an inquest three months prior to trial; and the fact that the jury was not sequestered until the time of deliberation."

As we had observed, the writer of the note said that the court's use of the "totality" approach has been its traditional method of adjudicating questions involving due process. These earlier precedents, particularly in cases involving criminal defendants, were analyzed. It was seen that inherent or presumptive prejudice was more important to the court than actual prejudice, which is generally difficult to establish. It was seen also that the court has often been unwilling to consider any one factor in a case by itself. Of course, this approach leads to contradictions and inconsistencies. Since the preservation of trial court discretion is important, there is a kind of jarring note when that discretion is disturbed, unless overriding considerations are shown. Reasonableness is to be considered, but it is not enough:

The major significance of *Sheppard* lies in the Supreme Court's assertion that, for the present, the trial judge has the primary responsibility of ensuring that an accused receives a fair trial, unaffected by elements external to the judicial process, and free from disruption within the courtroom.

The court did not indicate, according to the writer of the note, whether failure to take any one of the courses pointed out by Justice Clark might in itself be deemed a denial of due process.

The *Sheppard* opinion leaves unanswered the question of

what the Supreme Court will do if confronted by a factual situation where all the judicial safeguards suggested in *Sheppard* are provided. . . ."

Such situation might have arisen, the writer suggested, if Lee Harvey Oswald had lived to be tried for the assassination of President Kennedy. Would a change of venue have been enough, or would it have been totally inadequate in view of the national publicity? The same question might be raised in the Ruby case, but it was not suggested by the writer.

The writer's conclusion was a reasonable one:

It remains to be seen whether, in the face of increasingly pervasive mass communications media, the bench can maintain sufficient control of its own processes to ensure that every criminal defendant will be afforded a fair trial, unaffected by external or disruptive influences.

Once when I was privileged to breakfast with Justice Clark, and emboldened by his friendliness, I inquired about the famous school desegregation opinion, in which the Supreme Court had decided the basic constitutional issues unanimously. "We decided that way," he said, with more feeling than I had thought him capable of, "because we were right." The same unmistakable moral force informed the Estes opinion and, above all, the Sheppard opinion. Would not this fervor communicate itself to fellow Texans on the Texas Court of Criminal Appeals?

# 23

## THE MIRANDA CASES

JUST A WEEK after handing down the Sheppard decision, a bitterly divided Supreme Court, on June 13, 1966, spoke in a more controversial field and manner than it had in the Sheppard case. As the time for our argument before the Texas court neared, we read and re-read the historic words in the continuing hope of finding fodder in the mass of words to feed the Texas jurists. We found what we sought, not in complete measure, and not necessarily for that time and place. The group of decisions now known collectively as the *Miranda* cases would present a cheerful guide for us in a second trial, if we succeeded in getting a reversal of the conviction in the first trial.

The Chief Justice himself delivered the opinion of the Court in sixty-one printed pages. This time Justice Clark dissented in three of the four cases that were decided in the Miranda group and concurred in the result of the fourth case. In another opinion Justice Harlan, for himself and Justices Stewart and White, dissented. Then Justice White wrote his own dissent, in which he was joined by Justices Harlan and Stewart. This meant that Chief Justice Warren spoke for a bare majority of the Court; but five-to-four decisions, especially in landmark cases, are not unusual. In time they are just as decisive, just as much precedents for future rulings, as unanimous opinions of the court— unless they are reversed, which sometimes happens, too, in this highly charged field of constitutional rights. With admirable clarity the Chief Justice phrased the problem:

The cases before us raise questions which go to the roots of our concepts of American criminal jurisprudence: the restraints society must observe consistent with the Federal Constitution in prosecuting individuals for crime. More specifically, we deal with the admissibility of statements obtained from an individual who is subjected to custodial police interrogation and the necessity for procedures which assure that the individual is accorded his privilege under the Fifth Amendment to the Constitution not to be compelled to incriminate himself.

This very question was at the heart of our objection to the testimony of Sergeant Patrick H. Dean in the Ruby case. Assuming that Jack Ruby had said exactly what Sergeant Dean had quoted him as saying—and we bitterly disputed this premise—should the statement have been admitted in evidence over the objection of the defense? Was it not confessional in nature and obtained from a harried individual in the custody of the police? Was it not a breach of Ruby's Fifth Amendment privilege against self-incrimination?

The Chief Justice then recalled the Escobedo decision, handed down by it just two years previously: "Both state and federal courts, in assessing its implications, have arrived at varying conclusions. A wealth of scholarly material has been written tracing its ramifications and underpinnings. Police and prosecutor have speculated on its range and desirability."

Certiorari was granted in the four cases, grouped under Miranda, so that the court might further explore some facets of the problems in "applying the privilege against self-incrimination to in-custody interrogation; and to give concrete constitutional guidelines for law enforcement agencies and courts to follow." The Chief Justice insisted that the holding in Escobedo was not an innovation, but an application of long-recognized principles. He reviewed the precedents in the usual manner of the court. He summed up the Miranda holding with his usual clarity:

[T]he prosecution may not use statements, whether exculpatory or inculpatory, stemming from custodial interrogation of the defendant unless it demonstrates the use of procedural safeguards effective to secure the privilege against self-incrimination. By custodial interrogation, we mean questioning initiated by law enforcement officers after a person has been taken into custody or otherwise deprived of his freedom of action in any significant way. As for the procedural safeguards to be employed, unless other fully effective means are devised to inform accused persons of their right of silence and to assure a continuous opportunity to exercise it, the following measures are required. Prior to any questioning, the person must be warned that he has a right to remain silent, that any statement he does make may be used as evidence against him, and that he has a right to the presence of an attorney, either retained or appointed. The defendant may waive effectuation of these rights, provided the waiver is made voluntarily, knowingly and intelligently. If, however, he indicates in any manner and at any stage of the process that he wishes to consult with an attorney before speaking there can be no questioning. Likewise, if the individual is alone and indicates in any manner that he does not wish to be interrogated, the police may not question him. The mere fact that he may have answered some questions or volunteered some statements on his own does not deprive him of the right to refrain from answering any further inquiries until he has consulted with an attorney and thereafter consents to be questioned.

To most conservative law-enforcement officers and judges throughout the nation, these words had the effect of a sentence of death upon them, rather than upon some witless defendant. How could the court do this to them? Their reaction, in effect, if not necessarily in words, was that summed up on the "Impeach Earl Warren" sign which had so troubled Jack Ruby on the night of the assassination of President Kennedy.

The Chief Justice, who always has the courage and calm of his convictions, followed with a long analysis of the precedents which justified his viewpoint, including the famous Wickersham Report to Congress by a Commission

under President Hoover, the 1961 Commission on Civil
Rights, and other cases and studies which indicated that
"some policemen still resort to physical force to obtain
confessions." Unless there are adequate safeguards, such
official lawlessness is still possible, he said, and psychological force is as bad as physical violence.

Interrogation still takes place in privacy. Privacy results in
secrecy and this in turn results in a gap in our knowledge as to
what in fact goes on in the interrogation rooms. A valuable
source of information about present police practices, however,
may be found in various police manuals and texts which document procedures employed with success in the past, and which
recommend various other effective tactics. These texts are used
by law enforcement agencies themselves as guides. It should be
noted that these texts professedly present the most enlightened
and effective means presently used to obtain statements
through custodial interrogation. By considering these texts and
other data, it is possible to describe procedures observed and
noted around the country.

Out of the very mouths of the police, in a brilliant and
yet down-to-earth analysis, he documented the necessity
for the court to set down effective guidelines. When we
get too exercised over the escape of the guilty from the
clutches of the law, we should re-examine the Chief Justice's words; but, alas, they did not then, they do not now,
persuade all of his brethren or the people generally. The
Chief Justice sensed the storm that would arise and
anticipated it:

It is impossible for us to foresee the potential alternatives
for protecting the privilege which might be devised by Congress or the States in the exercise of their creative rule-making
capacities. Therefore we cannot say that the Constitution necessarily requires adherence to any particular solution for the
inherent compulsions of the interrogation process as it is presently conducted. Our decision in no way creates a constitutional
straitjacket which will handicap sound efforts at reform, nor

is it intended to have this effect. We encourage Congress and the States to continue their laudable search for increasingly effective ways of protecting the rights of the individual while promoting efficient enforcement of our criminal laws. However, unless we are shown other procedures which are at least as effective in apprising accused persons of their right of silence and in assuring a continuous opportunity to exercise it, the following safeguards must be observed.

He then gave in detail the safeguards and their justification which he had summarized earlier in his opinion. Over and over again, in a variety of ways, he repeated these safeguards and justified them, so that he would not be misunderstood:

After such warnings have been given, and such opportunity afforded him, the individual may knowingly and intelligently waive these rights and agree to answer questions or make a statement. But unless and until such warnings and waiver are demonstrated by the prosecution at trial, no evidence obtained as a result of interrogation can be used against him.

He demonstrated that society's need for interrogation of suspects does not outweigh the privilege against self-incrimination:

In announcing these principles, we are not unmindful of the burdens which law enforcement officials must bear, often under trying circumstances. We also fully recognize the obligation of all citizens to aid in enforcing the criminal laws. This Court, while protecting individual rights, has always given ample latitude to law enforcement agencies in the legitimate exercise of their duties. The limits we have placed on the interrogation process should not constitute an undue interference with a proper system of law enforcement. . . .

Over the years the Federal Bureau of Investigation has compiled an exemplary record of effective law enforcement while advising any suspect or arrested person, at the outset of an interview, that he is not required to make a statement, that any statement may be used against him in court, that the individual may obtain the services of an attorney of his own choice and, more recently, that he has a right to free counsel if he is unable to pay.

He cited the evidence, at home and abroad, in support of this optimistic view:

The English procedure since 1912 under the Judge's Rules is significant. As recently strengthened, the Rules require that a cautionary warning be given an accused by a police officer as soon as he has evidence that affords reasonable grounds for suspicion; they also require that any statement made be given by the accused without questioning by police. The right of the individual to consult with an attorney during this period is expressly recognized.

And the safeguards in Scotland, India, Ceylon, and elsewhere have not interfered with effective law enforcement. He seemed to be pleading for understanding of his views. We, who were representing Jack Ruby, understood them, and we approved. Were we to be dismissed as partisans? We also understood what Justice Harlan had in mind in the conclusion of his brilliant dissent:

Nothing in the letter or the spirit of the Constitution or in the precedents squares with the heavy-handed and one-sided action that is so precipitously taken by the Court in the name of fulfilling its constitutional responsibilities. The foray which the Court takes today brings to mind the wise and farsighted words of Mr. Justice Jackson in *Douglas* v. *Jeannette*, 319 U.S. 157, 181 (separate opinion): "This Court is forever adding new stories to the temples of constitutional law, and the temples have a way of collapsing when one story too many is added."

We could only hope that there would be no "collapse" before we had got the benefit of Miranda and Escobedo, as well as the specific Texas law which we felt had been violated by Judge Brown, misled by the State and his own lack of understanding.

# 24

## THE BRIEFS

IN THE NORMAL APPEAL in such states as New York and Illinois and, indeed, in most jurisdictions, state and federal, the party that is appealing, usually called the appellant, first files the record of the case within the period prescribed by the statute or the rules of court. Within a designated period, he then files his brief, customarily a printed document, in which he summarizes the facts, the issues, the points he wants to make, the legal authorities in support of these points, and the argument. At the same time, he files a printed abstract of the record, so that the court's search for facts will not be unduly difficult. Within a certain period thereafter, the responding party, usually called the appellee, files his printed brief and, if he thinks the abstract of the record is inaccurate or incomplete, an additional abstract. The appellant replies to the responding brief. The court sets down the case, at this point, for oral argument. By this time, the judges have had the opportunity to read the briefs and abstracts and, if they choose, the record itself. They may even have had their law clerks go through the material in a preliminary way. Thus, when the opposing attorneys stand before them, the judges, familiar with the case, will interrupt the flow of argument by appropriate questions or even by comments. The appellant generally opens and closes the argument, and the appellee is sandwiched between. It is only when there are new legal authorities available that either party may file additional memoranda, and then only by leave of court.

In the Texas Court of Criminal Appeals, and particularly

in connection with special cases, the practice is much more relaxed and informal. There is no need to file printed abstracts of the record and even the briefs are not usually printed, a considerable savings in time and money for the litigants. The briefs of both sides are filed simultaneously, either a few days before the oral hearing or even on the very day of the hearing. Thus, the judges will not be familiar with the points, authorities, and argument. They will be hearing the matter for the first time. They will be disinclined to interrupt the flow of the argument, lest they show ignorance rather than knowledge. The argument is tape-recorded, so that it may be referred to. Then, after the oral argument, the parties may file additional briefs within a period designated by the court. Ultimately, the court rules on the case, and successive motions for rehearings may be filed, briefed, and argued orally. In theory, at least, this assures fair consideration to every case.

In addition, the Texas court has what is called a State's Attorney, who may assist it, by filing briefs and participating in the argument.

This is at once more simple and more complicated.

## BELLI'S BRIEF AMICUS CURIAE

A year and four months before any other brief was filed with the Texas Court of Criminal Appeals, Melvin M. Belli, Sr., the discharged counsel for Jack Ruby, filed his *amicus curiae* brief of 166 pages. Whether it was read at that time, or later, by the judges of the Texas Court of Criminal Appeals we do not know. Curiosity, if nothing else, should have prompted them to peruse Belli's appellate brief. All my colleagues may not have read the very interesting document or profited from it, but at my request, Belli sent copies to me, and I read the brief carefully.

My feelings with respect to Belli himself are mixed. It is fashionable to blame him for the debacle with which the trial ended on March 14, 1964. Kaplan and Waltz, in their remarkable book on the Ruby trial, are unsparing in their criticism of him, and other writers about the case are vituperative. Belli, however, seems to thrive on conflict, as does Joe Tonahill. If he erred, as I believe, he erred in putting all the eggs of his defense into the basket of psychomotor epilepsy variant, even though I think he was right in attributing Ruby's crime to that aberration. Ruby (and Belli) would have fared better if more evidence had been offered to show the absence of premeditation and malice and the over-all role of happenstance; even then, given the attitude of the community at the time, the jury might have gone astray. Nonetheless, Belli and his associates did protect the record for appeal in most, if not all, respects. In Belli's fascinating brief, one finds many of the same arguments that we, his successors, later made. I freely confess Belli's brief is more exciting, although less persuasive, than the brief we filed. Belli's idiom is more piquant and picturesque and decidedly less sober-sided. His brief suggests an argument before a jury, rather than an orthodox appellate brief. It seems to have been dictated rather than researched and reflectively composed in a library. One can almost visualize him parading up and down the garish office in the Belli Building in old San Francisco, chuckling as he elaborates telling arguments, and poking somebody to punctuate the points. That is not a bad way to argue some cases, and certainly it makes lively reading. It would have been a memorable experience to have heard him argue the case orally.

The tone of the document is set in the almost excessively courteous, if not circumspect, introduction. There Belli explains why he is filing the brief and the difficulties under which he labored in preparing it. Many pages are then devoted to proving that "Ruby's 'confessions' and 'admissions,' in jail, forty minutes after arrest, not in writing, without a warning, without a lawyer, admitted into evidence over defendant's strenuous objections, reversible error, not 'res gestae,' violated the Escobedo rule." This telegraphese,

composed near Telegraph Hill in San Francisco, may not
be formal in manner, nor is the argument that follows, but
it is persuasive.

Then Belli argued: "It is reversible error for the trial
court to accept petit jurors, over objection, who have been
witnesses to the principal event being tried." And he
added: "The viccinage was contaminated." This was his
way of stating that those who had seen the shooting of
Oswald on television should have been ineligible to serve
on the jury, and that, in any event, the Dallas atmosphere
was tainted. This was argued strenuously under the further
heading: "It was reversible error to deny defendant a
change of venue from Dallas, a contaminated viccinage."
Thus Belli took the old English word for community and,
in a most modern and effective fashion, showed that there
was such prejudice in the Dallas community as to preclude
a fair trial and due process in the Constitutional sense.

It is especially noteworthy that although Belli castigated
Wade, Alexander, the president of the American Bar Association at the time, the press, and others, he did not excuse
himself: "It is true that this counsel did participate in daily
press and television and radio conferences about the course
of the trial and it is no excuse for his conduct in this regard
that 'everyone else was doing it.' . . ." He argued that, as
was stated in the Dallas *Morning News,* "Belli was tried,
not Ruby," and that this prevented a fair trial for the
defendant. Belli's first-hand account of what occurred is
of extraordinary interest and his castigation of the American Bar Association of great significance. This part of the
brief is superior to anything that appears in Belli's book,
which manages to make an amazing trial into an almost
pedestrian event.

Although the Supreme Court had not yet handed down
the Sheppard decision, Belli argued with remarkable forcefulness and prescience on this point. Then from this major
point he slid to a lesser one: "Alternation of judges when
trying fact issues without due process of law." This was a

rather clumsy way of saying that the inept Judge Brown should not have permitted Judge Wilson to take his place for a day during the picking of the jury and the continuing hearing on a change of venue. In the same minor key was the next point: "Reversible error to refuse right of opening statement by defendant."

Of much greater importance was the argument headed: "Jack Ruby's insanity never tried. He was incompetent to defend himself." This was Belli's way of stating that there should have been a separate trial of Ruby's sanity before his guilt or innocence was determined. In the same mood, Belli argued: "M'Naughton rule of insanity is error and outmoded." He wanted a Texas court to say that the Texas law on the test of insanity in criminal cases was no longer applicable, even if it was followed in almost all states.

"Multitudinous errors of law in the court's charge, improper quantum of proof, reasonable doubt and insanity law." The argument that followed was almost as short as the rather cryptic lead and did little to explain what Belli had in mind in the mouth-filling heading. It was clear only that he did not like what the judge had done.

The Conclusion summed up, rather shrilly and sometimes incoherently, Belli's grievances against the district attorney and the Dallas community, and expressed his fear that Ruby's mental condition had so deteriorated that his downward course could not be arrested. I felt, in reading this Conclusion, as well as the rest of the brief, that Belli had a deep concern for his former client, a shocked disbelief that he could have been condemned even in Dallas, a prayer that, somehow, matters would be righted and his own personal and professional sins remitted. I do not have it in my heart to condemn Belli.

### THE STATE'S BRIEF

The brief finally filed by the State in the Ruby case represented an enormous expenditure of time and energy. It

was 139 pages long and had, in addition, a fifteen-page
appendix. The brief was submitted, as is customary, in the
name of the criminal district attorney himself, Henry
Wade, and it bore the names of four of his best assistants
—William F. Alexander, James Williamson, Frank Watts,
and Wilson Johnston; and Leon Douglas, the State's Attorney, subscribed to it as well. The first fifty pages, more
than one third of the document, summarized the evidence,
witness by witness, from the State's viewpoint. The explicit references to the pages of the transcript of the trial,
the whole aura of this part of the brief, was calculated to
persuade the judges that the evidence overwhelmingly
indicated the guilt of Jack Ruby and made his conviction
and sentence of death inevitable. It was prepared graph-
ically:

### The Case in Brief

| | |
|---|---|
| The Charge | Murder with Malice |
| The Plea | Not Guilty |
| Verdict of the Jury | Guilty |
| The Punishment | Death |

All the Court of Criminal Appeals had to do was to write
with similar succinctness the word "Affirmed," it seemed,
and that would be the end of the matter!

The first few pages dealt, in general terms, with appellant's formal bill of exceptions, fifteen of them, all "refused
approval" by the trial court, Judge Brown, "after careful
consideration with the reasons for refusal to approve the
bills stated. . . ." The appellant [Ruby], the State declared,
took no action following such refusal to qualify the bills,
except for filing a so-called bystander's bill with respect
to one of them. For this reason, the State contended, the
Court of Criminal Appeals should ignore the bills of exception and must affirm on technical grounds. "However,
recognizing the seriousness of this cause and the maximum
penalty imposed, the State will cover in its brief those contentions urged in the defective bills of exception, consider-

ing them as informal bills or contentions of Appellant which should be disposed of by consideration of the Court." With this unction, the State went on to consider each of appellant's bills of exception in order, some at great length, some more briefly; all with a great show of authorities, drawn largely from the state of Texas and most carefully keyed to the record in the case. We would be involved in many fine points of the law, largely meaningless to laymen, were we to discuss *seriatim* the arguments offered by the State in opposition to these so-called bills of exception.

The State must have been greatly troubled by our contention that the viewing by jurors of the shooting of Oswald on television disqualified them. The top of one page of the State's brief tries to dispel the effect of this contention by capitalized emphasis. It is illuminating, as well as pictorially ornamental, to quote the words in full, exactly as they appear in the brief:

MERE FACT THAT THROUGH MEDIUM OF TELEVISION
A PROSPECTIVE JUROR EITHER CONTEMPORANEOUSLY,
OR THEREAFTER BY MEANS OF TAPED RERUNS,
SAW ON HIS TELEVISION PICTURE TUBE PICTURES
DEPICTING CERTAIN SCENES AND ACTIVITIES
PURPORTEDLY DEPICTING EVENTS WHICH OCCURRED
AT THE TIME AND PLACE WHEN AND WHERE
JACK RUBY SHOT OSWALD IS INSUFFICIENT
TO ESTABLISH THAT SUCH PROSPECTIVE JUROR
IS COMPETENT TO TESTIFY AS TO HIS OWN KNOWLEDGE
OF THE VERITY AND TRUTH OF THE SCENES AND ACTIVITIES
DEPICTED BY SUCH PICTURES, AND CERTAINLY IT IS
LEGALLY INSUFFICIENT TO ESTABLISH THAT SUCH
SCENES OR ACTIVITIES SO DEPICTED ARE MATERIAL
TO ANY DISPUTED ISSUE IN THE CASE

The brief then tries to answer our argument in minutest particularity—questions put to prospective witnesses and their answers and the objections of counsel, with telling words underscored. With glee, the words of welcome ut-

tered by Tonahill or Belli as each juror was qualified by
the court is quoted, for all the world as if the State did not
recognize that the defense attorneys were simply making
the best of a bad situation. Obviously, they had to butter
up the very ones they did not really want, after the court
had overruled objections with respect to the disqualification of those who had seen the shooting on television;
otherwise the prejudice of the juror would have been
compounded.

The testimony of Sgt. Dean and his fellow police officers
was of great concern because the State fully realized that
if that testimony was improperly received in evidence,
there had to be a reversal. The brief went into the minutiae
of the evidence introduced by both sides and considered
every possible legal theory under which it might be admissible.

The general tone of much of what the State had to say
was illustrated by the manner in which it disposed of appellant's bill of exception number twelve. That entire section of the brief is short enough to be quoted in full:

By Bill of Exception Number Twelve Appellant complains of
the refusal of the Court of admitting into evidence the medical
records pertaining to the mental history and condition of Appellant's mother, brother Earl Ruby, and sister Eileen Kaminsky
reflecting that the mother died while under commitment to and
in a mental hospital, and that Earl Ruby and Eileen Kaminsky
had received psychiatric treatment and showing thereby descending and collateral mental history relative to this Appellant.

The State urges and contends that no error is presented by
the refusal of the Court to admit the aforementioned medical
records for the reasons that (1) the medical reports referred to
in this Bill were not properly offered into evidence in that there
was not sufficient predicate laid therefor, and no sworn testimony that the persons named in the said reports were in truth
and in fact the relatives of the Appellant named in the medical
reports; (2) the said reports contained numerous matters im-

material, irrelevant, improper, hearsay, and further, the reports, in themselves, were not in fact relied upon by the expert witnesses of Appellant in forming their opinions as to the sanity of the Appellant and such medical experts did not have or use these medical reports at the time they completed the mental evaluation of Appellant . . . and; (3) all matters contained in the reports which were referred to or relied upon by any witness were admitted into evidence and in this regard such reports were merely cumulative of such admitted testimony; (4) such reports contained irrelevant and inadmissible matters and in this regard the Appellant failed and refused to point out and limit his offer of proof to those matters he deemed relevant or admissible and to exclude the inadmissible matters therefrom.

Translated into the ordinary language of laymen, this means that, somehow, the defense counsel had not complied with the purely technical requirements as to the admission of such documents and that such documents could be dispensed with, if one chose to dispense with them. It did not occur to the State, either then or earlier, when the trial was in progress, that in a death case one ought not to hem in an accused by legal niceties; that the substance, in such situations, should be inquired into, and not mere quibbles. The very documents sought unsuccessfully to be introduced at the trial were later published in full in the Warren Report and Hearings. They surely were relevant to an inquiry into Ruby's mental state, and, at worst, were cumulative.

The overruled motion for a change of venue, the subject of appellant's bill of exceptions number fourteen, predicated upon the publicity the case had received, troubled the State almost as much as it should have. Much of the argument was as fascinating as anything that one could find in a legal document. Here is one example:

By the first witness, Dr. Frederick S. Carney, an Associate Professor of Christian Ethics at Perkins School of Theology, the defense, by the use of ambiguous and lengthy leading questions, commenced the construction of a defensive theory, based on pure fantasy, that the City of Dallas was responsible for the assassination of the President; that the assassination and the subsequent murder of the Marxist Oswald were so closely intertwined that the City of Dallas—and not Ruby, was actually being tried.

By repeated reference to the fascinating term "oligarchy" mentioned in a paper written by Dr. Carney (which term "caught on" with national magazines and other news media), the defense made an abortive attempt to show the City of Dallas to be an evil and corrupt city completely controlled in every walk of life by an unknown and sinister group of business men who had the strange power to control every act of its citizens; the inference supposedly being that such power could control the action of the jury. However, Appellant's own witness, Dr. Carney, resisted the leading questions propounded to him regarding the "oligarchy" by saying that "it is a descriptive term, intended to point out the sociological, if you will, leadership of the community. The oligarchy in my judgment and in the judgment of others, apparently is predominantly business leaders." . . . Dr. Carney went on to say that "any community which is a constructive community, as I say, it has to have some means of carrying on its essential business. Every city will have some decision making center. I think that the decision making center in Dallas happens to be on most issues, the business leadership. Every city has a decision making center or it just falls apart." . . .

The recent holding of the Supreme Court in the *Sheppard* case was of concern to the State, and it purported to distinguish that case from the Ruby case. The State saw similarities only in the widespread publicity and interest in both cases; for the rest, it saw only differences:

The defense in the Sheppard case was alibi; in the Ruby case it was insanity. The homicide by Ruby was proved by direct evidence; in the Sheppard case it was circumstantial. Ruby was in police custody within two seconds after homicide; Sheppard

was arrested weeks after the homicide and only after extreme
pressure from news media directed toward law enforcement
officers demanding that Sheppard be arrested, tried and convicted. *Sheppard made a motion for continuance; Ruby made
none.* Sheppard's counsel made repeated objections to television and news coverage of the proceedings; Ruby and his
counsel held and encouraged press conferences at recess periods
during all proceedings to "sell" the Ruby point of view on
various issues. The cautious trial judge instructed the prospective jury panel on the first day of jury selection, February 17,
1964, not to read, listen to, look at TV or discuss the Ruby case.
Finally, it should be noted here that jurors in the Ruby case
were "locked up" from the moment they were sworn until the
verdict was returned. They were insulated and isolated from all
contact with the outside world and any form of news media.
The jurors in the Sheppard case went to their homes each
night during the trial and were allowed to receive telephone
calls and read and listen to publicity in connection with the
case.

The State promised a point-by-point analysis of the two
cases in the final brief it was going to file after our last
brief was in.

By a careful listing of only what was supposedly beneficial to Ruby in the newspaper publicity and by totally
ignoring what was harmful, the State tried to show that
Ruby was the beneficiary, rather than the victim, of the
press coverage. It is a wonderful example of what skilled
editing could do, if only the court would buy it:

Beginning with the killing of Lee Harvey Oswald by Jack
Ruby, which fact was uncontroverted, much of the publicity
was concerned with whether Ruby was of unsound mind or
suffered from psychomotor epilepsy at the time Oswald was
killed. Newspapers throughout the country constantly quoted
Ruby friends and/or lawyers to the effect that when Ruby
became angry, his hands would shake violently, that he got
extremely upset at the death of President Kennedy and that he

killed Oswald for Jackie Kennedy so that she would not have
to return to Dallas to testify. Numerous articles were published
quoting Ruby's sister to the effect that Ruby was a good
American, loyal to the United States and its President and
worried about the Kennedy children; that Ruby suffered more
from the President's death than he did from the death of his
own father. The papers also related Ruby's tremendous friendship, admiration and acquaintance of members of the Police
Department.

The papers quoted Tom Howard, Ruby's first lawyer, about
Ruby's love for the President and that Ruby had also suffered
head injuries in Chicago in 1940.

As soon as Belli got into the case, he constantly referred to
psychiatric testimony as being of great importance, of psychomotor epilepsy, the fact that Ruby was temporarily insane
and that the greatest psychiatrist in the United States did so
testify. There were statements from Belli to the fact that Ruby
would volunteer for a polygraph test and that Ruby was highly
agitated when he shot Oswald. There were quotations in the
press from Ruby's roommate concerning Ruby's peculiar
behavior the morning after the assassination of President
Kennedy.

There was an article in the Dallas Morning News to the effect
that the treatment and control of sociopathic personalities
would be expedited by the Oswald and Ruby cases and that
Ruby was a good example of sociopathic problems.

There were articles to the effect that Ruby would shed tears
while discussing the two events; that he was emotional; that
he loved dogs. There were numerous articles to the effect that
various psychiatrists employed by Belli said that Jack Ruby did
not realize what he was doing when he shot Oswald and that
there was a definite impaired function of Ruby's brain on a
physical basis. There were quotes from Ruby that he was a
changed man; that he had started reading the Bible and had
become a Bible advocate.

Throughout all of the publicity prior to the beginning of the
trial, Belli and Tonahill conducted news conferences in which

they sought to implant in prospective jurors' minds that Ruby was insane at the time of the killing of Oswald. Indeed, on the Sunday before trial was to begin on Wednesday, psychiatrists who were arriving to testify for the defense stated in a newspaper interview that Ruby was "as nervous as a cat," "deteriorating"; that he was becoming close to being incoherent and had an unconscious hatred for Oswald.

In the fifteen-page appendix to the brief, the State purported to summarize the news articles, excluding those articles which tended to prejudice the public and prospective jurors against the defendant.

Thus the brief wound its way to its laborious conclusion:

WHEREFORE, PREMISES CONSIDERED, there being legal and competent evidence sufficient to justify the verdict of the jury, and no error appearing in the record or the trial of this case, the Appellee, State of Texas, prays the Court to affirm this cause in all things.

## TONAHILL'S BRIEF

Joe H. Tonahill and his associate, Emmett Colvin, Jr., as friends of the court, filed their truly imposing brief for the appellant on the morning of the oral argument before the Court of Criminal Appeals. On the eighty-third, and last, page they certified that they had served copies "upon counsel for the State; Hon. Leon Douglas, State's Attorney; and Hon. Henry Wade, District Attorney for Dallas County, Texas." This pointed failure to certify that Jack Ruby's counsel of record had been served would have been a breach of the rules and of decorum, not to say professional courtesy, in other jurisdictions. Perhaps it was so even in Texas. Nonetheless, in the moments before the hearing, I wheedled first Colvin, then Tonahill, into distributing copies to us. That there was not time to study the many interesting pages did not trouble us much, because, in the order setting the case down for argument, the court had given us until August 1, 1966, to file additional briefs.

Tonahill and Colvin had put forth a tremendous effort to justify themselves and to show why the Jack Ruby jury verdict should be set aside. We were in their corner, basically, or they in ours; yet there was rivalry between the briefs. Would they cover points we had omitted, or would we touch upon items they had omitted?

Much in the two briefs was similar, much was dissimilar in treatment, if not in essence. They, like us, made much of the admission of the statements allegedly made by Ruby to Sgt. Patrick Dean. They supplemented this by objections to much in the testimony of police officers Archer, McMillon, King, and Leavelle. They, like us, made much of the denial of Ruby's motion for a change of venue and of the overruling of objections to the substitution of trial judges during the examination of jurors and the ongoing hearing on the motion for a change of venue. They asserted that there was error in the denial of a pretrial hearing on Ruby's sanity, in various parts of the court's charge to the jury, and in refusing Ruby additional peremptory challenges. In all, Tonahill and Colvin did well by Ruby and themselves.

# 25

## BEFORE THE COURT OF CRIMINAL APPEALS

DURING EACH STEP in our arduous ascent to the Texas Court of Criminal Appeals, we had to consider the effect upon each individual judge, and not simply the court as a whole. If we pleased one judge, we were likely to displease another.

In some states, politics does not affect the judiciary to any offensive degree; but in Texas even the highest courts are involved in power politics. These things we knew of the Texas Court of Criminal Appeals, but we were never quite sure of just what was brewing there that might transcend or obliterate the record. Why, for example, was Joe Tonahill permitted to associate himself with the case even when it was clear that neither Ruby nor his family wanted him to have anything to do with them or the case? Tonahill seemed to hint at times that he had a certain influence with the court. Discounting his boast completely, or confirming it of one judge rather than the entire court, the matter still warranted our speculation, because it could determine the ultimate result.

Judge K. K. Woodley was a key figure in our thoughts about the case. He had been in the court for fourteen years and was dominated by no one. He would not hesitate to speak out in dissent. In January, 1961, he had replaced Judge W. A. Morrison as presiding judge of the court, and for four years he had served in that capacity. In those days the court itself, a three-judge body assisted by two commissioners, selected the presiding judge. In January, 1965,

Judge Woodley was replaced as presiding judge by Judge W. T. McDonald who in turn was defeated for renomination in the spring of 1966. Judge McDonald, now a judicial lame duck, lined up with Judge Morrison at the very time we were scheduled to argue before the court, so that Judge Morrison presided on the last day of the term. Judge Woodley, often at odds with Judge Morrison, formally dissented from this unusual last-minute action.

There were three strong-willed gentlemen sitting in judgment on the Texas Court of Criminal Appeals. Their conflicting views and personalities were the subject of conversation within the profession, and with this we were familiar. We had to ask ourselves if there was some Hegelian synthesis that would encompass the views and personalities of all of the judges. Which arguments would transcend all differences? Which would aggravate a taut situation? And were there peculiarly Texan arguments as empathic as the yellow rose itself?

It must not be supposed that this is a game peculiar to Texas. In a sense, it is even more appropriate to the highest court of the land. Trained lawyers profess to know the workings of the great judicial minds in the United States Supreme Court. At one time, securing the approval of Justice Jackson automatically earned the disapproval of one or more of his colleagues, and vice versa. We are a nation of laws, and not of men; but those who determine the law are flesh and blood, with human predispositions and philosophies. Every great case must be handled with such personal foibles constantly in mind.

Excitement was in the air as the court convened for the hearing of argument before the Court of Criminal Appeals on June 24, 1966. Judge Morrison presided. If there was friction between himself and any of his colleagues, it was not visible. The audience, an unusual one, included judges from the State's Supreme Court and from the United States District Court and students and professors from the law school. Eva was, of course, ensconced near the front. The press, too, was present in larger numbers than at earlier stages of the reviewing proceedings.

Sam Clinton, opening the argument with a brief preliminary over-all statement of the issues, expressed himself effectively with a literary flair.

"There are a lot of things in this record to show that Jack Ruby did not have a tolerably fair trial," Clinton said.

"There were a lot of things on trial besides Ruby. Our judicial system was on trial; the Dallas community was on trial; it was trial by inflamed public opinion; there was trial by TV and newspapers before the case was called; there was trial by pamphleteers who passed out circulars around the court house; there was trial by picketing when pickets marched in front of the courthouse; there was trial by ritual when 11 of the 12 jurors said they saw it on TV, then went through the ritual of asserting they could set aside all preconceived notions . . . and there was trial by authors and book writers, not only the judge but by at least one counsel."

When Clinton finished, it was my task to evoke the circus atmosphere of the trial before Judge Brown, to present the Sheppard aspects of the case. Although I had many marked documents and an outline on the podium before me, my conviction that the trial had taken place in a poisoned atmosphere was so great that I scarcely needed to look at the material, except for an occasional direct quotation. I felt at liberty to refer to the record in the habeas corpus proceeding and assured the judges that, in considering the main appeal, all that was brought out in that case was before them.

"It is significant that in reaching its conclusion, the U.S. Supreme Court cited in the Sheppard case many circumstances similar to those in this case—the damaging publicity by the police . . . the district attorney's descriptions of prosecution evidence which was inadmissible," I said.

"Judge Brown had the strange notion he could not control what went on around the courthouse—that somehow he was powerless to act."

"The court doesn't consider merely the actual trial. It has to consider the total framework—everything which makes the atmosphere."

"We had a pervasive atmosphere which made a fair trial difficult."

I then quoted the comments made by Judge Brown during and after the trial, in which he said that he felt continued pressure from news media entering into the trial; and I quoted from the manuscript of Judge Brown's book in which the judge concluded that "Ruby did not get full justice."

"During the trial the judge repeatedly warned the audience to stop laughing and called for order and remarked that the courtroom was 'like a circus,'" I continued.

"What else went on in the courtroom? Matters far worse than were the basis for the reversal of the Sheppard case." I referred to the jail break which occurred in the building during the trial.

"It was the obligation of the court, as stated in the Sheppard case, to see that neither the defense nor the prosecution, nor anyone else participated in this kind of monkeyshine—this denial of a fair trial."

I referred to the false and misleading articles, claiming Ruby was a hoodlum, that he was connected with gangsters or with Communism and Fidel Castro.

"Almost every type of story that would poison the atmosphere was played up," I declared.

Burleson then dealt with other Sheppard aspects of the case, the jury selection, and a variety of points. He was so immersed in the case, so informed on the details, that his argument was highly effective, if not so fervent as those preceding his.

"The court said that everyone else in the state saw the television coverage and that the same problem would arise elsewhere. This was totally unsupported by any facts," Burleson said.

In the Rideau case, he pointed out, the Supreme Court reversed the verdict because four of the jurors saw the defendant confess over television.

"Therefore, we feel that, taking these cases and the Sheppard case into consideration, the Ruby case should have been removed from the locale of the crime and the court should have accepted as jurors only those who did not see films of the offense, and then, if no jury could be picked, a change of venue would have been in order."

Judge J. Frank Wilson had substituted for Judge Brown for one day during selection of the jury, and Sol Dann had been assigned this relatively minor point. He talked at considerable length on the matter and rather well. I do not think it counted for much in substance; but Dann's sincerity was so obvious that the air of solemnity was enhanced.

There was "no legally constituted court during one day of this trial," Dann argued. "It was just as fatal as if one juror was absent for one day."

Then Joe Tonahill came forth as a friend of the court. I feared what he might say, because of the animus created by the many months of contention. Given his style and diction, he was quite good, moving even, especially as he dealt with the wrongfully admitted and deadly testimony of Sergeant Dean.

"You don't have to go to the United States Supreme Court to find decisions on which to base a reversal. You have plenty right here," Tonahill said.

He labeled Dean's testimony "prefabrication and perjury."

As he lumbered back to his seat, I turned to him and said, with mixed feelings, "That was a very good argument, Joe." At first he looked startled, then his face lit up, and he patted me on the back. Later, a justice of the Texas

Supreme Court remarked to me, "That was a fine thing you did for Joe Tonahill. We think a lot of him here."

It was the State's turn to take up the argument. Bill Alexander, without looking at a note, began in triphammer fashion with a recitation of the facts.

"We of the district attorney's staff did not pick the audience before which this killing took place," he said. "Jack Ruby killed Oswald in full view of 140,000,000 people watching television. And the fact that hundreds of people in the immediate vicinity had cameras does not lessen his guilt one iota."

He argued: "Whatever the atmosphere might have been outside the courtroom, the jury was insulated and isolated from it," because it was locked up during the trial.

Williamson, who followed Alexander, was less plodding and far more winning than he had been earlier in the proceedings. He created the impression that Belli had actually welcomed the jurors as singularly qualified. Where, then, did this leave an argument about their disqualification? Ruby's counsel had wanted the case tried while emotions were still high, he said.

"Ruby and his devoted family and his defense counsel," he said, "felt the time and place to have a decision on his guilt or innocence was in Dallas—soon as possible after he took it upon himself to become an 'avenging angel' for President Kennedy and Gov. Connally."

"You're sane until you do something wrong, then you're temporarily 'blacked out,' then you're sane again—and you've got a first-class defense," he said.

State's Attorney Douglas, special court's counsel under the Texas system, spoke briefly, as if to indicate to the judges that he, too, wanted the verdict and judgment to be affirmed. Ruby's attorneys, if serious, should have asked for a continuance, he said. (He apparently had overlooked what the Supreme Court had said on this point in the Sheppard case, that it was the obligation of the court to continue the trial on its own motion when circumstances necessitated it.)

It now befell Kunstler, our anchor man, to answer the prosecution arguments. Bill at his best has a rhetorical grandeur that I find very warming, and on this occasion he was at his finest. (Eva, with typical candor, later assured me that he was best of all in the argument.) Taking up each of the points raised by Alexander and Williamson, he demolished them. He labeled Dean a liar, and proved it, we felt.

"Something delayed the transfer but how could Ruby have known that?" he asked. "If he had planned this in advance, Ruby would have been there at 10 A.M. Instead, he went up to Western Union to send a telegram about 11 A.M. And he had his dog in his car with him. Was that the act of a man planning to shoot another in a crowded basement, knowing he would never get out?

"The State can't explain this so they've invented a fabrication claiming he planned as early as Friday night to kill Oswald," he said.

"Ruby deprived Oswald of due process," Kunstler declared, "and we do not condone that. But it was the act of a sick, distraught man in [the] grip of rage—and we cannot destroy this man on this record."

Thus was the case submitted to the tender mercies of the court. Then, in a delightfully unexpected manner, Judge Morrison closed the hearing. He commended counsel for the care and skill with which the case had been argued and assured us that we were extremely helpful to the court.

The usual bout of press interviews and photography followed, so that we would know that this was, indeed, the Ruby case. My colleagues and I were delighted to be photographed as a group. By now we were indeed united in a kind of blood brotherhood.

From the courtroom I went to the criminal law class of a brilliant young professor who had invited me to lecture on the case. Buoyed in heart and spirit by the day's events, I spoke to the students as persuasively as I could of the inevitability of the reversal of the death sentence, and they seemed to be convinced. Later my young friend, who had attended the hearing in court, gave his perspective in a letter to me:

[T]he thing that impressed me most was how beautifully complementary . . . you all were to each other. Kunstler, the northern orator . . . ; Dann, the well-meaning; Gertz, always reasonable, always benevolent, always paternal. When it was all over, I felt that the *Sheppard* point could not fail. I remember being surprised that Tonahill seemed to display fifty times more than his reputed competence (but still considerably less than would have been desirable). I noted that your side was determined to remain gentlemanly toward him, and I believe this perhaps preserved the courtroom from potential unseemly conduct. I was sitting with Ruby's sister [Mrs. Grant], and as a consequence had a most difficult time absorbing the proceedings. However, listening to her was an experience in itself. Although I am a member of the Jewish community, I have never before heard the world so totally and comprehensively explained in terms of anti-Semitism. Even the simplest matter, to her, involved a clandestine conspiracy. . . . Ruby's sister attributed all of Ruby's woes to an anti-Jewish conspiracy.

A few days after the hearing, in a letter to us, Kunstler captured the mood that had enveloped us:

While I'm still imbued with the sense of satisfaction engendered by last Friday's hearing, I wanted to let you all know how much I have enjoyed our association. Much of our seeming success in Austin was due in large measure to the friendship and spirit of cooperation that has developed among us since our partnership began. I don't know how the rest of you feel but, as far as I'm concerned, I have been intellectually stimulated, emotionally surfeited (within limits) and professionally satisfied by our free-wheeling, easy-going relationship. Whatever the result of the appeal, we have scotched one shibboleth—that widely scattered, multi-religious lawyers with widely varying personalities and backgrounds can work together on a celebrated case without bickering, bitterness or blather. The Ruby lawyers have become an institution second only to the Smith Brothers, the Dolly Sisters and the King Family. Long may we wave.

# 26

## A PETITION FOR CERTIORARI

ON AUGUST 12, 1966, after the argument of the main appeal, we filed our petition in the United States Supreme Court for writ of certiorari to the Texas Court of Criminal Appeals in connection with the habeas corpus appeal.

In the petition we declared the first question presented was whether Jack Ruby was denied due process of law because the murder trial judge was contemplating or writing a book for personal profit on the case and its various post-conviction procedures. We then asked whether this rendered Ruby's conviction void and entitled him to a new trial.

After reciting, briefly, the sequence of events in the case, being careful to quote in full the letter that Judge Brown had sent to his editor on March 12, 1965—the letter in which he had confessed to prejudging the post-conviction matters referred to him by the Texas Court of Criminal Appeals and to lying about the writing of a book—we narrated the various steps we had taken to correct the situation and told of the resulting difficulties and frustrations. We dwelt particularly upon the habeas corpus proceeding and the basis for it, and since this was the reason for our petition, were quite explicit in setting forth all that was involved in it with the utmost detail. We described Judge Holland's reactions and how the Texas reviewing court had overridden the clear meaning of what he had said. We recited the reasons for granting the writ, grounded upon basic principles of judicial decorum and due process. We equated our case with *Estes* and *Sheppard* and older prec-

edents. We cited the canons of judicial ethics and Judge
Brown's breaches of them. While calling the Supreme
Court's attention to the appeal on the death conviction
still pending in Texas, we explained the technical reasons
for proceeding at that time in the Supreme Court. We
prayed that our petition should be granted and the judgments reversed or, alternatively, that the matter be held
in abeyance pending the final decision in the case before
the Texas Court of Criminal Appeals.

The State of Texas, through Henry Wade and his assistant, James M. Williamson, filed a relatively short brief
in opposition to our petition. Rather cleverly, the "questions presented" by our petition were rephrased by the
State in such slanted fashion as to make little of our contention that the disqualification of Judge Brown deprived
Ruby of his constitutional right to a fair trial in an atmosphere conducive to due process of law:

1. Whether Petitioner suffered retroactively the probability
of fundamental unfairness during the trial as to his guilt or
innocence by reason of the fact that, after such trial was completed, the motion for new trial was denied, and the case was on
appeal, the trial judge conceived the idea of writing a book
about the trial and thereafter contracted to write such a book
which is yet uncompleted and unpublished?

2. Whether Petitioner probably suffered, by reason of the
proposed book, any resulting prejudice depriving him of his
rights to a full and fair appellate review of such completed trial,
when under established Texas procedure Petitioner actually
must be and was furnished at State expense a full and complete
transcript of all proceedings in the trial court, which record the
Texas Court of Criminal Appeals is presently reviewing and in
accordance with established Texas procedure in death penalty
cases such appellate court will consider all errors claimed irre-
spective of any action which could have been or was taken by
the trial judge after the motion for new trial was denied?

The State contended that "the trial judge had *never*

*even thought* of writing a *book . . . until after* the trial on its merits had terminated"; that is, after the jury had returned its verdict, after the judgment was entered on it, after the motion for a new trial was decided, and after the notice of appeal was given, which resulted in the Texas Court of Criminal Appeals having sole jurisdiction of the case. In these circumstances, the judge's writing of a book could constitute no constitutional impediment. Snippets and snatches of the evidence at the hearing before Judge Holland were quoted and, in our judgment, distorted to show that what was done by Judge Brown with respect to the book, or otherwise, was legally harmless. It could not affect due consideration of the entire case in the Texas Court of Criminal Appeals.

The State made much of the fact that Ruby, as a person without means, was furnished a full transcript of the entire case at State expense. The various acts performed by Judge Brown after he entered into the contract with the publisher were minimized as having no relevance to the appeal. Ruby's defense was characterized, without truth and in bad taste, as built upon the epithet "that Oswald was a rat son-of-a-bitch," and that Ruby was simply an "avenger" or "exterminator." The actual defense of insanity was characterized as merely "formal," although, in fact, the bulk of the defense testimony dealt wth the effort to prove that Ruby was insane.

Seldom have I read a more distorted and inflammatory summary of the case. It seemed motivated by the belief that the Supreme Court justices would never read the record, but would decide the petition on some quickly formed impression. It seemed to us that this was self-defeating. The State should have recognized that in a proceeding of the dimensions of the Ruby case there was bound to be full consideration of all relevant facts.

Then the State characterized the issue of the disqualification of Judge Brown as MOOT (the capitals were the State's), since Judge Holland had replaced him in all matters after the order of the Court of Criminal Appeals, on February 24, 1965, had sent the case back for a sanity hearing to determine the matter of proper legal representation. The State's reasoning was that, while Judge Brown had in fact presided over several court hearings after that date, what he had done was, in effect, wiped out and had no constitutional consequence.

An effort was made, futile we thought, to explain away Judge Brown's "utterly incredible" letter to his publisher.

Our failure to participate in the sanity hearing was characterized as a "sit down strike." Jack Ruby's statement at the sanity hearing that he was not of unsound mind was offered in proof that we were in bad faith when, acting on the disclosures of our psychiatrists, we declared him to be insane.

It was proclaimed that Texas granted every defendant a fair trial, regardless of whether or not his case was "celebrated."

The right of Judge Brown to produce a book about the case was defended on the theory that Supreme Court justices also wrote about their cases.

The concluding paragraph of the brief, although somewhat muddied in language, set forth the State's ultimate contentions about our petition and especially our suggestion that the determination of it be held up until the Texas Court of Criminal Appeals could decide the appeal:

The grounds of this habeas corpus proceeding do not arise out of anything or in context with anything that happened during the trial proceedings now being reviewed by the Texas Court of Criminal Appeals. The petition herein is based solely on alleged *post-conviction extrajudicial* activities of Judge Brown. This petition raises separate and independent matters not enmeshed in the factual and legal issues involved in the pending review before the Texas Court of Criminal Appeals. Therefore, apparently it would serve no useful purpose to postpone or delay this Court's determination as to whether the petition herein has sufficient merit in itself to justify granting the writ of certiorari prayed for.

We felt that, except for the phrasing of the "Questions Presented," there was nothing in the State's response that shattered our theories on why the highest court should take the case. We thought we had disposed of the State's entire argument in one paragraph:

Respondent's argument that no action taken by the trial judge after the entry of verdict and the filing of a notice of appeal therefrom could deprive petitioner of fair appellate review is a clear misrepresentation of applicable Texas law and the entire concept of due process. In fact, one of the arguments advanced by the respondent before the Court of Criminal Appeals of Texas is that, since the trial judge did not approve the bills of exceptions tendered by petitioner in that proceeding, there is nothing for that Court to consider. Although respondent acknowledged here that there was, under Texas law, no distinction to be made between formal and informal bills of exceptions, it argued before the Texas Court of Criminal Appeals that only one of the fifteen bills of exceptions tendered by petitioner could possibly qualify as a formal bill, albeit it was allegedly so defective as to be unworthy of consideration. Respondent cannot argue before the Court of Criminal Appeals of Texas that in view of the trial judge's failure to approve petitioner's formal bills of exceptions there are no issues to be determined by that tribunal and then insist here that none of the trial judge's actions subsequent to the jury's verdict could possibly prejudice petitioner in his state appeal. The fact remains uncontradicted that the trial judge performed important discretionary functions affecting the appeal after he became disqualified, deciding all such matters against petitioner, thereby depriving him of a fair review of the case.

We thought, too, that we had disposed of the State's effort to minimize Judge Brown's book:

Respondent's argument that the trial judge could have had

no pecuniary interest in the outcome of petitioner's case because he did not think about writing his book until after the
jury's verdict is refuted by the facts. Not only did he inform his
publisher that the important post-conviction procedures in
which he was involved might make the proposed book "a much,
much better book than we had anticipated," but he knew full
well that petitioner's case was on appeal and that the post-
conviction rulings and publication by him of a book concerning
the case might improperly influence the appellate court. The
fact that it is impossible to determine in advance the number
of copies of the proposed book that might be sold does not, of
course, detract from the trial judge's obvious pecuniary interest
in the venture. Furthermore, it cannot be said that the disposition of petitioner's case on appeal would have no effect on its
sales since a reversal of the trial court's judgment and a new
trial would most certainly detract from the authority and interest of the first trial. This is a situation in which the consequences
are inherently so grave as to make unnecessary a precise inquiry into them.

We went on to point out that there was a world of difference between the writing by a judge of a book about the
law in general or about any other subject unrelated to
pending litigation in which he was or might still be involved and the writing of a book about actions taken by a
trial judge in settling the record required for review of
the case.

So the matter was left for the Supreme Court to decide
whether it would accept the case for review. We felt certain that the Chief Justice would disqualify himself because he had headed the Presidential Commission. We
regretted this. His compassionate bearing when he questioned Ruby after the death verdict indicated how deeply
concerned he was about human beings and their constitutional rights.

If, as we suspected, the Texas court would decide the
case as soon as its constitutional recess was over, early in

October, it might make unnecessary any further consideration of the case by the highest court in the land. If the Texas court affirmed the trial court, then we would truly need the most prayerful consideration of the matter by the Warren court. In that case, we would probably file another petition for certiorari, based upon errors in the main case, rather than the habeas corpus proceeding, and then ask the court to consider both petitions at the same time. Or we might have thought of another method of proceeding. By now, no one could accuse us of either a lack of persistence or limited resourcefulness.

# 27

## THE JUDGMENT OF DEATH IS REVERSED

AT LAST, on the morning of October 5, 1966, copies of the opinions of the judges of the Texas Court of Criminal Appeals were filed with the clerk of the court for distribution to the attorneys and the press.

Presiding Judge Morrison, who had been so gracious to us before the argument of the habeas corpus appeal, gave the unanimous opinion of the court. He began somberly: "The offense is murder; the punishment, death."

Then he decreed otherwise:

Shortly after noon on November 22, 1963, the President of the United States was assassinated within the courthouse area in the city of Dallas. A short while thereafter Lee Harvey Oswald was apprehended, but only after Patrolman Tippitt was killed in an effort to question him. Oswald was placed in the Dallas city jail. Two days later on November 24, in the basement of the city jail as Oswald was being transferred to the county jail, he was shot by appellant at close range, from which wound he died. Countless thousands witnessed this shooting on television. Four days later this appellant was indicted for Oswald's murder. His sole defense was that of insanity in that he was suffering from psychomotor epilepsy.

The court, like Judge Brown in the Mort Sahl interview, did not deem a defense of murder without malice as having been made. Judge Morrison continued:

On February 10, 1964, a change of venue hearing began in Criminal District Court No. 3 of Dallas County upon the motion of appellant to transfer the case to some county other than Dallas. The Court did not grant the change of venue; the selection of the jury began on February 17, was completed on March 3, and a verdict of guilty with punishment set at death was returned on March 14.

The voluminous record in this appeal finally reached this Court, and the case was set for submission on March 10, 1965.

Prior to submission a serious question arose as to which of many lawyers should be recognized by this Court as appellant's counsel on appeal. In view of this, we entered an order directing the trial court to hold a hearing to determine whether or not appellant had become insane since his trial and thereby rendered incapable of rationally selecting his counsel. Such hearing was held, and the record reached this Court containing a finding that appellant was presently sane, and we promptly set the case down for submission.

During the trial, over the strenuous objection of appellant that anything appellant may have said while in police custody constituted an oral confession in violation of the statutes of this State and was not admissible as res gestae, Sgt. Dean of the Dallas police testified as to a conversation which he had with appellant on the fifth floor of the Dallas city jail where he had been incarcerated, undressed and interrogated by other officers before Dean and Secret Service Agent Sorrells arrived at his cell. Prior to answering any of Sorrells' questions, appellant asked if his answers would be made available to "magazines or publications" and after being assured that he was being questioned only for police purposes, appellant replied, "I'll be glad to answer your question."

The time element which elapsed between appellant's arrest and the conversation in question varies between 10 and 40 minutes depending upon whether Dean's testimony at the trial or his written report made two days after the occurrence is accepted. Be this as it may, appellant was in a jail cell and had been interrogated by other officers prior to this conversation. Under none of the authorities cited . . . could this statement be held to have been spontaneously made.

Judge Morrison then went on to list a number of cases, legal authorities in Texas, "cited by appellant's counsel and counsel acting as friends of the Court." He continued:

The test in this State is spontaneity and these facts do not fit the test. One who is cautious enough to inquire whether his answers to the questions to be propounded to him are to be released to news media is not speaking spontaneously.

Sorrells questioned appellant about how he had been able to penetrate the police cordon protecting the transfer of Oswald. At the conclusion of this questioning and as they were preparing to leave, according to Dean's testimony he asked appellant a question and appellant told Dean that he had seen Oswald in a police line-up two nights before and that when he saw the sarcastic sneer on Oswald's face he had decided that if he got a chance to do so, he would kill him. Obviously this statement constituted an oral confession of premeditation made while in police custody and therefore was not admissible. The admission of this testimony was clearly injurious and calls for a reversal of this conviction.

What we have heretofore said makes it unnecessary to discuss in detail the error of the court in failing to grant appellant's motion for change of venue. Both Estes . . . and Sheppard . . . were decided after appellant's trial, but each case related to a state court trial held prior to appellant's trial and determines the law applicable to this case, and both are hereby controlling. It is abundantly clear from a careful study of both opinions of the Supreme Court of the United States and the record of this case that the trial court reversibly erred in refusing appellant's motion for change of venue. Not only are we bound legally by the holdings of the Supreme Court, but as practical public servants it becomes our duty to avoid the costs which are taxed against the State of Texas when one of our decisions fails to follow the rules announced by the Supreme Court.

To make the finding more palatable to a Texas public, he referred to a recent Texas case, and he disposed of our protracted effort to get rid of the original trial judge in a few words:

Judge Joe B. Brown, who tried this case, has recused himself from any further connection with the case and, we have concluded, properly so.

Thus the court was, in effect, saying that we had been right in the habeas corpus proceeding, although it had decided against us in the peremptory fashion previously narrated. Quickly and pointedly, Judge Morrison concluded his epochal opinion:

For the errors pointed out, the judgment is reversed, and the cause is remanded with directions that the venue be changed to some county other than Dallas. It is so ordered.

There were concurring opinions by each of Judge Morrison's colleagues.

Judge McDonald, agreeing with Judge Morrison in his opinion, wanted to elaborate on the error of Judge Brown in refusing to grant the motion for a change of venue. In a series of statements he specified the unsatisfactory conditions in Dallas at the time of the trial. Whole passages in Judge McDonald's opinion reflected the arguments that had been made earlier by Belli, Tonahill, and Brody, in their motion; by Burleson in his argument before the court; and by myself. The basic facts of the situation in Dallas, presented earlier in this book, were now summarized or paraphrased in Judge McDonald's opinion. He dwelt even on the "anti-Semitism against Ruby [that] was sparked by pretrial publicity that Ruby's name had been changed from Rubenstein to Ruby."

Against such a background of unusual and extraordinary invasions of the expected neutral mental processes of a citizenry from which a jury is to be chosen, the Dallas County climate was one of such strong feeling that it was not humanly possible to give Ruby a fair and impartial trial. . . .

After quoting, as had we, the words of Justice Frankfurter in the Dowd case, he continued:

Ten of Jack Ruby's trial jurors witnessed the shooting of
Oswald on television. They were challenged for cause under
[the Texas law] which prohibits a witness serving as a juror.
Such challenges for cause were summarily dismissed and disposed of by the trial judge with dispatch.

He summarized the examination of jurors Shields and
Malone:

Juror Shields witnessed the shooting on television. She was
objected to as being a witness to the offense as well as the
others who saw it on television. The trial court refused to grant
Ruby an additional peremptory challenge so that he could remove her as a juror. Ruby moved the Court to swear Juror
Shields as a witness and the Court refused.

The defense's effort to dispose of objectionable jurors
had not succeeded at the trial. Now it was influencing the
thinking of at least one judge of the Court of Appeals.

Juror Malone was a witness to the shooting on television and
was objected to as being disqualified under a provision of Texas
law. She knew that from what she had witnessed on television
that Oswald was shot in the Dallas Police Station November
24th and subsequently died as a result of being shot with a
pistol. *It was the most extraordinary thing she had ever witnessed.* [This was Judge McDonald's emphasis, as well as
ours.]
Nothing could remove her fixed knowledge of Oswald's being shot in the Dallas Police Station. The only thing she did
not know about the case as a fact was who fired the gun. All
other issues pertaining to the shooting of Oswald were firmly
and permanently fixed in her mind. She subsequently learned
from television that it was Ruby who shot Oswald.
The trial judge seated her as a juror over the protest of
Ruby's counsel who insisted upon being given additional pe-

remptory challenges in order that she might be challenged as an objectionable juror. . . . The Supreme Court of the United States in Rideau v. Louisiana, 373 U.S. 723, [another case cited in our briefs and argument] has held that such objectionable jurors as Shields and Malone were, in effect, witnesses to the offense. Further, that Court has held that even nonwitnesses who have been saturated with prejudicial news releases and rumors, and who hold a state of mind as objectionable [as] jurors Shields and Malone possessed were not qualified as fair and impartial jurors. . . .

There can be no difference to the competency of a witness who has heard via telephone or radio, or saw a matter through a mirror or field glasses, and a witness who has viewed a matter on television. A contrary holding would undermine the sound principles underlying the utilization of a scientific amplification and reproduction of sensory events, and thus unduly hamper the work and function of the triers of fact. In short, the television viewer meets the established criterion of personal observation required for a witness' competency. . . . The State operated from this inevitable and certain principle when it introduced the television film of the shooting of Oswald before the jury as direct evidence of the shooting.

The trial court could not, consistent with the due process, assume that the objectionable jurors Shields and Malone were endowed with a sense of detachment, so clear in introspective perception of their own mental processes that they could possibly exclude even the unconscious influence of their preconceptions as to all the established facts except identity of Ruby. Their mental processes were engendered by a pervasive pretrial publicity which denied Ruby his guarantee of a fair trial by a panel of "impartial, indifferent" jurors; because, "the failure to award an accused a fair hearing violates even the minimal standards of due process."

The judge again cited the Dowd case with the same words and in the same context that we had referred to it. He went on:

Against this background of crystalized opinions of the existence of the material issues with which the State was burdened to prove, Jack Ruby was forced to trial under the most adverse, unusual and extraordinary circumstances that this member of this Court has yet had occasion to consider.

This assertion we were ready to cheer. It was precisely what we had always contended. He underscored it by the very reference from the Estes case that, we felt, was determinative of the issue:

"A defendant on trial for a specific crime is entitled to his day in court, not in a stadium, or a city or nationwide arena. The heightened public clamor resulting from radio and television will inevitably result in prejudice. Trial by television is, therefore, foreign to our system."

It was established below on the hearing for change of venue, the jury voir dire, and the quick verdict that the firmly established legal principles of law in this state and nation cried out for a change of venue of this case, which would guarantee Ruby the fair and unprejudiced trial which he failed to receive. At the same time, such transfer would cast no reflection, indictment against, or a challenge to the honesty, integrity or inability of the Dallas citizenry to give such. . . .

We were delighted, smug even, at this adoption of our argument, until Judge McDonald suddenly credited Joe Tonahill with ably urging and pointing out "this basic principle of our jurisprudence which this Court has consistently followed." Yet he cited the cases that we had cited in support of the principle.

The general rule that a change of venue lies within the sound discretion of the trial judge has to give way when an unfair jury is forced on one charged with crime.

It is to be noted that all twelve of Ruby's jury entertained some conceptions of his guilt, one way or the other. The people of Dallas County had been exposed repeatedly and in great depth to the actual shooting of Oswald on television re-runs.

Just as we had, he referred to the Rideau case from Louisiana, where the Supreme Court of the United States "did not bother to look to the transcript of the [jury examination] in reaching its determination as to prejudice." He concluded:

This Court has been furnished with many outstanding briefs and many oral arguments were made by a battery of very able lawyers on both sides. This writer has been especially impressed with the conduct of Honorable Joe Tonahill. Through much stress and strain, misunderstanding among client and appellant's relatives, he has exemplified the highest standards of the legal profession, remained true to his duty, and done an outstanding job in briefing and presenting this case before this Court.

On balance, Judge McDonald had done extremely well in analyzing the prejudice which required a reversal of the death sentence. If he was excessively kind to Joe Tonahill, we could understand it: he, like Tonahill, had been repudiated by those on whom he had counted for support. Victory was sweet, even if Judge McDonald would compel us to share it with Tonahill.

Judge McDonald's adversary in the Court of Criminal Appeals, Judge Woodley, felt that he, too, had to explain the unanimous result. He began mildly:

The writer concurs in the reversal of the conviction because of the court's failure to change the venue and the admission in evidence of the testimony of the Witness Dean as to an oral statement of the appellant made while he was in jail, which statement, if made, was in the nature of a confession and inadmissible . . .

Though appellant's counsel did not seek a continuance and there is sufficient evidence aside from Dean's testimony to sustain the jury's verdict, the errors mentioned were such as to deprive Jack Ruby of a fair trial on the issue of the punishment to be assessed by the jury.

This aspect of the severity of the punishment was one that had not been labored by us; but it was clear, as Judge Woodley said, that if the jury believed that Ruby had premeditated his act, as claimed by Sgt. Dean, they were more likely to assess an extreme penalty.

Judge Woodley was more concerned about the history of the proceeding in the Court of Criminal Appeals and elsewhere.

"For a better understanding of the delay in the submission of the appeal herein, and of the claim that Jack Ruby's right to be represented by counsel of his choice was violated by the sanity hearing," he set forth in full "orders, quotations and facts" which he "deemed pertinent." From this sequence of orders and documents, Judge Woodley drew certain conclusions:

While the writer sees no denial of appellant's constitutional right to counsel of his choice, and does not agree with the contention that the sanity hearing was void or deprived appellant of any right, he remains convinced that there was no reasonable basis for inviting those who had been appellant's trial counsel but had been dismissed after notice of appeal to appear and present oral argument as friends of the Court after having denied a like right to his other counsel who withdrew or were "fired" before notice of appeal.

He also wanted to make clear, in the last paragraph of his concurring opinion, that he did not agree with another point that Judge McDonald had made:

In view of another trial and future trials, it should also be clearly understood that the majority does not hold that a juror who saw the shooting of the deceased on television is, for that reason alone, disqualified or subject to challenge for cause . . . as being a witness in the case.

Here was the possibility of error in the next round. It was an opportunity, too, to take the case to the United

States Supreme Court if there was another disastrous verdict. Surely, the highest court would want to take a look at this proposition. We felt that its ruling in the Rideau case from Louisiana made it likely that the court would reverse if a jury of witnesses tried the case.

# 28

## THE REACTION TO THE COURT'S DECISION

I SHALL NEVER FORGET the call from Dallas. Burleson, scarcely coherent in his joy, was saying, "We won!" The usually calm and unemotional Texan, deliriously happy, was a new and changed person. No, he had not yet seen the opinion. He would learn more soon. He would give me the details. We exchanged congratulations and discussed briefly those matters that required immediate attention.

Even as we began the conversation, my secretary began to signal me almost frantically: the communications media were on the trail, and they were seeking me just as they were seeking everyone of us—in Dallas, Austin, Detroit, and New York. A kind of emotional release follows any successful legal trial, and public acknowledgment of what has been accomplished is always a healthy restorative, particularly if for many months one has had for comfort only the knowledge of work done and still to do. Outwardly one may appear indifferent to the applause of the public, but, truly, one is never indifferent. One feels proud and happy. One wants to talk of the success and to think of it. As soon as I could, I called my wife, so that she might share this joy. Soon everyone knew, and many rejoiced with us.

When I turned to answer the queries of the press, I could express my feelings precisely. "The court acted exactly as it should have," I said. "The court had enough time to consider every aspect of the case, and it is in the American tradition that Ruby now will have the opportunity for a trial in an atmosphere conducive to a just result."

Had Lee Harvey Oswald lived, he would have been entitled to a fair trial, I said; now Ruby will get one. "All the believable evidence shows that the killing was on impulse and that Ruby did not go to the police station with the intent of killing Oswald."

I drew parallels between the Sheppard and Ruby cases, as had been done in the briefs and argument before the Texas Court of Criminal Appeals. "It is comforting that in the current hysteria about criminal cases, the courts can keep their balance and protect the rights of the defendant and the state as well."

In Dallas, Burleson interrupted Jack Ruby's reading of a book to break the news to him, "Jack, you won. You got a reversal today." Ruby received the news with the calm of disbelief, hardly grasping its significance. For about fifteen minutes Burleson tried, not too successfully, to discuss the various possibilities raised by the decision.

What did Ruby say on this historic occasion? Very little, so far as Burleson could recall. "Jack wasn't crying or laughing." "I'm kind of in shock myself," he remarked later, and Ruby's near nonchalance only enhanced the shock.

District Attorney Wade immediately let it be known that he favored a death sentence at the retrial. But he hedged by declaring that he would not agree to Ruby's entering a guilty plea unless the penalty would be a life sentence.

With as much grace as he could muster, in view of the hard-to-swallow reversal, he continued: "We will file a motion for a rehearing. We don't think there were any errors in the trial serious enough for a reversal."

Judge Brown refused comment.

Joe Tonahill, who "just happened" to be in Austin when the decision was announced, was jubilant: "I'm on my way to Dallas as soon as I can get a plane. I'm going to deliver a copy of the opinion to Jack, and tell him my obligation to him is now complete. I'm going to tell him to get a law school graduate to handle his business, because that's all he needs."

Jack Ruby, who had tried so hard to discharge Tonahill, thought otherwise. He would not permit his former counsel to see him. Nevertheless, Tonahill smiled. "I had no particular desire to see Jack Ruby," he said now, "but as a lawyer I thought it was my duty to give him a copy of the opinion." He left Dallas with the copy, on which he had written, "For Jack Ruby." "It may be he's just as sick as I've always thought he was," Tonahill remarked. "I still think he's paranoid. I can't see it any other way."

Melvin Belli, was in Houston when the decision was announced. He was not surprised at the result. "I'd filed a brief up there, the only brief on file for two years. . . ." Asked if he would return to the defense team, he replied quickly, "No, sir." He had had his fill of the case when the conviction was voted by the jury. "I wouldn't go back with this case now if I were asked."

"My heart feels a little lighter tonight," Eva Grant said, as she waited at the Dallas County Jail to see her brother. Sister Eileen, in Chicago, expressed herself as being "pleasantly surprised." "He's a wonderful person who wouldn't hurt anybody."

The mother of Lee Harvey Oswald was quoted as saying that she was glad Ruby's conviction was reversed because "the truth will now come to light." She expressed the hope that Ruby would not be freed on bond, because "he wouldn't live two minutes." Some indignant person (not herself) might kill him. She was against capital punishment, she said. She expressed delight that Ruby had been found sane. "It could lead to his taking the witness stand at a new trial and giving the other side a chance to cross-examine him."

Oswald's widow, Marina Oswald Porter (she had remarried after his death), said that she had never wanted Ruby to be electrocuted. "I think he's been punished enough already. I've always said that. He's a human being, too."

The members of the jury that had sentenced Ruby to death still insisted that Ruby had had a fair trial by an impartial jury, but those who were interviewed voiced no objections to the reversal of their judgment.

The foreman of the jury, Max E. Causey, a military electronics analyst, remarked: "Of course, we were all human. To completely deny that the jurors had any preconceived idea of his guilt would be getting into elements of the mind. I'm not even certain the appellate court is capable of doing that." This was tantamount, it seemed to me, to a confession of possible prejudgment, as we had successfully maintained in our appeal.

Told what the foreman had said, another juror, Mrs. Gwen English, a bookkeeper, said: "That's just one man's opinion. I don't think he has any way of knowing what the jurors thought or felt." How, then, had the jurors reached a unanimous verdict?

Mrs. Louise Malone, the last juror chosen, one of those whom Belli had tried unsuccessfully to challenge, declared the evidence against Ruby conclusive: "If the same evidence was presented in the same manner, I think any jury would return the same verdict." This was a strange concept, that manner governed a result. What Mrs. Malone said could be translated into the thought that if Belli, or someone else, had chosen another manner of presenting the same evidence, he might have gotten another result!

James E. Cunningham, another electronics engineer, and J. Wayman Rose, a furniture manufacturer's representative, expressed doubt about what might have happened had the trial been held outside Dallas. Rose, while believing that Ruby had had a fair trial, said: "I don't mind seeing anybody get another chance if he has it coming to him. Apparently, Ruby does, if the court decided it."

Jimmy Breslin, then a columnist for the *New York Her-*

*ald Tribune,* interviewed many people after the high court's decision, most of them in and from Dallas. He spent much time with Burleson, and he talked with Judge Brown. The latter professed to be surprised that he had been reversed in the matter of a change of venue. "Why, Belli and Jack Ruby asked me to keep the trial in Dallas. Anyway, I'm out of the case now for good. You can get old handling this case. I'm glad it ain't mine."

This prompted the enterprising Breslin to telephone Belli in Houston. According to Breslin, Belli exploded: "Judge Brown made his first mistake the day his mother told him to go to law school and he went there instead of staying home where he belonged. I asked for the trial to stay in Dallas? We spent two weeks making motions. I knew the decision would get thrown out because Brown wouldn't move the trial."

The American press, reflecting, I believe, the prevailing sentiment of the American people, generally applauded the reversal of the Ruby death sentence, but not always for the right reasons. I was appalled by the misunderstanding that still existed with respect to the pertinent constitutional provisions. Not unexpectedly, the Chicago *Tribune* found reasons to complain, but the utterly disapproving tone was surprising. The *Tribune* editorial, headed "A Mystifying Decision," was more mystifying than the opinions of the Texas Court of Criminal Appeals.

The holding of the court leaves us, frankly, bewildered. Millions of viewers saw the killing on television. They were not necessarily all confined to Dallas County, but covered the nation. How could a change of venue erase the recollection of the event? How could the fact of the killing be changed or even challenged when it was recorded imperishably on film?

Yet, as the *Tribune* pointed out, the majority of the court did not hold "that a juror who saw the shooting of the deceased on television is, for that reason alone, disqualified or subject to challenge."

And all of Ruby's jurors held "some concepts of guilt." The *Tribune* asked: "Was it possible to maintain some abstract objectivity when the act of killing was in full view not only of hundreds of witnesses at the scene but before an audience of millions?"

The editorial questioned the second reason for the reversal—the statements allegedly made by Ruby to Sgt. Dean. It then referred obliquely to Tonahill, but not by name, as "the lawyer who successfully appealed Ruby's conviction." It criticized his post-reversal statements as prejudicial. "If the court is going to impose bounds on pretrial utterance, it should apply them evenly to both defense and prosecution."

And it concluded with several misapprehensions: "The Ruby reversal is yet another of a long series of decisions stemming from the Supreme Court and passed down thru lesser courts which overbalance the scales of justice in favor of accused criminals. There cannot be the slightest question that Ruby committed the crime of which he was accused but here is another court which resorts to technical trivialities to deny an apparent fact."

The Chicago *Daily News* was scarcely more comforting. It declared that since the Ruby trial "was allowed to become a degrading circus, . . . reversible error was a near-certainty." "The two errors cited by the Texas Court of Criminal Appeals in overturning the conviction, however, are so technical in nature as to leave the layman still wondering—if not marveling—at the intricacies of judicial procedure."

It thought that laymen might well be forgiven for wondering "whether American jurisprudence is not caught up in a web that needlessly makes the simplest case incredibly complex." It opined that "Ruby's only defense was insanity, the only real question one of determining the degree of punishment."

It observed, disapprovingly: "Defense attorneys are already rubbing their hands over the prospect that Ruby may go free after a new trial under a Texas law that prescribed a minimum punishment for murder-without-malice." This "would be," it said, "an ironic ending to a tragedy. . . ."

The Minneapolis *Tribune* editorialized on the continuing battle over the coverage of criminal cases. It concluded, with possibly good sense: "But the Ruby case, while unique, demonstrates that there are often circumstances beyond the reach, or the right, of law enforcement officials to control. And equally beyond the news media's obligation to ignore."

The Detroit *Free Press*, in Sol Dann's bailiwick, was the most moderate and understanding of the metropolitan newspapers. It asserted that the Ruby decision was in line with the thinking of the United States Supreme Court and that it enforced the dignity of the judicial process. Ruby had not received a fair trial, it said, and therefore the reversal was appropriate. It put all of the blame on the trial judge, the hapless Joe B. Brown. Its analysis of the decision was a classic example of the clarity and precision of which the press is sometimes capable. Very sensibly, it said of the much maligned Supreme Court: "It has not set the rights of the defendant above the rights of society, but it has outlawed short-cut justice."

And it closed in an admirably balanced tone: "The Texas Court of Criminal Appeals did no more than was proper. Ruby does not go free now. But he will be tried, as he should, by the book."

# BEGINNING AGAIN

# 29

## PLANNING THE SECOND TRIAL

THE DAY after the opinion of the Texas Court of Criminal
Appeals was released, I went to Minneapolis. The trip,
planned some time before as a visit to the Guthrie theatre,
gave me an unexpected opportunity to judge the reactions
in a community far removed from the Texas tragedy. If
my reception was any indication, then Jack's plight had
begun to win him the sympathy of the American people.
Many small gestures and courtesies assured us of support
in our effort on Jack's behalf.

While I was in Minneapolis, all the communications
media continued to question me. It was as if I were still in
Chicago. Indeed, Chicago came to me through the electronic devices about which I have never ceased to marvel,
the same devices that had made possible the close collaboration between attorneys in far-flung places. Calls from
Detroit and Dallas told me of plans for another telephone
conference to discuss the consequences of victory. In the
end, we could not make contact with Clinton, but the rest
of us were available. We talked at length of the implications of the triumph and what it portended for the future.
Elation and measured confidence ran through the conversation, for we felt that the peril of the death sentence was
at an end, no matter what Henry Wade or Bill Alexander
said.

Several matters stood high on the agenda. What should
we say in reply to the State's motion for a rehearing? We
assumed it would be denied. Other questions would then
arise. Where would the second trial be held? Would Wade

agree to a plea of murder without malice? How should evidence be presented at the trial? Should we make an issue of Jack's sanity? These and many other questions concerned us now. Last, and not least important, was the desirability of continuing our efforts to influence public opinion so that Jack's case would get at least a neutral hearing on retrial. There was much work ahead for each of us and many problems to resolve.

One of the crucial topics in this conversation was a short conference that had been held between Burleson and Wade. Wade had insisted that the State was willing to try the case over again and would press for a harsh punishment. He had given Burleson a tough presentation of the State's view, taking the position that the mere fact that Sgt. Dean's testimony was no longer admissible was indecisive. There was, in Wade's opinion, other good evidence of malice that would lead to an extreme result, the death penalty even. Why, we wondered, was Wade taking such a position, since he had already expressed a willingless to urge commutation of the death sentence.

In a letter summarizing the telephone conference, Burleson led off the discussion:

We can point out to Wade that he has a legitimate reason for agreeing to murder without malice in that the Court of Criminal Appeals and other recent decisions of the Supreme Court have prohibited him from trying the case like it was tried the first time. . . . We can also point out that it is not our fault, nor anyone's fault that the Legislature has not made the punishment for murder without malice to be somewhere around 20 or 25 years. . . . I recall several years ago that Wade recommended to the Legislature that the punishment for murder without malice be raised to about 25 years and nothing more has been done. . . .

Burleson thought that we should persuade Wade that Jack Ruby had already suffered and been punished sufficiently. He had been kept in virtual solitary confinement away from other prisoners. The experience with Belli and Judge Brown had been traumatic in the extreme. Their writing of books about his case had been shocking. The struggle with Tonahill was even more devastating. His deprivation of counsel of his own choice, the aborted sanity hearing, these and other circumstances, had subjected Ruby to extreme punishment, far beyond the ordinary. He had, in effect, already served the equivalent of many years of imprisonment.

By this time I had obtained all the volumes of the evidence and exhibits of the Warren Commission, but had gone through them in only preliminary fashion, except for some sampling in depth here and there. It was clear, however, that this material would be indispensable to us in the retrial. It would also be of tremendous value in discussions with Wade.

I knew that there were important communications in the Warren volumes from Wade and others. (Finding them, however, was difficult, since, unfortunately, the indexing of the work is very bad.) All, or virtually all, of the witnesses at the trial also appeared before the Commission, and many potential witnesses who did not appear at the trial, such as Secret Service Agent Forrest Sorrels, had appeared before the Commission. With careful examination and analysis of their statements, we should be prepared for all eventualities.

We could therefore warn Wade of the consequences of a retrial—the impeachment of his witnesses through the introduction of material in the Warren Commission Report and the volumes of evidence. Some of the police officers had contradicted themselves scandalously. This would not make Dallas look good at a new trial.

Sam Clinton, who had not participated in the conference call, joined in the correspondence.

Frankly, since Wade has been so consistent in his public statements regarding his position on any "deal," I am pessimistic about getting him to change his view unless he is practically forced to do so in a way that permits him to point to some other development or outside consideration that justifies his doing so. . . . As I see it, the key is moving to quash the indictment upon which the original trial was had so that the matter can be presented to a new and different grand jury which, if properly persuaded, might be induced to return an indictment of murder without malice. If Wade is confronted with a potentially good motion to quash . . . he would be on fairly solid grounds in not resisting the motion. . . . Such a motion . . . would raise the points already outlined in one or another of your letters concerning lack of equal representation from all segments of the community, disqualification of grand jurors who saw the offense committed on television, and the like.

Burleson had given some thought to the schedule that might apply to the retrial. He gave us his best estimate:

October 5, 1966: Reversal in the Court of Criminal Appeals

October 20, 1966: State's motion for rehearing filed.

November 9, 1966: Rehearing submitted to Court of Criminal Appeals and oral argument by State.

December 7, 1966: Opinion of Court of Criminal Appeals overruling State's motion for rehearing.

December 16, 1966: Mandate issued to Criminal District Court from Court of Criminal Appeals.

December 19, 1966: Mandate filed in Criminal District Court No. 3 of Dallas County.

January 23, 1967: Change of venue hearing in Dallas.

February 10, 1967: Transcript prepared for sending to new county.

February 27, 1967: Pretrial hearing in new County.

April 24, 1967: Trial in new County.

As it turned out, this was an overstatement of the time at our disposal, and not alone because the legal processes were speeded up.

For our immediate consideration, there was the matter

of responding to the state's petition for a rehearing. Burleson was to prepare a rough draft and circulate it to the rest of us. Clinton, too, was concerned, when he saw the State's motion. "[It] uses such intemperate language in virtually castigating the Court . . . that the Court is more likely to be repulsed than impressed," he thought. "Therefore my own reaction is that our reply should be directed to bolstering . . . the holdings in the Court's opinion in simple and concise terms rather than castigating the State. . . . I believe that retaliation . . . should be avoided." And so it was handled.

On the matter of the change of venue, Burleson favored hiring someone, perhaps a young lawyer or law student, to visit cities to which the case might be transferred. I thought that perhaps the most reliable guide, and the most discreet, would be the examination of editorial comment and letters to the editor in Texas newspapers. Clinton, a resident of Austin, felt that Ruby could get a better jury there than elsewhere in Texas, although there were circumstances militating against selection of that city. He therefore thought Beaumont or Corpus Christi should be considered.

We had given some consideration to the pretrial conference with the judge, and what might be discussed then— whether we were going to raise the issue of Jack's sanity; whether we could use the provisions of the new Texas code on "discovery" (the legal term for acquiring knowledge of the facts before trial); and other matters.

I was greatly concerned about the presentation of evidence at the trial.

The difficulty with the first trial was that the proof of absence of malice was buried and obscured by other testimony, and the jury was led astray by Sgt. Dean. It would not be enough for us to rest content with the absence of his testimony from a subsequent trial. We would have to hammer away, as effectively as possible, on the theme of lack of malice, lack of premeditation, and the like. Jack's appearance on the stand might be helpful, but it would be a real risk.

How, then, were we to make our point? I thought we should bring in as many newspaper, radio, and television people as possible to prove that they were informed that the moving of Oswald would take place at 10 A.M., and not at any later hour. A parade of such witnesses would keep the fact constantly in the jury's mind. This would be preceded by our cross-examination of police officers and others, to bring out that the generally understood hour of removal was 10 A.M, and that Ruby could not have known of any other arrangements. At the same time of such cross-examination, we could negative his having received any aid from the police, either in knowing about the hour of removal or in getting access to the basement. We would also have the evidence with respect to the wiring of money to Little Lynn and we should make certain that this was so well developed as to be crystal clear to even the most prejudiced juror.

From my conversations with people everywhere, I knew that they were bothered by Ruby's carrying a gun. If he habitually carried it, there would be nothing special in his having a gun on November 24, 1963. This would have to be shown.

To make the jury more receptive to a light sentence, we could have testimony on the mental and emotional condition of Jack and members of his family. But it could not be the complicated testimony relied on by Belli. We would simply show that Jack was mentally sick and therefore did not know what he was doing or that it was wrong. We should have Jack quite unexpectedly appear on the scene, see Oswald, and, by mere reflex, shoot him. Anything more elaborate than that would do harm rather than good, in my judgment.

We also had to give thought to the selection of the jury. Obviously, in my opinion, we would try to eliminate "juror-witnesses"—those who had seen the killing on television. Unfortunately, the Court of Criminal Appeals would be no guide in this area, although one judge had noted that a majority did not rule that viewing the killing, in itself, disqualified a prospective juror. We also would have to think of the kinds of persons whom we would want to eliminate or select.

On the sanity issue, Clinton, for whom I had increasing respect, spoke to the point:

One of the most perplexing problems . . . is the sanity issue. Throughout these proceedings one of the primary considerations, as I understood them, was to keep Jack out of Rusk State Hospital for the criminally insane. But if he is acquitted of the offense by reason of insanity and is also found insane at the time of trial he will, in all likelihood, be sent to Rusk; if he is found to be sane at the time of the offense but insane at the time of trial the same unfortunate result obtains. It seems highly unlikely that he would be found to be insane at the time the offense was committed but sane at the time of trial—the only combination I can think of that would immediately free him. We all share the opinion that Jack is mentally ill, if not legally insane, and should be receiving competent psychiatric treatment as soon as possible. Thus we are confronted with a paradoxical situation: an offense has been committed and some punishment seems certain since acquittal by reason of insanity at the time of offense is highly unlikely yet to reduce the possible penalty we must inject the notion of insanity but not actually prove insanity at the time of trial in order to avoid commitment in Rusk. If I have correctly assayed the situation it would seem to follow that emphasis of Jack's mental condition at the time of the offense is to be stressed rather than at the time of trial. If this is so, then why raise the issue of insanity at the time of trial at all?

All of us had come to have a tremendous admiration, even affection for Judge Holland. Dann, however, was prepared to throw caution to the winds. He suggested that a bench trial would be better than a jury trial. I felt otherwise, and tried to explain my reasoning:

One reason to insist upon a jury, rather than a bench, trial is that we may object to juror witnesses. . . . If we are sustained on this point, we will have a better jury from our viewpoint. If we are overruled, then we have a constitutional point for appeal, if necessary. The corollary of this is that, unlike Belli in the original trial, we must object, in any event, to the introduction of films of the slaying. This is particularly important if we are overruled by the trial judge on the jury-witness point. . . .

We would have to explore the matter at our pretrial conference with Judge Holland. But it seemed to me that the best we could expect would be the combination of Judge Holland and a good jury.

Since a principal ground for reversal of the first judgment had been the adverse publicity in the Dallas community, all who were connected in any way with the retrial had to think of formulating ways and means, guidelines as it were, to create a better atmosphere for the second trial. It was a difficult task, we knew; but unlike the almost hopeless situation at the first trial, it was not an impossible one.

There were two cases to guide us. The United States Supreme Court had set forth standards in deciding the *Sheppard* case, and when Sheppard was retried, the presiding judge laid down rigid guidelines for the conduct of attorneys, the press, and others. This case gave guidance, however tentative and imperfect, to those who might be involved in other sensational cases.

For further enlightenment, there was the Richard F. Speck case in Chicago, involving the killing of eight student nurses in such circumstances as to chill the blood of an entire nation. When many people are prepared to rend an accused without benefit of a trial, how does one make certain that he will be treated fairly and accorded all the protection afforded by the Constitution? One of the psychiatrists chosen for the guidance of the court by Judge Herbert Paschen, to whom the Speck case had been assigned, permitted himself to be interviewed by the press. He made statements which were at best premature and at worst highly prejudicial to the defense. This was recognized as ominous. It had to be stopped at once. Mere admonition by the court was not enough. The Public Defender, representing Speck, and an assistant from the State's Attorney's office, representing the prosecution, agreed tentatively upon simple guidelines for the press and Judge Paschen approved them:

1. Only what occurs in the courtroom and is a matter of public record should be reported.

2. There shall be no seeking out of witnesses and questioning them prior to the trial for purposes of seeking information for pretrial publication.

3. Names of prospective jurors shall not be published.

These guidelines were subject to further refinement and clarification as the Speck case went from its preliminary stages to actual trial.

The court and counsel were to discover in time that they did not necessarily determine all the rules of procedure, that the press had certain rights which should not be interfered with by a zealous court. The Chicago *Tribune*, ever sensitive to the freedom of the press, insofar as it affected the *Tribune*'s opportunities to pry into and report what was going on in its domain, filed a special writ with the Illinois Supreme Court to compel Judge Paschen to relax some of his requirements. As it generally does in such matters, the *Tribune* prevailed.

Nevertheless, such ongoing circumstances will ultimately lead to workable guidelines for the trial of all cases of wide public interest. The retrial of Jack Ruby would undoubtedly attract world attention again, and we would have to do our best to prevent a repetition of the earlier debacle by careful attention to balancing the rights of the defendant against the privileges of the press.

Even as we were preparing ourselves for the retrial, fate was preparing to deal another blow to Ruby's counsel. On

November 15, 1966, Sol Dann was scheduled to make a plea in a Detroit court to disqualify a circuit judge from presiding over hearings on a bank merger. Before he could present his motion, Dann collapsed in the courtroom and was rushed to the hospital. There he appeared to be in critical condition, suffering severe heart damage. Thus, at a crucial time, he was secluded from all contacts with us. Dann, always exigent, took everything with such seriousness that it created physical repercussions in himself and others.

On the very next day the Texas Court of Criminal Appeals announced that it had turned down the State's motion for a rehearing. The retrial was coming on faster than we had expected.

# 30

## WICHITA FALLS IS CHOSEN

AFTER the State's motion for a rehearing was turned down, on November 16, 1966, Judge Holland said that he would not select a site for the second trial for at least three weeks. He wanted to meet the attorneys for both sides to see whether all could agree on a place for the retrial. Amarillo, Lubbock, Wichita Falls, and Fort Worth were reported to be among the cities under consideration. We had not joined the speculation, but we were quoted obliquely. Our opponents, it appeared, had been less coy.

Subsequently, Judge Holland advised us that he wanted to confer with us on Tuesday morning, December 5, about the retrial of Jack Ruby. In haste we planned to be in Dallas several days in advance so that we might first confer and prepare among ourselves. Dann, of course, was unavailable because of his illness, Kunstler could be present only during the week-end, Clinton on Tuesday. Only Burleson and I were able to be in Dallas at all times from December 1 to December 5.

As we were conferring in preparation for the sessions with Wade and Judge Holland, we read in the Wichita Falls *Times* an article that seemed inspired. The dateline was Montague; the language was explicit.

Lawyers for Jack Ruby will meet with the presiding judge of the 8th Administrative Judicial District Monday to possibly select Wichita Falls as the site of the Dallas night club operator's second murder trial.

Judge Louis Holland, of Montague, will meet with Ruby's

attorneys in Dallas to decide on a site and date for the trial
which was ordered to be held outside Dallas by the Texas
Court of Criminal Appeals when it reversed Ruby's death
conviction.

Members of the Dallas District Attorney's staff have indicated they would be agreeable to trying the case in Wichita
Falls. Holland, as presiding judge of the state judicial district
that runs from Fort Worth to the Red River, will make the final
decision on where the trial will be held after conferring with
defense lawyers, Elmer Gertz of Chicago, Ill., and Phil Burleson of Dallas.

Predictions in Dallas are that Holland will transfer the trial
to Judge Arthur Tipp's 30th District Court in Wichita Falls
with the Montague jurist to preside. Such a trial, if held here,
probably would be scheduled either in January or February.

Dallas District Attorney Henry Wade, the original prosecutor, has said he would seek the death penalty in a second trial
while defense lawyers have indicated they feel their client is
guilty of no more than murder without malice—a felony that
carries a maximum sentence of five years in Texas.

The Dallas newspapers, too, seemed to know the inside
story. They described Wichita Falls as a leading contender.
When questioned by local reporters, we would not
comment.

Others, like ourselves, were less certain of Judge Holland's choice. A distinguished judge called me, while I
was in Burleson's office, seeking my intercession in favor
of a Texas judge of his acquaintance. Our thoughts turned
immediately to the reports that Judge Brown had once
shopped around to see if he would travel with the case if
he granted a change of venue. There was mileage, we
knew, in presiding over highly publicized criminal trials.
This was one of the causes of difficulty in the *Sheppard*
case and, undoubtedly, in many others. We did not want
it to happen again in our case.

It was agreed that Earl would quietly go to Wichita

Falls that very day and see what he could learn about the community. Each of us gave him suggestions—whom to see, what to ask, and whom and what to avoid. He was to learn how the Jewish community reacted to the prospect of the trial being held in its midst, and he was to do the same for the general public. Was there prejudice against Jews generally and against Jack Ruby in particular? Was there a desire to exculpate Texas or themselves? Bill Alexander had come from Wichita Falls, and his brother was a physician there: would that hurt or help us? What would be the effect of the residence in Wichita Falls of Lee Oswald's older brother Robert? Were the press and the business leaders fair-minded?

Earl proved to be a good researcher and reporter. He overcame many unexpected difficulties. He found the name and address of the local rabbi, but when he went to the home he discovered that the rabbi had moved from the city. Did this denote that the Jews were an inconsequential or inconsiderable group? No, one of the leaders of the city was a Jew. He received Earl warmly and gave him a glowing account of what he might expect. He persuaded Earl that his brother would receive a fair trial, perhaps even a degree of sympathy. At any rate, it would not be a repetition of the old debacle. Earl brought back a highly laudatory account of Judge Holland, a man of great reputation.

In all, we were pleased with Earl's report. We could chance the initial selection of Wichita Falls, but we would make further inquiry through Burleson's associate, Tom Keane, and through other means. And we would watch closely all that appeared in the press.

That Monday morning we conferred with the district attorney. Burleson and I sat, as I recall, on opposite sides of Henry Wade's new desk in his new office in the new County Building of Dallas County. Earl Ruby sat on a couch facing Wade, silent throughout the conversation. Frank Watts and then Bill Alexander entered the room after the discussion had begun. We were sparring, rather than saying all that was on our minds.

"They tell me," said Wade, "that you like big, sensational cases."

"Sometimes," I replied. "Generally, the cases are mine-run ones—real estate deals, wills, common-law suits, nothing earth-shaking."

"They tell me," Wade began again, "they're raising a lot of money for Jack Ruby's defense in Jewish temples and synagogues."

"If they are, I have not heard of it," I retorted, remembering the failure of the Jack Ruby Defense Appeal. Then, with mock humor, I went on, "Henry, if you find out about the money that is being raised, let me know, as I want to get my share. I have received nothing thus far."

If Wade was skeptical, he did not show it.

Polite phrases expressed sympathy for Sol Dann, and the absence of Kunstler and Clinton was noted. "Sol is probably out of the case from this point on," I volunteered, "the others will be in it."

Still we were sparring. We wanted Wade to agree to a plea of murder without malice, carrying a maximum imprisonment of five years in Texas, and he wanted us to agree to a life term. No one would say what was truly on his mind. Later, later—this seemed to be the unexpressed thought.

Alexander declared that they would ask for the death penalty again. Then, in what would have been a sensational announcement worthy of banner headlines, if uttered publicly, Wade said that they would prove there had been a conspiracy and that Ruby was a part of it. We looked upon the statement as Wade's means of intimidating us. We would not bite; we would not be intimidated.

Where would the trial take place? The newspapers had hinted broadly that it would be Wichita Falls. Wade was impassive and noncommittal. So were we.

All, so far, was relatively friendly, and a bit foolish,

considering the seriousness of our business. Suddenly, Wade spoke frankly of the reversal of the death judgment by the Court of Criminal Appeals. He was vehement, angry, indiscreet, unwise, in his unwarranted attack upon the reviewing court. Never have I heard a district attorney speak so forcefully in criticizing the judges of his own state. What he said was extremely personal, acidulous. He would not forget; he would be avenged. It was almost as if he had been promised one result and presented another.

Much dirty linen was washed as the district attorney spoke his mind. Amazement and disbelief overcame me as I listened to the waspish comments. And it was in a state of semishock that I left when the session was over. No agreement had been reached, but I had got an eye-popping insight into the district attorney of Dallas County, Texas.

We met the next morning with Judge Holland in a conference room in the new court house. Clinton joined Burleson and myself. Earl, excluded from the conference of lawyers and judge, remained in the corridors to learn as quickly as possible what might be determined. Wade, Alexander, and Watts appeared for the State. I was beginning to wonder, and not wonder, at the nonappearance of Williamson.

Alexander and Watts had their usual grim, unfunny humor at my expense. "Perhaps we ought to bring in Ruby in the kind of cage in which Eichmann was tried in Jerusalem," said one. I did not, could not, laugh. "If you are going to enter a plea, you should do so now," Alexander said heatedly. "We won't entertain it at the last moment." Then he offered again to wager there would be another death sentence.

Judge Holland suggested what we already knew, that he preferred to hold the trial in Wichita Falls and that he, rather than the local judge, would preside. The courtrooms there were new and nice; the security provisions were good; cooperation could be expected. Although Earl's investigation had convinced us that Wichita Falls would do, we did not want to appear eager. Therefore we suggested that we would like time to look into the matter to determine whether or not prejudice existed. The judge said he would allow us ten days for this purpose.

We discussed various pretrial motions with respect to the indictment, witnesses, the suppression of various kinds of evidence, discovery, guidelines for the press, the time needed for preparations, everything of any nature that occurred to any of us. All was considered in a sensible and understanding fashion, and a schedule was agreed upon that would probably project the trial to some time in the spring.

We asked that Ruby be kept in the Dallas County Jail as long as possible to facilitate visits by the family and counsel and to obviate traveling to a less accessible city. The judge thought this could be arranged if there were some legitimate juggling with the date of the trial transfer order. Somehow it would be taken care of.

We listened to Judge Holland with mounting respect. It would be a privilege and a delight to try the case before him. Suddenly, we learned that he could be firm in the wrong as well as in the right. Would those who had viewed the Oswald slaying on television be barred from the jury? No, he would not exclude them for that reason alone. We might have argued further with him; to protect the record we would have to do so later. There was consolation in the thought that this decision might smooth our path to the United States Supreme Court—if there was another disastrous verdict.

When the conference was over, the press was permitted to enter. Judge Holland spoke to them in moderate terms, telling them what had been ordered and what had been discussed. He permitted the taking of pictures. There was none of the wildness, none of the taking over by the press, that had characterized the first trial and its preliminaries. There was decorum, good taste, legitimate activity. Here was a foretaste of what was to come. Judge Holland was human enough to enjoy the attention he was receiving, judicious enough to keep it firmly under control.

The reaction of Wichita Falls to Judge Holland's announcement tended to confirm his wisdom in choosing that city as the site of the legal drama soon to be presented, in revised form, to the American people. The lead editorial of the Wichita Falls *Times*, on December 8, 1966, convinced me that the community would be more guarded and yet more considerate than the hapless Dallas public.

Wichita Falls has been paid a rare compliment of historical significance in being selected by Judge Louis T. Holland, presiding judge of the 8th Administrative Judicial District, for the retrial of the Jack Ruby murder case.

The national and even international interest in the legal proceedings inescapably adds to the legal drama that will be taking place in the county courthouse here within two or three months.

While there isn't any doubt that Judge Holland will demand and insure the proper atmosphere in the courtroom that will provide a fair trial for the defendant charged with the slaying of Lee Harvey Oswald, identified by the Warren Commission as the sole participant in the assassination of President John F. Kennedy, there will be a responsibility on the part of the citizenship at large to see that dignity and decorum and the other essentials of an impartial hearing are maintained beyond the confines of the courtroom and courthouse.

In a very real sense, not only will the defendant be on trial but also will the legal system of this county and state and the American system of justice be on trial.

After a conference with prosecution and defense lawyers, Judge Holland affirmed the selection of Wichita Falls as the site of the new trial as a place "accessible to all witnesses" with "ample facilities" and a "multitude of good, fair, honest people."

It is a challenge to live up to that appraisal.

Wichita Falls Mayor R. C. Rancier, an attorney himself, was attending a convention of the National League of

Cities at Las Vegas when he heard that his city had been chosen for the trial. He was careful not to injure the feelings of Dallas or any other city in his comments. "Wichita Falls didn't seek to get the trial," he said. "Some cities did, perhaps because of the economic advantage of it. If I were in the motel business, I guess I would be interested in a great many people coming to town. But otherwise, the trial will not be of great import to the people of Wichita Falls." He said that he had been angered "when Dallas was unjustly criticized in the aftermath of the Kennedy assassination. It was an emotional matter. There will be no emotionalism in Wichita Falls over it at all."

Ruby could get a fair trial anywhere in the state of Texas, he said; the jury selection would be done painstakingly to assure this. "There's nothing distinctive about Wichita Falls in that regard. I couldn't say why our city should have been selected. The judge could just as well have selected Amarillo or Fort Worth." Wichita Falls, he believed, would take the trial in stride.

Everyone in Wichita Falls, it seemed, was asked to comment, and most were willing to talk. In this respect they were no different from the people in Dallas, only more circumspect.

Stanley Kirk, the Wichita Falls district attorney, agreed with Henry Wade that the death penalty was called for; the State had a solid case. He made it clear that he and Wade would work closely together. Around forty years old, a solid six-feet-one in height, easy-going and affable, Kirk did not hesitate to respond to questioning. Asked how he felt about the case, he replied, "I feel a little like the man who's being ridden out of town on a rail. If it weren't for the honor, I'd just as soon decline."

Sheriff Jim Voyles did not do much talking for direct quotation, but it was clear that he had considered all the security problems. Ruby would be kept in isolation in an eight by ten foot cell on the fifth floor of the jail. (The courtroom was on the third floor.) Many security details had already been arranged; others would be worked out later. Nothing was going to be left unguarded, but the star of the show would not be pampered. Ruby would not have a radio. He would be permitted to see his attorneys and a few others.

The press would be a problem, but it would be accommodated. The jury dormitory on the fourth floor might be converted into a pressroom if, as anticipated, hundreds of reporters showed up.

Jim Harwell, executive vice president and general manager of the Chamber of Commerce, was already preparing press kits for the expected crowd. "We hope that during boring parts of the trial some of them will write about our community," he said.

One resident in the community was less enthusiastic than others. Robert Oswald, the brother of Lee Harvey Oswald, was area sales manager of a brick company. He had moved to Wichita Falls in 1964. Unlike his mother and sister-in-law, he had talked to few persons since the assassination. He believed his brother was guilty of killing the President.

"It doesn't bother me personally to have the trial here in Wichita Falls," he said, "but for my family it is unfortunate."

He would not attend the trial. "It would serve no purpose for me to go. Naturally, I have an interest in it. But I'll follow the trial's progress through the newspapers."

He thought Ruby would receive a fair trial in Wichita Falls. He thought the trial in Dallas had been fair.

## 31

## JACK RUBY IS ILL

MANY OF US, unschooled in the complexities of modern psychiatry, still assume that a person is sane or insane all the time and on all levels of consciousness and being. Even when our minds tell us that men and women are more complicated than that, we shrink from the realization that we are all compartmentalized in one way or another and that we exist simultaneously on several levels.

Despite my surface sophistication in such matters, the hours spent with Jack Ruby always provided unsettling reminders of man's complexity. On certain commonplace subjects and at certain times, Jack seemed sane enough, if of no high order of intelligence. If we discussed a Jewish politician whose name was familiar to him, such as Chicago's celebrated Jack Arvey, or a figure in the prize-fighting world, he would talk with complete rationality. So, too, certain aspects of his case—the sequence of events, the personalities, and the like. But he could not cooperate with us in any meaningful way, and we soon learned to be on our own in the attempt to save his life.

Jack almost never dwelt on his own death sentence. He was concerned with the fate of the Jews—who were going to die because of him. One day he penciled a note to me:

Elmer, you must believe me, that I am not imagining crazy thoughts etc. This is all so hopeless, that they have everything in the bag and there isn't any chance or hope for me. These hearings are just to stall for time. What chance do I have, when I know at this time that they are killing our people here now in

this very building. you must believe me, as to what is happening they are torturing people right here.

Why should I continually repeat all these things over and
over

We were always fearful that our client, in this state,
would say or do some foolish or fearful thing. His wild
letters were smuggled out of jail by guards, and some
found their way into the catalogs of autograph dealers. We
would wince as we read the dreadful charges made by him
against President Johnson and others.

Bad as these things were, however, we feared even more
the quotations and misquotations, purportedly from Ruby's
lips, which might make it difficult for us to prevail in the
second trial. All of us were morally certain that Ruby was
not a part of any conspiracy, that he had acted on impulse,
that he was irrational; but conspiracy breeds on suspicion
and fear. Burleson, who was in Dallas all the time, had the
unhappy task of trying to supervise Ruby's visits and correspondence. On several occasions he took steps to halt the
kiting of material originating with Jack. The difficulty of
this assignment was compounded because Jack had an
uncontrollable urge to talk.

Dr. Manfred Guttmacher, a psychiatrist who had testified for the defense at the trial, has brilliantly described
this aspect of Ruby's personality, in *Crime and the Mind:*

Ruby talked readily, compulsively. He didn't talk to his aud-
itor, he just talked as he moved—physiologically, so to speak—
bobbing his head forward like a boxer, rolling up phrase after
phrase, which became entangled with malapropisms, flashes of
aggression, and self-aggrandizement. His verbalizing outdis-
tanced his ideas; it was circumlocutory, it was aggressive, paranoid, and just beyond the firm ground of reality. One had to
listen a long time to catch the thin line of inconsequentiality
and the confused thinking behind it. He spoke of himself as a
phenomenon, without conscious appreciation of any inap-
propriateness. A messianic tendency peeped through the tangle

of immature braggadocio: "Inwardly I was a representative of the Jewish people." Action and idealism were smudged in his mind: "I'm a guy geared to fight . . . a little Heb being a big guy. One fellow, Mac, he said I was the toughest Jew he ever knew." This latent paranoid trend gained strength as the years passed.

Indeed. No one who spent any time with Jack could fail to be convinced, sooner or later, of his mental confusion. Although the sheriff and members of the district attorney's office maintained that Jack was faking an illness, the evidence was all to the contrary, and it had been recognized by competent psychologists and psychiatrists, by defense attorneys, and by the family. (Even Jack's sister Eva, the last to be convinced, finally admitted that Jack was mentally ill.) Of the psychiatrists I had brought in, Dr. Werner Tuteur, who had spent hours with Ruby, firmly believed him to be demented, and Dr. Thaddeus Kostrubala, who had studied the psychiatric evidence, believed there was organic brain damage.

When the death verdict was reversed and I had to go to Dallas to confer with my colleagues about the retrial of the case, I naturally wanted to see Jack at the county jail at the earliest opportunity. I had not seen him in several months. The most recent proceedings had taken place in the Texas Court of Criminal Appeals in Austin and in the United States Supreme Court in Washington, and other matters had been handled by correspondence and conference calls with colleagues and by visits with Earl Ruby and the family. Then, too, I had taken a much needed vacation. During this absence my associate, Wayne B. Giampietro, who had worked with me on countless problems arising from the case, continued to work on it. Jack Ruby was never neglected by us, even when it was not possible for me to see him. Now, in company with Burleson and Earl, I went to see Jack again.

The familiar jailer of Dallas County was absent when

we arrived at the jail. After we were seated in the usual private visiting room (which Jack always believed was bugged, as indeed it might have been), Jack shuffled in, almost furtively. There was no bounce in his step and little life to him. At first glance I was shocked almost speechless. He was pale and pasty, and it was not simply prison pallor. He had the look of one stricken with a mortal illness. During the visit Jack coughed frequently and spit painfully into a bag. He complained he could not keep his meals down, that he had not been well for weeks. Carefully we inquired into the details. Then, to divert him, we tried to discuss the case and the retrial in particular. His answers to our questions were short. Obviously he was distressed, and we suffered with him.

We knew when we left the jail that our client was very ill and required immediate medical attention. Determining how serious the situation might be, however, was difficult. Eva, who saw Jack most frequently, saw him in unfavorable circumstances. She had no direct contact with her brother; as a visitor to the jail, she saw him in a restrictive environment. After comparing notes with her, we decided that we would have Dr. Coleman Jacobson, who had formerly attended Jack, visit with him professionally. The visit, however, would have to be cleared with Sheriff Decker, who was in the hospital.

Meanwhile Kunstler had arrived in town, and he also wished to visit Jack. Together we went to the jail. To me Jack looked as bad as before, if not worse. But an effort to pass a letter had an unanticipated effect, for Kunstler thought that Jack might be feigning illness in order to pass letters. This Jack did, giving Bill a letter intended for Earl.

EARL:

You must believe what I've been telling you for the past two and a half years. If you only would have believed me all along you would have found some way to check out what I said. You would have saved Israel, but now they are doomed, because they think the U.S. are for them, but they are wrong because

Johnson wants to see them slaughtered and tortured. Egypt is
making believe they are an ally of Russia, that is only to fool
Russia and the rest of the world. The Arabs are going to over-
run Israel. They are going to get help both from Russia and
the U.S. Its too late now to do anything, and we are all doomed.

They are torturing children here. If you only would believe
what I'm telling you. Phil was in on the conspiracy all along,
and he was very instrumental in the frameup they planned,
that I was in on the assassination of the President. Don't be
fooled by his working on the briefs, now that has done all the
dirty work, he put himself in a position to make every effort
that he is on our side. Please you must believe all I've been
telling you. Earl, they are going to torture you to death, and
you will witness your own family being put to death. Forgive
me for all this terrible tragedy I've caused. Love

I know you won't listen to me Earl, but if you go to a public
phone booth, they may be watching you, pretend that you are
going to a department store or a movie, and then give them the
slip. Try the phone booth and call some people in N.Y. you
know, and if you don't find them in, you will know something
is wrong. Try your family again and if they are not at home,
then try Eileen or Ann. If they don't answer then you know
something is wrong. Earl I know what I am talking about, and
I'm sure you think that I'm crazy. But don't forget the jury
found me sane, so I'm not crazy anymore! If you know your
family is gone, then you know that all is lost and you can't save
anything. But you still may be able to save Israel. By getting
to Miami either hitch-hike or some-way. You won't be able to
fly because they will be watching for you. From Miami you
must find a way to Cuba, by pretending to rent a boat to go
fishing, and get to Cuba someway. From there you must find a
way to Russia. Castro would get you there if he knew you had
information for Russia. Then you tell the Russians how Egypt
has been using them all along, but they are much closer to
Johnson, because of what is happening to the Jews in the U.S.
Then they will understand what kind of person Johnson is, and
then they may be able to save Israel.

Russia will then be in a position to tell Johnson, that there first move if any trouble starts is not to bomb the U.S., but to wipe out Germany, that one thing Johnson don't want to happen, because he is counting on them to be the master race, also all the other former Axis partners South America, Egypt, Italy and Japan.

Earl, as God is my judge, you must believe all these things I've been telling you. When you go back to your hotel, they may have a bug in your room. Don't say anything to Elmer, just take off without your clothes. Good luck and hope you believe me this time,             Love always.

If you should follow what I said, and you are hitch-hiking give a ficticious name, such Fleming etc. Try calling some local people, maybe they are missing already, Scheppo, Jacobson, Kaufman and others through the phone book. Please Earl, I know what I'm asking of you.

you must get to either Miami or Mexico City and then *to Cuba.* You may have lost your family by now, but there is nothing you can do about it now, and you can save millions of people who are doomed to be slaughtered. This country has been overthrown.

We concluded that Kunstler was mistaken with respect to Jack. He really was desperately ill, and action had to be taken at once. Arranging for Dr. Jacobson's visit was time-consuming, but ultimately clearance was obtained for a visit on the next Saturday, December 10.

After Jack's counsel had dispersed, Sheriff Decker himself was released from the hospital. And when the Wichita Falls sheriff arrived in Dallas to see the man who was expected to be placed in his custody during the second trial, Jack's condition had apparently thoroughly worsened. Sheriff Decker then had Dr. J. M. Pickard, the county health officer, visit Jack.

So it was that on late Friday evening, December 9, Ruby was taken to Parkland Hospital, where President Kennedy and Lee Harvey Oswald had died little more than three years before. Although the initial diagnosis of Jack's illness was pneumonia and his condition was described as serious, there was nothing unduly alarming in the doctor's statement.

Very soon it became apparent that his condition was more serious than had been supposed. An accumulation of fluid was found in his right lung. Some of this was removed to ease the congestion; some was set aside for pathological tests. The tests continued throughout the night.

Once again, as so often in the past, "responsible" officials felt it imperative to explain their actions. Why had not the jail officials done something earlier? Could not the jail doctor see that something was wrong?

Dr. John W. Callahan sought to explain. Ruby had had a "throat-tickling kind of cough," he said, but no fever. He had examined him at 10 A.M. on Friday, he said, and his cold seemed to be subsiding. "I thought he was improving." If it had been up to him, nothing much would have been done: he would have continued to give Ruby cough medicine and perhaps antibiotics. It was the visit by Sheriff Decker and Dr. Pickard that had resulted in the transfer to Parkland Hospital. "The sheriff can act any time he wants in a case like this," Dr. Callahan said.

The sheriff, too, minimized Jack's condition. "Jack said he had a bad cold and wasn't feeling up to par. I talked to Dr. Pickard and he suggested Jack should be taken to the hospital where he could be X-rayed, examined and tests made."

On Saturday, after Jack had spent a comfortable night, according to the hospital, and was "slightly improved," Dr. Callahan was a bit more troubled by Jack's condition. He had been giving Jack penicillin since Monday. "His temperature has never risen above normal, and normally in something as serious as pneumonia the body responds with a temperature rise." Now he said, "I think it was a good idea to send him to the hospital, however, because chest X-rays might reveal hazy areas that would not be apparent in the stethoscope examinations I have given him." Ruby had first begun coughing, according to the doctor charged with Jack's medical care, when the Texas high court reversed the murder conviction. "His guards also told me he was throwing up often, and he said he couldn't keep anything in his stomach." Ruby had had a coughing spell about a month before and had complained of chest pains. "I examined him and thought perhaps he had strained a chest muscle, so I gave him antibiotics and kept him in bed for two days. His condition seemed to return to normal."

At least one person was outspoken about Jack's condition. Eva had seen Jack on Friday and he looked "terrible, like a corpse. For three weeks, he's been deathly sick." Then, after visiting him in the hospital, she said, "I'm not leaving. I'll be here all night. I don't even trust the hospital. That guy's dying." She talked about Jack to everyone who would listen, and there were many.

Decker was disparaging. "She told me the same thing. I have doctors and nurses in the jail to care for prisoners. Anything about that would have to come from them." And to a reporter from New York who asked whether the jail was drafty, he replied testily: "The jail is a jail, not a pasture. It was built in 1914, made of concrete and stone, and intended to keep prisoners the same as they do in New York State. Jack Ruby is under my care and custody. I want him to have every right guaranteed by the law, and I want him to have medical attention if he needs it."

Very soon the bad news came. At a press conference called by the sheriff on Saturday afternoon, the attending physicians and surgeons announced that they had determined that a malignant and spreading cancer was somewhere inside Ruby's body. Jack was indeed a very sick man. His long-term condition was serious, and treatment was a matter of weeks, according to Dr. Jay Sanford, the head of the medical team caring for Jack. Dr. Watts Webb, like Dr. Sanford a professor at Southwestern Medical School, had removed a marble-sized lymph node from

Jack's neck. Discovery of a cancerous tumor in the lymph
system meant that the cancer had spread to other parts of
the body. The primary malignancy could be anywhere.
They would continue to probe to determine the source,
type, and extent of the malignancy. In any event, it was
unlikely that Jack would be able to go to court.

Eva, who had loosed a tirade on Friday, was even
angrier now. She was, she announced, going to call Washington so that "they" might determine what had brought
on her brother's condition. She would not charge definitely
that the illness was induced by the prosecution. "But there
is no history of cancer, diabetes or heart trouble in my
family," she said. "All of us live to be ninety and then you
have to shoot us to kill us." (She had forgotten, or deliberately ignored, that her oldest brother was suffering from
an arrested tumorous condition and had been operated on
because of it.)

The hospital was concerned about security measures to
protect their patient. "There are a lot of people in Dallas—
and the world, for that matter—who would like to see
Ruby dead," said one hospital spokesman. "Just think what
it would be like if it happened again. It must not be allowed
to happen again." Sheriff Decker had instituted maximum
security precautions when Jack was admitted to the hospital, and the hospital had guaranteed him assistance in
guarding Jack's personal safety.

From the very beginning of Jack's hospitalization I felt
that he was doomed, that he would be dead in a matter of
weeks. Others were optimistic. Phil Burleson at first found
it impossible to believe that the end was near, for the
doctors, speaking in the measured tones expected of their
oracular profession, seemed to offer a vague hope for Jack's
recovery. When the press first learned of Ruby's illness—
when the diagnosis was nothing more serious than pneumonia—and I was interviewed by Charles McCuen of the
Chicago office of the National Broadcasting Company, I
spoke in measured tones. When we were off the air and off

the record, McCuen asked what I actually thought was
going to happen. Intuitively I replied, "He is going to die."
Later, after the diagnosis of terminal cancer, McCuen
interviewed me again. Certain that I had heard of the
cancer before our earlier interview, he would scarcely
credit my disclaimers. But the truth is that I had doubts
in spite of my intuition. For death would rob us of the
prospect of the ultimate victory we sought. It was not
easy, after we had struggled so long, to admit consciously
that all would come to naught if Jack succumbed.

# 32

## THE SECRET TAPE

WHILE WE WERE IN DALLAS to confer about the pretrial
conference with Judge Holland, Burleson told us that he
had been consulted by Lawrence Schiller about a long-
playing phonograph record on the Kennedy assassination.
Schiller was known to us as a photographer for *Life* and
other publications during the fateful week-end of November 22, 1963, and he had played a role in connection with
Woodfield's ghost-written memoirs of Jack Ruby. A very
young man, equally brash and bright, with big ideas, he
had been preparing a series of documentaries for Capitol
Records on the death of Lenny Bruce, the use of LSD, and
homosexuality. This was essentially a reporter's job on
records, with exclusive interviews, commentaries, and the
like. He left prints of some of these documentaries with
Burleson and asked him to consider whether we would
permit Jack Ruby to be interviewed briefly for the record
dealing with the Kennedy assassination. He had already
interviewed many others—congressmen, the staff of the
Warren Commission, eye-witnesses—without paying for
the privilege; but knowing our need for funds for the
second trial, he was willing to pay for Ruby's interview.

Four of us attorneys and Earl discussed the matter.
Surely, money was needed, for Earl and other members
of the family had borrowed to the limit. In addition, Jack
had always wanted to proclaim the truth about his case.
This, then, we all agreed, would be a good means of accomplishing a dual purpose—fund-raising and vindication.
Because Burleson, on the scene in Dallas, was in a vulner-

able position and, besides, knew little about such matters, it was decided that I should carry on the negotiations in consultation with Earl. He and I would arrange the interview—if it could be arranged.

Schiller met me at my office in Chicago the next Saturday—as it turned out, the morning after Ruby was taken to the hospital. As we were negotiating the contract, I learned that Jack's illness had been diagnosed as terminal cancer. Schiller did not learn the substance of what I had been told over the telephone, but, certainly, there was an air of urgency in our conversation about the record, as if we both sensed that now or never was the time to tape Jack's recollections. Our task would not be easy, for the sheriff and the district attorney would be suspicious of anything that we might attempt. Of course, Schiller would pay only for an actual interview, and not for the bare hope.

So the contract was completed for the recording and use of Jack's voice in a personal statement, or apology, for history. All that remained was to secure the tape. We were certain that neither the sheriff nor the district attorney would cooperate with us in any way. We were just as certain that it would be disastrous even to ask permission of them. If they knew what we intended, they would make it impossible for us to proceed. True, Jack's attorneys had the professional, legal and moral right to confer with their client and to take down what he had to say at any time and in any manner they deemed appropriate; but what good was it to rest upon such right if, in a practical way, they could say nay to us? We knew that we had to move rapidly, not only because Larry Schiller and Capitol Records wanted us to do so, but also because how long Jack would be in the physical and mental condition to cooperate with us, or even survive, was uncertain.

Earl wanted me to go with him to Dallas for the taking of the tape. Since Burleson, who had to practice his profession in Dallas, could not afford to affront the sheriff, the district attorney, or any other authority, the recording had to be made by others.

On the appointed day I hurried to Dallas. Schiller, a master at such things, had a plentiful supply of recorders that could be concealed in attache cases and readily operated, and he had the equipment for playing and duplicating tapes. As an additional precaution, he had a qualified technician with him. Since Schiller could not be admitted to Jack's room, and any attempt to secure his admittance would only arouse suspicion, Earl and I would go to Jack's room in the Parkland Hospital together. We would each carry an attache case—I my usual one and Earl a special case equipped with the recorder. The recorder would function when the lock in front was pushed upward. Earl would question Jack, so that the dialogue would be easy and unforced and free from legal jargon. I would divert the attention of Decker's deputy or any others who might be in the hospital room. I drew up in advance a power of attorney from Jack to Earl to replace the one previously given to Eva. In fact, since the contract for the record was in Earl's name as Jack's agent, a new document was needed. I would place my case on Jack's bed, take the document from it, and explain it to Jack, who would then sign it. Earl's case, too, would be on Jack's bed, and Earl could then easily push the lock open and engage Jack in conversation.

Together Larry and I rehearsed with Earl the exact area to be covered by the interrogation of Jack. We tried to think of clear and precise questions that would best and most briefly bring out the essential facts about Jack's slaying of Oswald. We contemplated about fifteen minutes of conversation. Of course, we could not put words into Jack's mouth; for then it would not be his statement, and, moreover, there would be greater likelihood of complications and something going amiss. The aim was to stress the emotional state in which Jack found himself following the assassination of the President, the circumstances of his going to the Western Union office that Sunday morning, the purely happenstance nature of his going to the basement of the City Hall and being there at the very moment of

Oswald's arrival, the innocent nature of his having a pistol in his pocket, the lack of premeditation, his lack of any prior contact with Oswald other than the press conference on the night of the Kennedy killing, the complete absence of any conspiracy in these things. The very words of a dying man would serve to clear the air and persuade the American people.

We then tested the equipment, and to our dismay we found it lacking. The pickups were so indistinct and so bad generally that the equipment was unusable. Larry tinkered with the machine to give it greater fidelity. He could not get it to work as well as he wanted it to, but he did not dare go shopping for a replacement. He was well known in Dallas and if he appeared too much in public—particularly to shop openly for a recorder—word might get back to Decker or Wade. He made telephone calls to trace down possible sources, and having located what he needed at Neiman-Marcus, he sent an assistant for it.

At last, with the preparations complete, it remained only for Earl and I to visit the hospital to inform Jack of the recording and to see whether we might encounter any unexpected difficulties.

As Earl, Burleson, and I rode to Parkland Memorial Hospital that first time, I could not help wondering whether we were taking the route to the hospital that had been taken, three years before, by the mortally stricken President and Lee Harvey Oswald. I looked for familiar landmarks; they were there. Yes, we were going the same way, but at a much slower speed. The irony of the situation was less pressing than the immediate problems that we faced. Least important was the matter of the recording that we intended to take, not on this visit but the next. Most important was the future of our client and of the disposition of his affairs. Securing a fair trial for Jack Ruby was only a matter of time; but therein lay the difficulty. How much time was there? If there was little time remaining, there would be no second trial, and no need to prepare for it. If the time was long or uncertain, we might have to go through the motions of preparation, or seek to get Jack released, somehow, so that he might spend his last days or weeks in friendlier surroundings, perhaps even in Chicago, in the home of his sister Eileen.

Walking through the corridors of the hospital I was more oppressed than ever by memories of the catastrophes of November, 1963. The hospital seemed like a maw prepared to swallow up all who came within it. "This road, too, you shall travel," it seemed to say. Very soon we became aware of the circumstance that there was a special patient in the hospital. As we neared Jack's room, we had to be cleared by Sheriff Decker's deputies. They were taking no chances. They scarcely feared, I am sure, that their hospitalized prisoner would try to walk out. They were concerned with who would try to walk in, and what he might do. Their dread must have been of another repetition of past events.

At last we were in Jack's room. A deputy, discreetly quiet and almost inconspicuous, sat near the windows, reading a paperback book. He rose to learn who we were. One of Jack's sisters was already in the room, strangely quiet. A nurse, too, continually brought in and took out medications. Jack was propped up in bed, tubes of various kinds attached to him—and a television set in front and to the side. Newspapers and paperback books, including an engrossing one on gambling in Las Vegas, lay about. Jack looked at us, we looked at him, quizzically, all trying to conceal any hint of impending tragedy. Jack looked much better than I had anticipated, but he looked bad enough. He talked less, and more quietly and rationally, than I had ever observed previously. His conversation at times was of the prize fights he had watched the previous night and of inconsequential matters generally. In all, Earl and I visited with him twice a day during our stay in Dallas. At the beginning of each day, Jack seemed to be relatively strong, but as the day wore on he wilted appreciably.

Generally, the tendency was downward, with brief recoveries after the night's repose.

Although Jack appeared to be much more rational than when we had seen him in the Dallas County Jail, he still whispered, mostly to Earl, of his earlier obsessions. But now to the slaughtering of Jews induced by his act was added another strain—there was something conspiratorial about his illness. It had been induced, somehow, by the prosecution.

I asked him how he felt. "Like a dying man," he replied in an undramatic tone that almost belied the substance of what he said.

We whispered to him, in Yiddish, of our plans with respect to the tape recording. He understood and approved. He made it clear as to whom he wanted in the room and whom not.

We conferred at some length with the doctors, getting a clear and measured assessment of the situation. It would take several days, a couple of weeks, in fact, to be sure of the response to treatment and of the imminence of death. The doctors would insist upon Jack's remaining in the hospital for treatment; they would not countenance his return to jail; they would inform us of all medical and other developments. We were highly pleased, then and later, by the humane attitude of the doctors.

On the next day, with assumed nonchalance, Earl and I again went to Jack's room at the hospital. Eileen and Eva were already there, talking with each other and with Jack and the deputy sheriff. The hospital equipment contributed to the symphony of sound, sometimes making conversation difficult. Earl and I placed our cases on Jack's bed and I began talking to him; the women thereupon engaged with special vivacity in conversation with the deputy. It was as if they had been cued to their roles. Taking out the power of attorney that I had prepared, I explained it to Jack, got his signature on several copies, and then arranged, with some difficulty, to have some of the copies acknowledged before a notary public. The deputy sheriff cleared the matter with Decker, who sent over another deputy to pry into the situation, before consenting to the use of a notary public. This only confirmed our feeling about the futility of asking permission for the recording of Jack's statement.

Earl flipped open the lock in his case to set the recording device for us. In Yiddish, he explained that Jack should talk in the direction of "the thing." It was so sensitive that voices did not have to be raised. He began to propound questions and Jack to answer them. As either of them faltered, I filled in. Now and then, we peeked at the deputy, and he was completely oblivious to us. He was either talking with the women or reading a paperback. After a while, it was clear that Jack was tiring. We had got what we had come for and we were satisfied. We felt sure that it would please Schiller and, more than that, that we had made a rare contribution to history. The lock was flipped again, this time to close the case, and we left. As calmly as we could, we walked past the guards and to the parking lot, but our relief was complete only when we had safely delivered the tape to Larry Schiller.

The transcript of the complete tape, at least three times longer than what appears on the record, is given here in its entirety.

BACKGROUND NOISE—YIDDISH—Talk into the . . . here the device mechanical is in here, talk into the case.

A. When I went into the Western Union to try to send the money, and naturally the clerk took my money, and uh, and uh, turned away after he took the money, I turned away and walked out. I walked down the street, just natural strides, and as I

Q. Main Street?

A. No—Yes, Main Street, going west to Main Street, the south side of Main Street, as I walked toward the ramp, I noticed the police squad car at the head of the ramp and an officer leaning over talking to him with his back to me. All I

did was walk down there, down to the bottom of the ramp and
that's when the incident happened, at the bottom of the ramp—
according to the Western Union records—the time stamped on
the Western Union records—it's 11:17 the time the incident
taking place 11:21, it was 11:21.

Q. Did you walk slowly?

A. I walked my natural pace.

Q. You did not rush?

A. No.

Q. Did you recognize anybody when you reached the bottom
of the ramp?

A. No. I recognized the police officer in the car—that was
in the car—it was Lt. Sam Pierce, and this other man was just
talking to him, and why Sam Pierce had not seen me, I don't
know.

Q. Did you try to avoid him or anything?

A. No, I didn't.

Q. When did you finally realize that something had happened, Jack, when did you finally know?

A. Well, it happened in such a blur—well it happened in
such a blur, that before I knew it, I was down on the ground—
the officers had me on the ground.

Q. Had you realized you had done anything?

A. Well, really it happened so fast, and anything else I cannot recall what happened from the time I came to the bottom
of the ramp until the police officers had me on the ground.

Q. Have no recollection?

A. No. But, I knew they were holding my hand and grab-
bing for the gun.

Q. Had you ever known Oswald, Jack?

A. No.

Q. Ever know Oswald before?

A. Never had known him or seen him before.

Q. You never met him?

A. Never have, my Clubs were all money that either I borrowed for the family or self-accumulated. I was not obligated
to any other source, never had I attempted to ask anybody for

anything, so, I owe the government a little money at the time, but we were working out a deal on a compromise, those things over a period of years you pay off.

Q. Had you ever planned anything like this?

A. Had I ever what?

Q. Did you ever plan this. Did you ever think you were going to do this?

A. I don't know how to answer that. I was so emotionally upset for three days. At one particular time I had to have some money and I borrowed some money from Ralph Paul, and I gave him some stock in the Club to show good faith, that sort of collateral, for it.

Q. You did not try to sneak in the place, did you?

A. No, I didn't.

Q. Was there anybody at Western Union ahead of you?

A. Yes, one customer, one customer.

Q. Did you try to hurry up the people at Western Union?

A. No, I didn't.

Q. Were there other people at Western Union while you were there, Jack?

A. No, I didn't recall, I noticed only this one customer.

Q. Did you think that Oswald was already taken over by the Sheriff by the time you went to Western Union?

A. Uh, I don't know how to answer that, I don't know one way or the other.

Q. Do you remember when you drove by Dealy Plaza and saw those wreaths what you thought at that time?

A. What I saw?

Q. Yeah, what you thought?

A. The same thing I had gone through for the other two days, the letdown and remorse.

Q. Were you planning after Kennedy was shot to leave Dallas for a few days, Jack?

A. Yes, it came to my mind momentarily when I called my sister in Chicago, I said "Eileen, now I ought to come home for a few days," so the first thing she said was "who is going to look after Eve?", meaning my sister Eve just got out of the hospital, so she felt that she was convalescing somebody should be with her.

Q. Otherwise you would have gone home?

A. Well, there was a chance that I could of if Eileen would have talked me into it, you know.

Q. Is there any truth at all to the stories that Oswald had been in your Club?

A. None whatsoever, it's just a fabrication—in one particular incident that has never been enlightened to the public, I believe, is that a friend of mine, Mr. McWillie who invited me down to Havana, Cuba. I didn't come down, but he finally sent me plane tickets to come down as a good friendly gesture. So I accepted the invitation. I stayed with him for eight days, and then I left, and I had lived constantly with him the eight days, but then right after that he called me from Havana, Cuba and said "Jack, I want you to call Ray Brantley at Ray's Hardware store in Singleton Avenue and tell him to send me four Cobras"—a Cobra is a little revolver. So, I did call him and gave him the address. When I called him he answered and said, "Oh, I know Mr. McWillie very well" so that left it out of my hands. All I had to do was relay the message, but that is the only extent I ever had of any association with anything business dealings outside of the United States and that was only a message to relay.

Q. Normally you carried a gun with you didn't you, Jack?

A. Yes, I did.

Q. This was nothing unusual you had with you that day?

A. No. I always carried a gun because of various altercations I had in my Club then I carried pretty large sums of money at times.

Q. You had your dog with you, Sheba?

A. Yes, I did.

Q. Will you tell about Sheba, Jack?

A. Well, I was very fond of Sheba. She brought me a very large litter and I raised the litter by myself in my apartment, and I distributed the dogs to certain friends, but I kept Sheba and another dog called Clipper. Sheba was wherever I were go, leave the house, she jumped the door ready to go with me.

Q. She was with you that day?

A. Yes, I left her in the car. The ironic part of this is had not I made an illegal turn behind the bus to the parking lot, had I gone the way I was supposed to go straight down Main Street, I would have never met this fate because the difference in meeting this fate was 30 seconds one way or the other.

Q. When you were down there you didn't try to hide or conceal?

A. No, I didn't because if you checked the walking distance from the Western Union to the bottom of the ramp, you know it would have to be synchronized so perfect to the second, and to plan something you had in your mind premeditatedly. In that sense I didn't even allow myself one second of interval time. I never accepted a call at the Western Union. I presume there was a public phone. I never accepted a call for somebody to let me know what is happening.

Q. Did you know when Oswald was going to be moved, Jack?

A. I'll be honest with you, No.

Q. You had no idea?

A. Later on I found out he was supposed to be moved at 10:00.

Q. You were never told by anybody he was going to be moved?

A. No.

Q. Is there anything else you think I ought to know, Jack? Are you uncomfortable?

A. My rectum, I am bedridden, you know.

Q. You got sores, eh?

A. No, it's not sores—it's the pain.

Q. Jack, when you left the Western Union office what made you walk toward the jail house?

A. Because when I drove by I saw some people down at the ramp and the curiosity had aroused me because of the flash in my mind seeing the people there because before I went to Western Union as I drove by on Main Street.

*Q.* Is there anything else you can think of, Jack, anything else when you were walking by or going down there?

*A.* I don't know what to think—happened.

*Q.* Well, you are doing very well—just think a minute. Do you remember anything when you reached the bottom of the ramp?

*A.* Yeah, I did, like I said, a flash came to me from the point at the bottom of ramp at the time that I was grappling with the police officers for the gun. Actually, what had happened I don't know at that time.

The session in Schiller's room at the hotel was, in some respects, as dramatic as the experience at the hospital. As we replayed the tape, the suspense scarcely abated. Would it come out all right, or would we have to try again? Despite the surface noises caused by the air-conditioning and the conversations and the softness of Jack's voice, the recording was good. We had covered the right ground in the right manner. Jack's words were authentic. The task now was to select four minutes or so that would fit best with the material from other sources. Another copy of the tape was made, and from it passages were cut to preserve the original intact. The aim was to reduce the fourteen or fifteen minutes of the original to three or four. We knew that Jack was dying but we had to speculate that he might live. In the circumstances, was there anything that ought to be withheld? Were there prejudicial passages that would hurt him at a retrial? We listened to every sentence and word with extraordinary care. Now Eileen, then Earl or I, would be dubious about something or other. Words change their meanings when you listen to them too much or too well. Words have different meanings for foes and for friends. Larry Schiller had ideas of his own, and would sometimes argue with us. At last we wound up with the right words and the right length. Compare them with the full tape.

*Jack Ruby:* I went to the Western Union Office to try to send the money and naturally the clerk took my money. After she took the money I turned away and walked out. I walked down the street. And the curiosity had aroused me. Because of the flash in my mind seeing the people there before I went up to Western Union as I drove by on Main Street. On the south side of Main Street. So I walked towards the ramp I noticed the police squad car. On the head of the ramp and an officer leaning over talking to him with his back to me. All I did is walk down there, down to the bottom of the ramp and that's when the incident happened. At the bottom of the ramp.

*Question:* Did you recognize anyone beyond when you reached the bottom of the ramp?

*Answer:* No, but I recognized the police officer in the car. That was in the car. He was Lt. Sam Pierce. And this other man was just talking to him.

*Question:* When did you finally realize that something had happened?

*Answer:* Well, it happened in such a blur that, before I knew it I was down on the ground. The officers had me on the ground.

*Question:* Did you realize you had done anything?

*Answer:* Well, really it happened so fast and everything else, I can't recall what happened from the time I came to the bottom of the ramp until the police officers had me on the ground.

*Question:* Have no recollection?

*Answer:* No, but I know that they were holding my hand and grabbed one for the gun.

*Question:* Did you ever know Oswald before?

*Answer:* Never have known him or seen him before.

*Question:* Did you ever plan anything like this?

*Answer:* I was so emotionally upset for three days. . . .

*Question:* Is there any truth at all to the stories that Oswald had been in your club?

*Answer:* None whatsoever. It's a fabrication.

*Question:* Normally you carried the gun with you didn't you Jack?

*Answer:* Yes I did. I always carried a gun because of various

altercations I had in my club. And I carried pretty large sums
of money at times. The ironic part of this is that if I hadn't
made an illegal turn behind the bus to the parking lot, had I
gone the way I was supposed to go—straight down Main
Street—I'd of never, I would never have met this fate. Because
the difference in meeting this fate was 30 seconds. One way or
the other.

*Question:* Did you know when Oswald was going to be
moved Jack?

*Answer:* He was supposed to be moved at 10:00.

*Question:* Is there anything else you think that I ought to
know Jack? Are you uncomfortable?

*Answer:* My rectum is . . . I'm bedridden you know. . . .

*Question:* You got sores, huh?

*Answer:* It's not sores, it's the pain.

We have then the matter of the dying declaration made
by Ruby—the taped interview. Is this to be taken as so
reliable, so clearly the truth, that it could be admitted into
evidence in a court of law?

In Texas the question of the admissibility of dying dec-
larations is covered by a provision in the Texas Code of
Criminal Procedure. It allows the admission of such a
declaration in homicide cases where the deceased party,
the person who made the statement, is the *victim* of the
alleged crime. This statute has been held to be a codifica-
tion of the common law, and thus it must be made clear
that the statement was made with apprehension of death,
that the declaring individual was sane, that he had no
reason to state untruth, and that the interrogation was
directed toward certain expected answers.

Ruby certainly apprehended that he was near death.
Though there was serious doubt about his sanity, he
seemed to become more rational as death neared. And in
all fairness it must be said that he had reason to make a
self-serving statement. Only in a metaphorical sense was
he the victim of the crime, rather than its perpetrator. I
am afraid that there is no legal reason for accepting the

taped interview as true; but I believe it myself and I feel that factually it is true. It is a testament for history, and it is entirely regrettable that Oswald did not live to make such a statement.

On the whole, Jack Ruby's taped statement appears to be substantially correct. There is nothing novel or revolutionary in it.

To begin with, Ruby talks about going to the Western Union office. What he says is substantiated by the testimony of Doyle E. Lane, the Western Union clerk.[1] The Warren Report summarizes the clerk's testimony: "The Western Union clerk who accepted Ruby's order recalls that Ruby promptly turned, walked out of the door onto Main Street, and proceeded in the direction of the police department one block away."[2] Doyle Lane even describes Ruby's walking as a "just ordinary gait," which agrees with Ruby's description of his walk.

According to the Warren Report and what appears to be the best computation, Ruby's time estimate is correct.[3] The Report agrees with Ruby when it states: "after considering all the evidence, the Commission has concluded that Ruby entered the basement unaided, probably via the Main Street ramp, and not more than 3 minutes before the shooting of Oswald."[4] (Actually, it was much less than this.)

The question of any previous knowledge or acquaintanceship of Ruby with Oswald, denied by Ruby, was also answered in the negative by the Warren Commission. It found that there was no likelihood that the two were acquainted.

Ruby's discussion of his financial affairs is essentially correct: "At the time of the assassination, the United States claimed approximately $44,000 in delinquent taxes, and he was in substantial debt to his brother Earl, and to his friend Ralph Paul."[5] The testimony of Ralph Paul[6] supports Ruby's view of the kind of business transaction engaged in between himself and Paul.

Ruby says that he did not sneak into the police station,

although Judge Brown's book and the Warren Report suggest that Ruby was pretending to interpret or serve as a reporter for Israeli newspapers. This must have referred, if at all, to Ruby's appearance on Friday night in the police assembly room where a press conference was held. It could not be a reference to the events of Sunday morning. Ruby walked to the tragic spot without guise or guile.

Ruby's statement that he contemplated leaving Dallas after the assassination and that his sister Eileen talked him out of it because he had to stay with his recently hospitalized sister, Eva Grant, in Dallas, is corroborated by the testimony of Eileen Kaminsky.[7]

While Ruby was not completely coherent, his discussion of possible Cuban activities is essentially correct, although the Warren Report itself says, "There is some uncertainty about Ruby's trip to Havana, Cuba, in 1959." The FBI interview with McWillie[8] upholds Ruby's story.

As to any question of knowledge of the transfer of Oswald, the Commission Report cites the public communitions bulletins on transfer plans and the fact that the actual time of transfer could not have been relayed to Ruby before he left his apartment. The Western Union office testimony by Doyle Lane substantiates Ruby's recollection that there was only one other customer, and the evidence discloses nothing out of the ordinary; that is, it forecloses the possibility that any message might have been given to Ruby there.

A day or so before Larry Schiller and I completed the arrangements for the Ruby tape, Bernard Gavzer of the Associated Press telephoned me. He wanted to interview Ruby. If not Jack, then his brother Earl; if not Earl, then myself. For a variety of reasons, any interview would not be possible, I told him. When would I next be in Dallas? Perhaps that very week-end. Would it do any good for him to go down there and meet me? Maybe yes, maybe no. In that case, he would be there.

While Earl and Eileen and I were in Schiller's room at the hotel, listening to the tape, a note arrived asking whether Gavzer might see me. After conferring briefly with Earl, I went to Gavzer's room. At some length I talked with him about Jack Ruby—his personality, his conversation, his thoughts, his case. As I talked, Gavzer took notes. "You understand that these things cannot be printed until I give my approval?" I said, as the conversation came to an end. "I understand," he replied. "To make certain that you don't forget," I added, "I am taking away your notes. I will return them when I can."

After the tape had been edited, as Earl and I were waiting at Love Field for the plane to fly home from Dallas, we were startled to see Gavzer seated across from us. In our mutual embarrassment we said little. Our plane was delayed considerably, and Earl whispered to me again of the family's disappointment in what Gavzer had written at the beginning of the case. As I remembered the article (abstracted earlier in this book), it did not really seem to be a bad one, for Gavzer was a highly competent and honest reporter. The plane was delayed even more than anticipated. Suddenly Earl turned to me and said, "Why don't you talk with Gavzer?" I signaled to Bernie to sit beside us. Then for the first time intimate details of what had occurred were divulged. Gavzer was clearly excited and grateful for his beat.

At last we were called to the plane and took our seats. "Aren't you going to go to Gavzer?" Earl asked. "No," I replied, "if he wants to talk further, he will come to me." Gavzer did come, and Earl and I bit by bit revealed the story that was intended to give the American public a more sympathetic view of the dying man.

While nothing was said to Gavzer about the taped interview with Jack, we did dwell upon Jack's great desire to tell the truth to the world. To Gavzer Earl said, "Jack has told me a dozen times or more he prays to be given a final lie detector test so people will be convinced that there was no plan on his part, or conspiracy of any kind, to kill Oswald. It is his last wish."

Did Jack have any regrets about killing Oswald? Did he realize the enormity of what he had done in depriving the world of the opportunity to learn the full story of the Presidential assassination? I responded: "He has regrets, but they are not so much about Oswald. These are regrets about the havoc caused to his people. I don't think Jack mentioned Oswald's name more than a few times in the many times I saw him, and then it was as if Oswald was a figure beyond his comprehension. Jack saw himself as a kind of instrument. He did not have the delusion that God told him to do it, or that he was an instrument of any people, but that it happened without his conscious will. Jack reads the newspapers and magazines and watches television and is aware of the controversy about the Warren Report and all the books and articles which are constructing incredible stories of a conspiracy in which he is claimed to have had a part. He says, 'How can they think I am hiding anything or protecting anyone else? There is nothing to hide; there was no one else.' And he is bewildered that it is not plain to every one that it was a million-to-one chance that he would stumble into a situation in which it was even possible that Oswald could be shot."

How was Jack feeling? What was his condition and the prognosis? "Unchanged, resting comfortably," Earl Ruby said. Jack "seems to get worse in front of your eyes. I saw him in the morning, and then came back a few hours later, and you wouldn't believe the change in him. He looked like he was shrinking away. I don't think he could get finer treatment than he is receiving at Parkland. The hospital is doing everything in the world to take care of him and calling on the finest doctors and nurses."

Jack, he said, took joy in the sympathy expressed by the public, expressed in Christmas cards and get-well messages. This was reminiscent of what he seemed to feel after the shooting of Oswald, when he was beguiled by the messages he received in jail and mistakenly thought that all the world loved him and regarded him as a hero.

"He gets about 75 cards a day. They are first checked by Sheriff Decker before being delivered to him," Earl said.

I supplied a corrective, lest Gavzer form the wrong impression: "Jack still thinks millions of people believe there was a sinister plot to kill Oswald and he is preoccupied with wanting to prove there was not."

All was not bleak, I said. I told of his calling his favorite sister Eileen to his side and saying: "Eileen, do me a favor." He handed her a list for purchases of pastrami, corned beef, kosher dill pickles, rye bread, lox, cream cheese, green onions, bagels. It was the badge of his Jewishness, West Side Chicago style.

"The doctors didn't object," I said. "Of course, Jack couldn't hold that food down, but to deny it to him would be like denying a condemned man his last meal."

Then his mood changed, disastrously, to "black despair," as I told Gavzer. He said that he wanted to die at home—in a little room in Eileen's home in Chicago. He had had enough of Dallas.

In due course, Gavzer's article based on our conversation was spread across the front pages of hundreds of newspapers. He quoted us with complete accuracy, and the general tone was better even than we dared hope. The effect was tremendous. Earl and the others were pleased, where once they had been angered, by his reporting.

# 33

## AN "OFFICIAL" INTERVIEW

DURING THE PREPARATIONS for the second trial, we cast about for assistance from any source that bore upon Jack Ruby's case. One such person was Burt Griffin, who as junior counsel for the Warren Commission had worked on unraveling the threads of Jack's involvement on the weekend in November, 1963. He and his senior, Leon Hubert, of New Orleans, who was also charged with this responsibility, had come to believe that Ruby was not involved in any conspiracy. Both believed that Jack had shot Oswald in one emotion-charged moment, without premeditation or plan. Their research into Ruby's actions had been thorough. Thus it seemed that they might be of assistance to us.

Griffin I had come to know through a joint appearance on a radio program in Cleveland, and thereafter we had been in friendly, if not frequent, contact. I knew he was alert to information that would reaffirm or establish the truth about the assassination and its aftermath.

When Ruby's fatal illness became known, Griffin felt that something should be done to obtain a deathbed statement. He wanted our cooperation in this, just as we wanted his.

As a result of our correspondence, Griffin wrote to Barefoot Sanders to ask whether the Justice Department was interested in having someone speak to Jack. As Griffin wrote to me: "I believe that it is important to obtain a full length interview with Jack Ruby in order to complete the historical record. I would prefer that this be done by someone who is not actively engaged in the defense of his criminal case. At the same time, however, I would expect the confidentiality of such an interview to be preserved until it was clear that Jack Ruby would not be retried."

Griffin did not know that Earl and I were even then in the process of getting just such a statement from Jack on our own. We feared that Jack would not survive much longer, and the process of getting official authorization and then performing the interrogation would be lengthy and involved. Jack, in only a few days, might weaken and slip away. Nevertheless, to secure an official statement by an official agency, we were prepared to cooperate. That would be better than our tape, which was not "official" in the sense intended by Griffin.

Thus steps were taken to initiate the making of a polygraph examination. On December 27, 1966, Homer Garrison, Jr., Director of the Texas Department of Public Safety, wrote to Dr. Sanford at Parkland Hospital:

Attorney General Waggoner Carr, by letter dated December 22, 1966, has requested that this Department arrange a lie-detector test for Jack Ruby "provided his doctors are of the opinion that his mental and physical condition is such that they know of no reason which would preclude a reliable result."

As a doctor I am sure you know that the mental and physical conditions alluded to by the Attorney General are most important. It is recognized that a polygraph test to be valid must record the respiratory pattern, the galvanic skin resistance and blood-pulse of the subject under conditions which reflect the natural responses to question-stimuli of the subject. Any medication or physical condition which tends to inhibit or impair these natural responses detracts from the validity of the test and the examiner's ability to arrive at an opinion as to the truthfulness of the subject's answers.

. . . You indicated . . . that a conclusion as to the subject's ability to take the examination could only be given after a consultation on the matter by the group of doctors currently attending him. We, therefore, request that the results of such a consultation, when made, be made available to the Department of Public Safety, so that we can proceed with the examination as requested by the Attorney General. . . .

Garrison then outlined the procedures in administering the test. After the execution of a waiver, the examiner would conduct the examination "alone in the room with the subject." The examiner would be the sole judge and would "determine what questions, including the phrasing" to ask of the subject. In short, none of the test procedures that had been followed in the polygraph examination before the Warren Commission was to be followed here. Questions might be slanted, inadequate, indecisive, but Ruby's counsel was to have nothing to say about them.

As to the results: "Copies of the test questions, verbal responses, and charts will be furnished to the Attorney General of Texas, the District Attorney of Dallas County, and one set to the attorneys representing the subject." Copies of the examiner's report were to be furnished to the same persons.

Copies of Garrison's letter were being sent to the Texas attorney general, the Chief Justice of the United States, the district attorney and sheriff of Dallas County, and to each of the Ruby defense counsel.

We were not consulted, and did not respond. It all seemed like the playing of a tuneless melody. If we had thought that Ruby would survive, we could not have consented to the sort of certificate that was required for the test, one to the effect that the statements made in the polygraph examination could be used against Ruby. Since we would have no discretion over the questions propounded, we might have been signing away our client's life if we agreed to this procedure. The matter never came to an issue.

On December 30, 1966, Dr. Sanford replied to Garrison. The letter was a model of meticulosity. Dr. Sanford and his associates then knew that Jack Ruby would not live long. They had serious doubts about the consequences and utility of any polygraph examination, but they had to be circumspect. Dr. Sanford wrote:

At this time Mr. Ruby's medical condition varies somewhat from day to day and it is anticipated that it will continue to show variation relating both to his underlying disease process and to his treatment. Hence, at this time it is our opinion that the preliminary legal procedures outlined in your letter should be met prior to a consideration of the patient's mental or physical condition which may have varied significantly during the time interval in which these preliminary legal procedures are met.

The physicians involved . . . do not possess expertise in the conditions required for the performance and interpretation of a polygraph examination. Subsequent to the preliminary procedures, we would be willing to describe Mr. Ruby's physical and mental condition either to you or your designated representative. However, the decision as to whether or not his mental and physical condition is such as to preclude the reliable result requested in your letter, would have to be made either by you or your designated representatives who are expert in this type of study.

The letter was a polite way of saying little or nothing. But within days the matters was taken irrevocably out of the doctors' hands. The process was painful beyond words.

# 34

## IN ONE MOMENT

ON THE MORNING of January 3, 1967, Earl called me from the Parkland Memorial Hospital in Dallas. He had just been excluded from Jack's room, and doctors and nurses were rushing in and out. "I think Jack is dead," he said. All that day, and for days afterwards I was very busy. A new excitement had come over the communications media. And, for the first time, news of the taped last message of Ruby was released by Lawrence Schiller and the excerpts from the Capitol record were played throughout the country.

Later that day, with Jack's death confirmed, Earl and I discussed the making of an autopsy. Eva seemed to be opposed because of religious scruples, but Earl and I favored the most thorough autopsy: no questions should be left about the matter. We were not going to take a chance on the sort of controversy that still bedevils the Kennedy death. Experts from Dallas and Washington and elsewhere, governmental and private, eventually participated in the autopsy, which was detailed and lengthy. The autopsy report, when it was released, ran to many pages, covering every inch of the interior and exterior of Jack Ruby and showing that the malignancy had reached every vital organ. We learned, for the first time, that even the brain was affected. How long had the course of the cancer taken? It must have been swift, we were assured by doctors. There was the lingering thought that perhaps the origin of the cancer was deep down in the cells and had existed and been felt at the very moment that Oswald had been shot. The autopsy report told other revealing facts about Jack—his cleanliness, for example. Even as he lay dying the nails of his fingers and toes were manicured and well-groomed. The report was fascinating—and saddening.

To make certain that no one could claim that it was not Jack Ruby who had died, the press was permitted, briefly, to view the body, but not to photograph it.

Jack would be buried in Chicago, the city he always regarded as his home, even when he was a lost soul in Dallas. With much fanfare, the coffin was shipped to Chicago, and taken to the chapel.

Early on the day of the funeral, I was awakened by a telephone call. Whoever was calling was so disturbed that it was difficult at first to understand who he was or what he was saying. I finally made out the words: "Do you know what they are doing at the cemetery? It's disgraceful." The voice was that of "Jim" Harris, an old acquaintance, who ran Westlawn Cemetery in which Jack Ruby was going to be buried. The television people had shown Harris a document, signed by Earl Ruby, which authorized them to televise the funeral. They were erecting towers and spreading wires and placing microphones, and handling the arrangements generally as if they were covering a sporting event. As shocked as Harris, I could not believe what I heard. After telling him that I thought there was an error, and that, in any event, I would get the authorization countermanded, I telephoned the home of Earl's sister Eileen, thinking Earl might be there. Eileen and Eva were as upset as Harris and myself. "Call the police and have them thrown out!" Eva demanded. She gave me a number where I might reach Earl. I called and told him what I had learned. He, too, was upset, and puzzled, until he recalled that someone at the funeral parlor had said to him that it was necessary to sign a certain paper in connection with the burial arrangements. Without reading it, he had signed. Assured of his permission to proceed as I saw fit, I told him that I would try my hand at undoing the mischief.

Only then did I realize that I did not have Harris's telephone number. Furthermore, I did not know whether he was at home (wherever that was) or at the cemetery. When I did locate him and explained what had caused the television carnival, we agreed that Harris would ask the sheriff's police to remove all the offending paraphernalia at once, and that no one from the communications media would be permitted on the cemetery premises. Since the Ruby grave was not far from the cemetery fence, we could not control the public highway. The photographers could ply their trade from that distance, and some of them did. Later, as Harris supervised the removal of the equipment, he discovered that efforts had been made to conceal microphones near the open grave. They were going to miss not one word or sob!

Rabbi David Graubart, presiding rabbi of the Bet Din (rabbinical court) of the Chicago region, conducted the services at the chapel and at the grave. The dignity of his presence was as welcome as it was unexpected. The press and the curious were excluded (except for one reporter who had always been fair and generous). Only the family —all the faithful brothers and sisters—and their friends were present.

There was symbolism in the bearing of Jack Ruby to his final resting place. The pallbearers were the husband of his favorite, his youngest sister Eileen; a childhood companion, Joe Kellman; and four of the lawyers who had participated in the case that had now come to so dramatic an end—Michael Levin, the boyhood friend of the family; Phil Burleson, the one attorney who had stayed with the case from the beginning; William Kunstler, who had ignored his many other commitments to be on hand; and myself. As I accompanied the flag-draped coffin (for Jack had earned that right by his honorable, if undistinguished, wartime service), my thoughts encompassed every step of the way we had gone. I saw how fragile our grip on reality

might become, given the stress of emotional events. I saw
a vindication of our great American judicial system, in
which an impoverished nobody can receive justice, despite
the primitive forces that impede the way. Those gathered
about the coffin came from all parts of the country; they
were diverse men united in the one aim of bearing a fellow
being to the grave in peace and dignity. Dust to dust.
Nothing else mattered or had meaning, neither sins nor
virtues, greatness nor littleness. This is the common end
of the great and the humble, of slain Presidents and of
their avengers.

Rabbi Graubart quietly and solemnly enhanced the dignity of Jack's departure. "The eyes of the world are upon
us now," he said. "Jack Ruby linked himself with one of
the most tragic moments in American history. He acted as
a patriot, but as a misguided patriot and avenger."

He reminded the mourners of the scriptural image of
the avenger of the blood who pursues the slayer in heat
and overtakes him. "Jack Ruby," he said, "thought he could
acquire his spiritual world in one moment, to use the idiom
of the ancient rabbis. Jack Ruby unfortunately destroyed
his world in one moment."

"Shall we condemn him? No. I speak as a religionist who
believes that man is beloved of God because he is created
in His image.

"The ancient rabbis of old taught us not to judge our
fellow man until we come into their place. Jack Ruby was
a man who knew affliction, sorrow, and suffering. We dare
not condone this act, yet we dare not sit in judgment."

At the graveside, the three brothers recited the Kaddish,
the profound Jewish prayer that extols the Lord and His
works despite the ordeal of death.

Then the rabbi tossed the first shovelful of dirt into the
grave. Sometimes, the earth comes from the Holy Land in
sacred packets and is placed in the coffin as a symbol of
the messianic return to the ancestral land, but Jack Ruby's
coffin was sealed. He could not receive the proud and sad

homage of the holy dust. His brothers each bravely tossed
common earth upon the coffin. Their eyes brimful of un-
shed tears, all left the graveside and the cemetery.

At the home of Eileen they foregathered, the mood one
of reminiscence and, despite all, of relief. The long vigil
was over. A kind of immortality had come to a little man
and his little family.

# 35

## A CONSPIRACY?

AFTER THE ASSASSINATION of President Kennedy, public
shock and confusion were supreme, and increased day by
day. In the absence of any completely reliable report on
what had happened, in the face of incompetence by the
police, and with the death of the one person who might
have provided an explanation, rumor, gossip, malice, and
vast publicity, combined with an all-too-understandable
desire for absolute certainty, led quickly to the evolution
of theories about a conspiracy. How could three murders
within forty-eight hours be unconnected? How could single
individuals, unaided, have wrought such mischief?

It was in an effort to bring order from disordered events
and to reduce the area of uncertainty that President Johnson promptly appointed the President's Commission on
the Assassination of President Kennedy and persuaded
Chief Justice Earl Warren to head it. The credentials and
the reputations of the honorable men who served on the
Commission, the record of their endeavors in public service
on behalf of the American people, were not sufficient, however, to convince all the people that truth would out.

Even as the Commission and its staff were undertaking
a monumental examination of the events surrounding the
Dallas tragedy, speculative articles began to appear here
and abroad. Soon entire books were probing the public
record and analyzing what was said and done in Dallas, all
in search of hidden motives. These speculative ventures
were not halted by the appearance of the Warren Commission Report, nor by the publication of the testimony of the

witnesses and the documentary evidence upon which the
Report was based. The controversy continued. It may go
on forever. For some critics would not be convinced by the
evidence before them. And they would not heed the logic
of the arguments of those who desired only to learn the
truth, who had worked closely over the evidence.

Of the earliest works to appear, some shoddy beyond
belief, nothing needs to be said. The writers were compelled to rely upon hearsay, journalistic accounts, personal
visits to Dallas (in some cases), and (often) all too fertile
imaginations. With the appearance of the Report and the
volumes of evidence (twenty-seven fat volumes in all), the
attacks on the Commission, the Establishment, and American society as a whole did not halt. The focus was merely
shifted, for now the critics had available new weapons, the
evidence assembled by the Commission itself. (What a joy
to be able to condemn others by their own utterences!)

Thus the writings that appeared after the Report fall
into a distinct category.

Foremost among the critics has been New York attorney
Mark Lane. Lane, who has practically made a new and
profitable career through his lecturing and writing about
the events surrounding the assassination, began from what
must be considered a legitimate (if in this instance mis-
placed) concern. Like many other attorneys, he was
aroused by the violation of Oswald's rights while he was in
the custody of the Dallas police. Lane, however, could not
defend those rights while Oswald was alive, and the efforts
of others were belated. Nevertheless, after Oswald was
dead, Lane made the attempt. (He was encouraged by the
invitation of Oswald's mother.) That in doing this he
would have to impugn the integrity of many living people,
in much the same way Oswald had been mistreated by
exposure to the communications media, seems not to have
concerned him at all. He may even have welcomed it. To
Lane it has seemed right that, to defend Oswald, much of
the society should be accused.

In and of itself, of course, the provoking of questions about the conduct, integrity, or ability of a public figure, whether the President, the Chief Justice, or even a low-ranking local official, is legitimate, so long as it is not malicious. But the assembling of many insidious questions and the insinuating of doubt have the effect of sowing discord and suspicion everywhere. The consequence, and it is a most serious consequence, is that the whole structure of the society is undermined. If the society is corrupt, then it calls for exposure. But the critic should not react irresponsibly.

Lane, of course, has not been solely responsible for the devastating result, but he has been most active and most prominent. Many people have praised his work, and more have attacked it. Some have been knowledgeable, some ignorant; some cool, some passionate. Writers have come forward to support Lane's arguments about the events surrounding the killing of the young President. My concern here is not with whether Oswald did or did not kill the President, did or did not kill Tippit. My concern is Ruby, and since Lane has implied that Ruby was the "silencer," was in effect a part of a conspiracy, it is fair to consider Lane's presentation of the issue. An examination of what he has written, in *Rush to Judgment,* will go far to illuminate his methods in criticism of the methods of the Warren Commission. Is his work as free from question as he would obviously like theirs to be?

## THE SHOOTING OF OSWALD

Lane's description of the death of Oswald, admirably succinct, is a minor example worth examining in this light:

Ruby pushed through the crowd, pistol in hand, and placed the muzzle against Oswald's stomach. Oswald tried to protect himself by bringing forward both hands, but even so inadequate a defense was prevented by the handcuffs, and Ruby shot him once in the stomach. Oswald was dragged back into the jail office and there he began to bleed to death. The police started clearing the vehicles from the basement ramp, and when the ramp was clear, an ambulance was permitted to come in, pick Oswald up and leave.[1] . . .

This description seems clear and unexceptionable on its face. In truth, six issues of "fact" are in question.

1. *Did Ruby "push" through the crowd?*
2. *As he moved ("pushed") through the crowd, did Ruby have the "pistol in hand"?*
3. *Did Ruby place the muzzle of the pistol "against" Oswald's stomach? Did Oswald try to protect himself by bringing forward both hands?*
4. *Was Oswald "dragged" into the jail office?*
5. *Did Oswald "bleed to death"?*
6. *Was there an unreasonable delay in the arrival of an ambulance?*

The clear implications of what Lane wrote are destroyed if his sources do not support him. Those implications are that Ruby was intent on murder as he came through the crowd; that Oswald recognized he was to be murdered; that the police were derelict in their treatment of the mortally wounded Oswald (rough handling, delay in getting him to the hospital).

1. *Did Ruby "push" through the crowd?*
Lane's sources are the Warren Commission Report and the Hearings. Neither supports the claim that Ruby "pushed." The Report describes the event in these words:

After Oswald had moved about 10 feet from the door of the jail office, Jack Ruby passed between a newsman and a detective at the edge of the straining crowd on the Main Street ramp. With his right hand extended and holding a .38 caliber revolver, Ruby stepped quickly forward and fired a single fatal bullet into Oswald's abdomen.[2]

The photographs, reprinted by the Commission,[3] give no

indication of any physical contact until Ruby was subdued *after* the shooting of Oswald.

Lane, as usual, fails to cite the evidence in the Report and Hearings that does not support him.

Kenneth Croy believed that he saw Ruby at the base of the ramp before the attack on Oswald. Croy testified that the man he saw "near the railing" ran past him, but he did not mention any pushing or any collision between the man and any members of the assemblage. When Warren Commission attorney Burt Griffin asked a question concerning Croy's "pushing" the crowd back, Croy replied, "I didn't push them. I asked them to step back over there." Ruby was one of those who complied with this order.

James Turner, the most credible witness to Ruby's entry, testified before Warren Commission attorney Leon Hubert. Turner was certain that he saw Ruby coming down the ramp. His testimony was, in part, as follows:

*Hubert:* . . . Did he have to go through any great mass of people?
*Turner:* No . . .
*Hubert:* Did he have to push, or shoulder his way up there?
*Turner:* No.
*Hubert:* He could just walk up and get into position?
*Turner:* That's right.[4]

2. *As he moved through the crowd, did Ruby have the "pistol in hand"?*

Lane relies, as before, on the indicated pages of the Report and Hearings. Neither supports his allegations.

Neither Croy nor Turner, not cited by Lane, stated that Ruby displayed a pistol prior to the shooting, and since the best evidence indicates that Ruby was in the basement for a mere twenty-five seconds, their failure to mention a fact so material, which they would surely have noticed, would seem to be conclusive.

There is further evidence. A photograph reprinted in the Report[5] shows Ruby standing in the crowd immediately before Oswald's appearance. Had his weapon not been concealed, it surely would have been noticed by those near him. Ruby was able to get so close because of his relative inconspicuousness; an unconcealed pistol would have exposed him at once.

3. *Did Ruby place the muzzle of the pistol "against Oswald's stomach"? Did Oswald try to protect himself?*

For his muzzle theory Lane is still content to cite the same passages from the Warren Report and Hearings. Neither of these provides substance for the theory, and the already mentioned photographs disprove it at least in part.

For Oswald's alleged defensive reaction, Lane cites only page 216 of the Warren Report. No mention of Oswald's reaction is made there.

Certainly the most graphic, and perhaps the most effective, means of demonstrating the utter absurdity of both theories is to examine the photographs taken at the scene.

The famous picture by Jack Beers of the Dallas *Morning News*, taken immediately before the shot was fired, shows a space of about two feet between the muzzle and Oswald's stomach. In this photograph, it is clear that Oswald has not seen Ruby, and is therefore incapable of any reaction— defensive, recognitional, or otherwise. Indeed, no one in the entire assemblage saw Ruby at the time. As Beers explained to me, he had pointed his camera at the spot where Oswald was to enter the room. He did not know until later that he had actually photographed Ruby as he was about to shoot Oswald.

A second photograph was taken immediately after the shot was fired. The distance between the pistol and Oswald remains. Oswald's face is contorted with pain, his eyes are closed, or nearly so, and his left arm has jerked up over the wound. If his arm movements can be considered defensive, rather than reflexive, they are defending against a second shot, which never came. It should be remembered that Oswald's hands were handcuffed, and another pair of handcuffs linked his right wrist to Officer Leavelle's left wrist.

It is clear that the distance between the pistol and Oswald's stomach was about two feet, and this is substantially corroborated by Detective L. C. Graves, who was holding Oswald's left arm. He stated that the pistol was fifteen inches away from Oswald.[6]

Burt Griffin, a member of the Warren Commission staff charged with investigating Ruby's actions, replied to my inquiry on this point:

> You asked if we attempted to obtain any and all photographs of every kind, character, and description relating in any way to the actual shooting of Oswald. The answer is a most emphatic yes. To my knowledge we obtained all newspaper photographs and T.V. shots.
>
> I must have watched the T.V. film of the shooting at least a dozen times. If Ruby "placed the muzzle against Oswald's stomach" I never noticed it in all those viewings. Nor did I ever remember that Oswald tried to ward off the gun "by bringing forward both hands."

I myself viewed the television pictures over and over again—at their regular speed, then frame by frame, then backward—and it is my firm conviction that they utterly disprove Lane's assertions about the shooting of Oswald.

4. *Was Oswald "dragged" into the jail office?*

Lane cites the report of J. R. Leavelle, to whom Oswald was handcuffed.[7] The pertinent section states: "I turned my attention to Oswald, and with the help of Detective Combest, we *took* Oswald back into the jail office and laid him down. Handcuffs were removed and the city hall doctor, Dr. Bieberdorf, was summoned. We also called O'Neal ambulance. Oswald was placed in the ambulance and rushed to Parkland Hospital." Even Lane's own source does not justify his use of the word "dragged" to imply rough treatment or anything similar.

Again, Lane fails to mention other Warren Commission sources. Exhibit 2163 is an interview with Officer Leavelle, who states that he picked up Oswald "and *carried* him back inside the jail office to get him away from the area."

According to the testimony before the Warren Commission, Detective Billy Combest assisted Leavelle in transporting Oswald to the jail office.[8] The word he used was "took."

No support can be found for the implication that Oswald was handled roughly by the police after the shooting.

5. *Did Oswald "bleed to death"?*

Reference is made by Lane to Oswald's autopsy, which lists the cause of death as "Hemorrhage, secondary to gunshot wound of the chest." Lane also cites the report of Dr. Bieberdorf. This report contains no mention of Oswald's bleeding.

"Hemorrhage, secondary to gunshot wound of the chest" may, or may not, mean that Oswald bled to death. The implication that Oswald bled to death because he was manhandled after he was shot has no support.

6. *Was there an unreasonable delay in the arrival of an ambulance?*

The inference to be drawn from the Lane sentence, "The police started clearing vehicles from the basement ramp, and when the ramp was clear, an ambulance was permitted to come in, pick Oswald up and leave," is that a waiting ambulance was irresponsibly delayed while policemen moved several vehicles. In fact, only two cars had to be moved to clear the ramp, and they were moved well before the arrival of the ambulance.

Lane refers to Officer Brown's report, which states: "By this time, other officers had removed Lee Harvey Oswald and Jack Ruby into the jail office. I went back to my car and moved it back into the parking area so the ambulance could get through." Also cited is Officer Dohrity's report: "I then moved Capt. Fritz' car out of the driveway where the ambulance could get to the jail office." Nothing in these reports would indicate delay, since the cars were moved as soon as Ruby and Oswald were taken into the jail office.

The other citation which, to Lane, supports the inference is Dr. Bieberdorf's report. The doctor explains his treatment of Oswald and describes the arrival of the ambulance and its attendants while he was so occupied. While the doctor is Lane's own "witness" on this point, Bieberdorf actually stated that the arrival of the ambulance was "approximately five minutes after he had heard the gunshot."[9]

The conclusion is inescapable: Ruby walked, unpushed and unpushing, to the periphery of the crowd. At the critical moment he took several quick steps, drew the pistol, and fired the fatal shot before Oswald or his bodyguards or anyone else saw him. The shot was fired at close range, estimated at fifteen inches from its resting place in Oswald's stomach. Oswald reacted immediately to the shot by a contortion of his face and an upward jerk of his left arm. Officers Leavelle and Combest transported Oswald to the jail office, perhaps by carrying him, to protect him from the commotion in the basement. A doctor and an ambulance were summoned. The doctor arrived quickly and was in the process of treating Oswald when the ambulance arrived. The ambulance arrived within approximately five minutes of the time of the shot. Oswald died of "Hemorrhage, secondary to gunshot wound of the chest."

## MARK LANE'S JACK RUBY

Most of Mark Lane's comments on Jack Ruby are found in Chapters 16 through 24 of *Rush to Judgment*. Lane does not assume there the burden of demonstrating any positive theory concerning the murder of Oswald. He is content to point out what he considers to be flaws in the Commission's procedures and conclusions. Reasoning from his belief that those involved in the investigation performed their duties incompetently, he assembles a body of testimony that, standing alone, raises questions about certain findings of the Commission. (Only later did Lane begin to direct accusations against the CIA and other federal officials. When he became a part of the Garrison investigation in New Orleans, he became as vituperative as the district attorney himself.)

Since the material is not tightly structured, no chapter-by-chapter rebuttal can be attempted here. Nevertheless, the following examination of Lane's account will show that he is far from free of the faults he imputes to others.

### RUBY'S ALLEGED IMMUNITY FROM ARREST

Implicitly informing all the pages dealing with Jack Ruby is a theory that he used his police contacts to avoid civil and criminal prosecution. In particular, one should note Lane's statement: "Ruby was arrested eight times in ten years for violations of the nightclub regulations and other criminal acts including acts of violence. According to Commission Exhibit 1528, he was not convicted once."[10] The attached excerpt from the Commission's biography of Ruby takes a more comprehensive view.[11] It covers fourteen years and discloses five suspensions of Ruby's liquor license for violations of the nightclub regulations, the most recent in 1961, less than two years before the President's assassination. The record reveals twenty traffic tickets in thirteen years, with seven convictions and two six-month suspensions of his driver's license. Also noted are eight arrests for various alleged criminal and quasi-criminal matters, in three of which Ruby posted a bond. In another of the eight arrests, Ruby was adjudicated not guilty.

Certain observations can be made concerning this record. Most obvious is that Lane has substantially misstated the facts and their implication. Ruby was immune from neither arrest nor conviction.

Another observation might be drawn from ordinary experience. Police forces, composed as they are of fallible and susceptible human beings, are capable of minor acts of favoritism. Minor favoritism most commonly is manifested in the issuance of traffic tickets. Normally, a policeman is allowed a certain discretion over whether a summons will be given for a particular infraction. But Ruby, whom Lane would have us believe had the Dallas Police

Department in his hip pocket, could not even escape receiving twenty tickets in thirteen years, resulting in two long suspensions of his driving privileges and seven convictions.

Similarly, the five suspensions of his liquor license indicate that his commercial activities were receiving at least token scrutiny, and would appear to rebut Lane's allegations that Ruby was flagrantly violating the law with impunity.

The remaining blemishes on Ruby's record also seem to show a consistent pattern of prosecution, rather than the contrary. Ruby was certainly arrested. He may have been a law-breaking citizen. Nevertheless, that he was not convicted in every case cannot be used to support an allegation that he was guaranteed freedom from police restraints.

### POLICE ASSISTANCE?

Because Lane feels that the police did not prosecute Ruby with full vigor for his previous infractions, he reasons that the latter's presence in the basement may have resulted from the acquiescence or assistance of the Dallas police. He largely ignores the police testimony at the trial, which was responsible for the death sentence. He ignores the implications of Ruby's failure to accuse the police *after* the imposition of the death sentence. Why would Ruby remain silent if the police had aided and then double-crossed him?

*A Tip-off?* Because of the news media, the proposed time of Oswald's transfer (about 10:00 A.M.) was known to the public.[12] Ruby's testimony indicates that he had actual notice of this time.[13] No telephone calls from a policeman to Ruby's apartment could have informed Ruby of the later time, because Ruby was not at home after about 10:45, and no one (including Captain Fritz) could have known the precise time of the transfer until approximately 11:15.[14] Since news of the impending transfer was being broadcast contemporaneously, Ruby had no need to obtain information surreptitiously. (As a matter of fact, there is good reason to believe that when Ruby arrived in the area of the police station, he thought the transfer had already been made.)

*Police Acquiescence?* Lane relies exclusively on the testimony of one N. J. Daniels to show that Ruby's unauthorized presence in the basement was a result of police acquiescence.[15] Daniels stated that a man, whom he described, walked directly in front of Patrolman Vaughn, down the Main Street ramp, and into the basement. Daniels stated that Vaughn was looking in the man's direction at the time.[16]

Daniels' testimony contains some substantial, perhaps fatal, discrepancies. For example, his affidavits stated that the man was neither wearing nor carrying a hat,[17] but it is common knowledge, as evidenced by photographs, that Ruby wore a hat at the time of the shooting. Daniels thought that there were four policemen in Lieutenant Pierce's car when it ascended the ramp.[18] In reality, there were only three.[19]

Even more substantial is Daniels's vacillation over the chronological sequence of the car's appearance and the man's entry. The affidavits indicate that the man entered *a few minutes after* the car had exited.[20] In his testimony he originally said, with respect to this sequence, "I'm not sure," but stated that entry took place *before* the car came up.[21] Later in his appearance he again altered his story to conclude that he saw the man enter *after* the car had left.[22] Daniels never stated in his testimony or in the affidavits that the man whom he saw was Jack Ruby.

It can be readily appreciated that Daniels's testimony, even as briefly described, appears to be dubious. Two more factors must be considered in assessing the import of his revelations.

First, investigators, by examining videotapes, determined that only fifty-five seconds elapsed between the car's appearance at the top of the ramp and the time of the fatal shot.[23] Twenty to twenty-five seconds are required for a person to descend the ramp at a walk. Therefore Daniels's testimony is not merely unsure: insofar as he concluded that the man entered a few minutes after the car's exit, it is false, because events could not physically have taken place in the manner which he describes.

Second, Daniels was not the only person to testify concerning Ruby's entry. Ruby himself told Special Agent C. Ray Hall, in an interview, that he started down the ramp while Vaughn was watching for auto traffic and directing Pierce's car.[24] Kenneth Croy partially corroborates Ruby's story, because he claims to have seen Ruby at the base of the Main Street ramp before the shooting.[25] William Newman claimed that he saw a man, whom he could not identify, walking down the ramp about one minute before the shot was fired.[26] James Turner saw a man, whom he later discovered was Jack Ruby, descending the ramp immediately after the car left the jail basement.[27] He was positive in his identification.[28]

Standing alone, Daniels' testimony is vacillating and uncertain. Fortunately, it does not stand alone, but is effectively refuted by more reliable witnesses, accepted by the Commission.

### THE TESTIMONY OF NANCY RICH

Lane claims that the Commission minimized the close relationship between Ruby and many members of the Dallas police force.[29] He considers Chief Curry's statement that "no more than 25 to 50 of Dallas' almost 1200 policemen were acquainted with Ruby" to be the "germane" portion of the Report's section on "Police Associations."[30]

That the Chief's estimate was not taken at face value by the Commission is indicated, first, by the sentence following it: "However, the reports of Ruby's employees and acquaintances indicate that Ruby's police friendships were far more widespread than those of the average citizen."[31] The Chief's speculation is given similarly short shrift elsewhere in the Report: "Although Chief Curry's estimate that approximately 25 to 50 of the 1175 men in the Dallas Police Department knew Ruby may be too conservative. . . ."[32]

Lane cites the testimony of Nancy Perrin Rich as authority for the statement: "His bartender had standing orders to serve hard liquor to all police officers who came into the nightclub."[33] Since Lane has written an entire chapter concerning Mrs. Rich's testimony, her background will be examined in detail.

Early in her testimony,[34] Mrs. Rich gave Commission attorney Hubert a letter from Oscar A. Kistle, Chief Deputy District Attorney of Sacramento. She also described what she claimed to be her extensive career in police investigation work.[35]

Commission Exhibit 3058[36] yields the information that Mrs. Rich would more precisely be termed an occasional "informer" than an investigator. She volunteered her services and provided information leading to the conviction of an abortionist. The Department had no interest in hiring her.

She also assisted the police in Oakland, California, by securing a nightclub job for the purpose of informing on its owner. She was unsuccessful in this endeavor. While Mrs. Rich claimed that the Oakland Police Department had furnished her with a false police record,[37] Lieutenant Parker of the Department denied this.[38] After her failure at the nightclub Mrs. Rich had had no official dealings with the Department, and was known there as "a screwball" and "nutty as a fruitcake."[39]

An FBI report noted that Sergeant Dahl of the Oakland police force remembered Mrs. Rich's offering of "fanciful information." He advised that he would place "little credence" in her statements and that, "in retrospect," she was "emotionally unstable."[40]

Attorney Cy Victorson described Mrs. Rich, a former client, as a "habitual liar." Her husband was no more complimentary.

Mrs. Rich implicated Ruby in a plot whereby a group of conspirators planned to sell guns to a group in Cuba and evacuate refugees on the return trip (by boat).[41]

The impact of this testimony is weakened by the persuasive evidence on Mrs. Rich's lack of credibility. It is further debilitated by an FBI report on Dave Cherry, who was identified by Mrs. Rich as another of the conspirators. Cherry disclaimed any knowledge of the gun-running and described Mrs. Rich as "mentally deranged."[42]

A polygraph examination given to Mrs. Rich on December 5, 1963, was generally inconclusive because of her use of drugs, but the examiner felt able to state that he believed the Cuban arms story was untrue.[43] The examiner also offered his opinion that the lady in question was suffering from "delusions of grandeur."

Lane states: "When the Commission found material disconcerting, it often handled it in one of two ways. It either minimized the importance of the evidence . . . or it challenged the probity of the witness."[44] Concerning the first part of this statement, Mrs. Rich's material was truly disconcerting; it bordered on the ludicrous.

The Commission was entirely justified in omitting Mrs. Rich's testimony from the Report, especially since the testimony of other and superior witnesses was used on the nature of Ruby's favors to policemen.

The Report mentions those favors in two places. It notes: "According to testimony from many sources, he [Ruby] gave free coffee at his clubs to many policemen while they were off duty."[45] The Report also says, "Although there is considerable evidence that Ruby gave policemen reduced rates, declined to exact any cover charge from them, and gave them free coffee and soft drinks, this hospitality was not unusual for a Dallas nightclub operator."[46] Nor would it have been unusual anywhere in this country.

Andy Armstrong, the porter at the Carousel Club, testified that policemen in uniform stopped for coffee and that members of the vice squad were present regularly. He mentioned that police were among those who received a cut rate on beer.[47] Armstrong also revealed Ruby's "fear" of Officer Gilmore, a "strict" vice squad member.[48]

George Senator, Ruby's roommate and occasional employee, said that when police came to inspect, "Jack always offered them a coffee, asked them if they wanted coffee, a Seven-Up or a coke."[49] Senator testified that policemen who visited the club socially did not have to pay the entrance fee, and he corroborated Armstrong's testimony concerning the cut-rate price of forty cents on beer for policemen and other privileged persons.[50] Ruby himself admitted his waiver of cover charges and the lower drink price.[51] Curtis Laverne Crafard, a handyman employee of Ruby's, confirmed this, and added that the usual price of beer was sixty cents. He also mentioned that the police never drank alcoholic beverages when they were on duty.[52] Sergeant Jerry Hill,[53] Edward Pullman[54] and Jean Flynn[55] each confirmed this testimony.

The Commission wisely decided to rely on the internally consistent testimony of seven relatively reliable witnesses rather than upon that of one witness with a deserved reputation for unbridled prevarication. She is Lane's only source for the "hard liquor" theory and the "gun-running" theory. (Although Hugh Smith, a Dallas policeman, told of gifts of hard liquor,[56] he said nothing about the serving of any hard liquor at the club.)

### JACK RUBY'S TESTIMONY

Chapter 19 of *Rush to Judgment* deals with Jack Ruby's testimony before the Warren Commission. The selected portions of the record that Lane quotes are accurate, if out of context, and a reading of the testimony in its entirety is necessary for an evaluation of its content.

Given a full reading, and with proper perspective, a prima facie case develops for a theory that Ruby was mentally incompetent when he testified. He himself seemed to be aware that the natural import of his vocalizing would permit such an inference: "Do I sound dramatic? Off the beam?" ". . . and I am not a crackpot. . . ." "Do I sound sober enough to you as I say this?"[57] In this light, it would seem that one could readily discount Ruby's expressed fears for his safety and his hints at a conspiracy endangering the lives of the members of his family.[58] In addition, the Commission was in the most favorable position to assess Ruby's credibility, for it alone had the opportunity to observe his demeanor and hear his voice. In such circumstances it is usual for the reviewer to give some deference to the opinion of the fact-finder.

An examination of other testimony, given chronologically before Ruby's, indicates a substantial quantum of evidence showing not only that he was incompetent, but that his delusions were similar in quality to those that can be observed from the record.

Hyman Rubenstein, Jack's brother, discussed a December, 1963, visit with Jack: "Jack looked good, but he didn't act right. He looked disturbed to me." "He was worried more about the dogs than he was about anybody else." "You know, there was no logic there."[59]

Eva Grant stated in response to a question asking her opinion of Jack's condition: "I think he is mentally deranged. . . ."[60]

Sam Ruby's contacts with Jack in December, 1963, led him to a conclusion similar to those of his brother and sister.[61]

Even more corroborative evidence exists to indicate that Ruby was suffering from delusions, and it goes beyond any judgment derived from merely reading Ruby's entire testimony or even an opinion formed in deference to the superior position of the trier of fact. Those furnishing the evidence are members of a class that would be most sensitive to any major personality changes in Jack Ruby, since as a group and individually they had known him well for his entire life.

Lane complains that the presence of Sheriff Decker, District Attorney Bowie, and Deputy Storey might have inhibited Ruby in fully disclosing the truth.[62] If such were the case, Ruby did not object. Indeed, when Sheriff Decker offered to withdraw his men, Ruby declined the offer.[63] One can only contemplate Lane's reaction, and that of the public generally, had Ruby, left unguarded, attacked Chief Justice Warren or anyone else.

"There can be no sound defense of the Commission's refusal to bring Jack Ruby to Washington," Lane says.[34] Neither can it be shown that any conceivable utility would thereby have been derived. With hindsight, we may wish that it had been done—if only to prove the futility.

When I once asked Ruby what he thought of Chief Justice Warren, he replied: "A very nice man, but so naive." Warren had loaned Ruby his glasses during the interrogation. Unlike others, the Chief Justice had Ruby's full confidence.

### THE ALLEGED MEETING

Lane claims that a meeting took place between Ruby, Bernard Weissman (who placed the advertisement derogatory to President Kennedy in the Dallas *Morning News*), and Officer J. D. Tippit in Ruby's club on November 4, 1963.[65] Then he compares the available testimony and the Commission's conclusion.[66]

Concerning Weissman's presence at the Carousel Club, Lane cites the testimony of Bruce Carlin.[67] After being shown a picture of Weissman, Carlin replied that he was uncertain whether he had ever seen him before.[68] Lane also cites Crafard's affidavit, which states only that the latter had a "vague" recollection of a person named Weissman having been in the Carousel, but that he could have confused Weissman with someone else.[69] Karen Carlin ("Little Lynn") indicated that she had never seen either Tippit or Weissman talking to Ruby before the assassination. She further stated that a person vaguely resembling Weissman had worked at the Carousel *after* November 24, 1963 (when Ruby was already in custody).[70]

Bruce Carlin, Karen Carlin, and Larry Crafard are the only witnesses that Lane can muster to prove Weissman's presence at such a meeting. Their recollections are dubious at best and contrary at worst.

Weissman himself testified that he had never met Ruby and that he had never been in the Carousel.[71] Ruby testified that he knew an Officer Tippit, but not the one who was killed.[72] There were several Tippits on the police force. Lane himself was the Commission's source for the rumor concerning the alleged meeting.[73] Despite the most urgent request of the Chief Justice and the tremendous importance of the matter, he would reveal neither his source nor the ultimate source. In the absence of corroborative testimony, and in the presence of some that conflicted, the Commission could not rely on Lane's professed beliefs.

The strongest witness that Lane offers to indicate that Ruby and Tippit were acquainted is Harold Williams.[74] It is impossible to assess his credibility because no mention of him is made by the Commission in its Report or in the supplementary volumes. Nevertheless, even if Ruby was in fact acquainted with the Tippit who was slain, the question of the meeting remains a matter of speculation, with little if anything to support it. And it would not prove, or tend to prove, that Ruby had anything to do with his slaying.

## RUBY'S ACTIVITIES BEFORE THE SHOOTING

The Warren Report undertakes to catalogue Ruby's activities from November 21 to November 24, 1963.[75] Lane tries to read a conspiratorial import into these activities.[76]

The finding that Ruby, on November 21, "had visited with a young lady who was job hunting in Dallas"[77] is attacked by Lane as an oversimplification.[78] He correctly points out that Miss Connie Trammel was driven by Ruby to the office of Lamar Hunt. Miss Trammel also stated, however, that Ruby did not know Hunt.[79]

An attempt to place Ruby at the scene of the assassination is made by Lane when he notes that Don Campbell[80] last saw Ruby at the newspaper office at 12:25 (where, beyond doubt, he was at the moment of the President's fatal injury) and John Newman[81] did not subsequently see Ruby until 12:45.[82] Whether it would be possible for a person to be at the newspaper office at 12:25 and 12:40 and still be observed at the scene of the assassination is highly problematical, if not impossible. It is understandable that the Commission did not mention the theoretical possibility.[83]

Victoria Adams is cited by Lane as a witness to Ruby's presence at the scene of the assassination.[84] Her only comment was that the man she saw looked "very similar" to Ruby.[85] Her testimony indicated that the man she saw was probably on the corner for *more* than fifteen minutes, which exceeded the maximum time that Ruby could have spent there in order to return to the newspaper office on time.[86]

Jean Hill testified that a man whom she saw near the scene "looked a lot like" Ruby.[87] She admitted, however, that the man she observed "could have been smaller" than Ruby, and when asked whether she felt the man was Ruby, she replied, "That, I don't know."[88]

Lane attacks the Commission's finding that Ruby was not at Parkland Memorial Hospital.[89] The Report shows that Ruby was at the newspaper office until after one o'clock and that he had returned to the Carousel Club by 1:45.[90] The period in which Ruby could have been at the hospital was thus slight, but it is a bare possibility, and there is one perhaps credible witness, newspaper reporter Seth Kantor,[91] whom the Report discounts.[92] Another witness, Mrs. Wilma Tice, testified that she saw Ruby at the hospital, but her credibility was not so strong as that of Kantor.[93]

Lane's suggestion[94] that mysterious reasons lie behind Larry Crafard's disappearance on the morning of Oswald's slaying is rebutted by the Commission:

After Oswald was shot, FBI agents obtained from the Carousel Club an unmailed letter drafted by Crafard to a relative in Michigan at least a week before the assassination. The letter revealed that he was considering leaving Dallas at that time. On November 17, Crafard, who had been receiving only room, board, and incidental expenses, told Ruby that he wanted to stop working for him; however, Crafard agreed to remain when Ruby promised a salary.[95]

A bit of Wanda Helmick's testimony is accurately reproduced by Lane,[96] describing a phone call from Ruby to his friend, and financier, and associate Paul, which Mrs. Helmick overheard in her capacity as carhop in Paul's restaurant.[97] Lane neglects to mention, however, that Paul, while conceding that Ruby called him, flatly denied the substance of her allegations about the gun and his appraisal of Ruby's mental state.[98] Lane's technique, as we have observed, is to accept the less reliable witnesses if what they say can be distorted into an attack upon the Warren Report. He then rejects even the best Commission witnesses.

## DALLAS AFTERMATH

Witnesses whose testimony seems to Lane to contain a mysterious content are given the highest degree of consideration by him. Wilma Tice is no exception. The thought that she may have been threatened causes him to become quite solicitous.[99] Contrary to his assertions that the Commission was "indifferent" to stories that Mrs. Tice had been threatened, Counsel expressly asked Mrs. Tice about threats and received a disclaimer from her.[100]

Lane mentions four witnesses who, to him, cast doubt on the finding that Oswald murdered Tippit.[101]

Warren Reynolds, however, positively identified the man he saw on Jefferson Boulevard as Oswald.[102]

L. J. Lewis stated in his affidavit that he would hesitate to identify the man he saw as Oswald,[103] but he did note that the man was about thirty years old.[104] At the time, Oswald was 24, and Ruby 52. Even if Lewis could not state positively that he saw Oswald, he stated with implied certainty that he did not see Ruby, contrary to what Lane hints.

B. M. Patterson positively identified the man he had seen as Oswald, based upon photographs shown him by FBI agents on August 26, 1964.[105]

Harold Russell also positively identified the man he saw as Oswald.[106]

Warren Reynolds was shot on January 23, 1964.[107] A potential defendant was released because of an alibi furnished by one Betty MacDonald (Nancy Jane Mooney).[108] Lane claims that Miss Mooney worked as a stripper in Ruby's club and hints, as does Penn Jones, Jr., that her subsequent self-hanging and Reynold's shooting may have been related to the assassination.[109] One affiant, Patsy Swope, stated that Miss Mooney had told her she had worked at the Carousel.[110] That is the only evidence that we can find, but the Commission stated that it had no evidence that Mooney had worked for Ruby.[111]

We are unable to evaluate Lane's allegations concerning Mrs. Clemons, a supposed eyewitness to the Tippit slaying, because Lane relies on his personal interview of her.[112]

Lane is correct in his assessment that Amos Euins[113] was unable to testify with certainty about the race of the man whom he saw, and he is correct in stating that Euins altered his views on this point from what had appeared in his affidavit.[114] We cannot evaluate the truth of the allegation that Euins had been threatened because the report of the threats appears in an unsupported newspaper account.[115]

In any event, none of these things even begins to prove any connection between Ruby and the slaying of Tippit.

George Senator's testimony shows that he did call attorney Martin before he learned that it was Ruby who did the shooting of Oswald,[116] as Lane says.[117] Senator said that he called Martin "as a friend."[118] This would seem reasonable, Lane's insinuations notwithstanding.[119] Insinuation is no substitute for facts.

## CUBAN OVERTONES

Ruby, in an interview on December 21, 1963, told Special Agent Alfred Neely that he attempted to contact a man concerning the sale of jeeps to Castro. Police determined that the man was probably Robert McKeown.[120] The attempted communication took place in the late fifties, and apparently nothing resulted from it.[121]

The other principal whom Lane names as one of Ruby's "international connections" is Lewis J. McWillie.[122] The Report's summation of the Ruby-McWillie relationship is:

> In September, 1959, Ruby traveled to Havana as a guest of a close friend and known gambler, Lewis J. McWillie. Both Ruby and McWillie state the trip was purely social. In January, 1961, McWillie left Cuba with strong feelings of hostility toward the Castro regime. In early 1963, Ruby purchased a pistol which he shipped to McWillie in Nevada, but McWillie did not accept the package. The Commission has found no evidence that McWillie has engaged in any activities since leaving Cuba that are related to pro- or anti-Castro political movements or that he was involved in Ruby's abortive jeep transaction.[123]

Lane tries to link Ruby, McKeown, and McWillie in

nefarious activity.[124] McWillie told an FBI agent that Ruby was "apolitical" and had no connection with political figures in Cuba.[125] Thus Ruby's unsuccessful attempt to do business with McKeown in the late fifties and his social visit to Havana with McWillie are unrelated, one to the other, and to the assassination of Oswald. There is no persuasive evidence to the contrary.

The whole situation troubled Ruby himself, who did not conceal the associations. He constantly referred to it in conversation, for he feared the wrong inferences might be drawn by the uninformed or malicious.

### THE "PRELIMINARY REPORT"

Lane quotes [126] a memorandum from the Commission to the CIA: "It is possible that Ruby could have been utilized by a politically motivated group either upon the promise of money or because of the influential character of the individual approaching Ruby."[127] He refers to this memorandum as a "preliminary report";[128] however, the document does not describe itself in that manner.[129] It is labeled only as a "memorandum" of "pertinent information." An analysis of this memorandum reveals that it is essentially an outline for investigation, rather than the result of one.[130] The memorandum lists possible avenues for investigation, some of which were subsequently closed by the Commission's witnesses. (For example, a suggestion that Ruby might be linked to the "Las Vegas gambling community" proved to be unfounded.[131])

Lane alleges that "the CIA never grappled with the many serious questions posed in the preliminary report and asserted instead, quite gratuitously, that a search of its own files revealed no evidence that Ruby and Oswald were associated. . . ."[134] To the contrary, the CIA was not requested to investigate anything except its own files. Chief Counsel Rankin's letter, which requested information, merely asked the CIA to "submit to the Commission any information contained in your files regarding the matters covered in the memorandum, as well as any other analyses by your representatives which you believe might be useful to the Commission."[133]

As one looks into the progression of critics of the Warren Report, one finds that first they seize upon those areas in which questions may be asked. Propounding these questions with a solemn wink, they then proceed to make certainties of uncertainties. They no longer ask questions; they make charges—the less provable the charge, the more assured the manner of charging. Such judgments we are asked to accept in place of those pronounced, in measured terms, by the Warren Commission. What, then, are we to make of Lane's performance? Is it so free of fault or so full of error that one must wholly agree or disagree with the conclusions?

Judging solely by the correctness of his quotations or the accuracy of the citations of sources, Lane does not always meet respectable standards. Sometimes he quotes accurately; sometimes he omits highly pertinent language; often his citations are not to the point or persuasive. The vast number of references are the façade, not the reality, of scholarship. In many respects, he falls short of what might be considered the ideal, an ideal moreover that he explicitly demands of others. He is highly selective in choosing his sources and in crediting those whom he will believe, to the exclusion of others. Men will disagree, not only about the interpretation of data, but also about the data itself, and if reasonable men may differ, it is unfair— if not entirely outrageous—to look always behind the differences to find dastardly motivations. For all Lane's implications of conspiracy, criminal activity on the part of Jack Ruby, and profound secrets that could have been uncovered had it not been for the perverse blindness and incompetence of the Warren Commission and its staff, Lane has produced—nothing substantial.

Lane has not shown that there was a conspiracy in which Ruby participated, or discovered any member of it, in nearly five years of personal investigation. Although he continues to pursue the theory, he has got less near the truth than the Warren Commission.

The pursuit of "the truth" by Lane and others is but a manifestation of a bent of mind, an inclination that is both desirable and regrettable. The quest for truth has been the life's work of investigators who have contributed most to mankind, but it has also been the motivating force of those who have acted to frustrate diversity of opinion and belief. For Lane and the rest, the quest is not for truth in the human experience, but truth absolute and unchangeable, certainty now and forever.

Surely, in dealing with the problems arising from the assassination of President Kennedy and its aftermath, one must constantly ask, Is this true? But as Pilate knew, the truth is not easy to detect or to accept, because the very meaning of the word is not as clear as one might assume. Truth may be simply defined as "evidence sufficient to establish a thing as true, or to produce belief in its truth."[134] Of course, such a definition does not include certainty, for the very good reason that few things are certain. As a standard casebook on evidence suggests in discussing the problem of proof:

Evidence is produced at a trial so that an impartial trier can decide how an event occurred. Time is irreversible, events unique, and any reconstruction of the past at best an approximation. As a result of this lack of certainty about what happened, it is inescapable that the trier's conclusions be based on probabilities. . . . Fundamental, then, is acceptance of the fact that the results of adjudication are imperfect, that the rules represent a pragmatic attempt to come as reasonably close to the truth as the law's resources permit.[135]

In a criminal case, where theoretically the verdict is weighted in favor of the accused, what is true is only what

a jury concludes; and the jury's verdict may be set aside
through the protracted and complex processes of the law.

If we speculate about police involvement with Ruby,
for example, and the speculation shows no reasonable
suggestions of conspiracy, there is greater probability
about the truth than would be present in a formal adjudication by a court of lack of guilt. What we call moral
certainty means more than any verdict.

What we are dealing with should be called a question
of "probable opinion." Bertrand Russell deals with it in
this fashion:

In regard to probable opinion, we can derive great assistance
from coherence, which we rejected as the definition of truth, but
may often use as a criterion. A body of individually probable
opinions, if they are mutually coherent, become more probable
than any one of them would be individually. It is in this way
that many scientific hypotheses acquire their probability. They
fit into a coherent system of probable opinions, and thus become
more probable than they would be in isolation. . . . But this test,
though it increases probability where it is successful, never
gives absolute certainty, unless there is certainty already at
some point in the coherent system. Thus the mere organization
of probable opinion will, never, by itself, transform it into
indubitable knowledge.[136]

Thus the coherence of all facets of the accepted view of
what happened in Dallas during the tragic week-end of
November 22, 1963, particularly Ruby's activities, strength-
ens the probability of truth. In applying this passage from
Russell to the entire assassination, it might be said that
the coherency of the Warren Report suggests truth, that
it may not be indubitable knowledge, but that the probable lack of coherency of "conspiracy" views suggests the
lack of truth in such alternatives.

I have intentionally selected Bertrand Russell as a prime
source for my hypothesis because Russell is one of the
most vigorous critics of the Warren Report and, indeed,

of all views and personalities of the American Establishment. When the Warren Report was first released, Russell instantly poured vitriol on it, before he could have read it. This proves again the subjective nature of truth. "I believe, therefore it is true." Was it not St. Paul who said that "faith is the evidence for things not seen?"

The assassination of a political leader, whatever the intention of the assassin, is a political act, for the consequences are political. As events have shown, no citizen can remain unaffected. It is natural then that people should look behind the act of assassination to motive and intent and make the mental leap, in the absence of absolute truth, to certainty in things unseen, to conspiracies and plots. An earlier episode in American history, of might-have-been's and likely-was-so's, is instructive.

## THE ASSASSINATION OF LINCOLN

On the evening of April 14, 1865, General and Mrs. Ulysses S. Grant were to have accompanied President and Mrs. Lincoln to Ford's Theatre in Washington, D.C., for a performance of *Our American Cousin*. The President himself had urged the great military hero to attend, and the invitation had been qualifiedly accepted. The newspapers were notified, and advertisements announced an event that was certain to augment theatre attendance on what was normally a bad night, Good Friday.

Quite suddenly, the Grants begged off attending the theatre, excusing themselves by saying that it was necessary for them to return to their home in Burlington, New Jersey, to see their children. Had the Grants remained in Washington and gone to the theatre with the President and his lady, the General's armed orderly and perhaps others would have been on guard outside the presidential box, and possibly inside it as well. Neither John Wilkes Booth nor any other unauthorized or dangerous person could then have got within range of the President. With so many eyes on the hero of the day, it was unlikely that anyone would attempt the life of the President or get away with it. With the Grants elsewhere, the Lincolns had to make last-minute, less satisfactory arrangements for the evening. The result was disaster and martyrdom.

Students generally pass by this great "if" of history. In every event there are imponderables, and it sometimes seems the game of a child, not that of a scholar, to speculate over them. Dr. Otto Eisenschiml was the great exception. This enormously interesting man of the widest interests—chemist, businessman, historian, musician, baseball fan, and intellectual adventurer—was deeply absorbed in all aspects of the Civil War, initially because his father had been a captain at the battle of Shiloh. Dr. Eisenschiml probed deeply into the discourtesy of the Grants and found that their withdrawal was not as simple as had been assumed. With his usual thoroughness and imaginative resourcefulness, he determined the manner in which the Grants would have journeyed to Burlington. To do this, he dug up old railroad timetables and found, to his bewilderment, that the Grants had gained only discomfort by going at night. They had to travel in an ordinary coach and to transfer twice at very bad hours. If they had taken the morning train, they could have gone with the Lincolns to the theatre and still have seen the children at Burlington in the early afternoon. Surely the General, with all the available information at his disposal, knew this. What was the meaning of it?

Dr. Eisenschiml asked other questions as he delved further. Who, during that night of April 14, 1865, had tampered with the telegraph lines leading out of Washington, impeding communication when it was most necessary? Why did Secretary of War Stanton, on the flimsiest of excuses, refuse his Commander in Chief the company of the extraordinarily strong and alert Major Eckert? Why, instead, was an utterly incompetent and scatterbrained bodyguard placed at the presidential box, a man who went

to a nearby saloon, leaving the box unguarded? Why was
this man not punished, or even closely questioned, for his
gross negligence?

"Perhaps the most serious reproach against historical
writers," Dr. Eisenschiml concluded, "is not that they have
left such questions unanswered, but [that] they failed to
ask them."

Dr. Eisenschiml did ask these and many other questions.
He devoted many years and much money to amazing research and provocative writing on the subject. He did not
rush into print to capture headlines or catch pennies. He
was patient, scholarly, objective, nonaccusatory, even when
he appeared to have the most damaging evidence against
persons in both high and low places. Ultimately, he published one historical classic, *Why Was Lincoln Murdered?*,
two lesser books on the theme, *In the Shadow of Lincoln's
Death* and *The Case of A. L.—. Aged 56*, and several
articles.

Anyone who wants to consider, in perspective, the
severely critical contributions of Mark Lane and others to
the study of the latest presidential assassination should
peruse Dr. Eisenschiml's writings. I do not want to labor
the matter, but it is appropriate to highlight, briefly, a
few of the points made by the great student of the Lincoln
assassination and to supplement them by other material.

Take again the matter of the criminally negligent presidential guard, John F. Parker. He was a veteran member
of the Metropolitan Police Force of Washington, detailed
for such duty. He was to be armed with a Colt revolver
and to stand at the entrance to the box at Ford's Theatre,
permitting no unauthorized person to enter it and protecting the President through all hazards.

The stationing of Parker at the presidential box was
strange, indeed. True, until that time no President of the
United States had ever been assassinated, but threats had
been made against Lincoln from the moment of his election
—he had had to sneak through nearby Baltimore in un-

seemly fashion on his way to his inauguration—and there had been information leading to the belief that there were abduction plots and even plans to kill him. He, like Kennedy almost a century later, dwelt upon the death of Presidents. Washington was filled with dissidents of all kinds, from disappointed job-seekers to outraged secessionists. Common sense should have dictated the best possible protection for the President. Parker had earlier been charged with conduct unbecoming an officer; the use of violent, coarse, and insolent language; loafing and sleeping while on duty; insubordination; willful violation of the rules and regulations; intoxication; visiting a house of prostitution for as long as five weeks at one stretch; firing a pistol through a window while there; refusal to restrain some disorderly Negroes; and the like. Yet, on April 3, 1865, only eleven days before the assassination, a request was made on his behalf that he be excused from the wartime draft, taken off his usual beat, and detailed for presidential duty at the Executive Mansion. This request was made by Mrs. Lincoln, for reasons that have never been determined. The documentation, in her own handwriting, was found by Dr. Eisenschiml many years later, when he purchased the papers of the Civil War provost marshal of the District of Columbia. Parker went out for a drink or two at the very time when he was supposed to be at the presidential box, so that Booth was able to enter it, unmolested, and to shoot Lincoln. Mark Lane and others would have made much of any similar episode in connection with President Kennedy's assassination and its aftermath; they have made even more of lesser incidents. The Dallas police certainly took infinitely more precautions than did the District of Columbia authorities, and yet there was a similar series of disasters. Destiny does not respect blue coats in the plans of men.

Did the disgraceful Parker business indicate that there was a conspiracy to kill Lincoln and others? Parker remained on the police force, seemingly protected, as long

as Secretary of War Stanton was in office. When Stanton
was at last ousted by Lincoln's long-suffering successor
(whom Stanton had spied upon and betrayed), short shrift
was given to Parker. He was fired for less cause than had
existed. Until rediscovered by Dr. Eisenschiml, he passed
into oblivion.

There are conspiracies and conspiracies. Lincoln's slayer,
John Wilkes Booth, was part of a conspiracy, we know. It
included an assortment of odd human beings, none of them,
so far as is known with any certainty, in high public position, although Stanton charged the Confederate leaders,
from President Jefferson Davis down, with complicity. In
a very real sense, Booth acted alone in concocting and
carrying out his murderous act. The others were onlookers
and supernumeraries, in effect. These witless men to whom
he assigned other tasks, such as holding a horse for him or
slaying Secretary of State Seward and possibly Vice-President Andrew Johnson, funked and failed (except for Lewis
Paine), but they paid with their necks, just as did a possibly
innocent person, Mary Surratt.

Dr. Eisenschiml deals, in his writings, with all the facts
and inferences that might cause the Mark Lanes of history to conclude that Lincoln was the victim of as dire
a plot as is unfolded in *MacBird,* that unreal play in which
a Johnson-like character kills his predecessor, just as Mac-
beth killed King Duncan, to succeed him in office. Dr.
Eisenschiml proves that Stanton knew that Booth had killed
Lincoln shortly after the event, but did not make his name
public until 3:00 A.M. the next day; that while it was virtually certain that Booth was to attempt escape in the
direction of Richmond, Virginia, news of the assassination
and of Booth's role was not published there until April 17,
three days later; that every road out of Washington had
been barred except the very road the assassin was likely to
take; that no troops were sent in immediate pursuit of
Booth and Herold, his young associate, even though the
War Department knew they had crossed the Anacostia

Bridge and were racing away; that, in fact, when an officer asked for cavalry horses so that he might pursue them, he was refused; that news of the assassination was published in widely separated places before it had occurred; that it appeared—to go to an even more basic fact—that the war was not permitted to be won by Stanton until it was certain that slavery would be abolished and the Black Republicans could take over. There was much more besides. Yet Dr. Eisenschiml, not being a Mark Lane, very carefully pointed out that the logical inference that Stanton and his Black Republican associates were responsible for Lincoln's death has not a scrap of positive evidence to support it. This dark conjecture still haunts American history and holds lessons for those who speculate wildly over the Kennedy assassination.

It would seem that there is no mystery about the actual shooting of Lincoln by Booth, regardless of any other aspect of the case. True, nobody actually saw Booth discharge the gun; but he was seen in the presidential box at the theatre that night. He had jumped from the box to the stage, proclaiming *"Sic semper tyrannis!"* He had fled from the theatre and from Washington. He had proclaimed and believed himself the assassin. Why, then, should there be any question about the matter?

The direction of the shot, as observed by those who first saw the dying President, seemed to make it impossible that the fatal injury could have been inflicted by someone inside the theatre box. Booth, standing at the door to the box, saw only the right profile of Lincoln. But the bullet had entered the left side, not the right side, of Lincoln's head, the side that Booth could not have seen! And the bullet, entering below the ear, had coursed upward in the head. This would indicate, almost conclusively, that Lincoln must have been shot by someone in the audience, and not by Booth. But no such person had been seen, and it was inconceivable that he would have been unobserved by the throng.

It is true that very few people were aware of these strange facts at the time. One Washington newspaper reporter explained the matter in a way that did not truly explain. He thought that Booth had contorted his body before shooting the President, as if to create a mystery where none was necessary. He said that Booth had leaned over the railing of the box, "with the elbow of his right arm out of the box, his left hand on the balustrade," and in that unnatural position had used his gun with deadly effect. But this explanation did not satisfy even the reporter. Most people, including those in the audience, simply assumed that the bullet had penetrated the right side and did not credit any report that it was on the left. Dr. Eisenschiml presented the answer to this riddle, as to many others. It was supplied through James P. Ferguson, a restaurant keeper, a boyhood friend of Grant's, who had gone to the theatre to see the great general, not the President. He had never let the presidential box out of view. He saw Booth enter the box; he saw the flash of the pistol; and he, alone it seemed, observed Lincoln every moment. As Ferguson told it to the police that night, Lincoln's attention was attracted by some disturbance in the theatre. Pulling the curtain of the box aside, Lincoln turned his head toward the center of the theatre and looked down, in a rather contorted manner. It was at this moment that Booth fired. Thus the bullet struck Lincoln's head on the left side while it was twisted sharply to one side, and the course of the bullet was upward in Lincoln's head. Had Ferguson not observed these things, there would have remained a mystery to plague serious students and crackpots as well.

One must remember that mysteries often have ordinary explanations and are not necessarily conspiratorial in nature, as some would believe. As Hugh Kingsmill, an English writer, once observed, it is as much a form of gullibility to believe nothing as to believe everything.

There were other questions arising from Lincoln's autopsy. What course did the bullet take? Was it straightforward, or did it plow diagonally through the President's head? The doctors disagreed; but that was not the reason the patient died. The best modern medical opinion, as Dr. Eisenschiml has pointed out, and it is only an opinion, inclines toward the conclusion that the bullet took a diagonal course and stopped behind the right eye.

The autopsy showed that the upper bones of both eye-sockets of the slain President had been completely demolished; the plates were splintered in numerous places. These broken fragments pointed toward the inside of Lincoln's head, the opposite direction to that in which the Booth bullet had traveled. Examination showed that the bullet, arrested in its course, did not cause the destruction; it had not pierced the membrane separating the brain from the eye sockets. The bullet was unlike modern bullets. One could only seek expert testimony for tentative explanation; one could not be sure. The best opinion is that the low velocity of Booth's bullet, its relatively heavy weight, its having been fired at close range, these tended to produce a sudden highly forceful impact, as a result of which the eye sockets were shattered and the orbital plates broken down. Similar explanations may someday be found for the so-called mysteries of the Kennedy autopsy.

At exactly what time did the Lincoln shooting take place? The newspapers printed widely conflicting accounts. The many persons present at Ford's Theatre were apparently too shocked, or too careless, to look at their watches. Did Booth really shout "*Sic semper tyrannis*" as he jumped to the stage from the presidential box? Did he then explain, "The South is avenged"? How long was the jump to the stage? Did he walk erect or did he limp as rushed to the rear door of the stage? No two persons seemed to have the same answers to these and other questions. Some of the questions remain unanswered to this day, despite the best efforts of Dr. Eisenschiml and others. Some of these are important, others less so. Was Booth killed by Boston Corbett, or did he escape? In any event, Booth's associates, actual and alleged, eight of them, were tried by a military tribunal. All eight were convicted, and

four of them hanged, including Mrs. Surratt, about whose
participation doubt rages to this day. The lady was hanged
despite the tribunal's recommendation of mercy. The accused were clothed in hooded and heavy garments that
made life almost unbearable for them even before they
were tried and condemned; they were manacled and kept
in the hold of an inaccessible ship; they could not speak
for themselves or to their counsel. They did not have the
benefit of a civil trial. There was no Warren Commission,
no Congressional Committee of Inquiry, to examine into
the facts while they were still available. This was a blind
and furious inquisition in the cruel style of Oriental despots
of ancient days and not in the spirit of the martyred President of an enlightened land. It is a blot upon our national
reputation, recalled by few. How furious our latter-day
critics could well be, but Dr. Eisenschiml is almost alone
in his condemnation of what occurred. More important, he
sought for answers to questions, and he forewent dogmatic
answers.

Those who pursued Booth, a detachment of twenty-five
army men, were instructed to capture him and bring him
back alive to Washington. He was cornered, with David
Herold, in the tobacco shed at Garrett's farm. Young Garrett was sent into the barn to disarm the two men and to
persuade them to surrender. They would not do so. Herold
shortly afterwards left the barn and surrendered. Then the
shed was set on fire, so that the other occupant would be
compelled to leave. This man, presumably Booth, could be
seen through cracks in the wall of the shed. He seemed to
be moving toward the door when suddenly there was a
shot and he fell to the ground, a bullet in his neck paralyz-
ing his spinal cord. He died at sunrise the next day, April
27, 1865. So far as we know, he had been shot by Boston
Corbett, a sergeant in Lieutenant Doherty's detachment,
a religious fanatic who claimed that God had directed him
to countermand his military superior's order and to shoot
Booth. Later he said that Booth had been aiming at him
with a carbine, so he shot him. No other soldier in the

detachment, apparently, had seen Corbett shoot Booth; only one person, Garrett's twelve-year-old son, claimed, twenty-two years later, that he saw Corbett fire. The chairman of the congressional committee charged with determining who was to get the proffered reward for the capture of the conspirators said that Corbett was "an insane man" who "forsook his place, thrust a pistol through a crack and fired without knowing where the ball was going." It is possible that someone other than Corbett actually killed Booth, perhaps Colonel Conger, as Lieutenant Baker later claimed. But Corbett received the popular acclaim for the act and was feted throughout the country and treated as a hero. Audiences flocked to hear him speak, until they became bored by his Biblical bombast. His picture sold like the proverbial hot cakes; not even Phil Sheridan's heroic likeness sold better. Corbett was often interviewed, invariably giving God credit for his good aim. He was given only a small share of the reward and in time wandered off and was involved in various scrapes, including another divinely inspired shooting—an unsuccessful attempt to kill the members of the Kansas legislature. He was placed in an insane asylum, in time escaped, and was lost to history. Without laboring the matter, there are various respects in which he resembled Jack Ruby, who slew another President's assassin almost a century later.

He who would make much of a conspiracy in the death of President Kennedy would do well to reflect on this brief recital of the all-too-similar circumstances of the death of Abraham Lincoln. Events are not well ordered, the truth is not always knowable. And what is known is known provisionally, with some quantum of doubt appearing inconspicuously in the next phrasing. John F. Kennedy is dead, Lee Harvey Oswald is dead, and Jack L. Ruby is dead. These are certainties. That there is tragedy here is well established, but that there was or is a conspiracy is and will remain, in my opinion, beyond proof, for there are and ever will be in our midst individuals who disarrange history by their actions in a moment of madness.

# END NOTE

OF THE PERSONS involved in the Ruby case, a few last words must be said. Judge Joe B. Brown, the focus of much of the activity in the case, died in March, 1968, to little notice and no acclaim. He had outlived his role. The book he intended to complete was abandoned by his publishers and never appeared in print. No one much cared about Judge Brown after his actions were held up to careful public scrutiny, and he was happy to dissociate himself from the proceedings. The opposite was true of his able successor, Judge Louis B. Holland. Still presiding over his old district, Judge Holland remembers his association with this famous case with pride.

On the prosecutor's staff, much has changed. Henry Menasco Wade, who had expected to be named to the bench but was disappointed, continues successfully as the criminal district attorney of Dallas County, Texas. A. D. Jim Bowie, who left Wade's office in 1965 to serve on the bench, died in 1968. As should have been expected, his judicial record, during his short career as judge, was one of distinction. Bill Alexander went his vituperative way, contributing to Henry Wade's remarkable record of criminal convictions —until one day he declared that impeachment was too good for Chief Justice Earl Warren: the Chief Justice should hang. That was going too far, and after sixteen years as Wade's assistant, Alexander was eased out of office.

The attorneys who served Jack Ruby have gone their various ways. Joe Tonahill and Melvin Belli are still practicing personal injury law, less clamorously perhaps, but no less successfully. Belli has found a new legal partner—F. Lee Bailey, the hero of the Sheppard case, which so inspired us in the arguments before the Texas courts.

Sol Dann, before his heart attack, ran for judge in Detroit and lost. Now, with seeming unconcern for the risk he runs, he works as hard as ever at the law.

William Kunstler and Sam Houston Clinton, Jr., have continued to defend difficult clients in difficult cases, following the paths to which they have long been committed philosophically and emotionally.

Phil Burleson, who grew in stature as the Ruby case went on, quietly practices law in Dallas. The qualities he demonstrated in the case give promise that some day this young man may reach a position as a prominent national practitioner.

With the death of Ruby the murder indictment and the petition for certiorari in the Supreme Court were left in mid-air. It was far easier to terminate these proceedings than to commence or carry them through. The indictment was dismissed—not without a last effort by the unforgiving Bill Alexander to cast Ruby in a bad light. On our motion the Supreme Court dismissed the petition for certiorari. Thus did years of complicated litigation come to an end.

Of the Ruby case itself, and of its meaning, a few words are in order. The proceedings are at an end, but, unhappily, it is likely that there will be similar events in the future. Even as this record was being completed, other assassinations took place. To the extent that there is meaning in the Jack Ruby situation, a warning of the dangers to avoid in the handling of sensational cases, the story will have no end.

# NOTES

Throughout the book the sources of specific quotations, whether documents from the proceedings, personal correspondence, or newspaper reports, are cited in the text. In three chapters such textual citation was avoided, and it is assembled here. In the following notes abbreviated citations are used.

References to the *Report of the President's Commission on the Assassination of President John F. Kennedy* (U.S. Government Printing Office, 1964) are indicated by the capitals WCR followed by the page number.

References to the *Hearings Before the President's Commission on the Assassination of President Kennedy* (U.S. Government Printing Office, 1964) are indicated by volume numbers in roman numerals and the page number in arabic.

References to *Rush to Judgment* (Holt, Rinehart & Winston, 1966) are indicated by the capitals RTJ followed by the page number.

Chapter 4      The Testimony of the Dallas
               Police Officers      68-102

1. XII, 415-45
2. Dean Exhibit 5009
3. Dean Exhibit 5010
4. XIII, 56-83
5. Sorrels Exhibit 1
6. XX, 556-70
7. XIII, 37-55
8. XIX, 20-21
9. XII, 395-402
10. XIII, 1-12
11. VII, 251-60
12. XIII, 14-20
13. VII, 260-69
14. XX, 508-9
15. *Id.* at 507
16. XIII, 19

## Chapter 32    The Secret Tape    479-497

1. XIII, 211
2. WCR, 357
3. *Ibid.*
4. *Id.* at 219, 221

5. *Id.* at 365
6. XIV, 134, 141
7. XV, 275
8. CE 1697

## Chapter 35    A Conspiracy?    507-543

1. *RTJ*, 209
2. WCR, 216
3. XXI, 19-20
4. XIII, 132
5. WCR, 220
6. XX, 23
7. XXIV, 312
8. XX, 350
9. XXIV, 164
10. *RJT*, 236
11. WCR, 800
12. *Id.* at 224-25
13. V, 199
14. WCR, 224
15. *RTJ*, 219-24
16. XIX, 420
17. *Id.* at 419-27
18. XII, 230
19. *Id.* at 339
20. XIX, 419-27
21. XII, 232
22. *Id.* at 233
23. WCR, 219
24. XX, 56
25. XII, 192-93
26. *Id.* at 31
27. XIII, 136-37
28. *Id.* at 137
29. *RTJ*, 229-40
30. *Id.* at 230
31. WCR, 801
32. *Id.* at 224
33. *RTJ*, 230
34. XIV, 330
35. *Id.* at 337-38
36. XXVI, 615-17
37. XIV, 345
38. XXVI, 616

39. *Ibid.*
40. *Id.* at 617
41. XIX, 347-49
42. XXVI, 618
43. *Id.* at 632
44. *RTJ*, 231
45. WCR, 224
46. *Id.* at 801
47. XIII, 324-25
48. *Ibid.*
49. XIV, 312
50. *Id.* at 214
51. XX, 62
52. XIII, 434
53. XXII, 920-21
54. XXI, 272-73
55. XXIII, 136-37
56. *RTJ*, 233-34
57. V, 191, 196
58. *Id.* at 197
59. XV, 37, 198
60. XIV, 471
61. *Id.* at 500-501
62. *RTJ*, 243
63. V, 193
64. *RTJ*, 245
65. *Id.* at 249
66. *Id.* at 250
67. XV, 655
68. *Ibid.*
69. XXV, 530-31
70. XXVI, 482
71. V, 514
72. XIV, 559-60; V, 203
73. II, 58-61
74. *RTJ*, 253-54
75. WCR, 333-58
76. *RTJ*, 260-72

77.  WCR, 333
78.  *RTJ*, 261
79.  XXV, 194
80.  *Id.* at 205
81.  XX, 654
82.  *RTJ*, 261-62
83.  WCR, 334-35
84.  *RTJ*, 262
85.  VI, 193
86.  *Ibid.*
87.  *Id.* at 212
88.  *Id.* at 215
89.  *RTJ*, 263
90.  WCR, 335-37
91.  XV, 80
92.  WCR, 336
93.  XV, 392
94.  *RTJ*, 270
95.  WCR, 357-58
96.  *RTJ*, 271
97.  XV, 399
98.  *Id.* at 671-72, 675
99.  *RTJ*, 273-74
100. XV, 396
101. *RTJ*, 276
102. XI, 435
103. XX, 534
104. *Ibid.*
105. XXI, 27
106. *Id.* at 384
107. RTJ, 278
108. *Ibid.*

109. *Ibid.*
110. XXV, 872
111. WCR, 663
112. *RTJ*, 280
113. II, 207-209
114. *RTJ*, 281
115. *Id.* at 280
116. XIV, 245-46
117. *RTJ*, 282
118. XIV, 246
119. *RTJ*, 282-84
120. XXIII, 157
121. *Id.* at 160
122. *RTJ*, 301
123. WCR, 370
124. *RTJ*, 301
125. XXIII, 170-71
126. *RTJ*, 302
127. XXVI, 470
128. *RTJ*, 302 ff.
129. XXVI, 467
130. *Id.* at 466-73
131. *Id.* at 471
132. *RTJ*, 304
133. XXVI, 466
134. American College Dictionary
135. *Evidence-Cases and Materials*, MaGuire, Weinstein, Chadbourn and Mansfield, 1
136. *The Problems of Philosophy*, 140

# INDEX